STUDYING THE OLD TESTAMENT

STUDYING THE OLD TESTAMENT FROM TRADITION TO CANON

ANNEMARIE OHLER

TRANSLATED BY
DAVID CAIRNS

T. & T. CLARK LTD.,
36 George Street, Edinburgh

Originally published under the title *Gattungen im AT* by Patmos-
Verlag Düsseldorf in two volumes, 1972, 1973
Authorised English translation © T. & T. Clark Ltd, 1985

Typeset by Bookmag, Inverness, Scotland,
printed by Billing & Son, Worcester, England,
for
T. & T. CLARK LTD., EDINBURGH, SCOTLAND

ISBN: 0 567 09335 2

First printed 1985

CONTENTS

INTRODUCTION

Methods of Old Testament Exegesis

The Old Testament is not a book that fell from heaven; human beings wrote it, and it is important to understand the words of the writers. The Second Vatican Council has stated this clearly.

"Since God has spoken clearly in Holy Scripture through men, and in the manner of men, the expounder of Scripture, in order to apprehend what God wished to communicate, must carefully investigate what the sacred writers really intended to say . . . In order to discover what the sacred writers intended to say, attention must among other things be paid to the literary genre . . . If we wish to understand what the sacred author wished to say in his writing, careful attention must be paid to the forms of thought, of language, and of narrative, which were dominant at the time of the author, and also to the forms that were customary in everyday human intercourse at the time." (Dogmatic Constitution "Concerning the Divine Revelation", 12).

Anyone who wishes to understand the Bible must take the trouble to understand people who thought and spoke differently from ourselves. Modern Biblical exegesis has developed methods which can help to bridge the gap between us and the distant times and world of ancient Israel. These methods are set forth in this book. But not even the mastery of all the methods of exegesis guarantees a right understanding of the Bible, nor is it the only way to such an understanding. Else how could there have been so much profound insight into Holy Scripture in the days before the modern exegetical methods were known?

Knowledge of method is only one requirement, and not even the most important one, for people who wish to read the Old Testament with understanding. It is more important that they be familiar with the Bible, that they collect a store of experience of its contents. For this reason I would wish to do two things; to stimulate a consciousness of method, and also to encourage a continued searching of the Scriptures.

The history of modern exegesis shows that different methods are required to open up the Bible, while the monopoly of one method often only piles up difficulties. It is only two hundred years since the European Enlightenment taught us to value more highly insights gained by the individual than those which are supplied by an authority. This critical

1

attitude has influenced the modern age so deeply that we are no longer able to accept even the Bible without prejudice. For this reason methodical tools are indispensable. Some methods were first tried out on the Pentateuch, the first five books of the Bible. It was observed that these books ascribed to Moses contain sections which differ noticeably among themselves in style and use of language; that incidents are repeated (e.g. there are three stories about the exposure to danger of the ancestress; Gen. 12, 10-20; 20, 1-18; 26, 6-13); it was further observed that even a passage which purports to be a single narrative can contain repetitions, breaks, and gaps. (An example which can be easily verified is the story of the Flood in Genesis 6, 5-9, 19).

So long as the five books of Moses were regarded as an original unity, all this seemed inexplicable. Starting from suggestions in the work of earlier exegetes, Julius Wellhausen put forward, about the end of the nineteenth century, a hypothesis which in its main features has held the field[1] in Old Testament studies till the present day. The sources of the first five books of the Bible are four different literary works differing in date and place of origin. These were fused into a unity by the redactors, whose work passed through several stages. *Literary criticism* endeavours to restore as far as possible the underlying sources. In so doing it starts with the unevenness which can be observed in the Biblical texts. It regards this as indicative of places where the original literary units have been stitched together.

This method was finally applied to other books also. It is indispensable wherever the influence of different authors in one book has to be distinguished and a demarcation made between their contributions. But as soon as the attempt is made to give an explanation in terms of literary criticism of *everything* that seems incoherent to modern man, it becomes dangerous. The texts were broken up by the literary critics into the smallest units, half-verses and quarter-verses were ascribed to the different authors. Even the source documents were further divided, and regarded as compilations of different and still older writings. But even where an exegete guards against the over-refinement of the method, it can — if applied by itself — bar the way to an understanding of the text. The unity disclosed to us in the Bible, which took its rise from the source documents, is no longer appreciated in its true worth. At the time when this method was at the height of its popularity, the attempted reconstructions of many literary critics were compared by H. Budde to efforts to remove from ancient cathedrals, on which many generations had worked, everything that did not correspond to the original plan.

A new approach, for which Old Testament scholarship is above all indebted to Hermann Gunkel,[2] led out of the blind alley into which the over-refinement of literary criticism had brought matters: the *critical investigation of categories or genres*, often referred to as "form criticism". It shows that not all the unevennesses in the biblical writings are to be understood as the result of processes examined by literary criticism.

Nearly all the materials had already a long pre-literary life behind them before biblical authors set them down in writing. We must not expect from the ancient authors a smooth work, free from breaks, repetitions and changes of style, for in their work they felt themselves bound to what was given to them; they chose loyalty to the tradition in preference to a smoothly polished text.

This loyalty shows the power of the established form, which dominates the oral tradition. The oral transmission of everything that the fathers and earlier ancestors had said, did not take place in an uncommitted scientific spirit, but because the knowledge of earlier times was again needed in the present. The actual form which the transmission took from time to time corresponded to the needs of life. There were special forms in which law was enunciated, in which events in the life of the individual and the community were celebrated, in which the priest gave instruction to the people, and the father instructed his family; in which the group celebrating the eve of a festival entertained itself with stories, proverbs and riddles. Many subjects could only be spoken of in special prescribed formulae, and even the authors who arranged them within a wider context could not always deviate from these. The study of categories teaches us to understand smaller self-contained textual units against a concrete background. It asks where in its communal life Israel could use a text of such a kind. By so doing it permits us to go beyond literary forms and the individual authors, and to penetrate a remoter past, the life of the community which coined the forms and influenced the authors. It teaches us to contrast and to distinguish from each other small units which the authors embodied in their works. This method is particularly indispensable in the prophetic books. The prophetic tradition has only on rare occasions contrasted the units of discourse and distinguished them from one another. But where we know the laws of the prophetic genres, we can recognize the individual sayings and discourses.

But the study of categories too has its limits. Above all, it leaves one question open. How did the big literary units constructed from the many fragments of oral tradition come into being. How did the history of the patriarchs arise out of the individual sagas? How did the great historical picture come into being which coordinates the times of the fathers, the exodus, the desert wanderings, and the conquest of the land? When Gunkel speaks of collections of sagas, he seems to assume that the individual narratives had come together almost by accident. That may sometimes have happened, but gives no explanation of the unified picture of the history of Israel that presents itself to us in the Old Testament.

Therefore the *investigation of the history of traditions* was a necessary supplement of the study of categories. Here the principal instigators were Gerhard von Rad and Martin Noth.[3] The picture of the course of Israel's history was not first elaborated by the authors who long after the events, created the four principal written sources of the Pentateuch. This picture originated long before their day, in the pre-literary age. The events of Sinai, the making of the Covenant, and the divine leading to which Israel owed its possession of the land, were already elaborated long before this in Israel's religious festivals. The individual traditions of the tribes from which Israel took its rise were fused together into a single picture on the occasion of the shared festivals. The knowledge of the course of the people's history had become common property long before the authors appeared; it lived on in Israel's confession of faith.

Once the inquiry into the history of traditions had shown its value by the light it threw upon the Pentateuch, it also made a contribution to the interpretation of other books in the Bible. For example, important insights concerning the prophets are to be gained by asking which of Israel's traditions were important to them.

The more recent methods of investigation all direct our attention in the first instance away from the biblical text which lies before us. They inquire about older layers of tradition to which the version familiar to us owes its origin, about the original documents, about the different forms of community life which left their stamp upon the categories, about the festivals and the shrines where Israel's tradition was cherished. The *investigation into the history of the editing of the books*, or redaction-criticism has another purpose. For it, the text that lies before us is more than the point of departure which our interpretation soon leaves behind it. Those who provided the final version of biblical texts are not significant only insofar as they preserved more or less exactly what had come into being in the pre-literary stage. Among the strong-willed literary personalities, we meet groups with marked originality and a significant theological outlook. Even when the redactors contented themselves with ordering the material before them, and here and there commenting upon it, they are important witnesses for us as to how biblical texts were understood in ancient times.

A book about the forms of speech in the Old Testament could be structurally organized so as to follow the lines of development taken by scholarly investigation. The reader will, among other things, find traces of such an approach here, but they are not systematically developed. For our purpose here is less to give an introduction to methods of research, than to aid the understanding of the Bible reader.

History of the Old Testament Literature

It might have been possible to write a history in chronological order of the Old Testament literature. This history would have to begin with the *entry into Canaan*. It was only after the fusion of the language of the invaders with the local language of Canaan that the Hebrew language came into being. A further important factor for the beginning of Old Testament literature is the development of faith in Yahweh the God of the Covenant. This faith, to which Moses led the people, gave a new stamp to older traditions, and by so doing, destroyed them for us. Thus, if we had chosen this approach, we would have had to explain the connection between the Old Testament literature and the Canaanitic literature, and the fundamental differences between them.

After that, a picture would have to be given of the long *pre-literary epoch*, during which, in the various forms of the community, e.g., in the family and in the village, in the giving of legal decisions and in conversation, in prayer and in divine worship, a rich variety of forms of speech came into being, which preserved in themselves manifold traditions.

A decisive turning-point in the literary history of Israel was marked by the *Rise of the Kingdom* and the scribal office. Learned men, expert in the scriptures, interested themselves at that time both in the immediate past and in the oldest traditions of the people. The first great writings were composed. The internationally acknowledged "Wisdom" found a lodgement among these educated men and reshaped the popular wisdom sayings and family lore. Finally, in the course of the time of the kings the prophetic movement gained its greatest influence. It enriched Israel's literature with impressive forms of speech and possibilities of expression.

Another important turning-point of a different kind was brought by the *Exile*. After the banished Jews had all their religious and national institutions taken from them, everything that they could take with them in rolls of manuscript into banishment became of the first importance. With the exile begins a time of collection, sifting, and final fixation in writing. After a long preceding history it was only now, in this time, that the creation of the Bible as a book complete in itself began. None the less, even in the *post-exilic period*, new works came into being. But the oral tradition had now little significance in this context. Study of earlier writings, picking up individual themes from older texts and reinterpreting them, were the formative forces behind this literature.

It is not easy to determine the end of the history of Old Testament literature. The last books which were taken into the Canon of the Old Testament by no means signalized the exhaustion of the literary power of the Jews. Almost unnoticed there took place the transition to a rich post-Biblical literature. But even this possibility of depicting these forms of speech in their chronological order, i.e. according to their appearance in the literary history, has only been followed up in a sketchy unsystematic manner. Had the book been constructed on such a plan, the first chapters in particular would have been very difficult, since they would have had to pursue the inquiry in an area lying far behind the biblical text as we have it.

The Structure of the Book

For this reason I have chosen a way which leads from the smallest units to the greater ones, from the single word and sentence to the question of the unity of the whole Old Testament. Thus it is only the last chapters

5

which demand the wider perspective. At any rate no statement can be made which does not take account of the many layers of meaning of this book which through many centuries grew into the Old Testament.

A first step will lead us to *the peculiarities of the Hebrew language, the customary Hebrew ways of speaking and thinking*. A translation of the Bible always remains unsatisfactory. Anyone who is forced to undertake this task could see from a few examples that the language of the Bible was the means of expression of those who lived in a quite different world, and whose way of encountering the world was quite different from ours. Anyone who wishes to understand this language must free himself from modern conceptions of literature. In modern books an individual author addresses the individual reader. In the ancient world, however, the individual is much more closely bound up with society. "As the individual man in Israel would regard it as a crime to not act as 'One acts in Israel', so also the writer stands under the strong pressure of the style which is traditional for the category" (Gunkel).

The description of the customary categories of the Old Testament and their peculiarities forms therefore the second comprehensive part of the book. This description is problematic for a number of reasons.

1. We know only a very few of the old Hebrew descriptions of the linguistic categories of the Old Testament — e.g. "Petition", "Song of Praise". The meaning of most of them we cannot determine exactly — e.g. *Māšāl* means at one and the same time a saying, a sentence of moral teaching, a song of derision. Others can hardly be distinguished from related concepts — e.g. God's ordinances can be called *mišpāṭīm*, *ḥuqqōṭ*, *tōrōṭ*. Finally, many have such a breadth of meaning that they tell us little about the literary form — *dābār*, word. It appears that Israel never felt the need to grasp exactly by means of concepts the linguistic categories of which it made use. For this reason exegesis is forced to make use of modern concepts — and runs the risk that these are not exactly suited to the ancient material.

2. Of greater consequence is the fact that it cannot be easily determined what a linguistic category really is. What structural elements must texts have in common in order to belong to a category? Related motifs and stylistic characters are to be found even in differently formed texts; Psalms, narratives and prophets' descriptions of their own experiences, for example, represent the appearance of God in a similar manner, without its being permissible to subsume these texts for that reason as formally belonging to the same categories. Further, is not perhaps the unique element in a text much more important than the signs of its belonging to a category which it shares with other texts?

Linguistic categories cannot be apprehended when only unambiguous characteristics of the text are taken into consideration. Fixed forms of oratory and speech take shape in the communal life of a people, which is closely bound to origins and custom. There the community takes care that each individual so speaks as is the custom on certain recurring occasions. Texts of such a kind are basic constitutents of the books of the Old Testament. They bear the imprint of the manner in which Israel's groups and classes saw and experienced the world (the specialist terminology speaks of their *Sitz im Leben*[4]).

The rich variety of Israel's life is reflected in the multiplicity of the categories. A false conception of the truth of Holy Scripture misleads many people into reading it as if it contained only one type of writing — that of a historical record. It is believed that only so could it bear witness to the reality of the divine revelation. In this book it will be shown that the representations of historical reality in the Bible are just as manifold as the forms of speech. Human words also create reality: the reader of the Bible must also acknowledge this; it possesses its own truth just as does the world of things and events. For this reason we find revelation not only on the level of things and events, but also on this other level, the level of reality created by human words. There are many more forms than that of the historical record through which we can receive revelation.

3. Thus pure categories are at home in the oral tradition — they are extremely rarely to be found in the written text of the Old Testament. Forms taken over from the oral tradition are here brought into larger contexts of written material. This means that at least two different "categories" intermingle, two — usually even more — different attitudes of the speakers, the transmitters, or writers of the texts.

Therefore this work must lead beyond the investigation of categories. These alone cannot interpret the Old Testament. The small categories have their *Sitz im Leben* in the everyday life of the people — could the everyday life of Israel have been the origin of the faith to which the Old Testament bears witness? The picture of the stubbornness of the people and its continual apostasy which the Old Testament describes is probably in general correct. It is not the everyday life of Israel that is the source of faith. On the contrary Israel was repeatedly protected by great religious personalities from fusing its faith with that of the neighbouring peoples until the two were indistinguishable. For that reason we must listen to the text of the Old Testament, not only to hear what was said in the common converse of the community of the people. The following second part of this study-book inquires about the *influence of the great personalities* on the genesis of the Bible.

These great individuals are not, however, usually writers who composed the parts of the Old Testament; they are figures in Israel's history. This holds good above all for the prophets. Their intention was not to write books, but to make an impression on their people, to influence its fate. They did not wish to propound their own original thoughts, but to give new life and power to the ancient faith of Israel under conditions changed by time.

So it is hardly possible to speak of the influence of great individual personalities on the formation of the Old Testament, without at the same time taking into account the ancient *history of Israel's faith, its tradition*. The inner and outer development of Israel influence the formation of the biblical books. They are historical documents, not only in the sense that their content in the last resort refers back to historical events, but also inasmuch as the history of Israel is reflected in the history of their formation. This brings to our notice an important peculiarity of the revelation; it is a dynamic entity which we do not approach when we remain stationary at one point. The question, what did God entrust to Moses? is of little help to us. We must try to grasp what was the value of the great impulse which the work of Moses gave to the history of Israel. In the course of history continually new aspects of the revelation of God through Moses became evident. No single point in history casts full light upon it. The word of God also, which the prophets proclaim, is only rightly understood when we give it its place in the course of this history of faith.

No book in the Bible claims to be a new beginning; each claims to protect and transmit an older tradition. Thus a history could be written of the resumption, re-interpretation, and transmission of tradition, which would both concern itself with the great complexes of the transmitted faith, and also with numerous small motifs. This history permeates all the books of the Bible; in some of them it stands only in the background, in some it is fully effective.

The great *compilations of the Old Testament* which are considered in the fourth chapter, are testimonies to this continually renewed effort of the Israelite and Jewish spirit to preserve what is old and to demonstrate its present significance. But even in many smaller forms of speech the continual discussion has come to the surface. The last chapters will deal with this matter. The influence of the Old Testament writings upon each other, and their common loyalty to the inheritance of Israel, can help us to understand how the books that came into being in the course of the centuries came to be *one book*. For this reason Jews and Christians are right in regarding the Old Testament not as a library composed of different writings of ancient times, but as the one book of Holy Scripture. The Christian Church includes the New Testament in this unity. The interpreter must take account of this fact.

> Since the Holy Scriptures must be read and interpreted in the spirit in which they were written, the right evaluation of the meaning of the sacred texts requires that no less attention be paid to the content and the unity of the whole of Scripture. (Dogmatic Constitution "Concerning the Divine Revelation", 12).

In the Old Testament the living faith of many centuries took shape. Not even the written version received a fixed form; it became the basis of a history of interpretation. Since in the Old Testament many layers and many levels of interpretation overlap, it is not enough to ask for the original significance of an Old Testament text! Anyone who wishes to get to know an adult will find a photograph of him as a child useful, but he will not be contented with that. Anyone who wishes to understand an Old Testament text must keep in mind its whole life-story. He must follow the way the text took. In the two parts of this study book, the two different sectors of the journey are depicted separately. Yet only the interplay of all the inquiries that are here made independently can lead to an adequately rounded understanding of the text. The reader of this book certainly cannot expect a complete inquiry into the questions of Old Testament scholarship. Not even all the literary problems, and the problems dealing with the history of literature are dealt with. To me it seemed more important to lead the reader to consider in detail certain important questions of interpretation and to illustrate them by concrete examples, than to attempt even approximately to enumerate all the figures of speech, all the categories and forms of tradition. The foundation of work with the Old Testament, even at a school level, is the art of reading texts in relation to their literary form. My book does not set out to be more than an introduction to this art.

FOOTNOTES

1 Julius Wellhausen: *Die Composition des Hexateuchs*, 1885. Wellhausen speaks of the Hexateuch rather than the Pentateuch, because he includes the Book of Joshua in his enquiries.
2 Hermann Gunkel: *Einleitung in die Psalmen*, completed by Joachim Begrich, 1933. And Hermann Gunkel: (Handkommentar zum AT) *Genesis*. A short commentary on the Old Testament, 1910.
3 Gerhard von Rad: *Das formgeschichtliche Problem des Hexateuchs*, 1938. (Eng. tr. in *The Problem of the Hexateuch and Other Essays*), 1966. Martin Noth: *Überlieferungsgeschichte des Pentateuchs*, 1948. (Eng. tr. *A History of Pentateuchal Traditions*), 1971.
4 "Place in life" (of the community). The German phrase has become current in English. (Translator)

TRANSLATOR'S NOTE

With Dr. Ohler's approval, my general practice with regard to the Textual Examples and the other passages quoted from the Old Testament, has been as follows. I have used the translation provided by the New English Bible, though I have followed Dr Ohler's spacing and grouping of words, since such fidelity is often required to illustrate her argument. And in places where her own comments clearly show that her rendering of a passage differs from that of the New English Bible, I have substituted her rendering for its rendering, otherwise the reader would not have understood the English text of the book.

Only in one instance have I departed from this practice, in relation to the Textual Example recording the Call of Ezekiel (p. 180). Here the extraordinary nature of the text seemed to demand a direct translation from Dr Ohler's German.

David Cairns
Aberdeen, 1983

CHAPTER I

PECULIARITIES OF HEBREW THOUGHT AND THE HEBREW LANGUAGE

1. TEXTUAL EXAMPLE. THE REVELATION OF THE NAME OF GOD.
(EXODUS 3,10-15)

(God spoke to Moses)
(10) "Come now; I will send you to Pharaoh and you shall bring my people Israel out of Egypt".
(11) (Moses said to God) "But who am I, that I should go to Pharaoh, and that I should bring the Israelites out of Egypt?"
(12) God answered, "I will be with you. This shall be the proof that it is I who have sent you; when you shall have brought the people out of Egypt, you shall all worship God here on this mountain."
(13) Then Moses said to God, "If I go to the Israelites and tell them that the God of their forefathers has sent me to them, and they ask me his name, what shall I say?"
(14) God answered "I AM; that is who I am. Tell them that I AM has sent you to them."
(15) And God said further, "You must tell the Israelites this, that it is YAHWEH the God of their forefathers, the God of Abraham, the God of Isaac, the God of Jacob, who has sent you to them. This is my name for ever; this is my title in every generation."

In Christian prayers there are many ways in which God is addressed. (Father, Lord, almighty One, God . . .), but they do not use a name of God. The divine monition of Exodus 3,15 seems to have no validity for Christians:

> This is my name for ever,
> This is my title in every generation!

The prose text changes suddenly in this sentence into stately poetry, the narrator as it were puts the mnemonic into God's mouth. It is to be impressed unforgettably on the hearer what is at stake in this account, what was happening at that moment is to determine for all time how man can address God.

This challenge is not only forgotten among Christians. Many Christians will even refuse to name God with a name. Why should God need a name? In the case of the sun and the moon we regard a name as superfluous, for they are for us unique and not to be confused with each other. Zeus, Jupiter, Wotan, Osiris, Marduk, on the other hand needed names because there were many more Gods beside them.

15

Israel's Conceptions of God and gods

Up till prophetic times Israel assumed that in addition to Yahweh there were also strange gods the only point of importance was that Israel did not submit to them. Other nations might worship other Gods, for Israel there was only the one God.[1]

The Hebrew word *'elōhīm"* described all celestial beings: the God of Israel as well as his servants in the heavenly royal household, the gods of foreign peoples, even the spirit of the dead that returns to earth.[2] To us this may seem offensive, that for the one God the same generic description held good as for all divine beings. Did the Hebrews not for that reason need a name for God? And can we not all the more easily dispense with this name and disregard the injunction of Exodus 3,15 as time-conditioned?

If we make such a sweeping judgement, we shall not do justice to the significance of the name of Yahweh in Israel. We must inquire of the Old Testament more precisely what this name meant to the Israelites. The passage about the revelation of the divine Name to Moses can prove instructive.

Etymology of the name

In this narrative God names his Name, and interprets it: "I am indeed here as the One that I truly am." "Yahweh" is derived from the Hebrew verb *hāyāh* (to be indeed here). Whether this etymology of the Name is philologically correct, scholars are up to this day in disagreement. "Yahweh" remains for us the Name which cannot be interpreted or translated.[3] The author of this narrative however would not be satisfied with such a conclusion.

To us it seems interesting but inessential to know the significance of a name: who names his child 'Ursula' because 'Ursula' means 'the little bear'? In contrast with this the Bible frequently tells how a child is given a name full of significance, or how the name of a place originated in an event. Thus the biblical names "speak". Only after about 400 B.C. were traditional names chosen, which were given to a child because of an earlier bearer of the name, and not because of its meaning.[4]

The Hebrews also sought to understand names of obscure origin. Many of the approximately forty explanations of names which occur in the history of the biblical patriarchs alone are etymologically just as untenable as the explanation of the name Yahweh. The oriental delight in imaginative word-play found a wide scope here[5] but also an inclination which is to be found in the popular narratives of many peoples, to connect names with notable events. Names of places and men must for ever preserve in remembrance what had happened in Israel's history and prehistory. The etiologies of names thus become witnesses for the biblical faith that God intervened in the midst of world affairs, that he worked at certain places and through certain people. What at the first looks like playing with language, turns out to be an expression of Israel's faith.

Still less than in the case of the other popular etymologies of the Bible are we justified in thrusting aside the interpretation of the name of Yahweh in Exodus 3,14f. on the grounds that it is philologically incorrect. The author was certainly himself aware of the artificiality of this explanation of the name; he required three attempts to interpret the name; the connection of "I am that I am" to "Yahweh" does not come quite naturally even for him.[6] And yet he does not feel himself impeded from building up his interpretation upon this insecure connection of the verb *hāyāh* with the name "Yahweh". He was not put off by the fact that God here interprets his nature on the basis of a linguistically questionable presupposition about his name. In these days philological science in our sense of the word did not exist. The way these men related themselves to language finds many anologies in our folksongs and sayings; that "heart" and "pain" rhyme, that "love" and "suffering"[T] begin with the same letter — in these things people saw a connection in the realities described. So the relationship of the sentence "I am indeed here as the One that I truly am" with the name "Yahweh" — even if it seems artificial to us, is for these people of the greatest significance for the question who Yahweh is.

Three Modern Interpretations of the words "I am"

What does this sentence "I am that I am" intend to say? Western philosophical conceptuality has from ancient times mistakenly led to the view that this sentence makes a statement about God's eternal being (I am the one who eternally exists). Yet the Hebrew has no verbal form to express continual presence. The verbal form which is here used describes an action not yet concluded, a process not yet completed; we must often translate it with the future tense.

But also the statement "I will be what I will be" (Luther) says something different from the statement in its Hebrew form. Must we not see in the relative clause a rejection of every inquisitive question concerning the name, concerning the nature of God? No one can understand who God is, he will always be what he thinks it right to be.

Against this interpretation is the fact that the verb hayah has a wider range of significance than "to be". "Let there be (*hāyāh*) light, and there was light" (*hāyāh*) (Genesis 1,3). "It happened (*hāyāh*) towards the end of seven days that the waters of the flood came (*hāyāh*) upon the earth." (Genesis 7,10). Thus *hāyāh* does not merely mean "to be present, to be this or that"; it includes also "to come into being, to become", and "to take effect, to happen".[7]

The Hebrew does not believe that he can contemplate the world like a picture, in which everything stands still; he is more inclined to be interested in what it has come to be, what powers are at work in it. This

17

outlook on the world is reflected in the range of meaning of the verb *hāyāh*, "to be". We must pay attention to this if we wish to understand the sentence "I am that I am". This statement does not try to sketch God's nature in such a way that now we can contemplate it, completely at our ease. On the contrary, God's nature and his effectual working are closely interconnected. "I am the one who works, who works now and always."[8]

Even with this interpretation the meaning of the statement is not completely grasped. If we were to remain here, we would still be undecided as to what kind of action God's action is. We must try to understand the statement "I am indeed here as the One that I truly am" in its context. With this statement God introduces himself to Moses. What does this self-introduction mean?

Interpretation in the Light of the Context

Only a few sentences earlier, God had already once used the word "I am" (*'ehyeh* — first person singular of *hāyāh*). The narrator certainly chose beforehand this important word; he can take it for granted that his hearers take note of such assonances and understand them as guides for their interpretation. Moses had refused God's charge with the objection "But who am I?"; he had looked on himself as too insignificant and weak. But God instilled courage into him. "I will be (*'ehyeh*) with you" (Exodus 3,12). God says "I am, I am at work" and this strengthens the weak and spiritless man to help the people out of its extremity. God's being is being-on-behalf-of his own; his effectual power is intervention on his people's behalf.

In the central statement also we may understand *hāyāh* thus. The character of the whole narrative supports this interpretation; it is a call narrative, the easily recognized pattern of this geure recurs also in the accounts of the calls of Gideon, Isaiah, Jeremiah, Ezekiel, even in the narrative of the Angel's annunciation to Mary. Divine manifestation, (missing in the text here chosen), charge, objection on the part of the person called, strengthening, sign — these elements recur also in these contexts.[9] "I will be with thee" — with this word God strengthens the weak human being also in the other call narratives.[10]

The presupposition of this category of narratives is faith in the covenant of God with his people. God has bound himself to come to the aid of his people; the people on its side has acknowledged God as its Lord. In order to maintain the covenant, in order to save his people, or to remind them of their forgotten duties relating to the covenant, God commissions saviours and prophets. In point of fact, the story of the call of Moses ought not to be recorded as belonging to this pattern, for the covenant has not yet been made; Moses has yet to lead the people to Sinai. But for God the covenant is already a reality before Israel has entered upon it; God saves Israel out of Egypt before it has on its side affirmed that it is "God's people", indeed before it has at all experienced itself as an independent people. When God enjoins Moses to "lead *my* people out of Egypt" (Exodus 3,10) he anticipates a reality which he has yet to create by this deliverance from Egypt.[11] So we may hear in the word, with which God introduces himself to Moses, the obligation which God is going to take upon himself in relation to Israel, "I am indeed here, to save you".

By giving himself this name, God expresses his will to be in covenant. Yahweh is the God who wills to be there to help Israel. This understanding of the words "I am indeed here" can be supported by a further study of the context. Moses does not receive this word of God for himself alone. God authorizes him expressly to transmit the name and the signification of the name to the people. Further, it was not on his own initiative that Moses had asked for the name of God. He had put before God the people's question. It is fundamentally through the mediation of Moses that here the conversation between God and the people, the people and God, is carried on. This self-introduction of God is not meant for Moses, but for all Israel.

The Significance of the Name in the ancient World
But what could lead the Israelites to ask these questions concerning the name? They could have inquired about an unknown — yet Moses does not claim to bring news concerning an Unknown. "The God of your fathers has sent me to you." For what purpose should they still wish to know his name? Why are they not content to know him as the God of Abraham, Isaac and Jacob?

In this question concerning the name we can detect disappointment about the God of the fathers. This God did nothing to prevent their successors falling into slavery. What kind of a God is that? The question about the nature of God, about his significance for men, can in the ancient world take the shape of a question about his name.

In order to understand that, we must familiarize ourselves with what in those days a name could signify. Then, as today, the name is a description of the bearer of the name. What is known, can be named. The converse also holds good: what can be named is also known. When a child learns to speak, it learns of the existence, the peculiar qualities, and of the name of a thing at the same time. This close connection of name and name-bearer, is easily obscured to the modern consciousness; the name often appears as a label stuck on — it can be attached subsequently to a new product, in order to give it the most effective advertisement. But for the ancient peoples both thing and name together came into existence. "When the heaven above had not yet been named, the solid earth beneath had not yet been called by its name . . ." — is the beginning of the Mesopotamian epic of the world's creation. According to Genesis 2,19 Adam gives their name to the animals which have just been created

— he can name them because he is capable of apprehending their particular character; he knows that none of them can be comrades of equal rank with himself. The name and the nature of a thing belong together.[12] We may make a comparison with the modern formulae of chemicals. They do not only describe a substance, but give an insight into its structure, and make it possible for us to handle them correctly. In the ancient world, people were convinced that every name had a significance of this kind. We must be clear what this leads to in the case of people who think in terms of magic. The knowledge of the true name gives power over the bearer of the name. The man who can pronounce in the right manner the name of a god, can influence him.

It was in such a world that the Israelites lived. Egyptian magicians threatened gods who would not do what they wanted, that they would betray their names to the demons.[13]

Behind the question of the Israelites "What is his name?" there might on the one hand be the wish to learn the nature and the significance of this God, who once led the fathers, but to all appearance had forgotten their descendents: what kind of a God then is this God of our fathers? But they might desire to gain for themselves still more security; if they only knew the name, then they would be more likely to succeed in binding their God to themselves, to make use of his power; by what name are we to summon him?

The Old Testament gives in many places evidence of the conflict of true faith with magical ideas and practices of this kind. We find one example in the Book of Judges. The father of Samson asked the divine messenger who proclaims to him the birth of the child, "What is your name?" The messenger rebuffs him "How can you ask for my name? It is a name that cannot be disclosed" (Judges 13,16ff.).

God's Name as a Statement about his Sovereignty

Against such a background it must surprise us that God not only surrenders his name to the inquiring Israelites, but over and above this even teaches them to understand him in the right manner. But precisely this explanation lifts the otherwise uninterpretable name out of magical obscurity. The name "I am who I am" cannot be applied magically. It does indeed give comfort to the inquiring Israelites; it promises the effectual help of God, God has not forgotten the people, he is there to save them. But Israel cannot lay claim to his salvation. The relative clause of the formula of interpretation speaks of the freedom of God. "I am who I am". God depends on nothing earthly, only on himself.

A parallel is to be found in Exodus 33, 19, which sheds a clearer light on this significance of the relative clause. God speaks to Moses:

I will pronounce in your hearing the Name Yahweh
I will be gracious to whom I will be gracious,
And I will have compassion on whom I will have compassion.

20

Kindness and compassion belong so essentially to God that he chooses his name accordingly, but no one can demand kindness and compassion from God. God himself determines to whom he is kind and compassionate. The same thing is true for the divine name. "I am who I am". This name speaks of God's will to be in covenant. God is ready to come to the aid of his own. But these may not presume upon it as their right. This word is God's free promise. He offers his helping presence, he does not let himself be at the disposal of man.[14]

How seriously this reference in the relative clause to God's freedom is meant, becomes clear when we think that here an answer was given to the reproach contained in the question about the name. The Israelites had thought that this God had no significance for them: he had forgotten them. Such reproaches cannot apply to God. In fact, no person might say, "God is not here to help us." The man who says that has forgotten that God's presence to help is an impenetrable mystery of the divine nature. God is always there to help, the only question is whether he is there to be experienced as man would like him to be.

"I am indeed here as the One that I truly am" has however more to say; God is indeed dependent on himself alone, but not for that reason unaccountable. He is true to himself.

This interpretation of the name of God cannot be understood as the uncovering of the divine nature; it is, on the contrary, a hint of the inconceivable mystery of God. Through this interpretation of God's name Israel experiences three things; God wills to be present to help, he condescends to do this in full sovereignty; in this he always remains true to himself. All this God does not allow to be predicted of him; we cannot remind him of what is fitting for him and what not, by referring to this name. Israel experiences who God is, but in the future is compelled time and again to experience this God afresh.

We still have to reflect that the name of Yahweh is made known in the speech-form of the divine self-introduction. It is not without intention that the narrator puts the proclamation and the interpretation in the mouth of God himself. From God himself and from no one else can man learn who God is. God must introduce himself and make himself known.

Historicity of Exodus 3

Many exegetes assume that it was not theological reasons alone that made the narrator choose the speech-form of self-introduction, but that here there is still reflected a true historical knowledge of happenings in the time of Moses. It was only through Moses that Israel got to know this God; through Moses One who was hitherto wholly unknown introduced himself to Israel.

Against this we must first note that in the narrative Yahweh is the God of the fathers, not a strange God. It was only the name of this God, according to the belief of the biblical narrators, that Israel had not

21

hitherto known, or at least it had not known the meaning of the name. It is this that the narrator indicates, when he avoids the name of Yahweh in all the preceding sections.

Yet the witness of the Bible is not quite clear upon this point. In order to make this matter clear we must first be introduced to the author of our narrative. Scholarship has named the unknown man from the time of the monarchy "the Elohist", for the simple reason that he chooses in preference to describe God as Elohim. His work is not preserved in its purity, but has been interwoven with two other narrative works to make the Pentateuch, the so-called Books of Moses. These two other works however represent other conceptions of the call of Moses and the revelation of the name of Yahweh.

The Yahwist's work is older than the Elohist's. In the narrative of the call of Moses in the Yahwist, the revelation of the name of God is not mentioned at all.[15] According to the Yahwist, long before the Flood, men called upon the name of Yahweh (Gen. 4,26); already Abraham was building altars in honour of Yahweh's name in the land that Israel was later to inhabit (Gen. 12,7).

In Exodus 6, 2-8 there is a parallel account of the call of Moses from a much later time. This text of the Priestly Document certainly attests the revelation of the name of Yahweh to Moses — but knows nothing of an interpretation of the name.

Now, which is right? Did Israel learn through Moses the name of Yahweh and its interpretation, or only the name, or was the name known very much earlier? Like many other historical questions this one cannot be answered merely by the literary interpretation of the different texts. For this question did not interest the authors; they wished to answer quite different problems. The Elohist, in the narrative of the call, inquires about God's covenant with Israel: is God there to help Israel? The Yahwist dates the knowledge of Yahweh's name so far in the past, because his concern is to show Yahweh as the Lord of mankind; in fact mankind — not only Israel — should have called upon Yahweh. As will become clear in what follows, there are theological and not historical reasons why the Priestly Document does not take up the interpretation of the name of Yahweh with reference to God's will to be in covenant.

The historical question: since when did Israel know the name of Yahweh? — can only be approached when one uses other tools of inquiry than the mere linguistic exegesis of the text, combining many texts, and, going behind them, puts questions to them which were unimportant to the authors themselves.[16]

But one thing can be said with some degree of certainty: the profound interpretation of the Elohist hardly comes out of Mosaic times. Otherwise it would be inexplicable that it hardly finds any echoes in the Old Testament. Only the prophet Hosea, who, like the Elohist, lived in the Northern kingdom, assumes that his hearers know this interpretation. As God's messenger he uses the dissolution of the covenant as a threat

"For you I am One who is not truly here to help you" (lit. "I (am) a 'I am not truly here for you'") (Hosea 1,9).

Insertion into the Tradition of Israel

Thus the artificial etymology of the name of Yahweh was known to a small circle only, and for a short time. If Moses had communicated it to Israel at the same time as the name of Yahweh, this interpretation would certainly have spread more widely.

So, as for us, for Israel in general the etymology of the name of Yahweh was unknown. However, that does not mean that the name said nothing to the people. The name was highly treasured, quite apart from its interpretation being known. The knowledge of the name guaranteed to Israel that it knew the bearer of the name; it made it possible to call upon God. In contrast with this, the knowledge of its etymology was unimportant. Even without such interpretation the name had a rich content; everyone who uttered it could in so doing remember all Israel's experiences of Yahweh. Especially Yahweh's fundamental act of salvation by which he first created Israel, was evoked when this name was named.

I am Yahweh your God since your days in Egypt,
When you knew no other saviour than me (Hosea 13,4; 12,10).

The formula of self-introduction "I am Yahweh" is in its linguistic form different from the interpretative formula of the Elohist: "I am indeed here as the One that I truly am". The meaningful verb *hāyāh* does not appear in the formula of self-introduction. This is instead formed as a noun clause which contains no verb.[17] God's formula of self-introduction in the Elohistic narrative stands on the one hand in the broad stream of tradition, according to which God introduces himself as "Yahweh" — but it gives this tradition a very idiosyncratic form, by attaching the etymology of the name, and using it to make a profound theological statement. Thus the Elohist stands in a broad tradition.

History of the Formula of Self Introduction

Through the formula "I am Yahweh" Israel was repeatedly reminded of the source of its knowledge of the divine name; before Israel can call on God by his name, God must himself make this name known. Magical conceptions — that the invocation of the name has an influence upon God, brings him near — are thus made in principle impossible: it is not magic attached to a name, but God's free movement of grace towards Israel, that guarantees God's presence.

Wherever I cause my name to be invoked I will come to you and bless you (Exodus 20,24).

The formula of self-introduction is almost always conjoined with a proclamation of God's will. The best-known, and indeed the fundamental passage in this context, is the Decalogue.[18] It begins with the words:

"I am Yahweh your God, who brought you out of Egypt."

This statement, in its context is really very remarkable. For at Sinai, God is no longer an Unknown, for Israel has long since had experience of the powerful help of Yahweh. But even when the hearers already know the name, the statement "I am Yahweh" has a meaning. The name Yahweh is never spoken in vain, least of all when God himself utters his name. By proclaiming his name over the people, God declares his right to rule over the people. There is an analogy when the name of the victor is proclaimed over the conquered city (2 Samuel 12,28), the name of the husband over the wife (Isaiah 4,1).

We find this use of the formula "I am Yahweh" in the handing down of the law. One of the Old Testament collections of laws repeatedly authorizes particular commandments in this way.[19] When the priests read aloud the laws before the people, they proclaimed God's lordship over Israel.

"I am Yahweh" is here the public assertion of Yahweh's power over his people. At the same time, however, this statement speaks of the inconceivable mystery of the divine will. Israel's priests could give the commandments no justification, beyond the fact that they came from Yahweh, who had the right to give them.

It is this meaning of the formula which the prophet of the Exile, Deutero-Isaiah underlines; the name of God is an indication of the unfathomable mystery of Yahweh.

But on that day my people shall know my name,
They shall know that it is I who speak; Here am I.[20]

Deutero-Isaiah proclaims a new beginning to the people after the fall of Israel and Judah; God turns to Israel as Saviour once more. The prophet does not know of any argument with which to support this message of salvation, other than the indication that it is God himself who is acting. In this new beginning there can be experienced something of the inconceivable mystery of God, of his "name".

But in the last resort everything that Israel experienced in its history is to be interpreted in this manner. All the processes of history are for ever throwing fresh light on the mystery of the God who is at work in them. Ezekiel who, also in exile, preached shortly before Deutero-Isaiah, sees in this the goal of all God's activity. Israel and the nations are to "know that I am Yahweh".[21]

The Account in P.

To this time also belongs the account of the call of Moses in the priestly document. The whole narrative in Exodus 6, 2-8 is built around the formula of self-introduction. With the words "I am Yahweh" God introduced himself to Moses; with the same words Moses is to begin and close his message to Israel. The centre of this message also is the name of Yahweh.

"I will adopt you as my people, and I will become your God. You shall know that I, Yahweh, am your God, the God who releases you from your bondage in Egypt." (Exodus 6,7)

In the Elohist's account, God's charge to Moses was "Lead my people out of Egypt". Here, on the contrary, Moses is sent out, in order that the Israelites may "know that I am Yahweh". The deliverance from Egypt, the covenant which makes Israel God's people, and Yahweh Israel's God — all this happens only for the sake of this one goal. The name Yahweh must disclose its meaning to the people. It is noticeable that instead of the smoother statement "so shall you know me" the abrupt formulation is chosen "so shall you know that I am Yahweh". The name Yahweh includes in itself the mystery of God; this name is to become for Israel an eloquent name.

Israel did indeed learn from Moses that God's name is Yahweh — but that did not mean that it had learnt to know God's name once and for all. All the rest of God's further purpose for Israel, is to happen, in order that the people should penetrate further into the mystery of this name, that it may know "that I am Yahweh". The revelation of God's name to Moses was only the beginning of a great history, in the course of which Israel must penetrate ever deeper, ever anew, into the mystery of its God, who expressed himself in his name.[22]

Ineffability of the Divine Name

In the history of the name of Yahweh in the Old Testament, right from the beginning the thought of the incomprehensibility of God was important. It became more and more dominant. On the other side, the thought that God has revealed his mystery in this name, and will continue more and more to disclose it, fell into the background. The joy of knowing God through his name was replaced by the fear of that which, inscrutable to men, concealed itself behind the name.

"If you do not revere Yahweh your God, this honoured and dreaded name, then Yahweh will strike you and your descendants with unimaginable plagues, malignant and persistent, and with sickness, persistent and severe." (Deuteronomy 28,58f).

In the fourth century B.C. there begins a process which was not complete till centuries later: people dread to use the name "Yahweh". The Jews replace it by calling on "the Lord". Even the New Testament stands in this tradition, and so it comes that the name of God is scarcely known any longer to Christians.

Summary and Survey

We may today claim the right not to use the name of God any longer. But we ought to know what a special relation to God was possible in Israel through the use of the name of Yahweh. The man who speaks only

25

of "God" runs the risk of thinking only of an abstract deity, a supreme power. Yahweh was for Israel the mysterious God, incomprehensible and yet present in all historical experiences, whose will it is to give himself to be known in his deeper mystery. "Yahweh" was the God who had entered into covenant with the people, who had committed himself to Israel, and who at the same time, as sovereign Lord of the covenant, could not be called to account.

In the interpretation of the Old Testament texts of the revelation of the divine name, so many different approaches had to be used, that an unprejudiced reader of this section may ask himself whether too much has not artificially been read into the text. Were the narratives then not so composed as to be intelligible even to simple believers without many explanations? Even on us the elohistic narrative can have a profound effect, as soon as we read it for the first time. Yet we may not leave this impression untested, if we really wish to grasp what the biblical author means. For we have before us a translation which comes not only from a strange language, but out of a long past, and, by our way of thinking a really exotic world.

1. We were compelled to observe that the translator at times has no English word at his disposal which has a similar range of significance as the Hebrew. Then no alternative is left except to try to grasp the meaning of the Hebrew word, and to infer from the context what part of the range of the word's meaning fits the passage of the text lying before us. (Example: *hāyāh* — to be, Elohim — God).

2. The translation can mislead us because it does not exactly reflect the inner structure of the language. "I am Yahweh" and "I am indeed here as the One that I truly am" both contain in English "I am", but in the Hebrew the significant *hāyāh* is not found in the formula "I am Yahweh". Further "I am" is an inexact rendering of the Hebrew equivalent, because in this language there is no tense of the verb corresponding to the English present tense. For a right understanding of the text it was thus necessary to learn to know something of the structure of the language.

3. We were compelled to feel our way further into the special way of speaking of the ancients, and their relationship to language, in order to understand them. Word-plays, etymologies, names, mnemonics, repetition of significant words, affect us otherwise than they did these people.

4. All the phenomena mentioned hitherto which are strange to us — the different range of meaning of particular words, the different structure of language, the different relation of people to it — can be connected with another manner of seeing the world and things, and reflecting upon them. The succeeding sections of this first chapter will set these peculiarities of biblical language and ways of speech within a wider context.

With all this we have only seen the first layer of the text. We were compelled to observe that the laws of a particular kind of narration stamped the narrative, and that the same material in the Old Testament has been worked over several times. That led to the question about the relation between narration and historical happening. In conclusion we tried to "place" the text given us in the context of similar traditions. Later chapters will be concerned with these and further questions. What was immediately intelligible for the first hearers of the biblical texts, we must, as far as is still possible make intelligible to ourselves in the present by careful work. These people lived (just as we live today) within a context of relationships, about which they did not need to reflect further, but which influenced everything that they said and heard. We must try to concentrate our attention first on individual strands, and then to direct it to the whole fabric.

2. THE RANGE OF MEANING OF HEBREW WORDS

Greek, Roman, Egyptian and Babylonian plastic art and temples can give us light about the particular character of ancient peoples. But Israel, strangely enough, has not created any sculpture or architecture. Even Solomon's Temple was built by gentile artists according to gentile patterns. In order to know the mind of Israel, we must have recourse to its literary productions; in this field it cannot be doubted that Israel created original works, and even outstripped the neighbouring peoples.

The Picture of Reality in the Language
In spite of all the art of modern translation, the literature of Israel reveals its secret only to those who venture to search out the special peculiarities of the Hebrew language. The language of a literary work cannot be replaced by another language without the work suffering essential changes. Along with the other language there will appear another picture of reality. No one who speaks can see the world as it is. The possibilities offered to him by his language indicate to him the way he orders and understands reality. For the peasant there are in his fields only the many kinds of useful plants, and "weeds"; in the first account of creation only two kinds of plants are distinguished, those that bear seeds, and those that bear fruit, which conceal the seed in the fruit. What appears is not the manifold reality itself, but a picture of reality, seen through the "spectacles" of the words "Weeds", "Seed", "Fruit".

Job 4, 10f. distinguishes by five descriptions five different kinds of lion — while we on the other hand know only "the lion". Every language makes a different selection from the varied profusion of phenomena, and in so doing influences the speaker. The living conditions of the linguistic community stamp its speech and its picture of reality.

Now it could be objected that the world in which Israel lived has long since passed away. What is the use of knowing how reality was reflected in Hebrew speech? How much are we concerned, for example, when we speak of "atoms" to know in what sense the Greek philosopher Democritus used the word? And yet we cannot disregard Israel's understanding of

27

the word "God", what "grace" or "salvation" meant there. Even the Bible reader who is not interested in history but seeks in the Bible guidance for his life, must be required to think his way into Israel's understanding of reality which is concealed in such words. Only by doing this is it possible to avoid basing our faith on our own speculations instead of on the historical revelation. To take a relatively simple example: the beings whom we call "angels" are called in Hebrew *mal'āk*. The Old Testament does not know the category "angel" it names these beings after their task, "messengers". We must not pass over this fact unheeding, when today we speak of "angels".

History of the Hebrew Language

However, this by no means implies that Hebrew is better fitted than modern languages to give a picture of the reality known by faith. The rabbinic scholars and the Church fathers could still believe that Hebrew was the language of God and the first men, from which all other languages were derived. For long we have had another picture of this language. It is the result of a fusion of languages. The ancestors of Israel, who immigrated into Canaan, gave up their own language, which we do not know, and whose existence we can only conjecture, and adopted the language of the inhabitants. The Israelites themselves knew of this in later times: in Isaiah 19,18 Hebrew is called the language of Canaan.

Between the earliest and the latest parts of the Old Testament there lies about a thousand years. The song of Deborah in Judges 5 was composed about 1100 B.C. The Book of Daniel dates from the 2nd century B.C. One might think that the language would have altered much in this period; how hard it is for us to understand Beowulf or even Chaucer! But only a trained eye can detect linguistic differences in the Old Testament.[23]

What is preserved to us in the Old Testament is not the living vernacular of the people. Hebrew as a language of the people was supplanted by Aramaic in a process which took centuries to complete. At the siege of Jerusalem in 701 Jewish leaders asked the enemy envoy to speak Aramaic, in order that the people might not understand him. As little as a century later there are to be found some Aramaic peculiarities in the prophet Jeremiah. In the exile the banished citizens adopted the Aramaic language of the people among whom they were living, but in addition, held fast to the idiom of their home country. In this they were more loyal than those who remained at home. In the second century the Book of Daniel was written. The fact that it has been handed down to us partly in Hebrew and partly in Aramaic is a sign that Hebrew was still understood, but no longer spoken. At the time of Jesus, Hebrew was a language used only by scholars and in the cultus. When Jesus on the cross prayed in Hebrew the beginning of the 22nd Psalm (Eli, Eli, lama sabachthani?) the bystanders did not understand him. (Matthew 27,46f).

The history of Hebrew might have had a negative influence on the transmission of the Hebrew Old Testament. But the decay of the language was halted by the renaissance movement of the so-called Massoretes. These Jewish scholars took care with philosophical exactitude to preserve a pure tradition. For the liturgy of the Jews the preservation of the sacred scriptures was vitally necessary. The Massoretes also divided the text into sections for liturgical use, giving to it a uniform style of language, old-fashioned in comparison with the Hebrew of their day, in a way that was suitable for musical recital in divine service. The Massoretes added the vowel points to the text, which hitherto had been handed down only in consonantal form — this happened in general only in the 5th century A.D., and after that.[24] So we do not even know exactly in what form Jesus knew the Old Testament.

Anyone who knows this background will not believe that it is enough to know Hebrew in order to have access to "genuine" revelation. Even the Hebrew Old Testament gives only a picture of reality broken up into a multitude of reflections. This may be a consolation to the Bible reader who has in addition to cope with the further fragmentation of the picture in the English translation. But it may be of profit for him also to learn special characteristics of the Hebrew language, in order that he may be warned of the danger of prematurely reading his own feelings into biblical words. He is more easily alerted to the way in which other forms of life form the background of many ideas and conceptions.

Thus we understand "grief" as primarily a subjective feeling of the individual; while for the Hebrews it is primarily a social happening; weeping is part of the ritual-mourning for the dead; it can be produced at will.[25]

Even this one example shows that a Hebrew word can sometimes only be inadequately rendered in English, since we do not possess the background which makes it come to life.

Religious Concepts from the Realm of the Judicial Order

Many words from our religious vocabulary express to us principally the religious stance, the action and experience of the *individual*; love, grace, sin, redemption, righteousness. In contrast thereto the central concepts of the Hebrew's faith are set against the background of the *community* and its judicial order. This may surprise us, for "juristic thinking" in the religious sphere has a bad reputation with us. "Legalistic piety" is looked down on, yet we must reflect that for us, even in secular life the judicial order plays a quite different part than it did for the Hebrew. We hardly take note of it at all, except when we are forced to fear that we shall come in conflict with the law, and bear disagreeable consequences for so doing. But in that ancient world, people were so much more conscious how much they depended on the protection of the law. They experienced the judicial order as a blessing; only this order made communal life possible. Over and above this, Israel believed that it owed the whole system of judicial order to its God. In the covenant with Israel — "covenant" is a concept from the judicial realm[26] — Yahweh had promised to protect the life of the people. Israel's judicial order also served this purpose; it protected Israel from inner disintegration.

God the Judge

The picture of God the judge inspires us with fear. But the Hebrew considered rather that this judge can help the weak man to obtain his rights. The judge is the saviour; without him the weak man would become the unprotected victim of violence. Only so can we understand what is happening when the Psalmists pray God to be the judge (Psalm 7,9: 26,1; 43,1; 135,14). The picture of God as the judge can serve to interpret the course of events; the events take on the appearance of a court of law, in which justice must assert itself. David faces up to his persecutor.

"May Yahweh be the judge! May he make a just judgement between me and you. May he look upon and direct my case at law; may he help me to gain my rights against you!" (1 Samuel 24,12).

Punishment

And yet Yahweh's action is not in these pictures understood as rewarding the good man and punishing of the wicked. There is no word in Hebrew for "punishment", and that provides food for thought. God does not attach to the evil deed an additional punishment. What happens is rather that this action bears the seed of evil in itself; while the good deed already brings forth from itself salvation for man. The wickedness of a man falls back on his own head.[27]

Yahweh is not the God of requital, who is more concerned with a "just" balance than he is with good and evil men. He is not a judge who maintains an abstract administration of justice above mens' heads indifferently. On the contrary, the protector of the judicial order protects the life of men.

Redeemer

This thought is reflected in the use of the word "to redeem" (gā'al). It may surprise us that this concept also comes out of the judicial life of Israel. The "redeemer" was the man who in certain cases of need, was under the obligation of protecting the survival of the family, the life and freedom or property of a member of the family. The avenger of blood was such a "redeemer", as was the man who had to ransom an enslaved member of the family, or recover a mortgaged family property. Further, he was the man who, according to the so-called Levirate Law, had to marry the childless wife of his dead brother, in order to raise up descendants for his brother. Only against this background is it intelligible how bold the word about a Redeemer God is. It reminds us of the intimate connection into which God has entered with men. God is, so to speak, seen as a member of one's own family. Only the faith in the covenant of God with Israel could give men the courage to coin such a concept. The Redeemer does not assert an abstract "law", but secures the life and property of those who are his own.

God is the Redeemer, who protects the property of the fatherless. (Proverbs 23,11); he ransoms his people from slavery to strange nations, (Isaiah 52,3); he is even invoked by Job as the avenger of blood who himself after death — which indeed this same God has brought upon him — will appear on his behalf.

But in my heart I know that my vindicator lives
And that he will rise last to speak in court (Job 19,25).

Other words also, which describe the religious bearing of man, are to be understood against the background of judicial thinking. The thought of the community of rights in which Israel lives, is an undertone where the Old Testament speaks of the righteous man.

Righteousness

Righteousness is for us an absolute moral norm which always makes the same demand on men in different circumstances. The Hebrew calls righteous the man who fulfils the claims of the contemporary community. If need be, even the judgement of a court can determine whether a man is "righteous" (we would say "innocent") or not (Deuteronomy 25,1). That man is "righteous" whom no impediment excludes from the worship of the communal cultus (Psalm 15,1).

From this we can understand how Psalmists praying to God draw his attention to their "righteousness". This does not imply an overweening estimation of themselves, or the illusion that they are wholly perfect; their intention is only to say that they have not infringed the order of justice, and have not disturbed the life of the community.

Psalms and Wisdom sayings draw for us the picture of the righteous man who prospers, while the evildoer is unfortunate. We must not understand such texts from the standpoint of utilitarianism — "Act justly, so that you may not suffer penalty!" The harmony with society and its divinely-given order gives the protection which man needs for a happy life. (For this reason the expression of disappointment in some Psalms, and especially in the Book of Job, because the righteous man suffers, is the more violent).

Love of Neighbour

Besides the concept of religious righteousness, the thought of neighbourly love belongs also to this sphere. The injunction "Love thy neighbour as thyself" is to be found in Leviticus 19,18 in connection with directions as to correct behaviour in the legally constituted community. It also has reference to this society. It is only just that the Israelite should meet with love all who stand under the God-given order. To love our neighbour as ourselves is no more than right and equitable.

Religious Experience and Language

Anyone who concerns himself with Hebrew semantics i.e. with the question as to what spheres of reality were disclosed, ordered and mutually limited and demarcated by what words, will repeatedly observe that Israel's religious experiences have deeply stamped themselves on this language. This is not the only case where spiritual experience has stamped itself on the language of a society. Modern philologists maintain, for example, that Old High German took its origin from various German dialects, in the course of the ninth and tenth centuries, in order to carry out the programme set up by Charlemagne, the introduction of the Christian heritage into the areas where these languages were spoken. The struggle to reproduce in the vernacular ideas which the Germans did not know (*misericordia, gratia,* and others) brought into existence the one High German language.

Truth

Thus it can also be shown by taking different Hebrew words, how the best men of Israel endeavoured to express in words the people's experience of God. This holds good, for example, for the Hebrew equivalent for truth (*'emeth*). We moderns describe as "truth" that "which is", the statement which corresponds to reality is "true". We even tend to limit "truth" to what "really *happened*", and to apply this concept of truth to biblical texts. But ought we not to measure the Bible according to its own concept of truth?

The Hebrew word *'emeth* can also state that an account corresponds with the facts. The Queen of Sheba uses this word when she sees that the reports about Solomon are correct (I Kings, 10,6).

But that applies only to an outer fringe of the field of meaning which is described by *'emeth*. The accent does not lie on the objectively ascertainable facts, but upon the subjective trustworthiness and dependability of man. "Truth" in Hebrew can be ascribed to the state of affairs which is stable; "truth" is the word used when a declaration is reliable. Finally, the dependability and loyalty of a person can also be called "truth". This concept of truth is shared by Hebrew with other Semitic languages. But God's making of a covenant with Israel led to a widening of this concept.

Thy word is founded in truth,

And thy just decrees are everlasting (Psalm 119,160).

With these words a scholar of the later age of the Old Testament, looking backwards sums up everything that he has learnt of God's word in the sacred scriptures of his people. Here, too, a claim to absolute truth is made, but how different it is from what many modern Bible readers would like to understand by the absolute truth of scripture! The Psalmist does not look backwards; he does not compare the word handed down with something that happened a long time ago. He looks rather to the present and future. God's word has always inner stability, whatever may happen, events will never prove God wrong; what God has once decided (in the background is the picture of the course of events as a process at law, where God decides), retains its validity and effectual character; God is true to himself. But the essential decision on the strength of which the Psalmist, as a member of the covenant people, lives, is the election of Israel. To this act and the promises which are associated with it, God remains for ever true. The truth of God is his absolute loyalty to his promises.

Amen

To the same root as *'emeth* belongs a word which has been most widely adopted in modern languages, the word "Amen"; it serves to confirm what has been said. "Constancy", "security" is probably the fundamental meaning of the word's root, which branched out into *'emeth* and *'āmēn*, among other words.

Faith

Another twig of this stem was given religious significance by the prophet Isaiah. It is a verb, which we render in English with the word "believe". Among us a customary description of religious "faith" is the steadfast assurance of truth. The connection of the Hebrew *he'emīn* with *'emeth* and *'āmēn* must already remind us that this only reaches the outermost fringe of the field of meaning of that Hebrew word.

The event that moved Isaiah to open up the religious dimension of *he'emīn* is vividly described[28] in Isaiah 7. Enemies stand at the very gates of Jerusalem; the prophet comes face to face with the terror-filled king, and counsels calm and fearlessness; he confronts the wicked plans of the enemy with God's word; "This will not happen, or come to pass". He concludes the speech with an impressive play upon words which is hard to reproduce in English:

"Have firm faith or you will not stand firm" (Isaiah 7,9).

For a king of the House of David the verb of the main sentence must have a special ring. For the House of David had the promise given to it;

"Your family shall be established (stand firm), and your kingdom shall stand for ever in my sight" (2 Samuel 7,16).[29]

The prophet makes us observe that "stability" is not unconditionally promised to the son of David. But the king will also take note because of the word-play which Isaiah uses. In this statement the prophet brings two verbs into connection with each other, which are closely inter-related. We can approximately imitate this correspondence of the verbs if we translate rather stiffly: "If you do not make a firm stand, you will lose your standing".

Usually *he'emīn* in Hebrew means "to trust, to set one's hopes upon"; elsewhere it is linked with the object of the thing or the person, to whom trust is given. Isaiah widens this customary sense of *he'emīn*. On the one hand, through the linkage with the related verb "to have stability" (*'āman*), he leads it back to its concrete root-meaning, to seek a firm

33

standing. Further, he uses it in the intransitive sense, without connecting it with an object, and by doing so, gives it new weight.

The use of the verb without an object must not be so misunderstood as if Isaiah were refusing to say where the king might seek a firm standing.

The context of the speech will have shown the king where he can find security. Yet the prophet had begun his speech with the exhortation to inner constancy. "Be on your guard, keep calm, do not be frightened or unmanned" . . . (Isaiah 7,4). It is not his enemies that the king has to watch against, but his own cowardice. Only calm and fearlessness can save him; for his enemies themselves are in such danger that in any case they cannot hold out much longer — Isaiah compares them to "smouldering stumps of firewood". It is to this exhortation that the prophet comes back with his word-play at the end of the speech. Everything depends on the king's ability to look quietly on, while things develop. Isaiah has a strong help to offer him, so that he may come to such an inner fortitude, an unambiguous word of God about the enemy's plans: "That will not happen". Thus in the light of this passage "belief" would have to be paraphrased as a bearing of inner fortitude and calm, which owes its certainty to trust in God's word. For this reason faith confronts the development of events in a relaxed manner,

In a word not easy to interpret, Isaiah later once used *he'emīn* in the absolute sense;

"He who has faith shall not make haste" (Isaiah 28, 16f).

This statement is connected with a promise for Zion;

"Look, I am laying in Zion a corner-stone!"

The statement is to be connected with this promise. The man who possesses the inner composure which Isaiah requires from the believer, will not be impatient when he sees no sign of the fulfilment of God's word. Nor will he believe that he can himself bring about the fulfilment more speedily. But the prophet's cry of woe is addressed to the man who does not achieve this calm, which can wait in trust upon God's will:

Shame upon those who drag wickedness along . . .! They say "Let Yahweh make haste, let him speed up his work for us to see it" (Isaiah 5, 18f).[30]

From the use of *he'emīn* in Isaiah can be seen, how much effort it could cost a prophet to give expression to his utterances with the help of the Hebrew words available. An unusual use of language, a reference to a basic word-root through word-play of the word whose root has a kindred meaning, gave help to him in widening the usual meaning-content of *he'emīn* and the whole context of Isaiah's speech helped further. We can only grasp the range of significance of this word by taking into consideration all these data, and by making comparison with other utterances of the prophet.

Word Play

Among the devices by which Isaiah sought to broaden the meaning of the word, that of punning with the verb whose root is related to it seems strange to our ears. How such word-play sounds to us may be illustrated by an example from our own linguistic experience. Heidegger speaks of "thrownness" in order to express the fact that man does not himself create the fundamental situation of his existence, but finds it already in being. But in this situation, man has also unimaginable new possibilities, of which he can lay hold, or even invent, or devise. "And as thrown, Dasein is thrown into the kind of being which we call projecting".[31] This way of speaking seems contrived to us. But Isaiah's word, on the contrary, did not seem remote from life.

Word formation is a much more straightforward process in the Hebrew language than in ours. In the course of the development of the language, the law of triliterality, the law of three letters, had to a great extent carried the day. It means that in the case of nearly all words, a word-root of three consonants can be conjectured. (For example, the root 'mn belongs to he'emīn). Conversely, from the fictitious root (which of course never existed as a word) the different verbal forms can be deduced according to fairly well-established patterns. That the Hebrews were more conscious of such word-connections than we are, could be suggested by a popular Hebrew figure of speech: the use of the same root in different functions in the same sentence, the so-called Paranomasia: to counsel counsel; a speaker spoke; they struck him with the strokes of a single man (they all with one consent set upon him), etc. Isaiah, with his word-play used a figure of speech current in Hebrew.

The narrative of the creation of the first man offers us a familiar illustration of the popularity of the practice of linking together meaningful words whose roots were related. Man is called 'ādām because his origin was the 'adāmāh, the fruitful earth. 'Ādām and 'adāmāh are linked in fellowship from the first by a like destiny. The earth becomes fruitful because the man cultivates it — the man on his side lives from the fruits of the earth, and, finally the curse of man's deed remains on the fruitful field; it bears thistles and thorns on man's account.

This association of language can frequently give the Hebrews the first impulse to grasp a connection in thought. In such cases it is often enough if in relation to a word the memory of another word similar in sound, but not related in root, suggests itself. Amos sees fruit — qayiṣ — before him; with this sight he thinks of the end — qēṣ — of Israel (Amos 8,2). Jeremiah looks at the almond tree — šāqēḏ — and he speaks of Yahweh the watchful — šōqēḏ (Jeremiah 1,11f).

We feel that puns are inappropriate for something as serious as prophetic proclamation. It is only children who take their puns seriously, when, for example in riddles they exchange one homonym for another; but what serious-minded man in using the word "door-lock", thinks at once of the prince's castle?[T] In Job 9,30, on the other hand lye — bōr — is the subject of conversation — the poet thinks of the homonym — bōr — pit, and in the next half-verse sets down a synonym for it — šahaṭ — pit.

35

What lies behind such word-play? We can perhaps understand the mentality of the Hebrews, when we reflect how it annoys us when someone mispronounces our name. Isaiah uses these means to portray his vision of the hostile world power's march through Israel's towns,

He comes to stand *at Aiath*
. . .
Cry *yelling* Bath-*gallim*
*An*swer, *An*athoth
*Mad*menah *makes* off . . . (Isaiah 10,28ff).[32]

Such handling of language arises from another relationship to the word. It was not counted of no significance when words were like other words, for a similarity in words made the Hebrews thinks of a similarity in nature.

Word *(dābār)*

In this connection it is important to glance at the range of significance of the Hebrew word *dābār* (word). "These are but fine words" — with this statement we might reject a report. We understand a word as a reference to a fact, such a reference can sometimes be a mere signpost into the void. This shows the place that we allocate to words in the high-tension field between external reality and the mind of man. They are above all tools of the human intellect; they bear the meaning that man gives to them; they originate with man, and point to things.

In contrast, the Hebrew *dābār*" embraces both word and fact. The tension between word and reality is not so evident to the consciousness of the Hebrew. Fact and word correspond with one another; a word can correspond to fact. Mistrust of language, which might deflect our vision of reality, is not natural to the Hebrew. It is certainly worthy of note that the English equivalent of *dābār*, in addition to "word", is "*fact*" and not "thing". But even in the range of meaning which corresponds to "fact", *dābār* has a mental element; occasions, judicial matters and events are called *dābār*, as soon as man intellectually concerns himself with them. This Semitic use of language is reflected even in the Book of Acts, when the apostles call themselves "witnesses of these words" i.e. the events of salvation (Acts 5,32).

It is more important for our understanding of *dābār* that for the Hebrew the word also includes the act. To speak is also to act; a word brings operative forces into play. We most easily understand this when we think of a word of command. When we say "The king built this city", we understand building principally in terms of "speaking"; he gave the orders. According to the ideas of ancient times the power of the word goes much further than this. Even the man who has spoken it, can hardly subsequently cancel its effect. In Judges 17, 2ff the story is told of a woman who uttered a curse on the thief who had robbed her, certainly to the effect that the thief might have no joy of his stolen property. But then her own son returns to her the stolen money. She wishes to avert the ill-fortune from him, and makes out of it an idol for him. But soon a band of robbers steal from him the image, together with the priest whom he has taken into his service.

How important was the power of the word in the thinking of the Hebrews is shown — among other things — by their dividing up the field of meaning which we describe as "cursing" more precisely by means of several words. One of these words belongs to judicial language, *'lh*; it has two meanings; first the curse which is to compel the undiscovered thief, or receiver of stolen goods, or dishonest finder of them to restore the stolen property, and secondly the curse which secures oaths and contracts. Much more powerful is a second word *'rr*; such a curse can only be uttered by powerful men. To execute such a curse against Israel, the king of Moab on his own initiative fetched Balaam from far to help him. (Numbers 22ff). With this powerful word of malediction also secret crimes are visited, which never come to the light of day (Deuteronomy 27,15-26). But God can never come under the power of such a word; when the wicked curse God, that is done with the help of a third word, *qll*, (of course a curse of this nature can also be directed against men). Since the Hebrews were convinced of the effectual power of the word, they took puns, riddles, alliterations etc. very seriously. All this was more than mere trifling, for words could set in motion powers which brought into effect what they said.

God's Word

The range of meaning of *dābār*, like the content of many other words, is widened where the Old Testament wishes to speak of God. In the rest of the Orient also the idea of the effectual power of the word was used in statements about the gods:

If thy word sinks into the sea, the sea heaves,

If thy word sinks into the marsh, the marsh heaves,

When thy word drives along the heaven like the wind

It brings to the land abundance of food and drink,

When thy word goes forth upon earth, it causes luxuriant grass to grow.[33]

We find in the Old Testament similar sayings about the power of the divine word over nature.

By my word I dried up the sea (Isaiah 50,2).

Every reader of the Bible is familiar with the thought of the creative power of the divine word. We find this also in Deutero-Isaiah:

With my own hands I founded the earth,

With my right hand I formed the expanse of sky,

When I summoned them, they sprang at once into being (Isaiah 48,13).

But the point of origin in Israel for the conception of God's word is not the thought of the creative power over nature of the divine word. Oscar Grether has reckoned that in 93 per cent of all passages "the word of

37

God" is the technical term for the revelation of God to the prophets. It is from this viewpoint that we must understand the Old Testament concept. Through the word which God causes his prophets to speak he guides history. The narratives concerning the appearing of Elijah are instructive. His word summons the drought, his word also brings it to an end (I Kings, 17ff). Through Elijah Yahweh influences *natural* events in order to intervene in the *history* of Israel, to call it back from the worship of Baal.

The word of the prophets does not announce happenings which would have come even without this word. Rather does it set in motion the powers which bring the event to pass. The word of God is a power in history.

> Therefore I have lashed you through the prophets,
> and torn you to shreds with my words (Hosea 6,5).

Since the Israelites feared this power of the prophetic word, they tried to silence Amos (Amos 8,10ff). For this reason the king burnt Jeremiah's scroll with the prophecies of doom (Jeremiah 36,21ff). For this reason the prophet Uriah had to die (Jeremiah 26,20ff). But the prophets know that God's word is not impaired when it is persecuted and its proclamation obstructed. For God's word is much more than the prophet's word. Jeremiah says often that God's word which he must proclaim transcends his own powers, even oppresses his own will:

> I am reproached and mocked all the time
> for uttering the word of the LORD,
> Whenever I said, 'I will call him to mind no more,
> nor speak in his name again',
> then his word was imprisoned in my body,
> like a fire blazing in my heart.[34]

Even against the will of the prophet, God's will takes effect. Although the concept "God's word" is a prophetic technical term, the prophets see their own proclamation as an inessential element in the realization of the word of God. The prophet who proclaims the word does not need to be mentioned in this context:

> and as the rain and the snow come down from heaven
> and do not return until they have watered the earth,
> making it blossom and bear fruit,
> and give seed for sowing and bread to eat,
> so shall the word which comes from my mouth prevail;
> it shall not return to me fruitless
> without accomplishing my purpose
> or succeeding in the task I gave it.[35]

The concept "word" has an essential connection with "speaking". Here, however, there is no longer any thought of the "word of God" being also uttered aloud. "The word of God" becomes a description of the power of God at work in the world.

Deutero-Isaiah puts at the beginning (Isaiah 40,6-8), and at the end of his book (55,10f), the proclamation of the power of the word of God, which stands unshakable above the chances and changes of history. The word of our God endures for evermore. (Isaiah 40,8).

The older prophets were convinced that God spoke through them a word relevant to a particular historical situation. Deutero-Isaiah has developed this thought further in two directions. Neither the prophet nor a particular historical hour has to be mentioned when he speaks of the power of the word of God. The conception of the word of God has, so to speak, become more abstract. This explains why Deutero-Isaiah became the earliest witness for the thought of the creative power of the divine word in nature.

Mythological Elements

He can venture to imitate mythological forms of expression, for in his preaching there is no longer a great risk of their being misunderstood. An example will show this process of a more pronounced abstraction which is at the same time a more vivid depiction of the word of God:

Did you think my arm too short to redeem,
did you think I had no power to save?
Not so. By my rebuke I dried up the sea,
and turned rivers into desert (Isaiah 50, 2).

In the heathen myth of the struggle of the God Marduk with Tiamat, the sea-goddess Tiamat gives way before the rebuke of Marduk. But the prophet did not awaken any mythical conceptions in his hearers with this verse. The alterations in the mythical picture are significant. In the heathen epic Tiamat is not dried up, but put to flight. The drying up of the sea must have reminded the Israelites of the deliverance from Egypt. A memory out of the history of their own people mingles here with the echo of the heathen myth: the divine word is not a magical power that dominates nature, but powerful help for Israel; it possesses the power to redeem.

And yet even the memory of the Exodus from Egypt does not sound quite exact, for there Yahweh did not dry up the "rivers", (nor were "heaven" and "fish" involved) (Isaiah 50,2-3). Has Deutero-Isaiah transformed the motif to make it relevant for the Israelites banished into the land between the Euphrates and the Tigris? Now we encounter in other passages in the Old Testament the picture of a world-wide drought which Yahweh summons forth.[36]

Was there perhaps a mythical narrative which contained this motif? Even if Deutero-Isaiah has drawn his method of expression from such a narrative, his only concern is to give encouragement to the exiles; his purpose is to show that God's word has the power to help even them. The very mingling of the motifs indicates that his use of mythical elements was for him a means of expression, and not the content of what he wished to say.

The conception of "the word of God" in Deutero-Isaiah could be

39

dissociated from the concrete situation in which a prophet at a particular hour transmits to particular men the message of God. But for all that, the prophet is not speaking in pallid abstractions. The adoption of mythological motifs has reference to a concrete historical happening, permits him to continue speaking powerfully and vividly of God's word.

Emphasis on the Concrete

The reader of the Bible must always reckon with the Hebrew tendency to use vivid language. Words that for us are "sicklied o'er with the pale cast of thought" are often for him still firmly anchored in concrete contexts. What our speech distinguishes as "spirit", "breath", "wind", is held together in the Hebrew word *rūᵃh*. The divine spirit over the primaeval waters becomes visible in the picture of the storm over the sea (Genesis 1,2). And thus the creative power of the spirit of God can be concretely grasped, God's mouth needs but to breathe, and the stars come into being. (Psalm 33,6). Breath is a sure indication of life, and God's spirit works like the breath of life in the world (Psalm 104,30).[37] We must reckon with the fact that Hebrew passes easily from one nuance of meaning to another, above all, that for him along with a more abstract word there is still a resonance of the basic ground-tone.

This way of thinking and speaking may be illustrated by a further example. "The people" — this word basically describes an abstraction, which no one can clearly envisage. Israel, Moab, the Canaanites — how shall such entities be concretely grasped? The Israelite easily pictures the multitude who constitute a people as a single person:

Say to Pharaoh: thus says Yahweh:
Israel is my first-born son.
I say to you; let my son go, so that he may worship me.
But if you refuse to let him go, I shall kill your first-born son (Exodus 4,23).

The picture of the people as the son of God is linked with the concrete statement about the son of Pharaoh. The peoples become visible for the Hebrews in the forms of their ancestors. In the narratives about the latter he can hear also statements about the people who sprang from them. For example, what is said in Genesis 2f about Adam (Man), gives information immediately to the Hebrew about humanity, without his needing a special interpretation of the narrative for this purpose.

For a translator it is impossible to reproduce in his English version all the undertones which accompanied the words for the Hebrew. The modern Bible reader is therefore dependent on explanation, if he is not to misunderstand the ancient texts. In this section, it was only possible to indicate by examples how little we can spare ourselves the trouble of continually returning important words of the biblical text into their original context, and thus opening up their meaning for ourselves.

3. ANALYSIS OF STYLE AS A WAY TO THE UNDERSTANDING OF BIBLICAL TEXTS

The student of modern literature takes it for granted that in the analysis and interpretation of a text he should inquire about the style — what kind of words is chosen? What sentence structure? How is the text divided up? Are there peculiarities of rhythm or assonance? It is astonishing that hitherto in Old Testament exegesis there have been hardly any methodical introductions to the study of style. The man who investigates the style of a text, must make himself familiar with its individual form. In the exegesis of the Old Testament modern scholars are much more inclined to seek for what is typical in the literary productions. They tend rather to see in the Old Testament examples of textual categories than individual speech forms. They more often ask for what underlies the present text, for the traditions and sources out of which it has been formed, than about the final form which lies before us.

The Preference for the Traditional
The reason for this noticeable difference between modern Old Testament exegesis and modern literary studies relating to other fields of literature is to be found in the peculiarity of Old Testament literature itself. The authors of the Old Testament texts hardly strive at all for originality and individuality. They stick close to what is conventional. They wish to preserve the vitality of the ancient faith. It is in fact remarkable that it was possible to unite the Old Testament writings, which took nearly a thousand years to produce, within the confines of a single book. This was only possible because in Israel itself, in this long period of time, there were no intellectual changes so decisive as to break the bond with the older primitive traditions.

How can we understand this marked dependency of the Hebrew spirit? Whence does the traditional element draw such power? These people lived in much smaller communities than us. In a village, everyone knows everyone else; in these places there is no possibility of trying new experiments without being observed. In addition, they felt more than we do an encircling threat. They were possessed by a secret fear of nature. True, the creator had once divided the waters of chaos; he had locked it safely into the sea and above the clouds — but could it not break loose again? In the face of such fear they could only hold to the promise of God.

Never again shall the water be a flood (Genesis 9,14).
They did not even trust the rhythm of the seasons and days — they were not sure that day and night would come again, that there would be seedtime and harvest in the course of the year. God's word removes this fear from them — but not their own insight into the regular laws of nature:

> While the earth lasts,
> seedtime and harvest,
> cold and heat,
> summer and winter,
> day and night, shall never cease (Genesis 8,22).

These people found safety in the security of the great family. This alone gave them protection in case of need, protected the rights of its members. It was not for nothing that those who live without family, orphans, widows, foreigners, were in the Bible repeatedly taken under special protection.

The spirit of these people took delight in the adornment of the life of society. This life is hedged in with customs and festivals; the people find support in particular rules. There are unwritten laws even for conversation; every speaker intends to speak as "one speaks". In narrative, instruction, riddles, sayings and songs, rules are adhered to.

Individual Style-forms in the Old Testament

Texts which have been created in such an environment are certainly best to be interpreted by investigation of categories; their link with tradition is the strongest influence in their formation. And yet the texts were not transferred direct to the Old Testament from the mouths of these people. These orally transmitted linguistic fragments became literature. They were collected and sifted by highly educated people, who had so wide an outlook on the knowledge of their time that they could at least partially free themselves from their rigid subjection to the community. The prophets, who had to answer for every one of their words, were the first who really spoke a personal language. Analysis of style, which investigates the individual forms of speech, and the study of genres, which throws into relief what is typical, must cooperate in the interpretation of the Old Testament.

For yet another reason it is important to pay attention to stylistic refinements in the Old Testament. The hearers of these texts had an ear receptive to fine-sounding language; they took note of a skilfully constructed narrative, a well-turned phrase; they were ready to admit inaccuracies in the reporting of facts, even logical errors, for the sake of such things. When the young David was recommended to Saul, among all his merits emphasis was laid upon his eloquence. Even women in Israel understood how to speak cleverly and convincingly; the narrative about the witty Abigail and the woman of Tekoa certainly reflected the reality.[38]

The authors of the Old Testament texts could be certain that a good style of speech would be well received. They often consciously used rhetorical devices in order to influence their hearers. Works of scholarship today are seldom judged on their literary style. But in Israel poetry was reckoned as the only medium suitable for the impartation of "wisdom". Here, where we have to deal with "knowledge", the form is not a garment loosely thrown over an utterance; only in the fitting form does the utterance appear in the right light.

But how are we able to give any judgement at all of individual types of speech? Just as the Hebrews felt differently from us about language, so many means of expression had a different effect upon them than they have upon us today. Therefore we must ask what was normal in Hebrew speech, what attracted attention, what general possibilities were given by speech, and what was regarded as unusual.

Short Word Units

Statements which in our language are divided up into a number of words are often expressed in Hebrew in just one word. (Abraham says to his servant Eliezer "I want you to swear an oath" — to these seven words there corresponds one single word in Hebrew: $w^{e'}a\check{s}b\bar{\imath}^{'a}k\bar{a}$). Conjunctions and expletives are uncommon. This gives a Hebrew sentence the appearance of a structure of equally emphasized word units. This impression is further strengthened by the lack of subordinating conjunctions. The normal style of Hebrew speech lays equal emphasis upon coordinated sentences. Subordinate clauses are rare and there are few possibilities for logical structuring in main clauses and subordinate clauses of various kinds such as are exemplified, for example, with specially rich profusion in the language of Cicero. In narratives events are often strung together in long sequences by the means of "and".[39] The style has a ponderous effect on us. Short principal clauses are interrupted by frequent pauses, which allow the individual words to echo in the ear.

Long Sentence Structures

It is the more surprising, therefore, when we meet a long elaborate sentence. The second creation story begins with just such a long sentence:

On the day when Yahweh God made heaven and earth —
there was not yet any shrub of the field upon the earth
nor did there grow any plant of the field,
because Yahweh God had not caused it to rain upon the earth,
and there was no man ($'\bar{a}\underline{d}\bar{a}m$) to till the ground ($'^a\underline{d}\bar{a}m\bar{a}h$)
and a mist rose out of the earth, and watered all the face of the ground —
then Yahweh God formed a man ($'\bar{a}\underline{d}\bar{a}m$) out of dust of the ground ($'^a\underline{d}\bar{a}m\bar{a}h$).
he breathed into his nostrils the breath of life,
and thus the man became a living creature (Genesis 2, 4b-6)

We are accustomed to derive the second account of creation from popular saga. The picture of the Creator who forms man from moist earth from the ground, and blows breath into him, seems to point us in that direction, as does the picture of desolate chaos without rain and without cultivation, from which life upon earth originates. From this picture of a form of landscape, which often supplies the material for popular sagas, can be derived also the strange picture of rising mist,[40] which cannot be logically fitted in; the thought could be of a ground-water oasis in the desert. Finally the double word-play on 'aḏām and 'aḏāmāh seems also to point to a popular origin.

Though the material may come from this area, the style of the language is anything but popular: the given elements are brought together into a new unity in a great artistic structure of thought and language. The arch of heaven is spanned to include man; the creation of the world is only the back-drop before which the drama of man's creation is played. The bow is stretched taut between these two poles by means of the long insertion, a picture of the beginning and origin of creation.

Even in the matter of content this interpolation increases the tension. The ground of the field is still without life, for both God and man must first play their part in order that life may appear on it. Man must work together with God in creation — must he not be a miraculous work of creation? But this expectation is disappointed: the man who is to waken life in the fruitful ground is himself formed out of the ground. The word "dust of the ground" emphasizes his humble origin. The author even risks a logical inexactitude in order to be able to speak of "dust"; the ground was moist through the rising ground-water, and further moist clay, not "dust" is the potter's material.[41] Man is dust, of no account, and dead like dry earth which the wind blows away. The author takes up this motif again in Genesis 3,19; in death man returns to the dust. It is God alone who gives breath and life to this dead dust. On something so intangible and so fleeting as a breath of wind depends the whole significance of man.[42] And yet the construction of the sentences, which embraces the whole creation, is aimed at him.

It is no naive narrator whom we encounter here, but a man whose capacity to build up conceptual tension through the form of his sentences and the choice of his words, bespeaks his high culture. With this sentence begins the work of the so-called Yahwist, who in Solomon's time wrote a history of Israel which became one of the foundations of the Pentateuch as we have it. The very first sentence of his work shows his skill at giving new theological content to popular traditions.

A quite different type of sentence-construction — even more striking in the normally terse Hebrew style — is found in Deuteronomy:

> When Yahweh, your God, brings you to a rich land,
> a land of streams, of springs, and underground waters,
> gushing out in hill and valley,
> a land of wheat and barley, of vines, fig-trees and pomegranates,
> a land of olives, oil and honey,
> a land where you will never live in poverty,
> nor want for anything,
> a land whose stones are iron-ore, and from whose hills you will dig copper,

when you have plenty to eat and bless Yahweh your God
for the rich land that he has given you,
take care not to forget Yahweh your God,
and do not fail to keep his commandments, laws, and statutes which I
give you this day,
lest,
when you have plenty to eat,
and live in fine houses of your own building,
and your herds and flocks increase,
and your silver and gold increase,
and all your possessions increase too,
lest you become proud,
and forget Yahweh your God,
who brought you out of Egypt, out of the land of slavery,
who led you through the vast and terrible wilderness,
infested with poisonous snakes and scorpions, a thirsty and waterless
land,
who caused water to flow for you from the hard rock,
who fed you in the wilderness on manna which your fathers did not
know,
to humble you and test you,
and in the end to make you prosper,
lest you think;
"My own strength and energy have gained me this wealth",
but that you may remember Yahweh your God,
for he has given you strength to become prosperous,
so fulfilling the covenant
guaranteed by oath with your forefathers,
as he is doing now. (Deuteronomy 8,7-18).

This sentence is certainly the longest in the whole Old Testament, much too long for the hearers to be able to take it in as a *single* entity. Instead of causing tension, it invites us to linger by each individual clause of the sentence. The author is not content to speak of "the good land"; he breaks out, as it were into a hymn to this land. Five times he begins his praise anew: "a land . . ." and in each of these five sections the wealth of the land is named once more, at least with two synonyms, once with as many as five. The ancient rhetoric of the Greeks and Romans knew the figure of speech *amplificatio*: what could be said in a few words is blown up into a torrent of words. But this hymn to the land is more than an empty expansion of the word about "the good land". The wealth of Canaan is vividly portrayed in exuberant terms, with pleasing rhythm and resonance, in a variety of different word-sequences, of which no two are constructed in the same way. In his development by means of parallelism the author has carefully avoided repetitions of the same forms. When he comes for a second time to speak of the land of Canaan he does not look at the wealth of the land but at the wealth of its inhabitants; he does not see it all at once in the round, but pictures with deft strokes its growth. First comes the satisfaction of hunger; only after that the joy in beautiful houses — Israel becomes a cultured people — first the flocks increase, then the wealth is so great that it can only be estimated in gold and precious metals.

In spite of all the exuberance, the words are inserted sparingly. In the third great expansion the wanderings in the desert are not really described. On the contrary, significant catchwords bring again to life this memory, which was in the beginning familiar to all hearers of the statement.

But is the context not lost through the overloading of the different sections? We must first set before us in order the chief parts of the statement:

> When you become rich in the land, then do not forget Yahweh, and his commandments; do not think "I myself have won the wealth for myself, but think that in fulfilment of his promise God gave you the power to do so".

The Israelite hearers did not have so much difficulty as we do in grasping this line of thought. The fundamental pattern of the statement was familiar to them; they could easily recognize the decisive phrases in the framework that surrounds the particular parts. The fundamental structure of the statement is called in Old Testament exegesis "the framework surrounding the commandment". The part of the framework which precedes the commandment, refers to the taking possession of the land: "When you come into the land, remember this commandment!" The part of the framework which follows the commandment, traces it back to the Exodus from Egypt.[43]

In this case, however, no single commandment is put in the frame. On the contrary, all the "commandments, judgements and laws" of God are laid on the hearts of the hearers. This exhortation, which perhaps to us is by no means so striking as the colourful expositions which stand beside it, is the centre on which all depends, and the splendid frame is merely subsidiary to it. From this standpoint we can also recognize the situation on which this saying was uttered. It belongs to a sermon concerning the law, whose purpose is to indicate the actual relevance today of the divine commandments. The preacher thinks himself back into the time before the entry to the land, and speaks with the authority of Moses, as was customary in sermons dealing with the law. He places the ancient law in a new frame: Israel has become rich in the land. The exhortations which God's commandment contains for this situation he expresses in various ways; not to forget Yahweh and not to rely on one's own strength.

In the centre of the statement and at its end we encounter the word "today". If in the centre it can still relate to the time of Moses, (I, Moses enjoin upon you today the commandments), at the end of the statement "today" is the time in which Israel has become rich, and in which, consequently, God's promise is fulfilled. Essentially, however, we do not have here a telescoping together of two periods of time. The truth is rather that this statement is uttered in the situation of the perpetual "now" in which Israel stands under God's command.[44]

From this viewpoint we can also better explain to ourselves the length of the sentence. Since the time of Moses there was in Israel an unbroken tradition of the proclamation of the law. Fresh commentaries on the commandments were repeatedly written: the older commentaries were not in this situation completely put aside, but were made the basis of further commentaries. In this way, around the simple centre "Observe Yahweh's commandments!" there was built an increasingly splendid framework. In this sentence we have come to a final stage, which can hardly be surpassed. We can even still compare the immediately preceding commentary. It is preserved for us in Deuteronomy 6,10-25. Here too three stands in the centre the exhortation "Not to forget Yahweh who led you out of Egypt". The continuation betrays the origin of this exhortation, "You must not follow other gods . . . for Yahweh is a jealous God" (Deuteronomy 6,12. 14f). Here a commentary is given on the beginning of the Decalogue:

> I am Yahweh, your God, who brought you out of the land of Egypt,
> out of the house of bondage, You shall have no other gods beside me
> . . . for I, Yahweh your God, am a jealous God (Exodus 20, 2f 5b).

Thus the rich variety of the statement in Deuteronomy 8, 7ff is to be understood as a result of the history of continually renewed proclamation of the law. The sentence wears festal garments such as were never encountered in so rich and artistic a form on everyday occasions. The Israelites who understood this statement as soon as they heard it, had been schooled for generations to hear stately language in the worship of God. In the statement of Genesis 2, 4b we can see the work of a man who fitted together many kinds of popular traditions and made of them an arresting theological sequence of thought. On the other hand behind the statement in Deuteronomy 8, 7ff there stands the work of many generations of priests who pronounced the one exhortation "Keep Yahweh's commandments" with ever new and ever more refined methods.

Doublets

Such long sentences are the great exception in the Old Testament, and only come into existence under special circumstances. It is therefore more important to get to know the peculiarities of the terse style of sentence which, in the Hebrew language, with its small capacity for articulation, almost suggested itself to the speaker. A very frequent form of articulation is the creation of doublets.

> God is our refuge and strength (Psalm 46, 2[1]).
> beware of bowing down to the stars and worshipping them (Deuteronomy 4,19).
> I listened and heard (Jeremiah 8,6).

In the sequence of words of difficult meaning, such doublets allow the hearer a short pause and rest.

Alliteration and assonance often emphasize the kinship between such words.

There remains to him neither *name* nor *descendant*. (2 Samuel, 14,7; Isaiah 14,22).

Yahweh is stripping Jerusalem of every *prop* and *stay*. (Isaiah 3,1). (There is alliteration in the Hebrew of the words in italics.) This kind of doubling puts an audible emphasis on this part of the sentence, and helps it to make a stronger impression.[45]

Finally, the use of dyadic form became for the Hebrews a pervading habit of speech and narration. Joseph learns through two dreams of his coming greatness; he has to interpret two dreams of his fellow-prisoners and two dreams of Pharaoh. Gideon obtains two signs from God in confirmation of his call. (Judges 6,37ff).

In poetry the Hebrew formation of doublets is of the greatest importance. The parallelism of members — the division of a verse into two parts corresponding with each other — is its most important hallmark.[46] On a modern reader the continual recurrence of a dyadic structure may indeed have a soothing, if not actually tedious effect. But in Hebrew poetry quite different effects were also obtained from this stylistic device.

O sinful nation,	people loaded with iniquity!
race of evildoers,	wanton destructive children!
They have deserted Yahweh,	spurned the Holy One of Israel,

and turned their backs upon him.

| Where can you still be struck? | You will be disloyal still. |
| Your head is covered with sores, | your body diseased |

From head to foot there is not a sound spot in him,

| bruises and weals | and raw wounds |
| which have not felt compress and bandage | or soothing oil. |

Isaiah 1,4-6).

Apart from one unarticulated sentence, and one expression in triadic form, the twofold rhythm has asserted itself everywhere in this prophetic speech. The usual law of dyadic structure in the last two groups of words even overcome a triadic utterance — the last member is so enlarged that by itself it is able to balance the first two. Yet this speech is far from being carefully balanced in its symmetry. The expressions are short (mostly only two or three words in length) and weighty, the repetition has the effect of hammer-blows. Conflicting impression throng upon the hearers.

In the address, the prophet's intention is to make an immediate impact upon them. Israel must know that it is not only the prophet who denounces it. That is he inserts a statement in the Third Person, and no longer addresses Israel, but speaks as a witness before the court of law: the prophetic speech of denunciation is being heard before God's court.

The threat that is implicit in the question, changes into the description of the misery, which provokes pity; the direct address of Israel in threat and denunciation is once more replaced by the more remote assertion in the Third Person; Israel stands before the prophet like a severely stricken being. In addition to the dyadic rhythm with its short heavy phrases, the change of the form of utterance has become an important characteristic of the style.

But above all, the vividness of the picture of misery expressed in various continually repeated synonymous utterances, contributes to the effectiveness of the speech. The hammering rhythm and the picture of the blows that strike Israel correspond, and reinforce one another.

This ability to combine repetition with new elements to enrich it, to drive it home, and make the first utterance more vital and vivid, is shown repeatedly by Hebrew poets, and thus they make of the law of parallelism a subtle aesthetic form that can carry many contents.

The Hebrews were so accustomed to this dyadic articulation, that they must have taken note of every other pattern.

Triadic forms of articulation

But you, Israel my servant,
you, Jacob whom I have chosen,
race of Abraham my friend (Isaiah 41,8).

This threefold address of God to his people is followed by a speech constructed in the ordinary dyadic form. What caused the prophet to diverge from it at the beginning of the speech? The unusual content corresponds to the unusual triadic formulation. The prophet is speaking to exiled Jews, who saw in the overthrow of Jerusalem the end of salvation history, which long ago began with Abraham. These Jews said "Yahweh has forsaken me, my God has forgotten me" (Isaiah 49,14). They used for the fall of Judah the picture of divorce, God had given to his people a deed of divorce. (Isaiah 50,1).

Yet the prophet teaches them something better: God again speaks to the repudiated people. The remnant from the race of Judah is at this point even called Israel; in it the whole chosen people lives on. "Israel" however was the name of honour that God had given to the ancestor Jacob. In the exiled Jews, "Jacob" stands again before God, God's intention is to begin the election again.

The third, formally striking member of the triad is also the most striking in content. The name of the people "Israel" is of course familiar, its synonym "Jacob" occurs fairly frequently, but only seldom (and to my knowledge, not at all before this passage) is Israel called "race of Abraham".[47] If the Jews should not yet have ventured to take seriously the significance of this word addressed to them individually, the last doubt is removed for them: though they have believed that the end had come, it is God's will to take up with them again at the beginning.

The three synonymous names, Israel, Jacob, and race of Abraham, correspond to three synonymous amplifications. To our ears "servant" at least cannot be a synonym for friend. But in this word we must always be sensitive to the emotional undertones which at that time could vibrate in the word. *'ebed* (servant) can mean the slave, but also can mean one who finds security, trust and honour with one of greater power.[48]

Hebrew hearers took more notice of the third description, "friend". The title of honour as "God's servant", the "chosen one", still indeed included subordination to the mighty master. God had indeed spoken "face to face with Moses as a friend speaks with his friend" (Exodus 33,11). He did not wish to hide his thoughts from Abraham (Genesis 18,17ff). Even Deutero-Isaiah makes a distinction here: "friend" is something different from "servant", "chosen one". It is not used of Abraham's race, not applied to Jacob/Israel, but only to Abraham. But why does the prophet mention Abraham's friendship with God? Does he wish by this to indicate that the new election will surpass the old one, that Abraham's race are taken up into this friendship? Thus the striking third member apprises us of new contents of thought.

The triadic schema which we repeatedly find in Isaiah in the story of his call, in addition to the usual dyad, can have another origin. The thrice-repeated "Holy" of the Seraphim strikes the fundamental note of the whole representation. A schematic interpretation of the triadic schema cannot be given any more than of any other figure of speech. This makes the analysis of style difficult but illuminating for the interpretation of texts, because it always challenges us to make new attempts to see individual forms.

Forms of Repetition

The Hebrew hearer was particularly receptive of the most striking of biblical linguistic forms — the forms of repetition. Among them is the use of leitmotifs, the repetition of important words in a text. The Hebrew will certainly have heard that in the narrative of Jacob's wrestling at the Jabbok, the words "blessing" and "name" were repeated ("blessing" twice and "name" five times). The fundamental theme is the question, "How is God's blessing to be obtained?" Once Jacob obtained it by a deceit, now he wins it by a struggle. The second important question concerns the ancestor, Israel himself: what kind of a man is he? His name "Jacob" indicates him as a deceiver, but he has won for the people who are descended from him a name of honour. While we can only discover the purpose for laborious reflection, it was, as it were present to the senses for the Hebrew in the leitmotifs.[49]

The repetitive forms of style may indeed be reckoned as an especially striking expression of the Hebrew mentality. Repetition and variation make a statement impressive, and throw light on it from all sides, but can confuse a Bible reader who is looking for conceptually clear statements. Impressiveness, not precision, was what the Hebrew looked for in his speech. Even in the wisdom literature the repetitive style of speech is at home, indeed it comes there to its most impressive flowering. Even by itself, this preference for the repetitive style shows how different Israelite wisdom is from western philosophy. The very first sentence of the Book of Proverbs gives us an example:

The proverbs of Solomon, son of David, king of Israel,
by which men will come to wisdom and instruction and will understand words that bring understanding,
and by which they will gain a well-instructed intelligence, righteousness justice and probity.
The simple will be endowed with shrewdness and the young with knowledge and prudence (Proverbs 1,1-3).

Ten times we are told all that is meant by wisdom. We may see in this nothing. We may see in it mere flowery eloquence, and may even judge that the too frequent repetition of synonyms confuses the meaning. But we must in the first instance leave on one side *our* feeling for style. This is not a mere heaping up of words. What we have here is rather first a single description of the *whole* content. Then five more approaches are made to the *whole* theme; each pair of the six sections are more closely linked together. One might describe this way of speaking as unfolding and explanation, as deeper insight into the wealth of wisdom, as a viewing of this intellectual field progressively from every side, as a contemplative penetration of its variety. Instead of reproaching the Israelite authors as incapable of conceptual precision, the interpreter must try to understand the pecular mentality of these men.

Summary and Survey

The analysis of style as a means to interpretation of a text has the advantage that it can begin with observation concerning the text before us. But we must be very cautious in the way we interpret the peculiarities that we discover. We must know how the Hebrews reacted to stylistic peculiarities. We must reckon with another feeling for style, which has its origin in another mentality.

The great power of tradition over the men of the ancient world makes the conjecture at first plausible that only a few different individual language-styles were created. But the Old Testament presents us with a different picture. Most of the texts are characterized by a marked consciousness of style. We can often recognize in them the "signature" of distinguished authors who were in control of the merely traditional elements — without ever renouncing them. But we must also assume that the majority of the people had a fine sense of style.

Repetition and variation are the stylistic individual characteristics most frequently to be observed. These stylistic forms have a really musical charm. This fits in with the fact that the text of the Bible was normally heard, and not silently read. The oral tradition often decisively formed the texts before they were written down. But they were only transcribed in order to be read aloud again. The texts are meant to influence the hearers. For them repetitive forms are an impressive stylistic device: the repetition of sounds and resonances in alliteration and assonance:[50] the repetition of the same word-roots in the same sentence in word-play;[51] the repetition of important words in the leitmotif style; the repetition of the same word-sequence at the beginning or end of sections of a speech in a refrain or in like techniques;[52] the repetition of a statement in synonymous expressions.

How highly trained the ear of Hebrew hearers must have been, we can see from the fact that the writers can choose the very complicated structure which causes the themes to sound in the sequence ABCBA.[53]

If we are to make an analysis of the style, we must not only have a general knowledge of the original hearers' feeling for language, but also of the general possibilities offered by the language. There are few possibilities of structuring the Hebrew language. For expressing oneself in Hebrew the following devices are characteristic:

coordination

linkage in sequence

balance between phrases in the text

articulation in dyadic form, starting with the doubling of individual phrases and progressing to "parallelism of members".

Using these simple fundamental structures the biblical authors produce a varied range of powerfully expressive forms.

Passages with long sentences attract the attention of the Hebrew hearers. They mark for him e.g. festive language which has been built up through long usage in divine service (Deuteronomy), of the language of a man who is trying to integrate varied traditions into a single theological structure (Genesis 2,3bff).

4.   THE PREFERENCE FOR CONCRETENESS AND VIVIDNESS

The Author of Biblical Books

Sayings of Solomon, the Son of David, the King of Israel (Proverbs 1,1). Under this heading collections of wisdom texts are brought together from different centuries. These partial collections are made recognizable to us by further headings, as originally independent units.[54] How could the final redactor, who himself retained these headings, still ascribe the book as a whole to Solomon? We are faced by similar questions when David is regarded as author of numerous psalms,[55] and laws are put in the mouth of Moses.[56] For us the traditions of Israelite and Jewish schools of wisdom stand behind the Book of Proverbs, and psalmody, according to the views of modern exegesis, was practised in the song schools in the Temple, while generations of priests shaped the body of the law. For us, anonymous societies have taken the place of individual authors. But for his part, the Israelite looks behind these societies for the man who called them into life. This preference for the concrete, the direction of the mind towards everything that can be physically experienced, helps us to understand many other peculiarities in biblical modes of speech.

The Treatment of Numbers

For us a number indicates a quantity composed of purely identical parts. The Hebrew was less interested in the many individual units which had been numbered; for him the form of the number as such had its own significance. Four, for example, is the number of the world: four corners of heaven, four winds, four rivers in Paradise. The heavenly throne-chariot, which Ezekiel beholds, is constructed according to this number. Forty corresponds to four, the round number describing a complete period: the Flood lasted for forty days, Israel was forty years in the desert, Moses remained forty days and nights in Yahweh's presence. We can discover many cases of play with numbers in biblical reports, which today we can only point out, but whose meaning we can hardly indicate.

Abraham lived to the age of 175: = 7 x 5 x 5 years: sum of the digits 7+5+5 = 17

Isaac lived to the age of 180: = 5 x 6 x 6 years: sum of the digits 5+6+6 = 17

Jacob lived to the age of 147: = 3 x 7 x 7 years: sum of the digits 3+7+7 = 17

Since there are no special signs for numbers, but the letters of the alphabet could also have numeral values, the translation of words into numerical values, the so-called Gematria, played a part. The number of the men able to bear arms is given in Numbers 1,46 as 603551; that is the numerical value of the words "the sum of all the sons of Israel".[57]

Concrete Grasp of Mental Processes

In dealing with numbers the biblical writers show that with them the calculating understanding had less significance than the power of intuition. This accounts for the fact that the Hebrew word *yāda'* is much more at home in the sensuous sphere than the English equivalent "to know". The man who knows appropriates things to himself through seeing, hearing, feeling and touching, (for that reason also the sexual act can be described by the same word *yāda'*). The Hebrew has at his disposal a rich vocabulary for inner experience, for religious and moral behaviour; but these words remain concrete: "to believe" can still be understood as "to take a firm stand",[58] the man who broods "murmurs"; the man who reflects "speaks in his heart".

Pictures of Human Behaviour

The style of Hebrew narrative betrays the same tendency to remain with concrete experience. The characters are moved by passionate, often contradictory feelings. The divine commandment to sacrifice his only beloved son must have caused Abraham the most terrible inner struggle, but all that we are told of is his silent and exact obedience.

53

Abraham rose early in the morning and saddled his ass. (Genesis 22,3).

We hear not a word of Joseph's behaviour in the pit. There would be an opportunity here of depicting human behaviour; up to this point Joseph was pictured as the favourite son, who believed himself to be the chosen one among his brothers, but now he is deeply humiliated by his own brothers. But the narrator makes no use of this opportunity. And yet he is by no means uninterested in human behaviour. An outwardly visible gesture marks tellingly the behaviour of the brothers.

They threw him into the pit. The pit was empty and had no water in it. Then they sat down to eat some food (Genesis 37,24f).

But when, years later, the brothers came into distress in Egypt, the picture of Joseph in the pit comes up again — and this time Joseph's cries are not passed over.

They said to one another, "No doubt we deserve to be punished because of our brother, whose suffering we saw; for when he pleaded with us we refused to listen (Genesis 42,21).

The biblical narrators wish often to say more than is stated by them in words. We must read between the lines. The fear of the captive is not at first mentioned, because the brothers pay no attention to it. But it remains powerful and present in their conscience through the years.

In a famous comparison Auerbach has contrasted the biblical narratives with Homer's narrative style. In the Greek epic the present is fully illuminated, all the things and happenings are clearly, intelligibly, and vividly brought into the foreground. The biblical narrative, on the other hand, at first passes over the cries of Joseph in silence, and leaves it to the hearers to interpret the gestures of the brothers. It is not until much later that the narrator turns back, the new situation is seen against the background of the distant past, the narrative refers to the dimension of depth that underlies the present events, the endangering of Benjamin and the shameful deed done to Joseph are of a piece. The actions and behaviour of Homeric heroes, on the other hand, arise completely out of the present situation, and from spontaneous emotion. For them every day is as it were a new beginning. But the people of the biblical narratives are stamped by past events, and live in the hope of coming salvation. Even if the Hebrew may not succeed in portraying fear, hate, jealousy and love in detail, even if the narratives deal very sparsely in descriptions of mental and spiritual experience, the biblical narrations yet understand how to evoke pictures of complex psychological situations, and to give an insight into the profundities and conflicts of the human soul. Their hearers are meant to cooperate, i.e. to hear with them what they pass over in silence, and what only finds expression in gestures, actions, looks and speeches of the persons concerned.[59]

We find impressive pictures of intense human experience, not only among the great figures — Abraham who sets forth to sacrifice his son, Jacob who sets out to meet the brother whom he has deceived, David growing old and surrounded by intrigues — but also among the minor figures: the repudiated Hagar, who goes so far from her child as to be unable to see him die, but remains close enough to return immediately to him, is indeed an unforgettable figure. And so is Rizpah, Saul's widow, who in the hot season of harvest watches a day and night by the bodies of her executed sons, and the young swift Asahel who does not let himself be prevented from pursuing the famous commander in chief, so that the latter sees himself forced to kill him.[60]

These "pictures" of human behaviour are only lightly sketched in. What is important to the narrator is the impression, not the details. An exception is the narrative of the left-handed Ehud who kills the fat king Eglon. Here the exact description is important: the movement of the left hand to the right hip, where the dagger is concealed, the thrust into the stomach, the fat into which the dagger disappears up to the hilt. (Judges 3,15ff). Seldom do the biblical authors see things so vividly as this narrator. They are, however, entirely without the patience which contemplates happenings, forms, and things quietly from all sides. Even where we might expect detached descriptions, as in the case of the desert tabernacle, the temple, and the ark, the appearance is not described, but the making of it. The place of quiet examination is taken by the sharing of experienced events.

The World Picture

This holds good also for the manner in which the Hebrews looked on the world. They never asked "What exactly is the world?" Instead they asked about the story of its beginning. (Genesis 1). They saw in the world not so much the unchangeable cosmic order, which man can quietly contemplate, but instead the workmanship of their God, who created for man an ordered sphere to inhabit and continually protect it. Modern authors have tried to reconstruct the Hebrews' picture of the world. The orb of the earth is wholly surrounded by water, and floats upon the ocean of the abyss. Over this is arched the canopy of heaven, which holds back the heavenly sea. But the Hebrews never took the trouble to make for themselves a visible and coherent picture of the world. In different passages we do indeed find the conception of the firmament, an arch made of glass or ice which God has made secure, in order to hold back behind it the upper flood — but beside it there appears too the ironically exaggerated picture of the unruly child in swaddling-clothes, the primeval ocean which God has bound up with clouds and tamed. Thunder is interpreted as God's threatening voice above the heavenly waters, but the Israelites can also understand it as the upsurge of the upper ocean, or as the rumbling of the divine chariot over the firmament.[61]

The Hebrews have astonishingly little interest in a consistent world-outlook and interpretation of natural phenomena. So, for example, in Genesis 1, the author admits a flaw in the unity of his picture of the creation, in order to belittle the powers of the heavenly bodies, which even in Israel were often accorded divine honour. Light is first created, but the "lamps" (secularization!), the sun and moon, which in fact produce it, not until much later.

Merism

Nor did the Hebrews hold it necessary to coin a word for "world". Where we say "the universe, the world, everything" they mentioned only the part or the two outermost poles of the whole: heaven and earth, good and evil, death and life.[62] The knowledge of this figure of speech can protect us from misinterpretation.

"In the beginning God created heaven and earth" — heaven and earth here are not the first things created, upon which others follow, but stand as representatives of the whole creation. The first sentence of the story of creation is a summary of all that follows. The knowledge of "good and evil" which the serpent promises, is all-embracing knowledge, in which the gift of making ethical distinctions merely represents a subordinate realm. The fact that the Hebrews developed this figure of speech, the so-called merism, (in which a whole is described by means of its parts), is a new proof of the fact that they preferred to more universal and colourless concepts words which stand nearer to the concrete things which can be seen and touched.

But this tendency to concreteness does not correspond to a love for optical visibility. Not only the Hebrew world-picture, not merely the descriptions of the ark, the tabernacle and the temple, but numerous other biblical representations leave unsatisfied the man who would attempt to produce a drawing with their aid.

Images of Sound and Movement

The Hebrew prefers images of sound and movement to visual images. Powerful enemies, evil men, are metaphorically seen.

like the thunder of the sea . . . the roar of mighty waters[63]

In Psalm 29 the voice of God is exalted in the "image" of his voice, Yahweh roars from Zion.[64]

Such images are not visual, they do not clarify. The impression is more important than the visual image. The hearer of such comparisons, pictures, and metaphors must get the impression of standing before a reality which cannot be clearly seen, but only approximately apprehended. A picture of reality is evoked through indications rather than exhaustively portrayed. And yet Hebrew poets certainly possess the power to make the whole come alive through a detail. Thus in the poetry of Isaiah, out of two small individual details, one audible and one visual, there is created an impressive picture of war;

All the boots of trampling soldiers
and the garments fouled with blood. (Isaiah 9,4).

Only seldom are images introduced for clarification. More often, indeed, they serve to confuse. The mixture of various metaphors is here a means frequently employed. In one sphere of pictorial language in the Old Testament, the incoherence of the images is obviously employed with a purpose: in the use of mythological elements, which are borrowed from the world of images of heathen narratives.

Employment of Mythical Images

This also helps us to understand the fact that Israel produced no coherent world-picture. Israel refused to have such a world-picture, because, for the peoples in its neighbourhood it was closely bound up with the stories of the gods. What that signified, we can see, for example, from the Babylonian epic, *Enuma Elish* concerning the creation of the world. The land-god Marduk had conquered chaos and shown himself to be the greatest of the gods. He had divided the heavens into the quarters of the gods (constellations) and founded the temple of the capital city. There was an even closer link between the contemporary national life and the creation. The epic of creation was the ritual of the annual New Year Festival, whose central figure was the king. The order of creation was established anew by him. Thus the valid national order was not only traced back to the primaeval time, but at the same time finally'given fixed form.

Israel's faith has a different appearance. The essential thing that Israel has to hope for from Yahweh is not the guarantee of the order that has existed from the beginning. The primitive confession of faith is not directed to a creator God, but to Yahweh, who led Israel out of Egypt. Yahweh is the God of the Promise, whose purpose is to lead his people to unheard of new experiences. For this reason Israel could not allow itself to have a fixed attachment to a closed world picture, for to that picture belonged gods, who did not tolerate deviation from the primitive time-order.

Since the myths would have misrepresented Israel's experience of God, elements borrowed from the myths are never incorporated whole in the Old Testament. This will be the experience of everyone who would wish, for example, to try to get a consistent general picture of the process of creation from the Old Testament. Here references to God's struggle with chaos stand side by side with pictures of the cunning architect of the world. On the one hand the world has been wrested from chaos, but on the other hand built in sovereign mastery by God.[65]

Even more important is the observation that even in individual texts there are such breaks. In the account of creation in Genesis 1, creation by the word and creation by deed are united. Light and heavenly bodies are separated from each other. Further, Genesis 1,1 and Genesis 1,2 stand in obvious contradiction to one another; "earth" has in each of the two sentences a different meaning:

In the beginning God created heaven and earth.

But the earth was without form and void. Darkness was on the face of the deep.

According to Hebrew ideas "heaven and earth" could only proceed ordered and established from God's hand. It must have gone against the Hebrew mentality that here even chaos was drawn into the realm of created things.[66] Not even the author of this account was able to claim that "darkness" and "the deep" came into being through God's word. But at the cost of consistency he brings even the picture of chaos under the heading "In the beginning God created everything".

Modern exegetes have indeed claimed that the author was not able to distance himself from the normal conceptions of the ancient east, according to which chaos precedes the creation. They "save" the unity of the picture by translating the picture of chaos in the pluperfect:

At the beginning before God created all things, the earth had been without form and void . . .[67]

Yet the author has also distanced himself from the current description of chaos: if chaos in the myths was a goddess who can do battle mightily, here it is merely a condition of the world. We can also be confident that this author placed God instead of chaos at the beginning.

The biblical authors felt themselves free to choose out of the picture world of the myths what they liked. For example they by no means adhered strictly to Babylonian conceptions of the sea-battle with chaos. They took up also elements of Canaanite myth in which the sea-battle of God was not a prelude to the creation, but an image of the thunderstorm. And yet they connected ideas of creation with motifs from the thunderstorm battle.[68] This imbrimingling shows that elements taken into the Old Testament from heathen myths are no more than pictures. They are inadequate to portray God's working and so they remain incomplete, pale and not fully developed, and are combined with other pictures.

The Picture of the Manifestation of God

Ezekiel is a master of this style of blurring one image by means of another. The vision of the divine chariot-throne is the most explicit portrayal of a divine manifestation in the Old Testament.[69] Ezekiel's style is here so circumstantial and exact, that it no longer seems really suitable to describe the shattering experience of the encounter with God. This circumstantial character does not increase the clarity; quite the contrary, Ezekiel is actually at pains at once to relativize at once every visual characteristic. This is true not only for the central point of the vision, the appearance of God himself, but also for the marginal figures. As an example we choose the depiction of the wings of the living beings:

Underneath the "firmament" their wings were spread straight out, touching one another, while one pair covered the body of each. I heard, too, the noise of their wings, like the noise of a great torrent, like the voice of the Almighty. When they moved, there was a loud noise like the noise of an army camp, but when they halted, their wings dropped (1,23f).

Ezekiel in the first place describes the position of the wings as if he had figures before him, comparable with the figures of cherubs on the mercy seat (cf Exodus 37,7ff). While the wings of these cherubs are extended over the mercy seat, here the wings are under the "firmament", i.e. the platform of the chariot-throne.[70] That corresponds to Ezekiel's idea, that these living creatures carry the throne of God.[71]

However Ezekiel passes over at once from the visible to the audible, and thus brings confusion into his picture; the wings rustle, indeed at times they hang down. How then can they carry the throne? Even in the matter of what he has heard, Ezekiel will not definitely commit himself. For this reason he uses two similes at once. The noise of the wings was like thunder, but also like the sound of an army camp. He pushes the ambiguity still further by describing the thunder both as God's voice and as the tumult of the heavenly waters.

A picture is drawn of something that cannot be visualized; comparisons make ambiguous the reality which is brought into comparison. It might be asked, what is the purpose of Ezekiel in speaking pictorially at all, and in terms of comparisons.

It is this style alone that makes it possible for him to speak of his experience of God. The man who sees God must die; of this Israel is firmly convinced.[72]

> You are a stubborn people. Were I to journey with you, at any moment I might annihilate you (Exodus 33,5).

It was this word of God which once Moses in the desert had been compelled to transmit to Israel. And yet the confidence that "God is with us" was central to the faith of Israel. God's nearness and his remoteness belong together in Israel's faith. The pictorial language which describes the theophanies corresponds to this fact. Mighty natural phenomena reveal the approach of God and at the same time mark his withdrawal from man, who cannot bear the vision of God.[73]

For modern man these pictures of God's manifestation in the thunderstorm, fire, and earthquake, have become not only strange, but unreal. It may prove helpful to us if we perceive that even the biblical authors understood these mighty phenomena merely as their own inadequate means of portrayal, and not as means of which God himself made use. We can infer this from the fact that they are little concerned with the coherence of the images of theophany. Even in the portrayal of the theophany on Sinai, volcanic phenomena and phenomena of the thunderstorm stand side by side. Once more Ezekiel is the master of this use of language. He experiences God's approach like that of an approaching thunderstorm — but this is surrounded on every side by a splendour of light; what he sees in the first place are not shapeless nature phenomena. In these disguises he recognizes the divine forms of the living creatures, and even the form of God himself (Ezekiel 1).

But the Israelites were very far from regarding these self-contradictory images of the language of theophany as signs of the unreality of the appearances. On the contrary, they saw in the appearances of God a reality of such overwhelming power, that neither can man represent it adequately, nor can any nature phenomenon contain it.

The consciousness of the inability to express the reality of God in words, leads to two forms of representation of the appearance of God, whose extremes can be contrasted in two examples.

The earth heaved and quaked, the foundations of the mountains shook.

They heaved, because he was angry.

Smoke rose from his nostrils, devouring fire came out of his mouth, glowing coals and searing heat.

He swept the skies aside as he descended, thick darkness lay under his feet.

He rode on a cherub, he flew through the air; he swooped on the wings of the wind.

He made darkness around him his hiding place and dense vapour his canopy (Psalm 18, v.8-12 [7-11]).

This was what he showed me:

Yahweh was standing upon a wall, with a plumb-line in his hand.

Yahweh said to me: "What do you see, Amos?" I answered "A plumb-line" (Amos 7,7.8a).

The soberness and the composure with which the prophet receives the appearance of God are astonishing. Asked what he sees, he remains completely silent about it. In spite of the plethora of impressive imagery the Psalmist adheres to the same reticence. The mighty natural phenomena conceal God from curious eyes. It is notable that the poet cannot heap up too many images for that which is under God's feet: the heavens, the dark clouds, the cherub, the wings of the wind; then finally he says emphatically once more: God is concealed in darkness, God's nose, God's mouth are, of course, also invisible; if the poet nevertheless speaks of them, the images are of the intangible and the invisible.

In contrast with this, the sober language of Amos seems to betray more about God. It indicates that God appears in human form; he stands upon the wall, a plumb line in his hand. On the other hand "nose" and "mouth" in the Psalm do not give us indications of human form. The nose pours forth smoke, the mouth spits out fire; this picture is drawn in superhuman dimensions. Further, the snorting nose is for the Hebrew a common metaphor for anger.[74]

Anthropomorphism

We must often reckon with such metaphors when God's "arm" and God's "hand" are spoken of; what is meant is not a part of the divine

form, but God's power to help, his might. There is no anthropomorphism when God asks:

Did you think my arm too short to redeem? (Isaiah 50,2).

Metaphors (transferences from one special field of language to
another) have found a place also in colloquial English. We speak, for
example of a short-circuiting action, or, to remain in the field relating to
the parts of the human body which here concerns us, we say "head"
instead of cleverness. Instead of power, "a long arm". The Hebrew loves
to use such metaphors from particular fields, God inclines his ear, he
turns his face to us. In such sentences God's form is not described in any
way.

The majority of Old Testament anthropomorphisms do not depict
Yahweh's form, but his activity;

Yahweh spoke to you from the fire;

You heard a voice speaking to you, but you saw no form (Deuteronomy 4,12).

Thus the Deuteronomic preaching describes the event of Sinai.

In many passages of the Old Testament it strikes one that the Hebrews
placed less value on quiet contemplation than on experience, less on
seeing than on hearing. Vividness and clarity is less important to them
than powerful impression. This tendency helped them to apprehend how
man can encounter God; it is impossible for him to see what God's nature
is, but he is capable of experiencing his activity, and thus to learn what he
means for men.

The most significant anthropomorphism in the Bible is surely "God
spoke". With the help of this short sentence appearances of God are
represented in the narratives of the patriarchs: "Yahweh appeared and
spoke". Only occasionally a further sober verb is added, for example "he
stood and spoke"; "he came, appeared and spoke".[75] The narrators say
absolutely nothing as to the appearance of the divine vision. The only
thing of importance to them is that God is experienced, is heard. In this
way we must understand even more powerful anthropomorphisms. A
sober understanding may feel their inadequacy, but the Hebrews by their
help represent Yahweh as the partner of men, who commits himself to
discussion and participation with men.[76]

The commandment "Thou shalt not make an image of God" is
obviously obeyed also in the language of the biblical authors. God's
presence can be experienced through his help, through his will to be
man's partner. It can be represented in pictures of mighty natural
phenomena, or in words which in other contexts refer to human action
and behaviour. But the phenomena of nature, the divine activity and
speech, not only reveal God's presence — they also conceal God himself
from the curious gaze.

Against this background the statement "I saw God", which the
prophets Isaiah and Micaiah ben Imlah venture to use, and also the

statement "the elders saw the God of Israel" must sound very remark-able.

Moses, the elders, Elijah, were permitted on Mount Sinai to see God directly; the prophets saw God on the occasion of their call.[78] How seriously Israel took the exhortation not to make an image of God shows itself most clearly in these descriptions of the immediate vision of God. Even here God remains concealed. Moses is permitted only to see God from behind when he has already passed by. The elders see only the blue heaven under God's feet. In the depiction of Isaiah's vision even the fringes of his garment fill the whole temple; God himself remains incomprehensible. The descriptions of the vision of God might have given opportunities for speculation about his form and nature, but even here the Old Testament authors pay heed above all to what God requires of men and how he influences them.

The description of the vision of Ezekiel seems to form an exception which is also remarkable even for its length. The prophet depicts in detached and circumstantial manner heavenly figures and structures: the four living creatures, the fire in their midst, the wheels of the chariot-throne, its platform, and finally the figure of God. (Ezekiel 1,4-28a). The prophet and his task play no part in this long description. Its sole purpose is to portray God's reality. If, however, we take note of the literary style of this representation, it becomes clear that even Ezekiel remains true to the Israelitic tradition of reticence.

> High above all, upon the throne was a form in human likeness. I saw what might have been brass glowing like fire in a furnace from the waist upwards; and from the waist downwards I saw what looked like fire with encircling radiance. Like a rainbow in the clouds on a rainy day was the sight of that encircling radiance (Ezekiel 1, 26b-28a).

Ezekiel dares to say incredible new things about God — but at the same time he holds himself back with greater caution than do his predecessors. God comes forward into the prophet's presence so far out of his concealment, that he can compare his form with the form of a man. "Man" in Israel's thought is actually a word which is the contrary of God. Ezekiel is fully aware of the insignificance of man, and yet he is addressed by God as "man" instead of being called by his name — he is nothing but a weak creature.[79]

Ezekiel is the prophet of the exiles. It was the situation of desperate need which compelled him to make his bold assertion of God's human form. The exiled Israelites had lost the Temple and Jerusalem, the kingdom and their existence as a nation. There is for them no longer any institution through which God can approach them. In that situation God seeks for a way to be near them, which cannot be obstructed. He reveals himself as the one in the form of man, who comes to weak men.

A comparison with the first account of creation suggests itself. "God created man in his own image" (Genesis 1, 27). Nietzsche wittily turned this phrase round: God created man in his image — does there not lie concealed behind this fact that men created for themselves a God in their own image? Could not Ezekiel's vision have confirmed him in this opinion, since there God appears in human form?

For Israel at any rate this interpretation of Nietzsche would be unacceptable. The word "image", even in Genesis 1,27 is not there in the first place to be contemplated with curiosity. The image of the ruler represents his power — so, through the activity of man, God's power on the earth is meant to be present. The *effect* of an image is for the Hebrew more important than the impression which it makes upon a mere spectator.

The same is true of the bold picture of the God in human form. Ezekiel combines his boldness with the utmost caution. If other prophets ventured to say "I saw Yahweh", he speaks only of his own impression, of Yahweh's "appearance" — indeed, even this he can only reproduce approximately. He glimpses the divine form only in fire, light, and the sheen of metal. Only in a comparison does he speak of this form. God himself remains incomprehensible. This picture of God's manifestation is not meant to satisfy human curiosity, but to give consolation to the exiles: the Holy One can be near to them even in the unholy land of the heathen; he humbles himself to the point of showing himself in the form of weak humanity.

Our sober modern understanding is inclined to regard pictures and comparisons as mere ornaments of speech: if they were to be removed, the rationalist thinks, we would be left with the real meaning. But the picture language in which the Old Testament speaks of God, cannot be eliminated. These men can only experience God through images. It would be an impermissible speculation to remove the images in order to lay hold of the "substance".

But that is true also of other biblical images, even of those which originate in the rich mythical material of the heathen environment. We are not at liberty simply to discard these images, with the intention of finding the "authentic" statement. The biblical authors did not clothe abstract statements with images as an afterthought. Their thought was in images from the outset. With the aid of these images they sought to feel after realities which they were unable to find by other means.

Images of Death

Modern readers of the Bible easily and unjustly discredit pictorial language as "oriental fantasy".

The bonds of death held me fast,
destructive torrents overtook me,
the bonds of Sheol tightened around me.
. . .
(Yahweh) reached down from the height, and took me,
he drew me out of mighty waters,
he rescued me from my enemies, strong as they were,

63

from my foes when they grew too powerful for me (Psalm 18, 5.6.17.18 [4.5.16.17]).

The man who is threatened by enemies describes himself as one who is at the mercy of mighty waters, who is laid hold of by death. The two pictures for distress caused by enemies are not clearly distinguished from one another; the shadowy darkness of the underworld and the wild watery chaos intermingle. Death — in reality a destination which man is approaching — appears as a hostile power that seizes him. Images which can be quietly contemplated are rarely to be found in the Old Testament. Here even the bonds that bind the captive are seen as assailants. The inconsistency of the images might repel a classically educated artistic taste — but for the psalmist it is an expression for the instability which threatens his whole life. He cannot see how the extremity which he is experiencing is compatible with his relation to God.

It is not mere oriental exaggeration when the Psalmists repeatedly represent deliverance from illness, persecution and guilt as a resurrection from death. For the Christian death means a verdict concerning the achievement of his life which is now finally given. For the Hebrews death is nothing but the end of life: beyond it there is only a shadowy existence, far from light, far from happiness, and far from God. Here too we see that Israel above all directs its attention to what can be concretely apprehended; what went beyond life on earth was unimportant even for religion. It was quietly taken for granted that everyone must die in the end. But Israel's religious men were disquieted by the fact that the power of death invaded their life. Illness, persecution and guilt were experienced as an anticipation of death, as a banishment from living men and from God. Only a few pious souls in Old Testament times pressed forward to the belief in a life with God even beyond death. It was not speculation about the immortal created soul of man which led them to this faith, but trust in the faithfulness of God, who does not forsake those who wish to remain with him. This trust became habitual for all the Israelites who under the constraint of any kind of misfortune, cried to God as from the toils of death. A pictorial language which so deeply influenced Israel's life of faith cannot be thrust aside as a mere fanciful trimming.

FOOTNOTES

1   Faith in the one God was sharply profiled from the beginning, inasmuch as Israel was commanded to place trust only in the one God. Yet it was only slowly that Israel learnt that even beyond Israel there were not regions where other gods held sway. For this development cf.(1) Gen 35, 2.4; Josh 23.7; 24.2.14-16; the existence of other gods is acknowledged, but Israel must not serve them. (2) Deut 6.14; 1 Kings 11.5; 2 Kings 17; the other gods are weak in comparison with Yahweh. (3) Isa 44.6; 45.5.14.21; 48,9: "Apart from me there is no God". Even

this verse was at first probably understood as "Apart from me there is no powerful God who is strong to help, the other gods are practically nonentities."

2   Cf. 1 Sam 28,13; Isa 8.9; the spirits of the dead are called *ᵉlōhīm*.

3   Two modern attempts to interpret Yahweh etymologically may be mentioned — neither of these is significant in the Bible itself. The American Albright and his pupils (Freedman) understand Yahweh as the Third Person of the verb *hāyāh*. That is the way our text also takes it, but it thinks of the fundamental form (Qal) (he is); Albright on the other hand presupposes the causative form: "He brings into being". Against this Martin Buber starts with the abbreviated forms *Yāh, Yāhū*. (*hallᵉlū Yāh* means; Praise Yahweh!). He divides this abbreviated form into *Yā hū'*; claiming that the longer form was *Yā hūwā*. *Hū', Hūwā* is in Hebrew and in kindred languages the Third Personal Pronoun. According to Buber *Yā hū'* was originally the excited invocation of God, "Oh, He!"

4   The list of the kings includes for example between Jesse, David's father, and the last king in Jerusalem 22 names. In this list no name is repeated. Many Hebrew names are brief prayers (Zachariah [*zᵉkar Yāh*] = may God remember); others are names expressing a wish (*Benjamin [ben yāmīn]* = son of good fortune). But we meet also with derogatory names (Nabal = Blockhead) and names describing an occasion (Balak = Lightning; the child was certainly born in a storm).

5   So it does not signify, when a name is given two quite different interpretations, the one after the other; the child is called "Joseph" because God has taken away (*'āsap*) the reproach of the hitherto childless Rachel, and that he may grant further children in addition to this one (*yāsap*).

T   The German words are *Herz* and *Schmerz, Liebe* and *Leid*.

6   These three attempts are each time introduced by the words "God spoke"; (1) I am that I am (*'ehyeh 'ᵃšer 'ehyeh*) (2) The "I am" (*'ehyeh*) (3) Yahweh (*yahweh*). The hearer is led by the two preceding sentences, to think, when "Yahweh" is mentioned, of the Third Person of the same verb.

7   A specially remarkable use of *hāyāh* is to be found in the statement; God's word went forth (*hāyāh* = came) to someone; cf. Jeremiah 1,4 etc. Here too the meaning of *hāyāh* has the undertone of taking effect, what God says also happens.

8   In the German word "Wirklichkeit" (reality) a similar understanding of the world is reflected. "Realität" is different; this word has regard to the connections between things and inescapable facts (*res*). However, in contemporary linguistic use this distinction is no longer drawn.

9   On the category "Call Narrative", see below, Ch. II, Narrative Categories, 10.

10   Cf. Jer 1, 8; Jdg 6,16 (calling of Jeremiah and Gideon); cf. the angel's salutation of Mary (Luke 1,28) with the greeting of the heavenly messenger to Gideon (Jdg 6,12). Further, we meet this statement once more in the Call of Moses (Ex 4,11). The story of the Call of Moses existed originally in two versions, which are fused together in Ex 3f., In Ex 4,11 we encounter the "with thee" of the other version.

11   When in Ex 1-2,22 in the narrative about slavery in Egypt the word "God" with one exception is not mentioned, this means an indication on the narrator's part that it is not yet possible to speak of Israel in Egypt as the people of God.

12   Against this background the meaning of some derivations of names is also more easily understood. God himself gives the name, and by so doing determines the character and destiny of a man or a place. (cf. Gen 16,11; 17,19; Mat 1,21). Where God changes the name, he gives a new decisive turn to a man's fate (cf. Gen 17,5; Jer 20,3). It must have been specially important for Israel that even the name "Israel" came from God. It was bestowed upon the patriarch Jacob after his

struggle by night with the divine being (Gen 32,29; cf. what is said below about this narrative, chapter II, 6). Jacob had been forced to surrender his name to the opponent, and with it everything that was concealed in this name; Jacob was "the one who caught by the heel", the deceiver (Gen 25,26; 27,36 contain this interpretation of his name). But God gives to him the name Israel. In Gen 32 the name is interpreted "he has struggled with God". But the philologically correct etymology is "God shows himself the conqueror".

13   An illustration from nearer home is given by the fairy tale of Rumplestilt-skin; the evil dwarf has lost his power so soon as his name is known, i.e., his nature discovered.

14   Martin Buber tries to reproduce this meaning of the interpretation of the name in the translation "I shall be as the one that I will be". With this God promises to be present to help, but he reserves for himself the right to say how this presence will be experienced.

15   The Yawhist's account is combined in Ex 3 f. with the Elohist's account. On this way of working of the editors, cf. further Chapter II, Narrative Categories 7.

16   In favour of the conclusion that the name of Yahweh was introduced by Moses is the fact that about this time we begin to find names that include Yahweh, Yah, Yo — e.g. Joshua, Yahweh is salvation. (Jesus is a later form of this name.)

But there can be found arguments that the name of Yahweh is considerably older. In this context various biblical data are to be considered together.

From Ex 18, 8-12 it may be inferred that Jethro, Moses' father-in-law, was a priest at Sinai, the mountain of God.

According to Jdg 1, 16, Jethro was a Kenite.

According to Josh 15, 37; 1 Sam 27, 10; 30, 29 the Kenites joined up with Judah in Palestine.

According to 1 Chron. 2,55 the Rechabites were a Kenite group and were zealous worshippers of Yahweh. On this point cf. Jer 35.

In Gen 4, Enosh is named as the first worshipper of Yahweh. He was the father of Canaan (Gen 5,12).

Canaan is another form of the name Cain; the genealogies of Cain and Canaan in Gen 4, 17-22 and Gen 5, 6-32 contain the same names in similar forms.

Cain is reckoned to be the ancestor of the Kenites.

A possible inference from all these observations: Yahweh was worshipped under this name as early as in the times of the patriarchs. Among the Kenites knowledge of the name survived. It may have been passed on from Jethro to Moses, and from the Kenites to the tribe of Judah.

17   Noun clauses are also to be found in rare and exceptional cases in German: "Life a dream". In Hebrew they are frequent.

18   Cf. Ex 20, 2,5; Deut. 5, 6, 9; echoes of the Deuteronomic formulation are heard in Ex 15, 26; Jdg 6, 10; Ps 50, 7; Ps 81, 11; Hosea 13, 4; 12, 10.

19   "For I am Yahweh", cf, Lev 18, 2.4.5.6.21.30; 19, 4.10. 14; . . . 26, 1.2. 13 etc.

20   Isa 52, 6; 48, 12. Here too the verb "I am" is not expressed in the Hebrew, the significant $h\bar{a}y\bar{a}h$ of the interpretation of the name, does not appear.

21   Ezk 6, 7.13.14; 7,27; 11, 12; 12, 15. 16 etc.

22   It hardly fits with this conception of the authors of the priestly document that God should interpret his name at the first manifestation. The name is only one indication of the mystery of God, the ability fully to interpret the name, to know it, is only the final goal to which God purposes to lead Israel. Therefore the interpretation of the name by the Elohist, which was probably available to the authors of the priestly document, was not adopted.

23   There were certainly also Hebrew dialects, yet in the Old Testament these

are not to be noticed. Jdg 12, 1 ff. gives evidence of differences of dialect: the men of the tribe of Gilead can recognize their enemies from the tribe of Ephraim by the fact that the latter cannot pronounce "shibboleth". (Something similar happened in the Ardennes offensive in December 1944; Americans were able to recognize disguised Germans by their wrong pronunciation of "worth").

24   The vocalization of a text hitherto handed down by consonantal signs only naturally involves an interpretation. In English we can interpret the consonants R and T as rot, rat, root, rate, rote, etc. It is true that in Hebrew the consonants themselves are decisive for the fundamental meaning of a word in a way that they are not for us. Three consonants nearly always determine the fundamental meaning of a single word root. Because the language had this structure it was possible to keep it fixed for so long in a purely consonantal script.

25   In Gen 49, 29-50,14 Jacob's death and the mourning connected with it are pictured in a matter of fact manner which astonishes us.

26   On the concept of the "covenant" cf. Ch III.2.

27   Cf. 1 Sam 25, 39; cf. further the Wisdom teaching concerning the connection between acting and suffering, Chapter II, Poetical Categories 4, and the similar conception of the prophets in their announcement of punishment.

28   We discuss Isa 7 in another context (p.311.)

29   An examination of Isaiah's mode of address can support the conjecture that in his speaking about faith, he is thinking about the continuance of David's House. The speech had begun in the Second Person Singular; "Have firm faith and remain calm" the king alone was meant. At the end of the speech, we find the Second Person Plural. The king is here the representative of the House of David, who must stand firm if it is to stand.

30   About two hundred years later a successor of Isaiah, who knew and valued the prophet, proclaims how gloriously the old promise to Zion will be fulfilled: "Arise, Jerusalem, rise clothed in light". At the end of the great vision of Jerusalem's new splendour, he reminds us also of the warning of his predecessor against impatience: "I, Yahweh, will bring this swiftly to pass in its own time" (Isa 60,22).

31   Sein und Zeit, Tübingen, 1957 8th Edtn, p. 145 (Eng. tr., Blackwell, Oxford 1967).

T   In German there is here an untranslatable pun. Schloss = lock: Schloss = castle.

32   The sermon of the Capuchin in Wallenstein's Lager uses similar devices:
And the Roman Empire — God's pity! — I trow
Should be called the Roman Slumpire now,
The Rhine has been turned to a river of tyne,
Roisterers have pillaged the cloisters divine,
The dioceses have died and ceased . . .
But even here it is evident how different an effect puns have on our feelings. The Capuchin in Schiller's drama is speaking to rough soldiers, while in the Old Testament we encounter punning on a high literary level.

33   Cf. Falkenstein/von Soden, Sumerian and Accadian Hymns, Hymn no. 13 vv 30 to 32 and Hymn 44, vv 26-33.

34   Jer 20, 8f, cf; also Jer 5, 14; 15,16; 23,29.

35   Isa 55, 10f; also in Isa 8,7; in Jer 23, 29 there is no longer any thought of the prophet.

36   Isa 44, 26ff; Ezk 31,15; Nahum 1,4; 8 Isa 24, 4; 34,4.

37   Here only a small part of the range of meaning of the word $r\bar{u}^a h$ is considered. It is further important that $r\bar{u}^a h$ describes the spirit of God that comes upon Israel's deliverers, upon David and the prophets.

38   1 Sam 16,18; 25; 2 Sam 14.

39   This "and" is in fact only one letter (*w*) which is usually joined to the verb, so that the impression of uniformity is less strong than in a similar English narrative.

40   Could this humidity not take the place of the rain which was lacking?

41   We see again how badly the picture of the rising moisture fits into the present context. It conflicts with the picture of the waterless chaos, and with the creation of man from dust. In the lifeless condition of "heaven and earth" this "moisture" is the only active element before the appearance of man. It is not brought into connection with the Creator God, but seems, like God and man, to contribute to the creation. From all this can be inferred that for the writer of this account of creation, the "moisture" was known in older, more strongly mythical accounts of creation, as an independent power in creation; it was already so firmly anchored in the pictures of the creation, that he was unable to exclude it, in spite of all the difficulties which it created for him in relation to his own concept. But he fits it only loosely into his structure, and leaves it small significance in his total interpretation.

42   Cf. Isa 2,22: "Have no more to do with man, for what is he worth? He is no no more than the breath in his nostrils".

43   This explanation of the commandment is usually introduced by the child's question: "When your son asks, 'Why this?', then say . . ." Cf. Exod 12, 24-27a; 13, 3-10; 13, 11-16.

44   On this point cf. p.185.

45   In English we can similarly lay emphasis upon one part of a sentence: out of house and home, with bag and baggage.

46   On this point cf. below chapter II, Poetic Categories.

47   Cf. also the late additional conclusion of the Book of Micah, 7, 20 and Ps 105,6.

48   The mutual relations in which master and servant could stand are reflected in the narrative concerning Abraham's servant, who sought a wife for Isaac. (Gen 24).

49   Gen 1 is the passage most strikingly marked by leitmotifs. Even the repetition of whole sentences can indicate the essential thesis. Cf. in Gen 21, 1f: "As God has said". In Gen 24 the repetition of a whole section comes from popular methods of narration. Rebecca behaves as the servant of Abraham had prayed God that she would. Even here the repetition is an indication of the religious significance of the narrative: the servant sees the fulfilment of his wish as Yahweh's doing (Gen 24,21). Cf. the same kind of style-characteristics in I Kings 17, 14. 16.

50   On this point see p.27.

51   On this point also, see p.27.

52   Cf. Isa 2, 9.17; Amos 1; Isa 5, 8ff etc.

53   Cf. Jonah 1,4-6: A: 1, 4-6
                        B: 1, 7f
                        C: 1, 9, 10a
                        B': 1, 10b.11
                        A': 1, 12-16.

The long sentence from Deuteronomy quoted above is a portion of a text constructed on a concentric model:

A: Exhortation: Deut 1,1
B: Desert: 8, 2-6
C: Land: 8, 7-10
D: Exhortation: 8,11
C': Land: 8, 12-13

B': Desert: 8, 14-17

A': Exhortation: 8, 18-20

54   The proverbs of Solomon (Prov 10,1); the sayings of the wise (22, 17; 24,23); proverbs of Solomon transcribed by the men of Hezekiah king of Judah (25,1); words of Agur (30,1).

55   Ps 3; 7; 18; 34; 51; 52; 54; 56; 57; 59; 60.

56   Cf. on this p.190.

57   Cf. Exod 38, 26; Num 1, 46. References to other comments in the text: four winds: Jer 49, 36; Ezk 37,9; four rivers of Paradise: Gen 2, 10-14; vision of the throne-chariot: Ezk 1; forty days' flood: Gen 7, 4.12.17; forty years in the wilderness: Num 14, 33f; Deut 2,7; Exod 16,35; forty days before God: Exod 24,18; 1 Kings 19,8; on the forty years of peace in the time of the Judges, cf. p.290.

Another significant number is 7; it plays an important role in Gen 1. The 12 is also important, cf. Gen 35, 22; 42, 13.32; 49, 28; Num 1,44; Exod 28,21; 34,14; 1 Kings 18,31; Gen 17,20; 25,16.

When we reflect on the frequent symbolic chronology of biblical narrators, we must value the more highly the exact chronology of the historical writing of the Deuteronomist. On this point cf. p.290.

58   On this point cf. Chapter 1,2.

59   On this point cf. A. Auerbach, *Mimesis*. Auerbach starts with Gen 22, the story of the sacrifice of Isaac — the style of narrative which represents inner happenings in externally visible gestures, is to be found also in the New Testament. On this point we may compare the representation of the anguish of spirit of Jesus on the Mount of Olives (Luke 22,44). The portrayal of inner happenings in visible terms does not exclude a fine psychological understanding on the part of the narrator. A well known example of this is provided by the narrative concerning Paradise (on this point see below, chapter II, Narrative Categories, 4). Another example of this power of intuition in the biblical narrators, is to be found when we compare the narrative concerning the events after Saul's victory, with the report which Saul himself gives of it (1 Samuel 15, 9-15).

60   Gen 21, 9ff; 2 Sam 21, 8ff; 2 Sam 17.

61   References for the passages mentioned in the text: God establishes the firmament: Gen 1,6; Job 37,18; Proverbs 3,19; 8,27.

The sea is swaddled with clouds; Job 38,8f.

Thunder as the call of God: Ezek 10,5; 43,2; Ps 68, 34; as raging of the waters: Ezek 43,2; Hab 3,10; Ps 77,18; as rumbling of the wheels of God's chariot: Ps 77,19.

62   Gen 1,1; 3,5; Prov 18,21; 2 Kings 5,7.

63   Isa 17,12; cf. Isa 57, 20; 28, 2.15.17.

64   Amos 1,2; cf. also Amos 3,8.

65   Bringing of the waters of chaos by compulsion into the ordered creation: Gen 1, 6ff; Job 38, 8ff; 26, 5ff; Prov 3, 20; 8, 24; 30, 4; Ecclesiasticus 39,17; Jer 5,22; Ps 33,6f; 148,5; 24,2.

Construction of the world, stretching out the heavens, establishment of the earth, its pillars or foundations: Isa 40,22; 44,24; Job 9,8; Ps 136,6; Jer 10,12; Zech 12, 1b; Prov 3,19; 8,29; Ps 104,5 etc.

66   On this point cf. Isa 45,18.

67   Hebrew grammar allows of both translations the decision must be made in the light of the context.

68   Cf. Job 26,5ff; the chaos before the creation is here pictured neither as a watery chaos as in Gen 1, nor as a waterless chaos as in Gen 2, but in a picture taken from the world of the dead (26,5f). Then follows the motif of creation with

the image of God the cunning architect of the world (26,7). Only then follow pictures of the sea-battle, which only takes place in heaven (26,8-13).

69   On this point, p.62 p.197ff.

70   Ezekiel was indeed probably also thinking of the (invisible) throne of God above the wings of the cherubs on the mercy-seat.

71   But in addition Ezekiel also mentions the wheels of the chariot-throne. He describes its appearance in detail, but "forgets" the technically important detail: How are they attached to the chariot? What is their relation to the living beings, which also carry the chariot? Instead of an explanation, he gives us only the technically unsatisfying information that the "spirit of the living creatures" was in the wheels.

72   Cf. Gen 32,21; Jdg, 6,22f; 13,22; Exod 24,10; 33,20; cf. also the accounts of the mercy seat: Lev 16,2f; 2 Sam 6,6.

73   Jdg 5: Exod 19; Exod 15; Ps 15; Isa 30 etc.

74   Cf. Exod 15,10; Job 4,9; Deut 9,19 etc.

75   Cf. Gen 12,7; 26,1.24; 28,13; 1 Sam 3, 10.

76   God closes the ark behind Noah, he feels sorrow and grief (Gen 6,6; 7,16).

77   Exod 24,10; 33, 18-23; 1 Kings 19,8f; 22, 19-22; Isa 6; Amos 7, 1.4; 9,1; Jer 1,9; Ezek 1-3.

79   The English translations use commonly the description "Son of Man" in God's address to Ezekiel. But "Son" is only the normal Hebrew circumlocution for "one of the species". Ezekiel is called "one of the species Man", i.e. "man" (cf. in English "A head of cattle" — here also the circumlocution is necessary to form the singular out of a collective word). Examples of the deprecation of man's worth in contrast with God: Jer 31,3; Ezek 28,2.

CHAPTER II

MINOR CATEGORIES IN THE OLD TESTAMENT

NARRATIVE CATEGORIES

1. TEXTUAL EXAMPLE: THE BUILDING OF THE TOWER OF BABEL. (GENESIS 11, 1-9)

1) All the world spoke a single language and used the same words. 2) As men journeyed in the east, they came upon a plain in the land of Shinar and settled there. 3) They said to one another, "Come, let us make bricks and bake them hard"; they used bricks for stone and bitumen for mortar. 4) "Come", they said, "let us build ourselves a city, and a tower with its top in the heavens, and make a name for ourselves; or we shall be dispersed all over the earth." 5) Then Yahweh came down to see the city and tower which mortal men had built. 6) And he said "Here they are, one people with a single language, and now they have started to do this; henceforward nothing they have a mind to do will be beyond their reach. 7) Come, let us go down there and confuse their speech, so that they will not understand what they say to one another." 8) So Yahweh dispersed them from there all over the earth, and they left off building the city. 9) That is why it is called Babel, because Yahweh there made a babble (*bālal*) of the language of all the world; from that place Yahweh scattered men all over the face of the earth.

Contextual Situation

An unprejudiced reader of the Bible might think that the intention of the beginning of the Book of Genesis was to tell a connected story stage by stage, beginning with the creation of the world and of the first men, and leading up to the rise of the peoples, of which the story of the building of the tower speaks. Above all the linkage of the sections by means of lists of generations tempts us to arrive at such a conclusion. It looks as if there was an intention to present an unbroken account of the descent of mankind, in which the narrator occasionally pauses, in order to impart more detailed information about the original ancestors of mankind, Adam, and Noah and their sons, and, finally in chapter 11 an event in which the whole of mankind at that time participated.

However, a careful reading shows inconsistencies: according to Genesis 10,10 Nimrod's kingdom began in Babylon — in the following narrative it has yet to be built; according to Genesis 10 the nations descended from Noah's family, which had many ramifications — in Genesis 11,1 however, mankind is living together, sets off together on a migration, and plans a common work. According to Genesis 11 the world of nations is not formed in a process of slow natural development, as the family tree of Noah sees things — God's punitive intervention breaks up the unity of mankind at one blow into the many linguistic groups. Two different traditions of the rise of the peoples are here brought together without their contradictions being ironed out. We are following the intention of the author if we allow — just as he did — each of these traditions to stand on its own feet, if thus we regard Genesis not only as a part of the early history of mankind, but first of all endeavour to interpret this piece as an independent narrative.

If the story of the building of the tower gave an account of a historical period, we should have to ask: could this really have happened thus? In that case a contradiction with modern ideas concerning the beginnings of mankind and the origins of language would be inevitable; the event of Babel does not agree with our knowledge about the slow evolution of the families of languages.

The Category of Saga

Now however we have before us an originally independent piece. We must first of all determine its linguistic form. In so doing it will become clear to us that the question of historical reality is not at all relevant to the narrator's intention. Here a story is told which is true, but does not report an event which really happened.

The leading character in the story is the whole of mankind taken as a unity. Between the time of Israel's origin as a nation and the days when a group of people could believe that they represented the whole of mankind there must have intervened an immense interval of space or time. It is therefore inconceivable that a memory from these days should have reached Israel. One day, people had begun to tell the story of the building of the tower of Babel. What stands at the origin of this narrative is not historical event, but the conversation of people with one another — not indeed about pure fantasies, but about what these people had seen and experienced. Here it is not as if we were dealing with written narratives; for this kind of narrative no firm date of origin can be given. These stories lived in men's conversation as "saga" (what people say and pass on to each other).

And yet we can approximately read off from the Tower-Building Saga, when and where it was first told. The narrators and hearers of a saga know each other, and each can take for granted that the other has the same common experience and knowledge. To us, who do not belong to the same circle of auditors the narrative makes an imprecise impression. Where did the migration of mankind begin? Can the building of a city be a crime? Or is it only the building of the tower that is punished? On the other hand the remark about the building-material seems surprisingly exact; why was it particularly mentioned? In the human circle where this saga was at home, these questions did not exist; they told exactly the details that seemed remarkable to them (bricks and bitumen), but merely indicated what they could take for granted.

A Nomad Narrative

The exegetes are not agreed as to whether in the form of the narrative as we have it, a recension about the city and another about the building of the tower are conflated. Yet city and tower seem to belong to the same picture. The nomadic people, who told one another this story, knew the city of Babylon from hearsay, perhaps had even seen it. Its greatness, its inner working, and its variety, the large number of people living closely packed together in it (11,4: that we may not be scattered), was bound to shock the nomadic desert-dwellers. What was peculiarly striking was the strange Ziggurat. Originally the shrine had been built on a solid platform in order to protect it from high water. In order to exalt the dignity of the shrine, they built platforms in steps above each other. The original purpose was forgotten. Much less was it known to the wandering strangers from the desert. Like the whole city, the Ziggurat seemed to them incredible, what these men are able to do! (11,6: Nothing that they have a mind to do will be beyond their reach!) It is also inconceivable what should be the use of such efforts, if they do not serve as a proof of strength, and a way to fame. (11,4: We wish to make a name for ourselves.) From this saga speaks to us the nomad's inability to understand the culture of cities.

The Picture of God

Are we then to assume that God's word has taken human form in such a nomadic narrative? Is a sermon being preached to us, on the text that we should turn away from the achievements of culture? What kind of a God is this, who in this narrative speaks words that suit the mouth of a people who dwell in the desert, words of anxious amazement at the great achievements of men? (11,6: this is only the beginning of what they will do; nothing that they have a mind to do will be beyond their reach.)

The narrative should not be understood in the sense that mankind wished by building the tower to storm heaven, God's dwelling. The information, telling whence God descends to the town is omitted on purpose, in order not to confine God to one special dwelling place.[1] The gods of the heathen, on the other hand, have fixed dwellings. In these it is possible to attack them: the gods of the Babylonian Flood Narrative flee from the rising water into the highest heaven (Gilgamesh XI, 11). This God, however, has such pre-eminence that in confrontation with him the immensely great work of man is tiny. He must first descend, in order to see it better.[2] To us the word of God's descent may appear as illegitimate anthropomorphism — the intention of the old narrators was to express in words the superiority of God over the world. This superiority impresses itself upon them as the contemptuous side-thrust makes clear; this town is too small for God to be able to see it rightly from a distance.

In the context of the building of the tower, "heaven" describes not the dwelling of God, what the word describes is rather, in oriental exaggeration the greatness of the tower.[3] The narrative could certainly also be referring to the praise of the temple, which was customary in Mesopotamia: "O house, that like a great mountain reaches to the heavens".[4]

Some myths from the heathen environment of Israel also spoke of the punitive intervention of the gods. The gods threaten men, because they feel themselves threatened by them — so says an Egyptian myth. But on the other hand, the Babylonian narrative about the Flood never asks why the gods wish to send the Flood. According to the older Atrahasis epos, the noise of men was so burdensome to the gods, that for this reason they desired to destroy them.

Man cannot approach so near to the God of the biblical narrative that he has to defend himself against them. Even in punishment he is completely free. He had no need to worry himself about man's aggressiveness. It is his free decision "We will go down" (11,7)[5] — but, unlike the heathen gods, his decision is not purely capricious; he responds with punishment to the action of men.

The crime of men is not a conscious attack upon God. They have forgotten God, they think only of their praise and their strength. Through punishment God must remind them who in reality is the strong One. The fact that men do not understand themselves shows the saga of the building of the tower to be an exhortation not to forget to give him praise above all human praise, to whom in the last resort praise belongs.

Aetiologies

The origin of languages and peoples is thus explained. At the same time there is also given a popular explanation of the name Babel. These explanations are a special ornament of the narrative. The joy in the interpretative play of the understanding speaks in them. Some exegetes wished to see in these aetiologies the origin of the saga. The saga was, so to speak, invented in order to explain the origin of the peoples, the languages, and the name Babel. The theme here is not a past event, but an explanation of contemporary facts.

Yet the main interest of the narrative does not lie here. Its main purpose is to describe the behaviour of godless humanity, and God's answer. From this theme comes its power to hold us. For the aetiological questions we have long possessed better answers, but concerning the question of man's life before God and God's turning to man, the narrative can give us help.

The Glory of Man

It is not only here that the Bible warns us in our struggle for power and glory not to forget God. The achievements of culture and external power are in other passages looked on as a danger to faith. Here experiences from Israel's time of wandering continue to bear fruit. In the people's memory the time in the desert becomes a time of nearness to God; it is to the desert that Elijah goes to meet God there, (I Kings, 19), that Jesus goes before his work begins (Mark 1,12). The man who wishes to follow Christ is thereby challenged to distance himself in some measure from all the wealth of men, in order that he may bethink himself where the true riches lie. From God's point of view the great deeds of men appear small. The fact that men do not understand one another was to the old narrators a sign that in spite of all successes, mankind had not yet got very far.

Yet this warning is not the only word of the Bible about the cultural achievements of man. The same narrator who included this saga in his work tells us that, according to God's plan, man as a worker is a helper to God the creator. (Genesis 2, 4.15).

Those who wish to understand the story of the building of the tower must be familiar with many characteristics of biblical speech. Let us enumerate some of them in retrospect:

1) What appears to us as a continuous text may be a collection of originally independent minor forms.

2) The laws of the category of "saga" determine the form of expression.

3) The biblical narrative distances itself from the mythical way of thinking.

4) In connection with the saga, there are found two aetiologies. But they do not form its kernel.

5) The theme of this biblical text is varied and expanded in the course of the story of the development of the Bible.

6) The theme of this text is connected with other themes in the same composite work.

The two last points are discussed in more detail in the later part of the book. The others will be set in wider contexts in the following sections.

2.   THE EXEGETICAL DIVISION OF THE UNITY OF THE BOOK INTO A SERIES OF MINOR FRAGMENTS

The Pentateuch, a Collection of Individual Narratives

The narrative of the building of the tower was interpreted in the preceding section as not in the first instance a part of a historical book, but as an independent literary unit. The narrator himself gave us grounds for this by leaving visible the seams which came into existence when they were built into the text. There are many things that point to the conclusion that not only the primitive history, but the whole Pentateuch is a great collection of small individual fragments, so that we are compelled to admire the skill of those who were able to produce a coherent work out of such varied material.

Disparate fragments were mixed in various ways; narratives of different kinds, lists of names, places, etc., pieces and summaries of narratives, laws of varying structure which reflect the ordinances of different times. In the Book of Genesis are to be found short sagas such as bear the stamp of oral tradition (the sentences represent only the event itself, and omit the psychological processes, yet suggest them by means of gestures). Along with these we read too the long narrative of Rebecca's wooing, which is splendidly coloured though lacking in incident (Genesis 24). To this kind of narrative there corresponds another kind of audience, which is not only interested in incidents, but also in the art of embellishment and depiction. Such differences indicate that we are not dealing with works that come into being at a single blow, but with collections of fragments of different kinds.

Signs of Homogeneity

But these collections are not put together aimlessly. We can observe various signs of organization. All the narratives in Genesis 1-11 are "sagas dealing with mankind" i.e. in all of them the situation of the whole of humanity before God is represented; all of them deal with sin and judgement. Sometimes it is hard to find the reason for such organization. Why, for example are genuine narratives concerning the Promise confined to the Abrahamic tradition?[6]

Why is it only in this tradition that the stories are focussed on the son (Ishmael, Isaac)? Why is it that only in the Jacob stories a central role is played by holy places (Genesis 28; 32, 33ff), holy actions (Isaac's blessing) and covenants (Génesis 30,27ff; Genesis 29,15ff; 31,46ff)? Why is it that only in the Isaac-tradition accounts of well-digging and arguments about wells have an important place (Genesis 26)? Is it not singular that the groups of narratives about the three patriarchs turn their attention to different things in each case? To explain this striking fact the hypothesis was put forward that the narratives were kept alive in different societies with different kinds of interests, before they got into the collections of the biblical narrators.

Previous History of the Pentateuch

It might now be asked: why are we not satisfied with understanding the traditions as we now have them in their final form? Why do we concern ourselves with the previous history of a text? Should that not be left to the scholars? Goethe's Faust, Part I has also a previous history; the material first of all existed as a piece of popular tradition; Goethe himself also wrote a first draft of Faust. This previous history does not need to be known for us to understand the drama. That is all of one piece. The Biblical narratives, on the other hand, bear recognizable traces of their previous history; they are rough and flawed. For this reason, when we interpret them, we must take their previous history into consideration.

It is not possible to exaggerate the conservatism of the biblical narrators. They regard the text handed down to them with reverence. Genesis 28, as an account of the shrine of Bethel, probably did not look much different from the narrative we know. Contradictions, inconsistencies and joins and the sequence of the text prove how conservatively the collectors dealt with the traditions that confronted them.

To make this point some evidence from the primitive history should be given. How can Cain, when he is the son of the first two human beings, (Genesis 4,1) describe himself as a fugitive among all men (Genesis 4,14)? How, if he is condemned in the narrative to a nomadic existence (Genesis 4,12), in the family tree that follows, can he become the father of the city-builders (Genesis 4,17)? Obviously two different Cain-traditions have been artifically connected with the narrative about Adam and Eve, Cain being ascribed to them as their son. On the other hand the family-tree of Cain does not take account of the following narrative of the Flood, and makes part of mankind descend from Cain.

From this example two things become clear: the biblical authors treated the tradition with reverence, and for that reason made little or no effort to harmonize the texts. Both these things reveal their mental attitude. It is more important for them to adhere to traditions of their people than to prove their originality. They believe that they can only represent their own conception of the history of Israel if they look backwards for support to the tradition that has grown up in Israel in the course of history. Their works are not only stamped by their personal experience, but also by the experiences gathered by their people in the course of its history.

Historical Character

From this vantage point we must seek for an answer to the question concerning the historical character of the biblical texts. If we were to regard the really important thing to be, not the word of Holy Scripture, but the event underlying it, then we would really have to replace the Old Testament by a scientifically elaborated history of Israel (and correspondingly the Gospel by a history of the life of Jesus).

In spite of this the continual question about historicity is justified, for the biblical God has revealed himself in history. Yet the biblical texts, corresponding to their changing types of language, have each a different relation to history. To us the text may seem most valuable which seeks access to the historical event by critically testing sources and attaching itself to the most reliable. This kind of historiography is still very young. For a long time now people have been turning to their past to reflect upon it. Even the authors of biblical books have the intention of reporting truly the events of the past; they hold the collected texts to be genuine witnesses of that past. But of course they are unacquainted with any critical testing of the sources in the modern sense. They have another standard of judgement. Their criticism is directed to the witness which the sources bear to the faith. For the rest, inaccuracies and contradictions do not worry them. Our interpretation must do justice to this peculiarity of the biblical narratives. Therefore in the case of each independent language fragment it must ask in what special way it is "historical".

This point may be made clear in respect of the relation of patriarchal history to primaeval history. It is impossible that the memory of men should reach back to the beginnings of mankind, that in spite of the inconceivably great stretch of time between, these narratives should have been handed down to historical times and reached the biblical author in Israel. On the other hand it is by no means contrary to experience that in Israel genuine memories from the time of the patriarchs should be alive even centuries later. The oral tradition is particularly reliable in other cultures also when written sources for memory to rely on are lacking. Therefore it is no argument against the genuineness of the tradition about Abraham, that it was not fixed in writing till the time of the kings. In spite of wholly transformed temporal conditions (a settled life, a town culture) the narrative about the fathers truly describes the atmosphere of nomadic life, although the Yahwist closely links primitive history with the history of the fathers by means of the genealogical tree of Abraham's ancestry, we must assume that between them there is a gap in memory and tradition whose greatness cannot be estimated.

At the time of the biblical authors there still survived genuine memories of the history of the fathers. The way to primaeval history, however, could only be trodden with the help of imagination. But the writers did not rely upon their own powers of imagination. They adopted the stories that were told in Israel about the beginnings of mankind. But Israel had hardly an independent tradition concerning just these matters. In contrast with the rest of the ancient orient, in Israel the conceptions concerning the origin of the world played but a slight role. More important was the history since the election of the people by its God. Its thoughts about the origin of the world were borrowed from other oriental peoples. In the present form of narratives concerning primitive history the relationship to ideas of the other peoples is still recognizable.

But these narratives lived for centuries in Israel. The experiences that the people gathered in the course of its history, were incorporated in the process. In this form the Yahwist received them, in their light he sees the time of the beginning. So understand, it is legitimate to talk of the historicity even of this part of his work.

Summary and Survey

As we look back on our earlier reflections, three guiding lines emerge for the method of isolating minor categories.

1. The minor biblical categories arose predominantly out of the oral

tradition. They correspond to its need for brevity and impressiveness.

2. In our interpretation they are to be noted insofar as the biblical writer took them seriously, i.e. insofar as he lets them be recognizable as independent minor forms.

3. Since they were formed in the oral tradition, they cannot be regarded as the product of one author, but in the light of the ideas, thoughts, and convictions of the society which gave them life.

This method of textual interpretation was specially used in the narrative parts of the Pentateuch, but is also important for its other parts, and for other books of the Old Testament.

The books from Joshua to 2 Kings link up with the Pentatuech and carry forward the great historical pageant of Israel up to the Exile. Here too the picture is created from a conspectus of several originally independent sketches, and by means of the insertion of many originally isolated parts. Yet the oral tradition more and more loses its significance. For these later happenings, written sources can in part be used. It was natural from the beginning to write down the actions of the Kings. Even greater units were incorporated, which an author so completely shaped into a coherent work, that the material employed no longer possesses any independent value as evidence. This holds good, for example, for the history of David's successors on the throne, a famous piece of Israelitic historical writing (2 Samuel, 13-20 and 1 Kings 1-2); the individual traditions emerge still more clearly in the history of Elijah, which was inserted as a whole into the historical work (1 Kings 17-19 and 21 and 2 Kings 1-2). In other places the oral tradition continues to play a great role. The Elisha stories were, for example, first of all transmitted singly in the circle of the prophet's disciples, and are even now only loosely connected (2 Kings 2,19-22; 2, 23-25; 3,4-20; 4,1-17; etc). Even the narratives about Joshua's victories were at first orally transmitted at special places, where people were specially interested in them. A widely held hypothesis locates Joshua 2-9 at the shrine of Gilgal.

The remaining narrative works of the Old Testament were created in a time in which an author stamped his own intentions far more deeply on his work, and the written version gave decisive form to it. However the question about the minor forms is becoming once more acute in relation to two other kinds of books.

The *Prophets* did not compose books, but acted, exhorted and preached without at first thinking of a written version. It was only their pupils who collected their words and reports about their actions. Here too the oral tradition comes first. For this reason the textual units in the prophetic books are for the most part brief. And yet here the method of investigation according to categories is not in indisputed control. In the popular genres the typical laws of forms of speech express themselves forcibly. We see how strongly a community stamped these forms. What is typical predominates over the stamp given by an individual to the spoken utterance. Even the prophets used customary forms of speech. But certainly they frequently fill these with new meaning, or even, for effect, turn them in the opposite direction.

The *Psalms* present themelves from the outset as short textual self-contained units. They are, in addition, more to be understood as expressions of the faith and the feeling of the community than of an individual piety. Not even the prayers in "I"-form are spoken out of a unique situation. They can be spoken by many people together, or repeated by many in sequence.

The *Wisdom Literature* collected the wisdom sayings of the people. A series of popular poetic forms which in part have a long history of oral transmission behind them, is there preserved for us.

3. SAGAS

Man in our more civilised environment lives for the most part in several human communities, which do not as a rule overlap; in the community of the family, in the community of the place of work, in addition for one or another there will also be a circle of friends, a club, or the like. The original form of human life in community has another appearance. The same people live together, work together, have like destinies, share in the personal life of the other. It belongs also to the life of such communities that people are together in conversation, by the loom, in the village square, by the watch-fire, or in the extended family. Here live stories which are passed on from generation to generation, without anyone thinking of writing them down and giving them a fixed shape.

These stories are told for hearers who have the same horizon of experience as the narrator. Similar stories are known, and references are understood which remain a closed book to strangers. Often they are attached to a special place, whose peculiarities play a part in them. Usually they are striking features of the landscape, in which the narrators live; the bond of the community with its home finds expression here. At one place one of their number was encountered by something uncanny, at another an ancestor proved a hero; a striking natural phenomenon of the environment is to be traced back to strange events, etc. The landscape is peopled by familiar and uncanny forms. At the same time these narratives bear witness to the common views of these men. They betray what one thinks, by what standard one judges. All this allows us to draw from such a narrative inferences concerning the society in which they originated, but not inferences about an individual author. They are not individual creations; they belong to the life of the fellowship. No one is interested in the man who first told them.

Of course people do not think, where such stories are concerned (fairy tales, sagas, legends, anecdotes, short stories, myths, etc) of obeying strict artistic laws. For it is not the art of story-telling that the hearers admire; what is primarily important for them is the story that is told. The content itself, so to say, itself stamps these forms of speech.

A. Jolles distinguishes them according to the manner in which the people in them encounter the world; fantastic exaggeration of reality marks the fairy-tale, insecurity and tragic despair the saga, liberating laughter the jest.

Sagas in Israel

The traditions of Israel's past lived on for the most part in communities such as we have just described. So it must not surprise us if even the idioms of speech which are created in such communities, are met within the Old Testament. The final version often bears traces of the long oral transmission. We can recognize in what type of human community the traditions grew up and were passed on. An example of nomadic story-telling is given us by the saga about the building of the tower. Even the form of landscape in which the story-telling community lived, can be conjectured: trees, wells, springs — striking points in a country that has little water — often play a part in these narratives.[7]

Comparison with Sagas about Heroes

We shall here describe the literary form of the popular narratives embodied in the Old Testament by the term "sagas". This term is filled with meaning for us when we think of the "Sagas of Classical Antiquity", or the "German Heroic Sagas". We see Siegfried and Achilles, the splendid heroes, who succeed in everything — and yet bear the mark of vulnerability. Heracles, the performer of many labours; the wily Odysseus; human greatness does battle with a hostile world. Even in their overthrow the Burgundian princes keep their honour.

Sagas of this kind are unknown to the Old Testament. It will hardly be possible to number great deeds of Abraham. In the Greek and German epics human greatness authenticates itself even where it can find no success. Old Testament sagas lay emphasis on quite another side: failure. Abraham's lack of faith seeks in the son of a maid a substitute for the promised son, who fails to appear (Genesis 16, cf. also 15,3). Jacob deceitfully obtains the blessing (Genesis 27).

In the Moses tradition and the tradition of the occupation of the land, and the time of the Judges, many interpreters see the heroic sagas of Israel. But even here the story told is one of human failure. Moses and Aaron are rebuked and punished by God. (Numbers 20,12). What happens in the Old Testament narratives is not that man vindicates himself in a situation of need, that he stands up strong and free in his conflict with all difficulties. In the Israelite saga man stands before the face of God. Therefore the heroes venture little on their own initiative. Gideon ventures an attack after he has obtained an encouraging vision in a dream (Judges 7,9-15). Moses is victor over Amalek without having touched a weapon. His persevering prayer decides the battle (Exodus 17,8-16).

An essential motif of the heroic sagas, the pursuit of honour and great deeds, does not fit in with the views which stamped the sagas of Israel. Among Israel's neighbours, on the other hand, we find this motif again in unbroken force. Gilgamesh and his friend Enkidu have performed astonishing deeds. When Enkidu dies, Gilgamesh learns that in one point he is still inferior to fate. This the strong man does not tolerate. For this reason he sets out to ask of the sole survivor of the Flood concerning the mystery of eternal life.

Sagas about the Spirit World

With the concept of "Saga" we further connect ideas that come from a kind of folk-narrative which till today lives predominantly in oral tradition. These are narratives in which man is confronted with an uncanny no man's land between this world and the beyond. Outside of the realm of human habitation, in twilight and in darkness, man can encounter the occult, dead men, devils, spirits, uncouth monsters. Often man does not return unscathed from the encounter, but bears all his life long on his body a sign of this encounter.

In the Old Testament, belief in the power of demons, spirits, ghosts, and the dead is held in check, for where these have scope for their activity, the realm where God rules is constricted. But even in Israel this uncanny borderland is known (cf. Isaiah 34,11-15), but in the old narratives the fidelity of the collectors has retained references to it in only three places. Jacob and Moses are assaulted by God himself, as by a hostile demon; the spirit of the dead Samuel appears to Saul (Genesis 32, 33ff; Exodus 4, 24ff; I Samuel 28)

Fairy Tale Motifs

Israel's sagas war very strongly marked by faith in Yahweh. For this reason we find neither sagas about demons, nor pure heroic sagas, and also no genuine fairy tales. Fairy tales are set in a fantasy-world and for this reason they cannot give expression to faith in the God who makes himself known in the historical experiences of the people. On the other hand, Old Testament authors do not hesitate to use fairy tale motifs; the weak conquers the strong (David and Goliath; cf. of the fairy tale about the gallant little tailor). God roams incognito over the land (Genesis 18, cf. the fairy tale of the poor man and the rich man).

We tend not to take quite seriously narratives that take up fairy tale motifs. The Old Testament narrators thought otherwise. They take away from the fairy tale motif everything of fantasy. Goliath is a powerful man, David a supple young man. The hero is a historical figure. For the rest the narrative can quietly allow for the luck and skill of the weak, and the overthrow of the arrogant Philistine, who despises God's army. (1

Samuel 17, 26) Thus transformed, the fairy tale motif is serviceable to faith. So the adoption of a fairy tale motif does not prove that the author did not wish to take heed of the historical; on the contrary he shows by the way in which he transformed this motif, that Israel's faith orientates itself by historical events.

Of course here the old narrator cannot be concerned with historicity in our sense. The narrative represents pictorially how Israel experienced the historical struggle with the Philistines. Through God's blessing even the weak becomes strong. Historical experience is reflected here; the most faithful representation of the events is not aimed at.[8]

Mythological Motifs

The Old Testament rejects myths still more sharply than fairy tales. All the concepts which attempt to describe the linguistic categories of ancient popular traditions are blurred, because it is impossible to grasp naturally imprecise linguistic forms according to exact laws. Further, the concept of "myth" is loaded with further imprecision because it has been used to describe the whole way of thinking of prescientific times. These times apprehended the world not by means of the laws of continuity and causality, but as it offers itself to the senses and is reflected by the power of human imagination. A familiar example is the ancient picture of the world, according to which the disk of the earth rests upon the water, and the heaven arches above it.

A whole exegetical school concerns itself with "demythologizing" the Bible. Its intention is to detach the biblical message from these old patterns of ideas. That in itself is the aim of every exegetical method. But the detachment should not go so far that in the end every concrete idea is renounced. Carried to such lengths this method negates an essential need of even modern man. Especially in the fields which concern him intimately, in friendship, love, and the life of faith, he could not wish to rely on merely abstract reflections. He needs lively, vivid conceptions. But the exaggeration of this method also contradicts the essence of the biblical message, which culminates in the fact that in Jesus the perfect image of God lived among men.

Advocates of radical demythologizing might be tempted to appeal to the Old Testament commandment, "You shall not make an image for yourself". They might think that all talk of God in images was forbidden, because it draws God too closely into the world of our conceptions. Yet this commandment did not hinder the Israelites from talking and speaking of God in images. What was forbidden to them was rather to attempt to obtain magical power over God. (It was thought in those days that a person was so truly present in his picture, that one had him in one's power if one possessed his picture.)

The Old Testament resists such efforts, even when it speaks of God in pictorial terms. The picture is not a means of getting possession of God; on the contrary, it makes clear how little God can be conceived. Only the use of pictorial speech allows us to speak of the incomprehensible.[9]

In the old sagas another way of speaking about God is found. They speak of God making it possible for man to experience him. They talk not of man's understanding, but of his capacity for experience of God. God thrusts deep into the personal life of man. He claims love, and bestows security, he disturbs man, and causes him fear, he gives him joy, and allows him to despair. All this, man experiences otherwise only through men who are near to him. Therefore the Old Testament pictures the meeting of God and men through the use of language which is taken out of the human sphere, in anthropomorphisms.

He was sorry that he had made man on earth, and he was grieved at heart (Genesis 6,6).

God is represented by these naratives as the partner of men, who commits himself so deeply to them that he can be disappointed.

It may seem even bolder to us when the Old Testament exploits heathen myths as an arsenal of colourful figures of divine action. Yet the Old Testament, in doing so, breaks up the mythical narratives into the smallest fragments. How far this destructive process can go, became clear when Canaanitish myths were discovered (excavations of Ras Shamra — Ugarit 1929). It was discovered how many fragments of these myths the Old Testament used — and yet it would have been completely impossible to reconstruct these myths from the fragments before their discovery.

What is the reason for this hostile attitude to the myth? The myths of Israel's neighbours represent the gods as a part of the power of nature. Their dwelling-places in the constellations, at the zenith, in the lower waters, are part of the earth. The expressions of their life can be grasped in the life of nature. So long as the god of fruitfulness is in the underworld, drought prevails. In the thunderstorm he flies over land in his journey through the clouds. They must wrest their lordship from other divine powers, and maintain it continually in conflict with them — Marduk is king as victor over Tiamat, the power of chaos.

Far otherwise is it with Israel's God. He is not a part of the world, but superior to it. For this reason the old narratives avoid speaking of heaven as his dwelling-place. His life is not bound to the life of nature — drought is the sign of his power, not of his weakness. (I Kings 17,1). He rules without limitation. When he punishes men in the story of the building of the tower, it is not out of fear for his position as ruler.

Among the peoples that were Israel's neighbours the myths were intended to allow man to influence the gods; the Babylonian narrative of creation was portrayed in a drama at the New Year in order to secure the continuance of the stability of nature. This side of mythical religion is ridiculed in I Kings 18,25ff: the prophets of Baal try to waken the god of rain from his sleep of death, so as to end the drought.[10] Because Yahweh is withdrawn from human influence, faith in him cannot tolerate a coherent mythical narrative. Only individual elements from these myths, set free from their original context, are made serviceable for the illustration of this faith.

But even in this the old narrators are very cautious. People were still not sufficiently emancipated from the myths as to use them as a picturesque decoration for their speech. The old narratives use a peculiar technique in dealing with such motifs. This can be shown by giving two examples:—

(a) In Genesis 15, 7-21, Yahweh makes a covenant with Abraham. He uses an old covenant ceremony; the partner to the covenant steps through the space between the halves of sacrificed animals. This gesture is the graphic representation of a curse. If the partner were to break the covenant, the same thing will happen to him as happened to the animals. Yet it is not Yahweh himself who performs this ceremonial, but a fiery appearance; it remains completely obscure what this has to do with Yahweh.

(b) Genesis 18 might have as its foundation a narrative of gods visiting men and sharing a meal with them. But of Yahweh himself no other thing is said except that "he spoke" and "he appeared". In order to make this possible, the narrator leaves vague the relationship between Yahweh and the three men. Thus in these examples the mythological elements serve to avoid intrusive statements about God himself. Although a suggestion of a connection with God is made for the hearer, the narrators carefully avoid specifying what this connection is and consequently the narratives remain in semi-obscurity.

Mythological elements play a greater and a different role in the later texts of the Old Testament from that given to them in the old sagas of Israel. In relation to them there is less reserve; the use of mythological elements is regarded by the author of the Book of Job as a proof of scholarship. The use of clearly recognizable mythological elements is a nearly infallible sign of a late, i.e. exilic or post-exilic origin of the text.

Aetiologies

The aetiological motif occurs much more frequently than the mythological one in the old sagas. Aetiology answers the question about the origin of what is to be found in the present. Many exegetes have assumed that such questions were the origins of most of the sagas of Israel. Exodus 13,14 names the situation in which such an aetiological question is put and answered. A child has observed a usage and now asks his father its meaning — here the meaning of the redemption of the first-born. The father answers by telling the story of the Exodus from Egypt.

But a narrative is always more than the answer to such a question. A narrative is created when the story is told of an event which contains in itself a tension, and leads to a solution — that is another matter than the aetiological question and the answer given to it. There is no such thing as a pure aetiology in which the line of the narrative coincides with the line of the aetiology. The aetiology is always merely one theme in a narrative, not its essential core.

87

The question about the relation between aetiology and narrative is important for another reason. One might in fact be induced to consider aetiological narratives as essentially invented narratives. In that case only the condition for which an explanation was being sought would be regarded as historically tangible (multiplicity of language, redemption of the first born), and not the events which were thought to explain the situation (building of the tower, death of the Egyptian first-born). But when it is observed that the aetiology is often only an appendage to a narrative, then we realize that the question of historicity is not to be solved in such a wholesale manner.

Saga and History

This brings us again to the question of historicity. One might advise against the use of the word "saga" for biblical narratives, because to our way of thinking "saga" and "history" are contradictory concepts. We think of figures like Siegfried or Brunhild, of dwarves and water-spirits that play a part in the Nibelungen Saga. Although Siegfried is reared in Xanten, he does not seem to be quite at home in this world, the splendid hero who falls a victim to dark machinations might be a figure that is moulded on the myth of the struggle of darkness against light. Or Brunhild; the magic fire protects her. What place in history might she find?

On the other hand, historical figures also have found their way into the Saga. Attila and Theoderich meet us in the Nibelungenlied. A saga can have the same object as a historical writing. It is distinguished by the fact that its theme is more limited. Writers of history interpret a series of events as a coherent whole. The saga writers place no value on historical coherence. In their narratives are reflected the living stuff of history, the experiences of the past.

We may sum up our conclusions about the sagas of the Bible as follows:
1.   The concept of "Saga" names the narrative after the place where it is at home; it lives in "saying" from mouth to mouth.
2.   Saga is fitted, in a way different from fairy tale and myth, to keep live even historical traditions. a) It is easily connected with certain times and places; b) its "stage" is the environment known to the narrators and the original hearers; c) it certainly is happy to show that a superhuman power intervenes in this world.
3.   Saga is more fitted than anecdote and farce to be the bearer and expression of faith; since it inclines to show man in serious encounter with the world. A total claim is laid upon him, the issue is often of life and death.
4.   The hearers of a saga are originally and chiefly interested in its content. A more detailed description of the biblical sagas must thus concern itself with their content (cf. the following sections).

4. SAGAS OF MANKIND

Comparison with other Types of Saga

Usually it can be seen from a saga what interests moved the society which gave it a home. This is true even of the narratives in Genesis 1-11. The narrative of Paradise speaks from the perspective of the countryman; the man is a farmer, taken out of the fertile earth, Adam taken from the Adamah; his task is to complete God's work of creation by tilling the soil (Genesis 2,5.15). The narrative of Cain and Abel prefers the shepherd to the farmer. The tower-building saga lastly, only becomes intelligible when we take into account the failure of wandering desert-dwellers to understand the city culture which confronts them.

In some points, however, these narratives are different from the type of saga which the previous section sought to describe. They are not located in a determinate place. The time in which they are set is, even for the consciousness of the narrators, immensely distant. About the location of "Eden" we find only contradictory indications,[11] Ararat (Genesis 8,4) and Babel (Genesis 11,9) lie in foreign territory.

But above all the narratives in Genesis 1-11 are distinguished by the width of their horizons; all of them are concerned, in the last resort, with the whole of mankind. When decisions are taken about the life or death of Adam and Eve, Abel, Cain, and Noah, then what is at stake is always the same time the life of the whole of mankind that is descended from them. In the narrative of the Tower of Babel, the whole of humanity becomes visible.

Comparisons with Myth

They share this width of interest with myth. In the victory of Marduk over the monster Tiamat, the fate of the whole world is decided; in the victory and decline of Baal the fruitfulness or drought of the whole land is at stake. These narratives are more closely akin than other Old Testament sagas to myth. As an attempt to influence God and to draw him into the world, the myths are repudiated here also. Yet the Israelites are children of their time, and of the culture of the ancient east; we must not wonder that they take on the characteristics of mythical thinking which do not seem repulsive to them.

Just like myth, the narratives of Genesis 1-11 seek to describe the present condition of the world. In so doing they even adopt the same methods as myth does. We explain to ourselves conditions which are presented to us by seeking to link them, causally with a series of events that preceded them in time. The method of the myths is different; they derive given conditions in the present from unimaginably distant events in the worlds of the gods. Two examples may make that clear:

(a) After creating the world, the gods wished to enjoy rest in their dwellings; for this they required servants, and therefore they created men (Tablet 6 of the creation epic, *Enuma Elish*).

(b) Not only natural events but also political conditions are traced back to the mythical primaeval time: at that time kingship came from heaven and settled in Babylon. Babylon has the precedence over all cities because there the gods built for Marduk at the very creation the temple Esagila.[12]

Narratives about Creation

The narratives in Genesis 1-11 have a similar aetiological slant. The conditions of the Creation certainly cannot within the scope of faith in Yahweh be derived from exciting narratives about events of primaeval times, for there is no collaborator or competitor with the creator God — since at least two persons are necessary for a narrative, there is in the Bible no authentic story of creation. In the Babylonian myth the chaos dragon had first to be overcome before the world was formed out of his body. Against the background of such creation myths the biblical account of creation, Genesis 1,1-2, 4a and 2,4bff came into being. But in their present form there remain only feeble suggestions of the view that the will of the creator God was not the only agent in calling the world into existence.

The narrative of Genesis 2, 4bff[13] tries to describe the situation before the creation, by enumerating everything that did not yet exist. It is a world without bushes and vegetables, without rain and cultivation by men. Thus the desert appears which Palestine's inhabitants knew when the rains fail, or the earth is not cultivated. Chaos is not portrayed in the manner characteristic of the myths or as the domination of mighty, supernatural powers. A picture taken from the daily experience of the narrator makes chaos palpable.

A part of this picture of the desert is the "moisture" (a word very rare in the Old Testament, and one not clearly definable: '*ēd*); it corresponds to the rising ground-water which creates oases in the desert. This water is serviceable for creation; God forms man out of the moist earth. The narrative is very careful to ascribe all creative power to God. Here, however, this thought is not carried through consistently, the "moisture" obviously exists before God's creative act intervenes.

Genesis 1,1-2,4b is not a narrative, but a confession whose source is a sober piece of doctrine. Systematically all the parts of the creation are enumerated and explained as God's work. Even this piece of doctrine does not refrain from describing the state of affairs before the creation. Here too, the Israelites are children of their time. Our philosophical concept of "nothing" cannot occur to them. For this reason Genesis 1,2 has recourse to the mythical conception of the watery chaos, which precedes all creation. But chaos is here only a condition of the world, not a rule of personal powers. It has no might of its own that could oppose itself to the creator; it is mere material for creation. Even this text breaks free from the ancient oriental tradition, in which men told each other of the struggle of the creator god against hostile figures of chaos.

Aetiology

Aetiological narratives, which explain the origin of creation, are not to be found in the Old Testament — but there are narratives of a similar kind, whose purpose is to explain certain circumstances in the world of man: the inclination that man and woman have for one another (Genesis 2,24), the tedium of work, (Genesis 3,17ff) and the pain of child-bearing (Genesis 3,16), the enmity between snake and man (Genesis 3,14f): the multiplicity of peoples, who do not understand each other (Genesis 11,7ff). Here narratives can be created; here man appears as collaborator and antagonist of God in a way unknown in the myths of the ancient orient.

The aetiology in the Paradise narrative (Genesis 2,4b-3,24) differs from that in many other sagas. It is not a mere appendage. Here we certainly have a special kind of aetiology before us. A whole bundle of aetiological questions is concealed in this text. These questions are all directed to one experience — the contradictory character of human life. Man the tiller of the earth comes from the earth, he wakens life in the earth through his labour — yet his bond with the earth reminds him also of death.[14] Work is seen as cooperation with God the creator, but also as labour on accursed ground (Genesis 2,5.15-3,17ff). The mutual relationship of the sexes has the power to bind the man more strongly to his wife than to his father's family; thus love can burst the strongest bonds that the ancient orient knew (Genesis 2,24) — and yet her bond with the man can be for the woman a degrading subjection, and can mean sexual bondage. (Genesis 3,16). Pregnancy and birth, which are properly causes for joy, bring pains and distress. These contradictions lead to the aetiological question; whence come the distresses of mankind? Surely the creative will of God cannot have called them into being? Why does a curse beset human life?

Guilt and Punishment

It must be admitted that this last question underlies the narrative of Genesis 1-11 only in an indirect manner. All these narratives deal with guilt and punishment — what seems to hang over man as a curse of fate, is, because of their guilt, rightly inflicted as punishment.

The aetiological style of narration is natural for myth: in everyday life only the aetiological interest is tangible; the event which caused the present state of affairs is not accessible to man's everday life. But the transformation of the aetiological question to which we have just drawn attention, bears witness to a way of thinking which is far removed from myth. Gilgamesh loses the plant of life through carelessness. Adapu despises the water and bread of life through ignorance; the myth does not know why the gods send the Flood — here death and fear of chaos in fact

91

weigh upon mankind as a curse. How inevitable this fate is, is testified by the myths in which men throw away the few possibilities of liberation from it. In myth the gods are the powers who determine man's destiny, man is only the object of their action, and is not counted as their partner.

Very different is the conduct of the God who intervenes to punish Adam and Eve, Cain and the whole of mankind. Here it is shown that aetiology is only one of the many concerns and overtones of the sagas that deal with mankind. Their purpose is not only to explain the present condition of mankind, but also to disclose who this God is for men. By punishing, he holds fast to his original will as creator, from which man has turned aside. Man ought to work together with God in the creation, not against him. The punishment of God is also meant to protect the life of men; he clothes Adam and Eve, protects Cain, after the Flood promises security in the face of chaos.

These narratives would be misunderstood, if we were to reduce them to the triviality of aetiology. For example if the story of Paradise had only dealt with answering the question about the sufferings of humanity, why would it have employed the vivid pictures of the garden and its trees, or the motif of the divine knowledge?

No Mythical Exaggeration

These narratives owe their vividness to the incorporation of mythical elements which have here played a much more important part than in other sagas. The material of the Flood story had a history in Mesopotamia before it was told in Israel. It is not so easy to discover what elements of the narrative of creation and the Fall come from myth. Myth knew wonderful things about the first man (Job 15,7; 38,21); stories were known about the fall of exalted beings who were privileged to dwell in the divine realm (Ezekiel 28,11ff; Isaiah 14,12ff).

Ideas of this kind are behind the saga of Genesis 2,4bff, but only in a very indirect manner. Its subtle psychological understanding expresses an enlightened attitude; the serpent wins the woman to its side by first giving her the possibility of defending God. Eve learns by stages the benefits of the tree. The tastiness of its fruits is what she first notes, then she recognizes its beauty, lastly she ventures to think of its real significance: it gives "knowledge". Adam and Eve are not miraculous beings. Properties that all men can possess are illustrated in them: superiority over the animals, the gift of finding a fitting partner; it is not only for Adam and Eve that it can be said that all-embracing knowledge tempts them.[15] Not even the garden that God plants is something different from one of the astonishingly fertile oases in the desert. According to Ezekiel 28,13 on the other hand, the first created being lived "on the holy mountain of God among fiery stones".

The story of the Flood also avoids mythological exaggerations. Utnapishtim, the Babylonian Noah, tells how in the early morning a black cloud came up, in which the storm god thundered. His heralds went before him. The god of the underworld opened the doors. Demons held torches high, to blind the whole land. Darkness, earthquake and storm took away the courage even of the gods. They fled. According to the Biblical account it rained forty days and nights (Genesis 7,12).[16]

Such a sober attitude on the part of the narrator is most to be expected in sagas. The movement of the action is determined in these narratives in a different manner from that characteristic of myth. It is determined by man who are at home in this world. Therefore, in spite of all differences, the term "saga" is fitting for these narratives also.

Outside of the primaeval history there are no more sagas of this kind in the Old Testament. At the most, the narrative of the destruction of Sodom would be comparable. Here too we encounter the motif of guilt and punishment; in this narrative too the aetiological explanation of a strange phenomenon of the present plays an important part; as in the mankind-sagas the narrator has no immediate access to the time in which this phenomenon — the Dead Sea — did not yet exist. Yet in this saga the wide prospect on the whole life of humanity before God is missing. At the same time it only forms the background for the family history of Lot, Abraham's nephew.

5. FAMILY SAGAS

People and Corporate Personality

The narratives collected in Genesis 12-50 represent the beginnings of the people of Israel in the guise of a family history. To us it appears strange, that a people should descend from a family. Historical science has long since made it probable that groups of different origin were fused together in the people of Israel. Yet the theory above mentioned has its meaning. In it is expressed the conviction that a common destiny in the past and in the future unites them. The individual Israelite cannot imagine that he has any significance apart from his membership of the people. He cannot abstract from the fact that he is a member of this society.

What consequences follow from this can be made clear from the prophetic preaching about punishment. The prophets seem to distance themselves from their people, whom they threaten with disaster; for example, they speak of "this people" (Jeremiah 6,9; 29,13). But the word that meets us is put in God's mouth. God is here separating himself from this people. (At the same time God is adopting the form of a speech at law in which the accuser, turning to the judge in authority, speaks of the accused in the third person).

But the prophet himself does not separate himself from the sinful people. In the vision at his call, Isaiah himself draws this to our attention:

I am a man of unclean lips,
And I dwell among a people of unclean lips (Isaiah 6,5).

Hosea experiences in his own family the sin of Israel; his wife bears on her body the signs of an adherent of the fertility cult; the names of his children preach judgement daily: "Not my people" and "Without mercy" (Hosea 1).

The indissoluble bond that united all members of the people finds its fitting expression in the fact that the national name of Israel was at the same time the name of an individual, the name which Jacob earned for himself (Genesis 32,23f). The prophets sometimes spoke of the people as an individual person!

When Israel was a boy I loved him,
I called my son out of Egypt (Hosea 11,1).

Sagas about the Ancestors

An expression of this kind was familiar to the people. In their sagas it had long been customary to personalize qualities and destinies of the community in one ancestor. It is noticeable how much the old traditions endeavour to bring the catchword "red" (*'āḏōm*) into connection with Esau, and how they delight to picture him as a very hairy man (Genesis 25,25.30; 27,16). This is a side-glance at the Edomites, whose ancestor Esau became (Genesis 36,1). The saga of the unnatural intercourse of Lot's daughters with their father reflects horror at the fertility rites of Canaanite peoples, who are supposed to have arisen from this union (Genesis 19,30ff). The blessings of Jacob for his sons, (Genesis 49) are in large part understandable only when it is realised that they held good not for persons but for tribes.

And yet the sagas of the ancestors cannot be reduced to an embodiment of the characteristics and destinies of peoples. Conflicts and experiences which only the individual can have are pictured. And yet the Israelitic custom of seeing the whole future people summed up in the ancestor expresses itself even in the explanation of such sagas as do not materialize in individual form characteristics of collectives. The people of Israel realizes that in the events which are related, its own destiny was at stake. Had the sacrifice of Isaac been carried through, where then would be the people that descends from him? The narrators knew that they were stamped by the decisions that had been made at that time. Abraham trusted God — that meant that the destiny of the people whose father he became was laid in God's hands.

Much evidence can be adduced to show that the reduction of the ancestor sagas to tribal sagas, i.e. to the personalization of characteristics of the society in its ancestor, is not an adequate explanation. To name only one thing: how is the figure of the decrepit blind Isaac to be explained? He believes that he must himself see to the continuance of the divine promise by transmitting the blessing to the eldest son; deceived by wife and son, he has to learn that it does not depend on his initiative at all.

The Historicity of the Ancestors

And yet the interpreter must not fall into the opposite mistake, seeking to enter more intimately into the thoughts of the figures in the saga than the text, with its sparsity of personal information and the gaps in biographical detail permits. The text itself may entice us to ask questions whose purpose is to close such gaps; what moved Abraham to remain in Mamre so long? What were his inner feelings when he thrust out his son Ishmael, as he prepared himself to sacrifice his son Isaac? Questions of such a kind can find no concrete answer. They are directed neither to the saga itself, which is in fact silent on these matters, nor do they allow us access to Abraham as a historic figure. We know Abraham only as the sagas reflect him. The fact has led to result that for long scholars assumed that "there was no historical knowledge to be got about the patriarchs."[17] Today this position is no longer maintained. Admittedly we cannot immediately read off from the sagas what the historical personality Abraham (not the figure in the saga) thought and believed. The way into the historical time of the fathers is harder to find. The sagas about the fathers must be compared with extrabiblical texts from the time of Abraham to find evidence about people who lived on a similar cultural level. In this way, for example, A. Alt comes to the hypothesis that the patriarchs worshipped a God who had linked himself with the nomad family. He was not, then, worshipped at a definite place, like the gods of Canaan, but as the God of the father of the extended family, the God of Abraham, the Fear of Isaac, the Strong One of Jacob.[18] This of course is not an explanation of the biblical sagas. Their interpretation does not lead back to the faith of the historical Abraham, but shows his experiences of faith in the light of the experience of God of the later Israelite narrators.

A tradition which was orally transmitted through centuries is, as we might suppose, so transformed in the process, that practically nothing any longer leads us back to its origins. Yet the memory of illiterate peoples without a written tradition proves to be astonishingly reliable. The names of the places and people in the sagas of the fathers are an infallible indication that these narratives still preserve genuine memories. One might think it natural that names would be used which did not become customary till later, that places would be named which did not exist at the time, that usages would be passed over in silence which had become strange at the time of the narrators. It is precisely here that the sagas show their historical reliability.

Prehistoric Character of the Family Sagas

In spite of this the sagas must disappoint the historian. They are concerned with birth and death, with strife and reconciliation, with events that are important for the continuance of a family, but leave no historical traces behind them. They are narratives out of a prehistoric world in which not the people but the family is the greatest social grouping known to man. In such a world the question whether a child is born is just as decisive as is in our world the continuance of a people (Genesis 16;18). Against this background we must read the narratives about the imperilling of the mother (Genesis 12,10ff; 20) or of the child (Genesis 21,9ff; 22). The whole human fellowship in which these people live, can thus be called in question.

Abraham, himself never in danger, would lose with his wife or his son the meaning of his life. In the events of the sagas he is not the one who acts and decides, but the participant for whom all is at risk. When he himself undertakes to secure the continuance of his family — and here he is following the wish of his wife — he created terrible confusion. (Genesis 16).

In the saga-circle dealing with Abraham, mother and child stand in the centre, in the Jacob-circle, on the other hand, it is the brothers. Both have a relatively large place in the book of Genesis, but that should not hide from us the fact that only a few traditions of the fathers are contained here. The same theme is taken up several times, in different forms. We encounter three themes several times in different forms.

1 Promise and birth of the son:	a) 18,1 ff + 21,1 ff
(Parallel to this, but not genuine narratives):	b) 15,1 ff
	c) 17, 1ff
2 Imperilling of the ancestress:	a) 12,10 ff;
	b) 20, 1ff
(Parallel to this, but from the Isaac circle):	c) 26,1 ff
3 Hagar in the desert:	a) 16,1ff;
	b) 21,8 ff

Twice we are told how Jacob obtained the precedence by stealth (Genesis 25,27 ff and Genesis 27). The story of the exchange of the birth-right for a mess of pottage is best described as a jest; the incongruity of the price raises a smile. Other ideas about family rights underlie the parallel narrative. It is not the right of the first-born, but the father's blessing which ensures precedence in the family. This institution of the father's blessing is unknown both to the Abraham narratives and to the times in which the sagas of the fathers were set down in writing. However the Jacob narrative in Genesis 48 again reminds us of it. Here we have an example of the way in which the old sagas preserve the memory of legal forms of past times, even when the narrators and collectors of the saga no longer know them, and when they see that in other sagas these are replaced by other institutions. (Further the presence of parallels of this kind gives us a clear indication of the fact that sagas of different origin were collected.)

The old family sagas are short. Only two or three people appear at once. The narrative concentrates itself on what is happening; it is silent about what went on in the minds of the people concerned. But the signs speak clearly of the thoughts and feelings of the character in the saga: Abraham gives Hagar and Ishmael provender for their journey into the desert — but far too little; he sets out in the morning for the sacrifice of his son; when it comes to climbing the mountain, he himself carries the fire and the knife, so that his son may not injure himself. Short and always self-contained, these sagas correspond to the style of oral narration.

Linking of Sagas

In the text of the Bible today indeed, they no longer encounter us as single narratives, but as part of a continuous story. This linkage is chiefly the work of the collectors who set down the sagas in writing. Thus, for example the family saga of Genesis 18 has subsequently been linked with the saga of the destruction of Sodom. Two of the three divine messengers who had appeared to Abraham, went on their way to Sodom, one remains behind in conversation with Abraham.

Another type of linkage is to be observed in the narratives of Genesis 27-33; they are united by the theme "Blessing". Deceit has made Jacob the recipient of the blessing; he is forced to flee from the brother whom he has deceived; the vision of God assures him that even in a foreign land he will not be forgotten by God. Does the blessing hold good even in the foreign land? From this question the Jacob-Laban-stories gain their suspense. And when Jacob returns and encounters the brother whom he has deceived, it comes to the unexpected end, that the bearer of the blessing solemnly casts himself in the dust before the unblest one, as men were wont to do in the orient to show obeisance to a prince.

Even before the collectors put together the individual sagas to make one picture of the history of the fathers, individual saga-cycles had already been created, which clustered around certain figures. For interpretation is it true that the individual narrative has primary significance, but its position also in the whole story must not be neglected. Even when this general context was only created by the subsequent linking of individual sagas, and thus does not portray the course of history, it can reveal to us how the old narrators and collectors understood the sagas.

By the side of sagas rich in content and poor in verbal style are also to be found individual sagas which present another picture. The event which is recorded in Genesis 24, could be adequately reproduced in a summary: Abraham caused a wife to be brought for his son from the land of his forefathers, Rebekah, the daughter of a nephew of Abraham. The vivid descriptions which adorn this long narrative, are a transition to the narrative form of another time. The hearer is more interested in the variety of life than in a closely packed plot. In the narrative of Joseph and his brothers there are many characters and side-plots, and in addition there is an interesting stage in distant Egypt. Delight in the exotic, in ornate style, and in complications of the action give this kind of narrative its charm. The individual narratives are here almost fitted together into a kind of biography. The old sagas have as their content only a single happening — here, on the contrary, the story of an unusual life is told, a

97

story covering many years. Further, the happenings here are placed in a different light from that of the old sagas; there is no encounter with God; it is not the blessing which is the cause of the quarrel of the brothers; Joseph who stands in the centre of the stage, is not the man to whom the blessing of Jacob is to be transmitted; the place of immediate leadings and promises of God is taken by ambiguous dreams: from a purely external point of view we seem no longer to be dealing with the life of man in the presence of God.

And yet this narrative too draws its intensity from a theological concern. The way in which God's will is effected leads through situations in which God has apparently forgotten the human beings. But in the end it is precisely the humiliations which prove to be the unavoidable way to vindication. Joseph could only come to honour in Egypt, because his brothers sold him, because he had to leave the respected position with Potiphar to go into prison, because he was there so long forgotten in spite of the agreement with Pharoah's officials.

6 TEXTUAL EXAMPLE; JACOB'S STRUGGLE BY NIGHT (GENESIS 32,22-32)

22) During the night Jacob rose, took his two wives, his two slave girls, and his eleven sons, and crossed the ford of Jabbok. 23) He took them and sent them across the gorge with all that he had. 24) So Jacob was left alone, and a man wrestled with him there till daybreak. 25) When the man saw that he could not throw Jacob, he struck him in the hollow of his thigh, so that Jacob's hip was dislocated as they wrestled. 26) The man said, "Let me go, for the day is breaking", but Jacob replied, "I will not let you go unless you bless me." 27) He said to Jacob, "What is your name?", and he answered, "Jacob". 28) The man said, "Your name shall no longer be Jacob, but Israel, because you strove with God and with men, and prevailed." 29) Jacob said, "Tell me, I pray, your name." He replied, "Why do you ask my name?", but he gave him his blessing there. 30) Jacob called the place Peniel (God's face) "because", he said, "I have seen God face to face and my life is spared." 31) The sun rose as Jacob passed through Penuel, limping because of his hip. 32) This is why the Israelites to this day do not eat the sinew of the nerve that runs in the hollow of the thigh; for the man had struck Joseph on that nerve in the hollow of the thigh.

The original independence of the Narrative
The saga of Jacob's struggle by night interrupts the narrative of Jacob and Esau. In fear of the revenge of the brother whom he had deceived, Jacob had fled alone and penniless. Now after many years he returned, blessed with a large family and numerous flocks. Yet he fears his brother who is coming to meet him with four hundred men. He takes double precautions; he divides his caravan, so that Esau can attack only one half of it,[19] and he sends gifts to meet him.

The questions, with what intentions Esau was approaching, and what effects the gifts were having upon him, remain for the present unanswered. The tension of interest is interrupted by the account of Jacob's experience by night in the crossing of the Jabbok. This narrative is so complete in itself that it is meaningful even without the Jacob-Esau story. After this interpolation the story of the meeting of the brothers continues, but not at the same place. We hear no more of Jacob's two caravans: the gifts for the moment play no further part. The narrator does not reflect that even the flocks intended as gifts had to cross the dangerous ford. The narrative of Jacob's experience by night has obviously been subsequently inserted into this context.

Genesis 32, 22-32 is recognizable as an independent piece even in its present textual context. That has consequences for the interpretation of the narrative. It forbids e.g. the question whether the change of Jacob's name corresponds to an inner change in the man through his struggle with God. In Genesis 17,5 Abram too received from God a new name. In all the following narratives he is now called Abraham. Jacob's new name "Israel" on the other hand is now apparently forgotten. This gives us even less justification for constructing a connection with preceding and subsequent Jacob stories, in order to interpret this story of the changing of his name. Only when this narrative is interpreted as an independent unity, can we ask why it was interpolated at this place.

As in many other places in the Pentateuch, two layers of interpretation overlap in this story also. A story originally independent is given a function within a greater whole. But when we look more closely, further layers become visible. As times changed, this saga has been repeatedly given new interpretations.

Elements of the Ghost Saga

In some characteristics it resembles sagas about devils, demons, and spectres. During the night a mysterious figure attacks Jacob. He remains nameless, the narrative speaks only of a "man". This corresponds to the vague manner of speech of many German sagas about "the white woman". The imprecision of the expression is intended to convey that here something inconceivably menacing is intervening in the life of man. In such sagas the bright day drives away the hostile spirits. As in Grimm's fairy tale of the "grave mound" the first rays of the sun drive away the devil, so here too the dangerous struggle ends with the dawn, as in that German fairy tale the soldier has won riches from the evil power by deceit, so here Jacob gains a blessing from his mysterious opponent. But Jacob does not emerge from the encounter unscathed; he halts upon his thigh. This motif also recurs repeatedly in ghost sagas.

Although individual motifs of this saga are also to be found in narratives of other peoples, it is a saga belonging to a locality, firmly attached to a definite place in the land east of Jordan. The dangers of crossing the river are made palpable in the form of a demon who lies in wait here for men.

99

Elements of the Saga relating to the Cult Centre

This saga became a narrative relating to a cult centre. The aetiology of the name of the place — Penuel — God draws near, the face of God — was added to the narrative. But this also meant a change in its meaning. Even the heathen inhabitants of the land east of Jordan would not have dedicated such a cult centre to a ghostly demigod so now the narrative is no longer concerned with a demon, but with a great God. It explains the singularity of the God of Penuel; man must first get the better of this God, before he is graciously approached by him.

Glorification of the Ancestor

When Israel settled in the territory near Penuel, they took over the cult centre, and worshipped their own God there. With this the cult centre narrative changes again. The Israelites were repeatedly made to wonder that their God wished to be so near to them. They knew that no man could stand before him. "Woe is me, I am lost . . . for with these eyes I have seen the King, the LORD of Hosts." (Isaiah 6,5). To suffer deadly fear in the presence of the deity is a fundamental human experience. It can be a first step to the experience that God is not satisfied with a small share in man's life. He claims the whole man.

In the legend of the cult centre at Penuel the Israelites found the possibility of giving expression to their astonishment that the great and dreadful God was present with his people. Indeed the narrative does not so much express wonder at God's condescension as wonder at the greatness of the man who can bear this nearness. The ancestor Jacob must have had almost superhuman power to survive this struggle.[20] In fact the story at first told was one of a victory of the ancestor. He won himself the name of victor. "You shall be called Israel, because you strove with God and with man, and prevailed" (in reality Israel means "God rules").

Reinterpretation of Jacob's Victory

This conception of the victory of the ancestor no longer fits the later Israelite conception of God. Yet even the "authors" of the final version of scripture did not venture wholly to excise the older form of the narrative. They certainly take good care that it is not God himself that wrestles with Jacob. For this reason they retained the indefinite expression "man" and do not speak of Yahweh, but of "Elohim". "Elohim", a divine being, does not only describe God himself, but also the gods, the divine beings of the heavenly court, even intermediate beings like the spirits of the dead.[21]

Now the whole narrative is marked by vagueness. Only thus could the traditional narrative be left almost intact, and still understood as an expression of a purified concept of God. It is true that the divine opponent cannot defeat Jacob; it is true that he must ask the lamed ancestor to end the struggle; it is true that he must yield to Jacob's request for a blessing — but in all this he preserves his superiority. At first he pays no attention to Jacob's demand for a blessing, and asks him instead for his name. But the man who surrenders his name discloses by so doing his nature. Jacob is forced to confess his guilt, for his name betrays that he is the deceiver (Jacob, the one who skulks after, dogs another man's steps). The divine being gives him a new name and thereby proves that he is his master. On the other hand the information about the divine name is withheld. When, only after this interplay, Jacob receives the blessing, the latter is not the result of dominance and victory, but a free gift.

The statements of the narrative now no longer fit very well together. Jacob emerges from the struggle undaunted and defeated, injured and the receiver of a gift, as victor over the deity, and as a man reminded of his limitations. The prophet Hosea knew this narrative, though, it would appear, in a rather different form. But to him also the figure of the defeated victor seemed essential:

> He struggled with the angel and was victorious. He wept and begged favour. (Hosea 12,5a).

This contradictory character of the narrative took shape in the history of its development.

The Jacob saga interpreted for the people of Israel its name, and so its nature. Its ambiguity made it a picture, with whose help the people could once and again meditate about its relation to God; it reflected God's incomprehensibility and nearness, man's greatness and weakness.

Insertion in the Jacob-Esau Cycle

Genesis 32, 22-32 is enclosed in the framework of the story of the encounter of the hostile brothers. The text neither needs this framework in order to be understood, nor does the Jacob-Esau story need this insertion; on the contrary the Jacob-saga is interrupted by it. And yet the collectors of the narratives very deliberately chose this place. This is shown by the verse which follows this interpolation, Genesis 33,1. Jacob has only just put behind him this encounter, both dangerous and rich in blessing, when he looks around him again, and sees Esau approaching. The encounter by night with the divine being, according to the opinion of the collector, is meant to prepare him for the encounter with his brother.

The theme of the blessing has brought the Jacob-Esau stories and the Jacob-Laban stories into one cycle. Blessing, too, is the theme of the Penuel narrative; that also was clearly a reason for including it in this cycle. Through overreaching and deceit Jacob has already cheated his brother of the blessing. With the cunning of a sly shepherd he has won great riches from his master Laban. His success has marked him out as the fortunate man who succeeds in everything. So long as these narratives were passed from mouth to mouth among the people, they certainly expressed above all the delight of the Israelite shepherds in the superior cunning of their ancestor. But later, surely, the question was asked whether the blessing was really due to cunning and human adroitness. This question may have caused the insertion of the Penuel story at this place. When he is face to face with the divine assailant, Jacob's strength and superiority avail him nothing. He then speedily realizes whom he has before him, and decides to take advantage of the situation. But he must humbly receive the blessing as a gift. The receiver of the blessing has no cause to be proud of his excellence. So the conflict of the brothers can end with the humble obeisance of the one who has been blessed, before the one who has not.

Summary
The following stages of development have left behind their traces in the final version.

1) It contains accounts of the manifestation of spirits and demons, such as are indigenous among different and independent peoples.

2) The narrative of the dangerous river demon is connected with the ford Jabbok.

3) The legend of the cult centre explains how the God of Penuel encounters man.

4) The saga of Jacob the mighty ancestor tells us that not even the deity overcame him.

5) The influence of later reflection makes it a narrative of the greatness and the weakness of the man whom God can encounter.

7. LAYERS OF GROWTH IN BIBLICAL TEXTS

The Old Testament traditions and texts were for centuries continually reinterpreted. The oral tradition and its fixation in writing, the remodelling of scriptural texts to form greater units, the making of copies, use in divine worship, and interpretation for a later age, left behind their traces. Thus many texts do not belong to one historical point in time. Beneath this final form the interpreter must seek to learn the history of the text. Three principal kinds of stratification can be distinguished.

Layers from the Time of oral Transmission
Layers of the text which originated within the oral tradition can indeed be recognized, but can no longer be clearly separated from one another. An example is provided by the saga of Jacob's struggle. Another is to be found in the story of paradise. At a first glance many things here are not in order. Although the tree of life stands beside the tree of knowledge, (Genesis 2,9), Adam, Eve, and the serpent do not seem to notice it. Only after their punishment is the tree mentioned again. The man and the woman must not touch it, therefore God drives them out of the garden

(Genesis 3,22). This unevenness betrays that the narrative had a still older form. Once the man and the woman tried in vain to win everlasting life from the tree of life, but now access to the tree of life is barred to them for all time coming. Such a story of paradise would have been a narrative parallel to various myths of the ancient orient. The water and bread of life the plant of life, had been nearly within the reach of mortals, but in the last moment the attempt fails, eternal life remains for ever unattainable (cf. the narratives of Adapa and Gilgamesh). In the form of the paradise story handed down to us, the tree of knowledge has suppressed the tree of life. That radically alters the story. It does not lead up to the lament for the inevitable fate of human mortality, but to the testing of human behaviour in relation to God. Knowledge is indeed not made essentially inaccessible to man, like eternal life (Genesis 3,22). Yet men have unjustly appropriated it. Therefore they are not exalted by the wisdom that they won, but by means of this wisdom they learn what they are without God, naked, helpless and dishonoured beings.[22] And yet the redactors of the saga have not completely expunged the motif of the tree of life. Thus the elements of the narrative are no longer fully consistent. Thus we are given free room for meditation. Has not the fact that the tree of life is, so to speak, the disregarded witness of sin, something to say to us? Does God not bestow eternal life on the man who listens to him?

This inner spaciousness of many Old Testament narratives has kept them alive, and continually suggests reinterpretation. Yet such reflection leading to further application must on the whole be limited to cautious questioning if we are not to incur the danger of reading more into the text than it permits. At times there will be nothing left to do but to state that an unevenness is not to be smoothed out, and not to be explained. The old narrators indeed also often accept traditions without reflecting about them in all their details. Were this not so, how, for example, could the messenger of God, who in the narrative of Jacob's struggle, caused Jacob to feel the power of God, be afraid of the morning light?

Exodus 4, 24-26 too has been left unchanged, like a fragment of primary rock surviving from the time of a still partially unclarified faith in Yahweh. During the night's rest Yahweh seeks to kill his emissary Moses, but is hindered by the circumcision which Moses' wife hastily performs. It was always known in Israel that the encounter with God could have a fatal outcome for man (Isaiah 6,3), but here God attacks from an ambush like a demon.

Exodus 4,24ff reports the narrative of Yahweh's attack only briefly in its chief points. Such reports and relics of narratives are perhaps often preserved as the last traces of complete stories. In this form we learn of the encounter of Jacob with the messengers of God (Genesis 32,1f) or of meeting of Joshua with the armed angel (Joshua 5,13-15). In Genesis 6,1-4 the fragmentary tradition of the narrative of the marriages with angels is to be explained as the product of the Old Testament's dislike for myth.

103

Layers dating from the Time of the Committal to Writing

Even when the texts of the Old Testament were already committed to written form, their history had not come to an end. The first written collection of oral tradition was made about the time of Solomon (10th-9th century BC) by the so-called Yahwist (J). About a hundred years later came the collection of the Elohist (E). The original form of both collections can be reconstructed only in part. A redactor fitted E into his fundamental document J in such a manner as to give the outward impression of a homogeneous work (R^{JE}). Judging from a modern standpoint we may regret this procedure, since it could disfigure older traditions. But for the believing Israelites the critical comparison of these texts was not important. For him they were all equally confessions of faith in Yahweh, and guidance for life in his presence.

The composition of J and E did not mean the drying up of the oral transmission. Some time before R^{JE} Deuteronomy was created out of the still living tradition. There was an older, probably written kernal around which in the course of time traditions about the journey through the desert, laws, and sermons about the law grouped themselves. The unmistakable originality of this work did not permit it to be confused with R^{JE}. It was attached very late and almost completely intact to the older collection.

Even the Priestly Writing (P), which came last, could still appeal to very ancient oral tradition. It provided for a redactor the basic material into which he could fit R^{JE} and D.

Thus even the history of the fixation in writing of the Pentateuch lasted for centuries. The four basic works contain layers from different times, and themselves bear witness to the different times in which they were created. Additions brought up to date the four basic writings and enriched them. The final version of the redactors acknowledges that the older writings are just as relevant as the later ones. The observant reader notices many indications of the complicated history of development. Repetitions and pleonasms, inconsistencies and contradictions are characteristic of the texts in which two versions are conflated.

This fact may be illustrated by the example of the Flood narrative. Twice God commands Noah to take beasts into the Ark; once, in so doing, he makes a difference between clean and unclean beasts (Genesis 7,2f), once not (Genesis 6,19). Twice we are told that human beings and beasts went into the Ark (Genesis 7,7-9; 7,13-16). According to Genesis 7,4.12 the Flood is created by a tremendous rainstorm, according to 7,10f by the fresh outbreak of the primal waters which are otherwise held back by the firmament. The redactor, who conflated the Flood stories of the Priestly Writing and the Yahwistic version, gives us sufficient evidence to reconstruct both parallel accounts, each in its own individual character. Therefore the modern interpretation of the text follows its own intention when it once again distinguishes these layers from each other and compares them with one another.

Not only the Pentateuch has been worked over by redactors. *Redactional expansions* are repeatedly to be found in the Bible. They bear witness to the fact that the believing Israelite never regarded the biblical message as belonging to the past. Thus prophetic sayings, which were originally intended for the northern kingdom of Israel, were transformed by additions into sayings for the southern kingdom of Judah, so that even after the end of the southern kingdom they still remained valid. (Hosea 1,7; 6,11 etc).

It seems to be a fundamental trait of biblical texts, that they remained alive over long periods, and continued to grow. There were always people who with their help wished to understand themselves and their relation to God. The layers added by the growth of these texts bear witness to this.

8. NARRATIVES OF THE ENCOUNTER WITH GOD

The theme of man's encounter with God has found expression in different categories. In sagas, in stories telling of dreams and visions, in prophets' descriptions of their own experiences, in song. Yet the common content marks these forms so clearly, that many kindred elements are to be found in them.

Cult Centre Sagas

A number of narratives about the fathers still betray the fact that behind them are cult centre sagas, which would show that it was possible to meet a special divinity at each place. In these sagas man was met by the god of a spring,[23] of a tree,[24] of a ford,[25] of a striking feature in the landscape.[26] But in the tradition of the fathers these sagas have changed their meaning. The God of the fathers is not confined to one place. Even in Egypt he cares for Abraham; he stands on the side of the man whom he as blessed even in Mesopotamia (Genesis 12, 10 ff; 29 ff). Israel did not believe that Yahweh wished to confine himself to one fixed place. The people experienced God's presence in the cloud which travelled with them,[27] in the tent which could be taken down and put together again,[28] in the Ark, which could be carried from shrine to shrine, and went into battle with Israel.[29] David's plan to build God a permanent house, was not easily put into operation. (2 Samuel 7, 5 ff). Faith in the presence of God with the men who belong to him thrusts far into the background conceptions of his presence at a special place in Israel. What that means is that there are no longer real cult centre sagas. Usually it is only the attachment of the aetiology of a name which recalls this older form of the narrative. In most cases the place no longer plays a part in the course of events. Just as little do the old sagas inquire in what manner man then experienced God's encounter with him. Customarily they content themselves with saying that God appeared and spoke.[30]

105

In some of the Jacob narratives this reserve is broken. The rock-fragments of Bethel (Genesis 28, 10 ff) and the dangerous Jabbok ford, (Genesis 32, 23 ff) give as it were the first impetus to the encounter with God.

But the divinity with whom Jacob wrestles, is not the Lord of Penuel, but the Lord over Jacob's whole life; he compels Jacob to divulge his name, and gives him a new name. Even in Genesis 28 the God that appears is by no means a local god. Bethel indeed means "House of God", God is in this place. But it is at the same time called the "Gate of heaven". From this place there is open access to the divine realm, which is inaccessible to man. From heaven God rules over a much wider realm than merely the one place Bethel. The range of his lordship is so wide that constantly messengers with messages from him descend and return. Thus neither of these two narratives is any longer a pure cult centre saga.

Dream and Vision

As if it were not enough to make a gap between God and man to correspond with the gap between heaven and earth, the narrative of Genesis 28, 10 ff makes the encounter with God, in addition to this, take place in the sphere experienced in dreams. Often the biblical authors do not venture to say more of the encounter of God with man than "God spoke". In dream and in vision on the other hand man can experience God's presence in vivid images. Narratives of dream and vision permit us to ascribe to the power of the human imagination which seeks to draw near to God, that picture of God's presence.

God's Hiddenness

It is however to be observed that even in these narratives God himself does not become visible. The narrative of the dream itself in Genesis 28,10 ff does not say more about God himself than "He stood", "he spoke". In the vision of Abraham in Genesis 15,7 ff it is left to the reader and hearer to make the connection between the fiery appearance and Yahweh. According to Exodus 24,10 the elders and Moses see only the heaven under God's feet. In the vision of Isaiah, even the fringes of his garment filled the whole temple (Isaiah 6,1). Ezekiel indeed ventures a bold utterance about the figure of God, which he sees, but emphasizes with all caution that he can portrary only what is external, the appearance, the impression, not God himself (Ezekiel 1,26).

God the King

In Genesis 28, God appears as the King, whom the heavenly court serves. We meet a similar picture in the visions of Isaiah, Micaiah ben Imlah, Ezekiel and Daniel.[31] Even this picture gives the possibility of withdrawing God from the all-too-confident grasp of human imagination. In the mythical religions of Israel's environment, men represent God the king in a symbolic play on the occasions of the yearly celebration of an enthronement festival, and thus attempt to influence him to favour them. But God the King of Israel is withdrawn from human influence. He uses troops of messengers for the wide realms of his domain (Genesis 28, Daniel 7); he confuses men (1 Kings 22); he brings destruction on sinners (Isaiah 6); he is free to appear where he will (Ezekiel 1).

The Journeying God

Only in the few visions of God the enthroned king, and in the isolated relic of a narrative (Exodus 24,10f) does God appear at rest in one place. Otherwise God encounters man only as a traveller, the God who sets himself in movement. Yahweh always decides freely whether he is present or not. Ezekiel adopts this conception even into the picture of the throne of God; it has globular wheels, which can roll in all directions, and the beings who carry it have faces pointing in all directions — God can travel without effort in all directions.

God is only seldom pictured as omnipresent, much more often as the one who repeatedly and anew visits his people. The word "to come down" which is frequently used in this context, can indicate that God normally is in heaven his distant dwelling-place. But beyond an indication the Old Testament does not in general go; it is silent as to the place from which God comes down. The heavens, the dwelling-place of many heathen gods, do not, for the believer in Yahweh, seem great enough for their God.[32]

But, above all, the conception of a heavenly dwelling-place contradicts the experience of Israel's faith that its God is near and with his people. Therefore later descriptions of the descent of God emphasize that Yahweh has the power to open the heavens, to bow them down, or to divide them.[33] This God thrusts aside all hindrances, even the separating wall of the heavens, in order to be with his own.

Israel can rely on this, that God is inclined towards his people, but it remains conscious that it cannot simply take his presence with the people for granted. When the people needs his help, God of his own will approaches. Yahweh made in the desert the covenant with Israel. Since then Israel's history is the place of meeting with God. Yahweh comes to the place where Israel's fate is decided. Of this we are reminded by texts which describe how Yahweh repeatedly travels along the desert road of his people, in order to be present as the helper of Israel.[34]

The Old Testament recognizes a series of signs and pictures of the approach of God: natural phenomena like thunderstorms, earthquakes and tempest show that he is present.[35] To the author of the Elijah epiphany in 1 Kings 19 this way of depicting the divine presence seemed unfitting; it is not in mighty signs, but in an almost inperceptible happening that God encounters man. Later biblical authors use mythological images; God comes riding on the cloud, he fights against the sea and its monsters when he appears.[36] In all these texts great care is taken that only figures and signs of the divine presence are accessible to man, and

107

that God himself remains concealed under them from men. God appears to man, but is not himself seen. In the Elijah theophany the author avoids the statement which the reader expects, that God finally comes in the still small voice.

A further motif has grown from the effort to picture the God who wishes to be so near to man, as at the same time the inconceivable one, the motif of God passing by. Yahweh does not stay still beside Moses and Elijah, as he appears to them. Moses cannot get a glimpse of him until he has already passed. When God passes by, Elijah hides his face (Exodus 33 f; 1 Kings 19). The Old Testament speaks in different terms of God passing by, an event which men only notice subsequently, when misfortune has occurred.[37]

God in the Temple

Thus the Old Testament knows various ways of expressing the faith that God can never be grasped at any place or time. This strong tradition stamps even the texts which tell of God's presence in the temple and in Jerusalem. In the cloud which conceals God, God descends into the holy place, in order to dwell there in darkness (1 Kings 8, 10f). Isaiah indeed sees Yahweh in the temple, but his form towers unimaginably far above the building, the very train of his garment fills the whole temple (Isaiah 6). The powerful tradition of the greatness of God, which no place can contain, makes it finally easier for Ezekiel to speak of God's departure from the temple. Yahweh departs from Jerusalem in order to come to his exiles (Ezekiel 10, 18 ff). The faith of Israel that God will ever and again come to his people, awakens the hope that in the consummation of the last times, God will for ever dwell in the midst of his people.[38]

9. MIRACLE NARRATIVES

Rationalistic Explanations of Miracle

The miracles of which the Old Testament tells, are today often denuded of all extraordinary features — in this way the interpreter believes that he has proved that "the Bible is right after all." The marshy sea of reeds could be made passable by a hot wind from the desert. (Exodus 13, 17 ff). A landslide could for a short time stem the course of the Jordan (Joshua 3). The wind can deflect flocks of quails from their way, so that they sink to the ground exhausted in the desert and are easy to catch (Numbers 11, 31 ff). There is one good thing about these explanations; they prevent the interpreter from applying the modern concept of miracle to the old narratives. The men of old times did not regard as miracles only events in which God breaks the laws of nature. On the other hand the rationalistic explanations obscure the meaning of the miracle stories; the latter do precisely intend to speak of the unusual event which transcends human limitations. But the older narrators regard what men experienced in this event as more important than the event itself. It was for Israel a sign of the presence of God, who was at hand to save his people. It is this experience which makes the event a miracle.

The Miracle of the Exodus

The particular nature of the Old Testament miracle narratives is especially visible in the leading of the people out of Egypt. This theme runs through the whole Old Testament; ancient texts and authors of the later time both understand it as the pivot of the history of Israel.[39]

In Exodus 1-15 this theme is expanded at length in narrative terms, and embellished in many ways. Wherever in the Old Testament the theme of the Exodus is sounded, there accompanies it the reference to the miraculous character of this event: "with signs and miracles", "with a strong hand."[40] God set free his own people. The narratives in Exodus 1-15 are equipped with a whole apparatus of wonderful events. The passage through the Red Sea alone has seven miracles belonging to it: the changing position of the pillar of cloud (Exodus 14,19), the light that shone on the side of the Israelites, the darkness on the Egyptian side (Exodus 14,20), the drying up of the sea (Exodus 14,21), the division of the water, and its consolidation into two walls (Exodus 14,22), the confusion of the Egyptians (Exodus 14,24 f), the obstructing of the war chariots (Exodus 14,25), the flowing back of the water and the destruction of the Egyptians (Exodus 14,27).

This accumulation of miracles — some of them mutually incompatible — indicates that in this text there is an overlap of layers added by growth. The drying of the sea and its division and its consolidation into walls of water, the flight of the confused Egyptians and their overthrow in the sea, into which they were pursuing Israel, cannot all have happened at the same time. Two versions of the narrative of the passage through the sea have been laid together, without the redactor giving preference to one of them, for the sake of logical consistency. For him it was more important that both of them spoke with one voice of the same experience of Israel, that in this happening God's power had manifested itself to man (Exodus 14,17). God alone is acting here, Israel must stand still (Exodus 14,14);[14] all that is required of it is fearless confidence (Exodus 14,31). The consequences of the event are acknowledgement of the divine power, and trust in his guidance (Exodus 14,31). Taught by its experience, the people acknowledges the fact that it owes its existence to God's intervention.

It would however be wrong to regard the whole miracle narrative as an illustration of the teaching that God protects the life of his own. Such spiritualizing interpretation of a miracle story is indeed attested for the miracle of the manna in Deuteronomy 8,3:

> He humbled you and made you hungry; then he fed you on manna which neither you nor your fathers had known before, to teach you

109

that man cannot live on bread alone but lives by every word that comes from the mouth of the LORD.

But the miracle of the Reed Sea never became an illustration exemplifying a religious doctrine. This narrative was not created by the faith in God's life-preserving power. The fact is rather the reverse; the Old Testament faith in Yahweh who secured the existence of his people appeals to what happened at the Reed Sea. (So, for example in Isaiah 51,9ff, the prophet awakens the memory of this miracle in order to strengthen confidence, even in the time of the exile).

In the course of time the miraculous elements in the Reed Sea narrative were more and more heightened. The old Yahwistic version still spoke of the hot east wind that dried up the sea, and the flight of the Egyptians in confusion; the later one spoke already of the dividing and solidifying of the water and the overthrow of the whole combat force of the Egyptians; finally, according to Exodus 15, 1-18, a hymn about this event from exilic or post-exilic times, God's mighty breath of tempest builds up the sea. The more unhappy Israel's situation was, and the more confidence in God's power to preserve needed strengthening, the more the Old Testament authors tried to emphasize the power of God by accentuating the miraculous element. So in Isaiah 51,9 ff the passage through the sea is connected with motifs dealing with the binding of the floods of chaos in primaeval times. From the beginning of the world, the God who called Israel into existence by the deliverance out of Egypt proves his might. He is also powerful enough to lead his people home again from exile.

The miracles of the journey through the desert are also experienced as signs that God preserves the life of his people. He gives manna as food, takes care to provide water and meat, according to Deuteronomy 29,5 even clothes and shoes. The priestly narrative's version of the manna narrative makes clear by illustration that God's saving intervention should be answered by trust on the part of the people. Each man must only collect as much manna as he uses in one day. Anyone who, against instructions, wishes to provide for later days, finds that his supply goes bad.[42] Here we are reminded of the command to "stand still" which is issued to the Israelites on the occasion of God's miraculous intervention at the Reed Sea. Human planning and action must be wholly relegated to the background, where God's wonderful work is to be experienced.

Miracles in the Holy War

Even the events in the conquest of the promised land and in the early stages of the defence of the new possession are understood in the Old Testament as signs of a wonderful salvation of the people by God. In this time Israel is waging "holy wars". They are "holy" not because they are wars of religion whose aim might be to enforce and propagate the faith of Israel. What is at stake is rather the defence of Israel's existence. These wars are "holy" because they are waged, not by Israel, but by God.

Israel's task is to rely on God's help. Here it is as it was in the case of the miracle of the Reed Sea, and in the manna story of the priestly document. Yet here it is clearly shown that this reliance does not mean leaving it all to God. The armies which God uses to wage the holy wars are formed of the freemen of Israel. They express their reliance on God by conducting the wars according to a fixed ritual, like an act of worship, ascribe the victory to God alone, and consequently dedicate to him his part of the booty. This view of the conquest of the promised land finds expression, among other things, in the description of the fall of Jericho (Joshua 6,1-27), and Gideon's war against Midian (Judges 7).

Miracles for an Unworthy People
The narratives of Israel's salvation by God's miraculous intervention are confined to the time from the deliverance from Egypt to the final settlement in the land. In Israel this time was later judged to be remarkable. It ought to have been a time in which the people responded to experience of wonderful divine help with full trust. But obviously Israel had experienced all the miracles in vain. They repeatedly rebelled against God's intention, were discontented, and turned to other gods. So in the narrative of the time in the desert of Ezekiel 20,1ff; Psalm 78; Psalm 106, the refractory and disloyal people are condemned. But we find similar judgements also in the books from Exodus to Judges.

With this is connected a new interpretation of the miracles. God really does not work them for the people's sake. The people had deserved destruction, and not salvation. It is for his own sake that he stands up for Israel, remains true to his decision to protect the people as his own. He saves them for his own reputation's sake, that foreign peoples should not despise Israel's God (Numbers 14; Psalm 106,8; Ezekiel 20,14). According to the older accounts we were able to describe as "miracle" an event in which the people experienced the salvation of its existence through God's intervention. On this later view it is principally the foreign peoples and their gods who are to behold the miracles of Yahweh (cf. also Exodus 15,11).

It is this understanding of miracle which has formed the narratives of the Egyptian plagues. The plagues contribute only indirectly to the salvation of the people. Their main purpose is to prove the superiority of God to the foreign princes. (The accumulation of miracles points here also to the fact that we have to deal with several layers of growth, and increasing embellishment of the narrative). Yet even here we cannot apply a modern understanding of miracle; even these proofs of God's powers do not consist merely in the breaking of natural laws. Swarms of locusts are frequently blown by the hot east wind out of the desert into the land (Exodus 10,13) — had the swarms e.g. come from the sea, then Pharaoh would have been forced to grant that a supernatural power was involved. It is not possible to decide by "objective" criteria whether an event is a miracle; the question to be asked is whether man acknowledges

111

it as a proof of God's power. For this reason an Old Testament teacher of wisdom can conclude by praising all the facts of creation as divine miracles. (Ecclesiasticus 42, 15-43,33).

The Miracle Worker

We must distinguish the narratives which centre round a man who works miracles from the narratives about miracles which praise God's works for his people, and extol God's mighty works before the peoples, the gods, and all the world. The former type of narratives is dealt with in the next section.

10. NARRATIVES ABOUT EXTRAORDINARY MEN

The Role of Man in the Sagas of the Fathers

The old sagas of Israel dwell only seldom upon deeds of cunning and strength. Most of the motifs providing this kind of pleasure in narration have attached themselves to the figure of Jacob. Cunning as a shepherd and cleverness help him to win wealth in his dealings with Laban and to win a blessing in his dealings with Esau. Yet Jacob only wins what God has planned for him from his birth. He cannot ascribe the blessing which he received after the struggle at the Jabbok to his own powers, but only to divine grace. There are individual elements which still at a distance indicate the picture of an unimaginably strong Jacob. He survives the struggle with the divine being; a great fragment of rock, such as is to be found at Bethel, can serve him as a pillow to prop his head at night. But it is not the ancestor, but God, "the mighty one of Jacob",[43] who is the victor. Jacob has indeed outwitted Esau, but for that reason he must flee into a strange country; he has indeed returned home from abroad blessed with riches, but he casts himself at the feet of his unblessed brother.

. . . in the Narratives of Saul and David

The general picture given by the narratives of the Books of Samuel and Kings is entirely different. God does not appear to intervene at all in the quarrel between Saul and David (1 Samuel 18-2 Samuel 1). The friendship of Jonathan, the support of priests and prophets,[44] even of brigands and Philistine enemies of Israel, his own cunning, adroitness and courage, and finally also Saul's misfortune help David to gain the mastery.

Unique, unrepeatable life-situations of Saul and David are depicted — there is no room for the thought that tribal qualities are being exemplified in a typical figure. The fate of Saul can only be explained as arising out of an unrepeatable historical situation. He is not able to bring the political requirements of his still new kingly office into harmony with the old religious traditions (cf. especially the narrative of Saul's sacrifice).

His counterpart, the favoured young David, is an equally unmistakable figure. He has good fortune, everyone loves him. He can even console Saul, and help him to forget his sufferings, but on the other hand he makes more poignant his consciousness of misfortune.

Thus the relationships between the people in these narratives are not straightforward. Ambiguous feelings also motivate a figure like Jonathan, who is loyal to his father and to Saul's opponent David. The human behaviour is complex, and can only be understood as the result of several different motives. David prefers to go out of the way of his rebellious son Absalom rather than to oppose him. In any case, in view of the successful rebellion, no alternative was possible for him (2 Samuel 15,12 ff). At the same time he retreats without a fight, in the hope that his fortunes may take a turn for the better, if only he submits patiently to the will of God (2 Samuel 16,12).

Nevertheless he braces himself for the decisive conflict, but would still wish to spare his son (2 Samuel 18,5). He accepts the proposal of his military leaders, to keep himself out of the battle; in the first place he sees that in this situation, the chief thing is that his life must be spared, and secondly he can thus avoid an immediate conflict with his son. Yet after he had agreed to keep away from the dangerous conflict, he later wishes that he had died in the place of Absalom. But he can again conceal his grief, so soon as he is exhorted to secure his authority (2 Samuel 19).

Many causes must cooperate to bring about such an event as David's success in the conflict with Saul. And the consequences of an event too are confusingly varied. Because David loves Bathsheba, Uriah must die. David is accused and repents. This love is also the reason why Bathsheba's son Solomon has precedence over David's eldest son Absalom, and his second son Adonijah. Revolt in the kingdom, strife in the royal family, political murders after Solomon's accession to the throne, are the result.

The Authors of the Narratives about David

The Israelite authors of the time of the first kings clearly achieved new powers of narration. It is obvious that the changed condition of the time offered new possibilities to the human spirit. Here we are no longer listening to the old saga narrators whose wish was to entertain, instruct and edify their acquaintances in the circle of the family or the tribal or village community with stories from the past. The domination of the central kingship which took the place of a loose tribal bond required an army and a structured group of officils for the exercise of government, the collection and administration of the finances of the state. It had become essential to educate the men for such offices. The art of writing became important for the performances of many of their tasks. But this created the possibility of portraying a complex series of events like those in the books of Samuel and the Kings. It is only the committal to writing that makes possible for the author such a finely elaborated representa-

113

tion of men, their motives and actions, their collaboration and conflicts. The themes of these narratives can only be treated in longer units than are possible in the oral transmission of the sagas.

The most famous example of the new art of narrative is the story of David's succession to the throne, which forms a long complex in 2 Samuel 6-1 Kings 2. A good knowledge of the events depicted and temporal proximity of the writer to them is betrayed in the manner of the narration. His theme, superficially, is no longer the enforcement of the divine will, but the human history which determines human willing and human suffering. The place of the narrator of sagas is taken by this writer of history.

Events which take place only on the human level could now for the first time be regarded as worthy of notice, because the new form of government had created an attitude of mind corresponding to itself. The royal government had to take account in the annals of the actions of the Kings;[45] lists of officials and solders had to be there for the finding.[46]

Comparison with Ancient Oriental Records of Kings

Yet this by itself is not an adequate explanation of rise of the new art of narration. Tasks of a Government Office of this kind could indeed sharpen the vision of educated people for matters of fact, but they did not create also from the beginning the capacity to grasp and portray complex historical phenomena. It was not in this official realm that Israelite historiography developed. This is shown with all clarity by a comparison with historical texts of the ancient orient — which had already been much longer acquainted with royal chanceries.

What predominates there are the reports of the kings, written in the first person. These are not to be found at all in the Old Testament. The Accadian annals do not go beyond a list of the deeds of the king. Enemies are only interesting as the objects of these glorious deeds — the enemies of the Israelite kings on the other hand appear as personalities with a character of their own. In the place of the boastful enumeration of deeds, there stands in the Old Testament the depiction of an often complicated action, in which what we are told of the king is by no means only to his credit.[47]

In Israel's environment in the ancient east, the figure of the king is entwined with splendid mythological imagery. The narratives of Saul and David in contrast portray the king in his often honourable but also often shameful human behaviour. The king is only distinguished beyond other people by the fact that his failure casts him deeper into unhappiness and suffering. Saul, forsaken of God, is almost driven crazy by his suffering. Circumstances compel him to act, but his action entangles him more deeply in misfortune (1 Samuel 13;15). David's flight from Jerusalem is the climax of the human tragedy of an ageing man who is forced to observe how the love of the people turns from him and towards his rebellious sons, but who is too weak to control in time the assaults of his sons.

Above all, the history of the succession to David's throne portrays the weakness and failure, human dignity and greatness of the king without making value judgements. Only the character of the portrayal moves the reader to participate inwardly. The stories which other peoples tell of their kings always unambiguously take the side of their mighty king, the darling of the gods. The author of the throne-succession story avoids any commentary.

God's Plan in History

Is history here recounted merely for its own sake? If this were correct, then in this new art of narrative something would have emerged not only wholly different from the histiography of the rest of the ancient world, but also something wholly new in contrast with the older Israelite contemplation of the past. Israel had always had a strong interest in history. But that history was never look on as completely past, it remained effective to the present day (cf. Exodus 13,9). Many of the roots of the historiography which became prevalent in the time of the kings in Israel, can be found in the old Israelite sagas. The saga narrators too sometimes without commentary showed man in a situation of extreme need, only the nature of the representation awakened in the hearer's participation in the fate of the characters. As in the case of the old narrators, so is it with the author of the throne succession history; his final concern is to show the working of God in human destiny. Only the conception of the nature of divine activity has changed. Every happening can be derived almost without a gap from human motives, actions and reactions. God had commanded Abraham in his time to go forth from his home, to sacrifice his son. But now God no longer intervenes with commands in the course of the action. And yet his will embraces the whole confused tangle of human action.

This concealed background of historical happenings is disclosed by the narrator of the throne succession story at three places only: 1) David's crime against Uriah displeases God; 2) David's son Solomon pleases him; 3) God causes Absalom to disregard the good advice of a man who had fallen away from David, and to listen to a secret supporter of David (2 Samuel 11,27; 12,24; 17,14). At none of these points does God immediately take charge of events. David's crime bears in itself its sinister consequences; it leads him at last to the unhappy experiences at the hands of his rebellious sons. That Solomon from his birth is "the one loved by God" (Jedidiah as the prophet Nathan names him) becomes visible not in a miraculous manner but in the "natural" course of events, when on the insistence of Nathan and his mother he is finally named as David's successor and is able to establish himself in his kingly office. The same procedure of the narrator is to be observed at the third point: when God causes Absalom to accept the wrong advice of David's friend,

David's fortunes take a turn for the better. Exactly in this manner David's prayer has succeeded in obtaining this change — but the prayer is not answered by a miraculous divine intervention, but by the cleverness of David's friend, who deceives Absalom.

Narratives about the Prophets

In other narratives of the books of the Kings and Samuel too, it is only the eye of faith which perceives that God's plan guides secular history. His will is not made known directly, but only through the prophets, to the men of action. The prophet Ahijah appoints Jeroboam as ruler over ten of the tribes of Israel, and therewith as initiator of the division of the kingdoms (1 Kings 11,29 ff). But the prophet's words is fulfilled in a purely secular manner: Solomon's successor embitters the people by his hardness, and thereby smooths the way for Jeroboam. But in a single sentence the narrator discloses the real background of the event; God had willed that Solomon's successor should act in such a way that the word of the prophet was fulfilled. A second example: Elijah strives successfully with King Ahab, who tolerates heathen syncretism (1 Kings 17,ff); he receives the commission of anointing kings in Aram and Israel who will fulfil God's judgement (1 Kings 19,15 ff). Elisha, his successor, fulfils the commission, and by so doing gives the usurpers an important impulse really to seize the kingdom for themselves (2 Kings 8, 7 ff; 9,1 ff). There is nothing miraculous in the intervention of the prophets in historical events. It is only their interpretation of the events that reveals that in the last resort in secular affairs, the most important thing is the will of God.

God also allows individual men to do what displeases him, without being thereby deflected from his own purpose. The story of David shows this with particular clarity. The reader has just learnt that Michal, David's wife, remained childless (2 Samuel 6,23), when the story is surprisingly told of Nathan's prophecy to David and his successors (2 Samuel 7). But will it be possible for this prophecy to be fulfilled? Through David's sin, his crime against Uriah, the fulfilment comes nearer. True, the son born of the adulterous intercourse with Uriah's wife dies, but on the other hand Solomon, the beloved of God, is born of the marriage. Human guilt is indeed punished, but it does not prevent God from fulfilling his intentions in just this way.

The Sombre Picture of Man

The picture of man in the Israelite historical writing is sombre. In this, also, it is akin to the older Israelite narratives. After the climax of Nathan's promise there follows immediately the failure of David, which draws in its train all the sombre happenings at the end of his life. Soon after Saul's coronation as king there follows his rejection by God and the story of his decline. The figures of the Judges are drawn in a like manner; Gideon has triumphed over the Midianites, but with the victory comes at once his doom he makes for himself from the booty a golden oracle-object which leads him and his family into misfortune (Judges 8,24 ff). On his return home after victory, Jephthah is fated to see that the sacrifice which he devoted to God in the battle is his daughter (Judges 11,34).

Even more sudden appears this turn for the worse in the Samson stories. Through his wonderful birth, his special dedication to God, Samson is a figure that promises great things. He also plays many mischievous tricks on the Philistines, Israel's enemies. But in so doing he takes revenge each time for defeats that were intended for him personally, and not for Israel — in relation to which he himself was not blameless. He ends, in chains and blinded, an object of the mockery of his enemies. Yet in his death he wins his greatest victory over his enemies (Judges 16,30).

The aim of all these narratives is thus by no means the glorification of great men. The judges, David and Saul are no spotless heroes, still less are they exemplary legendary figures. At first sight they are only outstanding among the others through the fact that God makes use of them to save his people. In so doing God gives free room not only for human courage, the cleverness and greatness of Saul and David, but also for their errors — even the deviations of the easily misled Samson.

Comparison of Sagas about Deliverers and Narratives about David

The narratives about the rise of David and Saul, and the succession to David's throne, have also much in common with the older narratives about the judges. But there are still more things to distinguish these two groups from one another.

In the centre of these narratives about the judges stand the conflicts with Israel's enemies. Of the same type are the narratives about Joshua, and certain narratives about Moses and Saul. In them is reflected the special structure of the covenant between the tribes of Israel in the time before the kings. Only in time of danger did the free men come together under the leadership of a man called by God. Their conflicts counted as "holy wars". God is the true hero. Untiring prayer and miraculous divine intervention[48] confuse the enemies and drive them back. Human courage is only a sign that God is with the warrior.

The "heroes" of these narratives are hardly set before our eyes as living figures, each in the special circumstances of his life. It is not their personal capabilities which are decisive for victory. The heroes are not "great" in themselves; they become heroic, because God's spirit comes upon them. But he gives them power only for one single great act of deliverance, and only because of this one deed are they outstanding.[49]

Here indeed we can see the decisive difference from the larger cycles of stories about Saul and David and from the "throne succession story". These "heroes" are typical figures. They stand in the centre of one single great event. In contrast, David and Saul are individual figures entangled in complex varied interrelations of event and fate. In the narratives about the judges it is not the human involvements that are of interest, but the salvation of Israel by God — in this these men are only tools in God's hand.

The name "judges" does not suit them. It was only given to them subsequently by the collector of these narratives, who put them together to form a picture of the time before the kings. It would be more to the point to have called them "deliverers of Israel".

We cannot, however, ascribe the deliverer-narratives to "history writers", as we can, for example, in the case of the "throne-succession story". Here there are no writers of history at work, who are interested in human complexities. What we have here are narrators of sagas. These always pay undivided attention to the one great event — without paying attention to the complicated connections of secular affairs. For what they wanted to depict was the manner of God's intervention in earthly realities.

Now, however, two types of narrative have been attached to the deliverer-figures, from which one might infer an interest in human biography: the tales of childhood and of vocation. But not even these are meant to represent individual figures and destinies. They are narratives whose purpose is to declare what made these men outstanding figures — just like the motif of spirit possession; they are not great on their own account, but through the election and call of God.

Narratives of Vocation

We must here study more in detail the vocation narratives. These do not in any way depict individual experiences, but the typical human reactions to the challenges of God: Gideon refers to his weakness and wishes for a sign: with this the narrative represents him as the little man who is really not worthy of the divine call. Moses behaved just so; as Gideon answered to the call of God so do even Jeremiah and Ezekiel. In the Gospel of Luke we still meet the same motif in the answer of Mary to the message of the angel. God calls a weak human being, but the latter is strong because "God is with him".[50]

A second type of stories of vocation tends rather in contrast to suggest that the man is astonishingly great, so great that God deems him worthy of a commission. In a vision the man sees God in the midst of his servants and messengers. But it is not the heavenly beings, but the man whom God sends out under his commission. This form of vocation is clearest in 1 Kings 22. The same pattern already underlies Genesis 28. Jacob sees God in a dream; messengers unceasingly go from him and return to him, but it is not to them but to the man that God turns. Although Isaiah 6 coincides almost word for word with 1 Kings 22, the type of the story has changed decisively. The heavenly beings are no longer counsellors and messengers; their sole function is to give glory to God. The man, on the other hand, thinks of himself as lost; as a sinner he is not worthy of such a vision.[51] It is only a divine intervention which enables Isaiah to offer himself as a messenger. Ezekiel emphasizes much more still the human weakness of the man who is called. He cannot even stand and listen unless the divine spirit supports him (Ezekiel, 1, 28-2,2).

With this Ezekiel has inserted a motif out of the deliverer-sagas into the narrative of his call, the motif of endowment by the spirit. Here too, Ezekiel can have had recourse to prophetic tradition — Elisha becomes a prophet when he receives the "spirit" of Elijah.[52] Moses too, according to tradition, possessed the prophetic spirit; when God caused something of this spirit to come upon the seventy elders, they fell into prophetic ecstasy (Numbers 11,24-30). The mention of the gift of the spirit in the vocation narratives is an attempt to explain how a man can ever accept divine tasks. In man himself there is little that could form a point of contact for God.

Yet another motif of the vocation narratives points to the following fact. The call lays hold of a man unexpectedly. Elisha is engrossed in his daily work when he is called by Elijah to be his disciple. It is in exactly the same manner that God's call breaks into Saul's life. When he hears the news of Israel's defeat, he kills the cattle with which he is ploughing, in order to follow God's call. Gideon is threshing when the heavenly messenger speaks directly to him: "You are a brave man, and God is with you".[53]

In 1 Samuel 9 f the motif of the irruption of the call into the life of every day has almost a fairy-tale quality. Saul sets out to look for his father's she-asses and finds the kingdom. And the transformation of the man Saul is just as strikingly described: "As Saul turned to leave Samuel, God gave him a new heart" (1 Samuel 10,9).

Filled by God's spirit, Saul falls into ecstasy. All the narratives of the sudden departure of the man called from his daily work know the motif, that a messenger of God[54] transmits the call of God to the man for whom it is meant. This happens with Saul too, not merely through a word addressed to him, but by means of a special rite of anointing.[55]

Like Saul, David is anointed by Samuel; like Saul, after the anointing he is filled with the Spirit of God. Saul's inspiration by the spirit leads to prophetic ecstasy; the deliverers of Israel were empowered by God's spirit to do one great deed — but not so David.

Then the spirit of the Lord came upon him, and was with him from that day onward (1 Samuel 16,13).

The narrator here lets himself be guided by the hopes which, since the promises of Nathan are connected with the anointed king in Jerusalem (Messiah = the Anointed). Through the promise, it was claimed, an enduring presence of God would be bestowed on the people.

Summary and Further Comments

To sum up, once more we must distinguish between historiography and the sagas about the deliverers and hold them apart. The characteristics of historiography are:

1 A written text
2 Concentration on the secular realm
3 Portrayal of complex human motives, of varied presuppositions and tangled consequences of events
4 Portrayal of unique human situations
5 Reserve in the matter of value judgements
6 Disclosure of the fundamental divine plan
    a) by rare indications of God's attitude to the event
    b) by prophetic interpretation and exercise of influence

What is common between this kind of historiography and the narratives about the judges, is the sombre picture of man. But while Israelite historiography traces all situations exclusively to the interplay of human powers, these narratives give to man a much more insignificant part to play in the course of history. God's spirit makes the judges capable of their achievements. The wars are decided by miraculous divine intervention. The different types of stories of vocation show how insignificant man is. But this belittling of human endeavour distinguishes these narratives not only from the Israelite historiography, but also from the hero-sagas of other peoples. They are in conflict even with the ancient Israelite family sagas. God's dealing with the individual man, with Moses, Joshua, the judges, is lastly here no longer with the individual but with the destiny of the whole people. For this reason it has no significance for the forward march of history, when the individual fails. God can always use another man for the deliverance of the people.

These narratives were passed on from mouth to mouth in different circles in Israel. It was not until much later that they were fitted into larger literary compositions.

The concept of "legend" is not to be applied to them. We are accustomed to call by the name of legend particular coherent stories from the life of the saints. They repeat biographically vivid, but also often insignificant details; when a man is pleasing to God even little things are significant. The sagas of the deliverers have no interest in biographical detail — their purpose is rather to show how man from time to time behaves in God's presence. Further, unlike Christian legends, it has no very high opinion of the men who are chosen by God.

For this reason even the Samson narratives are not to be included among the legends. We have indeed many vivid, often witty details, but the narratives are not edifying. Rather even when we are confronted by the greatest victory of Samson on the occasion of his death, our final reaction remains one of disquiet when we consider how little a man gifted by the spirit corresponds to the figure of a saint. The Samson narratives have this trait in common with legends, that the actions and behaviour of the man chosen by God do have interest. In the deliverer sagas on the other hand the figure of the man remains vague, since it is indeed God alone who acts. But Samson's adventures are unlike the actions of the saints; they cannot please God. At most one might compare these narratives with anecdotes which, in certain incidents that are not in themselves decisive portray essential characteristics of a man.

Among the narratives about the deliverers of Israel, the childhood stories are still the nearest to legend. Like the vocation stories, these also are meant to ascribe the greatness of these men to divine election alone. This urge becomes even clearer here. God has already chosen these people for himself, when they themselves could not yet show their worthiness of this distinction. They are "chosen, before God formed them in their mother's womb" (Jeremiah 1,4). These great men owe not merely their greatness, but their very existence to the divine intervention. Moses is protected from certain death, Samson and Samuel are the product of barren wombs.[56]

As in the vocation stories, so also in these narratives typical motifs of narration are used. The motif of the mother's unfruitfulness is to be found in the story of Sarah, as in that of Michal, David's wife. The motif of the rescue of the child from the water (Moses) is also to be found in the birth-story of the Accadian king Sargon. Comparable is the narrative of the saving of Romulus and Remus by a she-wolf. There is of course no connection between this saga and the biblical tradition. It seems to be a favourite play of the human imagination to picture oneself that a great man was nearly not born at all.

Imagination also decorated the typical characteristics of Old Testament childhood stories. Here belong, among other things, the tar-covered rush-basket of Moses, his cunning mother, who arranged to be entrusted with her own child like a foundling, the self-forgetfulness of the praying mother of Samuel, which caused offence, the incredulity of Samson's parents, who wanted to hear the promise of the birth, once more, together. It is this loving attention to detail which makes the childhood narratives akin to legend.

If anything in the Old Testament has legendary characteristics, it is the Elisha narratives. Vivid stories from his life are told with the purpose of glorifying the prophet. He is the great miracle worker. These miracle narratives have nothing in common with the miracle stories of the Book of Exodus. The theme of these narratives is not the deliverance of the people by God's mighty hand, but the glorification of the man of God who can help himself and others, and tolerates no ridicule. Of course these miracle narratives do not lose sight of the fact that Elisha draws his miraculous power from God. But the full light falls upon the exceptional man to whom God has given such power.[57] The Elijah tradition on the other hand stands more in line with the stories about the deliverance of the people. The miracle on Carmel happens by God's agency: he confuses and destroys his enemies. Elijah is only cooperating with God (1 Kings 18).

11. Lists

The modern reader in general will not waste much time over the lists of names which we often encounter in the historical books of the Old Testament. The layman finds it hard to think that they have anything to say to him. We could find comparable lists in our administrative offices. For example, in a business there must be lists of the names of the employees, and lists of the goods produced; in the Treasury there must be a list of those who are liable to pay tax, etc. Lists of this kind must have been made too in the Government Offices of the kings of Israel. Parts of these have been included in the Old Testament, as, for example the list of "David's heroes".[58] These lists constituted a first naive kind of historiography.

Even before the central royal administration required exact bookkeeping, such sketches existed. Joshua 15-19 is based on geographical lists of the possessions of the tribes which date from the time of the 11th century to the time of the monarchy, and bear traces of continual revision. In Numbers 33 a list of stations in the desert is preserved, in Genesis 36,31 ff a catalogue of the kings of Edom.

The Bible reader will find the many generation-lists much more striking. Even the Yahwist, who composed his historical work in the first years of Solomon, can base himself on extended genealogical material. It may appear remarkable to us that people wished to represent the course of history by genealogical lists. The same kind of thought which here finds expression underlies also the sagas of the fathers. The course of history appeared to antiquity under the guise of the evolution of a family. Even the Hebrew language reflects this peculiarity of their thought. The Israelites name themselves "sons of Israel", i.e. descendants of the patriarch Jacob = Israel.

In individual cases such lists could have been formed with many different, often no longer clearly recognizable intentions, and taken up, for a different purpose, into the context of a narrative work in the Bible. The intention can be, for example, to exalt the fame of a man by connecting him with an ancestor of the greatest distinction; thus Heman, Ethan, and Asaph, David's temple singers, to whom also many psalms are ascribed, are presented in 1 Chronicles, 6 18ff as descendants of Levi. In the same way in our cultural milieu there were members of the nobility who traced back their descent into a very distant past, to Charlemagne, for example.

Another purpose for which lists can serve (e.g. lists of Popes) is to prove an unbroken connection. When the chronicler at the beginning of his work represents the time from Adam to David only by means of lists of this kind, his purpose is to show that the Davidic age is the climax of the whole history of the world.

But quite other concerns may underlie the lists. The so-called Kenite list (Genesis 4,17 ff) tells of the development of human capacities and arts. Genesis 29,31-30,21 pictures by means of the enumeration of the births and names of the sons the tension and conflict between the two wives of Jacob to obtain precedence as mothers.

The purpose of Genesis 10 is to give a survey of the whole world of nations as known at that time. The peoples do not stand over against one another without connections; they can be placed in distinct groupings according to degrees of relationship.[59] If such an outlook on universal history is in itself astonishing in the world of the ancient orient, even more surprising is the fact that Israel is concealed only in the unknown name of Arphachshad, who, according to a later genealogy, was one of the ancestors of Terah the father of Abraham. Israel did not trace its descent directly back to the great figures of primitive history. The genealogical tree which leads to the father of the race of Israel runs concealed in a people that has no other significance.

The list of peoples in Genesis 10 is evidence that Israel had a modest estimate of its own origins. It was the descendant of other groups of peoples, which did not win its independence till late. This judgement is historically correct. But it goes against the efforts of many other peoples to depict their own lineage in the most splendid terms. Rome traced its lineage back to Troy. German kings claim to be descended from the gods;[60] the Japanese emperor, from the sun. People thought along similar lines in the old oriental world. The list of the primaeval kings of Babylon begins "When the kingship came down from heaven the kingship was at first in Eridu" (the Babylonian palace)[61]. But Israel does not possess its greatness by nature, it is only God's call that distinguishes it.

A number of genealogies of different form, origin, and probably different intention also, have been inserted as a coherent whole into the priestly writing. We find here eleven times the formula "this is the history of the origin (the history of the beginning of the family) of . . ." But in every case the originally wider field of vision of the historical picture is concentrated upon one important line — from the whole world upon humanity, upon Noah, upon Shem, upon Terah, upon Abraham, from whose sons Isaac is chosen, from whom descends again Jacob; in conclusion the list leads to the climax, the priestly representatives of Israel, Moses and Aaron.[62] If the priestly document adopts this barren framework of the generation lists for its historical work, that is one of the means it chooses to make clear that God's activity was real and tangible. The sequences of generations of fathers and sons bear witness, as it were, with their names, to this fact.

CATEGORIES OF THE TRADITION OF THE LAW

1. TEXTUAL EXAMPLE: THE DECALOGUE (EXODUS 20, 1-21)

(1)   God spoke, and these were his words:

(2)   "I am Yahweh your God who brought you out of Egypt, out of the land of slavery.

(3)   You shall have no other god to set against me.

(4)   You shall not make a carved image for yourself nor the likeness of anything in the heavens above, or on the earth below, or in the waters under the earth.

(5)   You shall not bow down to them or worship them; for I, Yahweh your God, am a jealous God. I punish the children for the sins of the fathers to the third and fourth generations of those who hate me.

(6)   But I keep faith to the thousandth generation with those who love me and keep my commandments.

(7)   You shall not make wrong use of the name of Yahweh your God, for Yahweh will not leave unpunished the man who misuses his name.

(8)   Remember to keep the sabbath day holy.

(9)   You have six days to labour and do all your work.

(10)   But the seventh day is a sabbath of Yahweh your God; that day you shall not do any work, you, your son or your daughter, your slave or your slave-girl, your cattle or the alien within your gates.

(11)   For in six days Yahweh made heaven and earth, the sea, and all that is in them, and on the seventh day he rested. Therefore Yahweh blessed the sabbath day and declared it holy.

(12)   Honour your father and your mother, that you may live long in the land which Yahweh your God is giving you.

(13)   You shall not commit murder.

(14)   You shall not commit adultery.

or the alient within your gates.

(15)   You shall not steal.

(16)   You shall not give false evidence against your neighbour.

(17)   You shall not covet your neighbour's house; you shall not covet your neighbour's wife, his slave, his slave-girl, his ox, his ass, or anything that belongs to him."

18)   When all the people saw how it thundered and the lightning flashed, when they heard the trumpet sound and saw the mountain smoking, they trembled and stood at a distance. (19)   "Speak to us yourself", they said to Moses, "and we will listen; but if God speaks to us, we shall die." (20)   Moses answered, "Do not be afraid. God has come only to test you, so that the fear of him may remain with you and keep you from sin."

(21)   So the people stood at a distance, while Moses approached the dark cloud where God was.

A Many Times Re-Edited Text

In this text it is difficult to find the Ten Commandments and it is not remarkable that the Jews and Christian Churches extract them from this Old Testament text in different versions, Exodus 20, 1-21 bears traces of repeated revision: the commandment to keep the Sabbath is given detailed justification in sermonic style;[63] the commandment relating to parents is connected with a promise, the veto on misuse of the Divine Name is connected with a threat of punishment; there are several elucidations of the range of significance of the word "image", as also of the types of behaviour indicated by the prohibition of images.[64] In relation to the last prohibition there is repeated enumeration of who and what belongs to the neighbour's "house".[65] (As the most important member of the house, the wife is named first; thus no depreciation of the wife is intended by naming first the generic concept "house", but it is clear that the commandments are meant for free men, who have possessions.) Finally in 20,2 and in 20, 5a-6 there are two more self-descriptions of God that belong to the text. From all this it is evident that an originally shorter list of Commandments was enlarged in the course of time by all sorts of additions.

How restricted this series must have been can still be seen from 20,13-16. Yet an original version cannot be reconstructed with sufficient certainty. Probably at first it consisted merely of ten prohibitions. However, in the version known to us, the commandments concerning parents and the Sabbath are positively formulated;[66] and are consequently expanded: it is now not a matter of concern even to determine whether the boundaries set up by God have been observed; in every minute of the Sabbath, in every type of converse with one's parents, God's will must be observed. The positive Commandment is not satisfied to lay down external limits, its function is rather to guide all the steps of man.

The fundamental form of the Decalogue was certainly short and impressive, the commandments could be counted on ten fingers, and were easy to keep. They were shaped by people who wished Israel to lay these commandments to heart, and to make them understandable; preachers of the law have inserted their commentaries into the text.

But how is Exodus 20,1 to be understood against this background?

God spoke all these words.

Can "all these words" at the same time be God's word from Sinai, and a text many times revised by men?

An Originally Independent Text

We can know the Decalogue only as part of the narrative of God's self-manifestation at Sinai. That seems also to be its fitting place; when God appears to men, he does so in order to speak to them. So also here: God comes to Sinai in order to proclaim the Commandments.

But on a closer inspection, breaks in the text show that the connection

125

between the Decalogue and the Sinai event was only established subsequently. According to Exodus 19,18 f. God descended in fire, smoke, and earthquake in order to converse with Moses — not with the people. This conversation transcends human proportions.

Moses spoke, and God answered by a peal of thunder. Could the people understand such words of thunder? The reaction of Israel in 20,18-20 is understandable. In deadly fear they ask that in God's place Moses should speak to them.

But Exodus 19,10-25 fits in badly with the picture of God's words of thunder. Once again we are told that God has come down to Mount Sinai to converse with Moses. Once again Moses appears as a mediator between God and the people, but now in a strange manner: Moses climbs up the mountain to hear God, and comes down again to speak to the people. He has then to go up again, in order to receive further words of God.[67]

Even before Moses can carry out this command, there follows God's speech to the people itself, the Ten Commandments. It fits in neatly with neither of the other layers; the direct address of God to the people does not tally with either of them.[68]

1 God speaks to Moses in thunder (Ex. 19, 18 f   20,18-20).
2 Moses goes hither and thither between God and the people (19, 20-25;   20,21).
3 God speaks to the people (20, 1-17).

It becomes evident that the Ten Commandments were only placed in this context subsequently. Whence did they come? Why were they so important to the preachers of the law in ancient Israel that time and time again they proclaimed them, expounded them and expanded them?

Apodeictic and Casuistic Formulations of the Law

A first answer to this question is to be found when we follow up an observation of Albrecht Alt.[69] Two formulations of the law side by side in the Old Testament are to be compared.

Exodus 21,18: When men quarrel and one hits another with a stone or a spade, and the man is not killed but takes to his bed; if he recovers so as to walk about outside with a stick, then the one who struck him has no liability, except that he shall pay for loss of time and shall see that he is cured.

Exodus 21,12: Whoever strikes another man and kills him shall be put to death.

Both formulations deal with the same theme; fighting between men. They vary in length. The first formulation — in Hebrew there is only one sentence — represents a case and its consequences at law. A man has been injured. But no one has lain in wait for him, for the weapon involved, a stone or a spade with which one returns from working in the fields, might be accidentally at hand. The injured man was confined to bed. He did not need to recover completely; it is enough that he recovers sufficiently to be able to get around again, i.e. can take part in the life of the village. For this case that is exactly set out a definite stipulation is made how the court is to give its verdict. The injured man is entitled to a compensation for his inability to work, and for the costs of his healing; over and above this his opponent is not punished.

In order to be able to determine all these circumstances exactly, the Hebrew language must have violence done to it. If in other cases the course of speech in Hebrew is marked by block-like sequences lying side by side, in this sentence a more general case at law is further differentiated into parallel subordinate clauses, in order that, finally, when the conditions have been specified, the legal consequence, the punishment, may be named. Such a degree of exactitude presupposes a long tradition of juristic schooling. Israel did not originally possess this tradition: we can see this already from the constructions of the sentences, which are unusual for Hebrew. Everything indicates that when Israel occupied the land it adopted a legal system of this kind from the inhabitants of the cultivated territory, and thus accommodated itself to an already old juridical tradition in the ancient East. Disputed cases, such as may occur in a village community, are settled by laws of this kind. It is striking that cultic and religious questions are not touched; this is true also of the legal system of Hammurabi. It was by guidelines of this kind that the assembly of freemen in a village society let themselves be directed, when it was summoned to settle a case at law.[70]

This kind of law is related to the legal formulations which are in use in our society today. Then, as now, it was necessary for the maintenance of public order to establish exact legal precedents for cases defined unambiguously and with the highest degree of precision. Since Albrecht Alt this form of legal maxims, of which there is evidence throughout the ancient East, is called "casuistic".

The second legal formulation, Exodus 21,12, uses a completely different style of language. The Hebrew sentence uses only five monosyllabic or disyllabic words; the two subordinate clauses necessary in English are in the Hebrew part of one single main clause. The utterance is short, its rhythm is emphatic and composed wholly of words of obscure significance. One of the words is indeed only a repetition of the verb. Together with the use of the verb at the end of the sentence — a situation uncommon in Hebrew — this reinforcement lays the chief emphasis of the sentence on the threat of punishment. The aim of this solemn language is not to describe a situation at law, but to underline the gravity of an obligation, its deadly seriousness. A. Alt speaks of "apodeictic formulations of law".

Could such a formulation be utilized in the practice of the law? The nature of the death penalty is left undetermined, without inquiry concerning the degree of personal guilt and the more precise circumstances, the gravest threat is at once uttered. The legal thinking of this kind of

127

formulation is far removed from that which finds expression in causuistic law. If one could ask how the circumstantial and exact formulations of casuistic law could be held in memory at all without being set down in writing, the formulations of apodeictic law are intended from the first to make an unforgettable impression on the hearer. The purpose of these legal formulations is not to judge a particular situation according to legal principles; they are intended for solemn proclamation, in order to impress on all men that they are subject to an inexorable will for justice.

The impression they make is strengthened by the fact that they are continually set together in longer series. Exodus 21,12, for example, is flanked by similar unqualified threats: the man who strikes his parents, who robs men, who curses his parents — he shall die yes die. (Exodus 21,15-17).[71]

What imperious will for justice here claims recognition is clearly shown by the apodeictic formulations in Deuteronomy 27,15-26. Even the man who sins in secret cannot escape this will. The apodeictic law proclaims Yahweh's will. Hence the impressive language. Where Yahweh's unconditional lordship is at stake, there is no place for juristic refinements. It was the priests who in the place of God read aloud and drove home these commandments.[72]

This would indicate a place which might have been the original home of the Ten Commandments. By the width of its outlook the Decalogue shows that it belonged to the group of apodeictic formulations of law. While in other cases the individual groups collocate only the secret crimes, or those worthy of death, or Yahweh's privileges, the Decalogue endeavours to place together ethical requirements for the whole life of man.

Albrecht Alt sees in these legal formulations an original creation of Israel; they are without parallel in the ancient East. He claims that they took shape from the belief in Israel's special standing in the sight of God. From its time of wandering in the desert, Israel brought with it this legal thinking into the land of cultivation. There, more complicated forms of community life required quite a different type of legal thinking, which finds expression in the casuistic legal formulations.

The Jealous God

If with Albrecht Alt we understand the Decalogue as a series of apodeictic formulations of law, this has consequences for its message about God. This God demands his rights unconditionally; he takes no account of the manifold conditions of human life. One of the old preachers of the law emphasized this in his expansion of the First Commandment:

> You shall have no other god to set against me . . . for I, Yahweh your God, am a jealous God. I punish the children for the sins of the fathers to the third and fourth generations of those who hate me. But

I keep faith with thousands, with those who love me and keep my commandments (Exodus 20, 3.5-6)

The preacher who inserted this elucidation of the First Commandment did not formulate it himself, but, as the fixed formulae which he uses show,[73] has adopted them from the traditional material of his people. To us this formula of divine self-introduction sounds intolerably stern. The worst element in it is the thought of God as the avenger. Does he take revenge on families? — We should indeed note how unequally punishment and grace are dispensed: God's faithfulness is granted to thousands, his punishment touches only the four generations of one family, who are living at the same time. Further, a true observation underlies the saying: in bad as well as in good things, we share the fate of the generation into which we have been born. But does the melancholy fact that children have to pay for the guilt of their parents, correspond to God's will? Even within the Old Testament this antiquated stern picture of God's operation is corrected.[74] If we were compelled to understand the Decalogue merely as a series of apodeictic formulations, as the expression of God's unconditional claim to sovereignty, then it would be no more than evidence for a happily outworn stage of faith in God as the hard, unrelenting Lord.

The Formula of Retaliation

How Israel itself outgrew an older type of legal thinking — perhaps brought with it from an outworn nomadic time — can be seen from the context in which the so-called "formula of retaliation" is placed in Exodus 21,24 f,

. . . eye for eye, tooth for tooth, hand for hand, foot for foot, burn for burn, bruise for bruise, wound for wound.

In wild times of arbitrary cruelty — cf Genesis 4, 23f — such a legal formulation may hold back unbridled revenge. Within the framework of the Old Testament it has another significance. It is surrounded by laws whose manner of procedure is entirely different: in some cases the punishment is much less than the harm the guilty party has caused (an abortion is to be paid for by a money fine, Exodus 21,22). In some cases it is much higher (where an eye has been put out, or a tooth, the slave is to be set free, Exodus 21, 26 f). Within this context the old saying insists that for every single injury a just compensation should be determined. It might be paraphrased: justice must be maintained.

Contractual Characteristics of the Divine Covenant

But it was not necessary, in the handing down and the continuing reinterpretation of the Decalogue, that first an older stage should be surmounted, in which these Commandments had borne witness to a faith in God as the inexorable avenger, which Israel had perhaps brought with it from the desert. It became evident in the course of investigation that an important presupposition of Albrecht Alt's was not tenable. Series of apodeictic commandments, short categorical commandments of the Lord are to be found not only in Israel, but also in important texts of the people of the ancient cultures. We find them also in inter-state treaties which kings of the ancient orient made with their vassals. The earliest examples of this were found in Hittite treaties. The structure of these treaties reminds us in many points of God's Commandments to Israel: they begin in the preface with the description of the Hittite king, who grants the treaty — so God introduces himself at the beginning of the Ten Commandments. A historical prologue tells of the history preceding the treaty. In the same way the story of how the people were delivered from Egypt and led to Sinai belongs to the law of Israel. Then follow different concrete demands, the substance of the treaty. In the heathen treaties, the gods are summoned as witnesses, a thought which naturally has no place in Israel's thinking about the Covenant. The treaties are closed by the announcement of blessings and curses, as happens at the end of the Deuteronomic law book in Deuteronomy 28.

Structure of a Hittite Sovereignty Treaty (ca. 1500-1300 B.C.)	Parallels in O.T.
1) Introduction of the great King. "These are the words of the sun, Marsillis, the great King, king of Hatti.	"I am Yahweh, your God"
2) Historical prologue; earlier relations between the partners to the Treaty	who freed thee from Egypt" (Exodus 20,2)
3) Details of the Treaty	Decalogue, collections of laws.
4) Clause about safe-keeping of the document in the temple and regular reading of it publicly.	Deuteronomy 31,10-13.
5) List of the divine witnesses to the treaty.	Absent.
6) Curse and blessing.	Exodus 23, 20 ff; Deuteronomy 28.

These Hittite treaties are not yet available in modern translations. For this reason a treaty from the seventh century B.C. may serve as an example. The Great King of Assyria concludes a treaty with his vassals, in which the latter undertake to acknowledge the Crown Prince as his successor. Extract from Esarhaddon's treaty with his vassals, ca. 670 B.C.

1)   Treaty which Esarhaddon, King of Assyria has concluded with you before the great gods, in favour of the designated Crown Prince . . .

2)   When Esarhaddon departs from this life, you shall raise Assurbani-pal to the kingly throne.

3)   If you do not fight for him,
        do not tell him the whole truth,
        do not make things easy for him . . .

4)   If you do not have the intention of keeping Esarhaddon's treaty . . .

5) Then may Assur, the King of the gods decree to you an evil fate . . . may the gods make your soil like iron, so that no one can plough it, so that rain does not fall on it out of a bronze heaven, thus may rain and dew not come to your fields and meadows.[75]

Here also we find challenges in a negative form (compare no. 3). Down to individual details the curses at the end of the text are comparable to the curse on the law-breaker in Deuteronomy 28,23.

Keeping the Commandments: a Question of life and death

What message from God do the Commandments contain, if we understand them as the stipulations of God's Covenant? Stipulations in a contract can have a fatal significance. Everyone will know this who has signed too quickly a contract to purchase, without consulting the part in small print — the stipulations of the contract. One can stumble here, and one has to pay the penalty oneself.

Are the Ten Commandments to be understood thus? Has God here laid a trap for the unwary, that brings down the man who does not keep the Covenant? The Old Testament curses on the law-breaker seem to confirm this interpretation.[76]

But can God's purpose be the destruction of the man who breaks the Commandments? Should we not be more inclined to hold by later Old Testament texts?

Have I any desire, says the Lord Yahweh, for the death of a wicked man? Would I not rather that he should mend his ways and live? (Ezekiel 18,23).

Does the curse on the lawbreaker also belong to an outdated stage of the biblical message, which we can forget, and have the Ten Commandments as stipulations of God's Covenant lost significance for us?

This false impression can only arise if the analogy of the Old Testament law with the stipulations in treaties made with vassals in the ancient east is pressed too far. These great kings made treaties for their own advantage, their sole aim was to have loyal vassals. Therefore their demands regulate only the relation of the subjects to the great king. So long as the tribute is paid, and no revolt raises its head, they could not care less how conditions are in the subject state.

With the Decalogue, things are quite different. From the Commandment about parents onward, it does not regulate the relationships of men with God, but the community life of man. There are in the Old Testament many laws which teach Israel to regard the natural society as a sacral sphere in which nothing unholy may happen.[77] At the beginning of the great Old Testament collections of laws, however, stand the Ten Commandments, as, so to say, a summary and guide to the understanding of what is to come. Here, above all, there is concern for the ordering of human society. God intervenes in human affairs. He has made a covenant, but not like the great rulers of the ancient East, for his own advantage, but for the advantage of men. The curse against the man who

131

breaks the covenant shows how seriously God takes also the evil will of men. The man who ruins human fellowship is the one whom God allows to live in this ruin.

The Fatherly God's Counsel for Life

The further advance of investigation warns us not to lay too much weight on the comparison with the stipulations of treaties. The schema set out above is enough to make its weaknesses clear. We must gather together from the most different texts of the Old Testament the elements that relate to the vassal treaties. The Old Testament has not handed down to us an actual covenant-treaty between God and the people.

Further, it was found that apodeictic commandments in the culture of the ancient east are not found only in such treaties, but also in quite a different place, in the instructive speeches of the wise men.

From the Teaching of Amenemope (ca. 1100 B.C.)

Mock *not* a blind man
and despise *not* a lame man,
do *not* make hard the lot of a paralytic,
do *not* make fun of a man who is in the hand of God (insane),
and be *not* roused against him, when he has done amiss.

In Old Testament collections of sayings also, prohibitions are strung together in series in this manner.[78] The wisdom speeches let us discover where this kind of speech had its origin. The teacher of wisdom calls himself "father", and he addresses his "son".[79] A source from which the wisdom literature draws are the counsels for life which were passed on in families from father to son.

Anyone who observes parents dealing with small children, will also today be able to discover how frequency "apodeictic commandments" are given: "Don't run across the street!" Advice given by parents even to grown-up children can take this form, when the latter make themselves independent: "Do not strike up a friendship after one glass of beer." In spite of their brief negative form no one will understand such formulations as "apodeictic commands", no one will believe that here an inflexible legalistic will is seeking to find expression. Nor will anyone understand them as the conditions of a contract in the sphere of the family: "Only so long as you hold by these rules will you belong to the family". But just because these commandments are uttered in the context of the family, they are to be understood quite differently. They are the expression of loving care for the future of the person addressed, their intention is to help him to preserve his freedom and his life.

The origin of the Ten Commandments might lie in such rules of life, to be handed down in the family. From this standpoint it would also be understandable why they are marked by the width of their outlook. The parents might be anxious to prevent their children somewhere transgressing the boundaries outside of which human communal life becomes impossible. Therefore the relationships within which life can be lived are comprehensively and fully described. It was possible to understand such commandments as God's teaching about life, as soon as Israel saw itself in faith as a family of God, as son of the God who exercises fatherly concern (cf Hosea 11, and the tradition of the deliverance from Egypt which underlies the passage, and also Exodus 4,22).

The first clause of the Ten Commandments, God's first description of himself, thus is given special importance:

I am Yahweh, your God, who brought you out of Egypt, out of the house of bondage (Exodus 20,1).

Now that is not a "historical prologue" — as it appears in comparison with the ancient oriental treaties with vassals — but the most important statement of the Commandments, in whose light they are to be understood. In the Commandments there speaks the God who has set Israel free; he shows Israel how it can preserve this freedom.

When in many Christian Catechisms the Ten Commandments are used as a test for the examination of conscience, that is a misuse. Here there is no examination of wrong behaviour in the past, here the intention is one of fatherly care for the future. Here tiny transgressions are not being stigmatized; what we have here is a warning against transgressions of the outer boundaries.

Old Testament Words for the Law of God

We have been accustomed to take our cue from the language of the New Testament, and to speak of the Old Testament "law" — but the Old Testament has a variety of concepts for it; the word of God, the covenant, testimony, the ordinances of righteousness, the way, instruction, etc. Only seldom are the manifold divine ordinances comprehended under one concept, as the New Testament does with the word "law".

Most important of all, the word "law" never serves as such a general description — a first indication of the fact that juristic thinking alone can never do justice to the Old Testament "law". An old collection of laws is described as the "Book of the Covenant", the Ten Commandments are called the Covenant "Words". Correspondingly the two "tables" that God gave to Moses are "The Tables of the Covenant", or "Tables of Witness".[80] The context against which the word of the covenant can be understood in the Old Testament has already been described. Two other concepts or categories which the Old Testament uses to describe its laws must now be dealt with.

Torah

Instruction, tōrāh, became for later Judaism the chief description of the law. Tōrāh means the instruction of the ignorant. For example, the oral answers of the priests to questions put by laymen, questions as to how they should behave in cultic or ethically problematic situations are called tōrāh.[81] Tōrāh retains also a concrete practical meaning when God

133

is considered as the issuer of *tōrāh*, and the teacher of Israel. When Israel described the divine ordinances by this name, its thinking was far from juristic. God's commandments appeared, not in the first place as obligations imposed upon Israel, but rather as teaching concerning right behaviour; the ignorant will be glad of this instruction.[82]

God's *tōrāh* is not instruction about everything in general, but about what it is vitally necessary to know. Everyone in Israel had a concrete picture of the neighbouring desert; it is necessary for the survival of the traveller to get instruction about the path in it; the man who disregards the signposts in it is the prey of death.[83] The commandments are such signposts or, to use another figure, they are the boundaries within which men can live with God and with each other; the man who transgresses them, strays into the realm of death.

The Word of God

One more description of God's ordinances found especially in the later law-piety of the Old Testament is "The word of God".[84] It gives expression to something which was contained from the beginning in the tradition of Israel concerning the law: Israel owed the ordering of its life to God.

On the famous stele containing the law of Hammurabi (ca. 1700 B.C.), the lawgiver is represented as standing before the sun god, the supreme judge. The parallel to the biblical figure of Moses (ca. 1300 B.C.), who receives the laws from God, is obvious. Yet the role of the god Shamash in the law of Hammurabi is not comparable with the significance of Yahweh for the law of Moses. The prologue of the law code of the ruler of Babylon interprets the laws not as the words of his god, but as a human work, created in accordance with the god's instructions.

> Shamash instructed me, Hammurabi, to cause the laws to be published in the land . . . so that I may seem to the dark-haired race like Shamash and enlighten the land and create prosperity for the land.

The law code of Hammurabi has nothing to do with the sacral. There is nothing here about the relationship of men to the gods.

The case of the Old Testament law is different. Though the priests amplified the Decalogue with their own commentaries, they recited it as the word of God. Its fundamental form, too, a collection of short rules for life could have had its origin entirely in human insights. What does it mean, when, in spite of this, the Old Testament repeatedly puts its laws in the mouth of God?

In the Old Testament, "word" is a form of expression borrowed from the prophets — instruction, *tōrāh*, belongs to the priest, counsel to the wise man.[85] Prophets proclaim God's word as messengers, they impart what men cannot know of themselves. But in this sense the Commandments are also God's word. To be sure human intelligence can find without divine help and with certainty an ordering of life, that guarantees harmonious life in society. But men cannot by their own powers know that God makes a right communal life his own concern.

Books of Laws

From this point of vantage it is understandable why the Old Testament contains no systematic law codes. The purpose of a systematic law code is to leave if possible no loophole open for the man who is injurious to society. Israel's law-books pursue another goal; God's instructions were collected and preserved with gratitude. It was immaterial to the collectors that incidentally contradictions could be lying side by side.

In the "Book of the Covenant", Exodus 20, 22-23, 33, is preserved for us the oldest collection of this kind. Different forms of law, each of which presupposes a different type of legal thinking, are lying here cheek by jowl. Casuistic and apodeictic formulations are found relating to the same theme; the formula of retaliation is given a new interpretation, being changed to a principle of determining what is just through adequate compensation. Thus even already this oldest collection in the Old Testament is to be understood against the background of an earlier historical coordination of different kinds of judicial thinking.

In our day laws generally do not become binding until they have been written and published. For the most part the laws of Israel had a long history of use behind them before they were set down in writing. Such laws are also gathered together in the ancient collection of "The Law of Holiness" (Leviticus 17-26).

The authors of Deuteronomy wished yet once again to offer an independent summary of the divine instruction. But even they did not here create a systematic book of laws. In the seventh century, when the overthrow of Israel loomed ever nearer, they attempted to create a new foundation for the continued life of their people, by giving new life to old laws.

About 400 B.C. Ezra went to work in the same way. His intention was to create a legal foundation for the life of the new Jewish community, as the Persian great king had required (Ezra 7,12 ff). The intention was that after all the errors of the people, the returning Jews should again live under the ancient law of Yahweh. All these collectors were less concerned to compass the life of the national community in all its departments, than to hand down as loyally as possible old forms of tradition, even those which — by our way of it — were in contradiction with other Commandments, which had become outdated, or were no longer understood.

Law — State — People

To our way of thinking there is a close connection between state and law. Institutions of the state have legislative power, and watch over the administration of the laws; many laws regulate the obligations of the citizen over against the state. Nothing of this kind is to be found in Israel.

135

On the contrary, religion and justice interpenetrate. But the constitution of the state, which did not come into Israel until late, is forced to fit in with this order which has come down from the ancient past, and often seems to be a foreign body in it. The Deuteronomic law concerning the king, which is the nearest thing to a state law, sets limits to the powers which the king might appropriate to himself, on the basis of the given order, instead of giving him legislative or judicial power (Deuteronomy 17,14-20). When King Ahab wishes to have Naboth executed on a charge of high treason in order thus to acquire his vineyard, the false case against him is not made by the king and officials, but is brought by the elders and notables of the town before the people. When the punishment of stoning is inflicted upon Naboth, even the execution of the penalty is left to the people.[86] The people itself is to ensure that no one lives in its midst who has broken away from the fellowship with God.

The purpose of the laws is to protect the people, not to guarantee the institution of the state. From this point of view the social tendency of Israel's laws can be understood. God's commandment gives special protection to the man who has little public standing, and therefore can easily lose a case at law. As early as the Book of the Covenant, we find a series of commandments of this kind (Exodus 22, 20-26). Deuteronomy especially strengthens this tendency of the law.

The fact that the Old Testament laws are not state laws, imposed on a people from above, influences even their formulation. They are, in fact, laws given by God which form the basis of the national community. In the laws of the ancient east, explanations and justifications are unknown. But in the collections of Old Testament laws, we meet with them frequently. These collections were not intended for specialists, who only needed to know and to apply the law. They were written for the people, who were to take them to heart.

POETIC CATEGORIES

1. TEXTUAL EXAMPLE: PSALM 31

   1) To the Chief Musician. A Psalm of David.

Flight from Distress to the protecting God
   2) With thee, Yahweh, I have sought shelter,
      let me never be put to shame.
      Deliver me in thy righteousness
   3) bow down and hear me, come quickly to my rescue;
      be thou my rock of refuge,
      a stronghold to keep me safe.

4) Thou art to me both rock and stronghold;
   lead me and guide me for the honour of thy name.
5) Set me free from the net men have hidden for me;
   thou art my refuge,
6) into thy keeping I commit my spirit.
   Thou hast redeemed me, Yahweh, thou God of truth.
7) Thou hatest all who worship useless idols,
   but I will put my trust in Yahweh.

A Promise of Thanks

8) I will rejoice and be glad in thy unfailing love;
   for thou hast seen my affliction
   and hast cared for me in my distress.
9) Thou hast not abandoned me to the power of the enemy
   but hast set me free to range at will.

A Description of Suffering

10) Be gracious unto me, Yahweh, for I am in distress;
    and my eyes are dimmed with grief, my soul, my body.
11) My life is worn away with sorrow
    and my years with sighing;
    strong as I am, I stumble under my load of misery;
    there is disease in all my bones.
12) I have such enemies that all men scorn me;
    my neighbours find me a burden, my friends shudder at me;
    when men see me in the street they turn quickly away.
13) I am forgotten, like a dead man out of mind;
    I have become like a pot that is thrown away,
14) For I hear many men whispering threats from every side,
    in league against me as they are
    and plotting to take my life.

Trust in Yahweh

15) But, Yahweh, I put my trust in thee;
    I say, "Thou art my God".
16) My fortunes are in thy hand;
    rescue me from my enemies and those who persecute me.

Prayer for Help and Vindication in the Sight of Enemies

17) Make thy face shine upon thy servant,
    save me in thy unfailing love.
18) Yahweh, do not put me to shame when I call upon thee;
    let the wicked be ashamed,
    let them sink into Sheol.
19) Strike dumb the lying lips
    which speak with contempt against the righteous
    in pride and arrogance.

Song of Thanksgiving
20) How great is thy goodness,
 stored up for those who fear thee,
 made manifest before the eyes of men
 for all who turn to thee for shelter.
21) Thou wilt hide them under the cover of thy presence from men in
 league together;
 thou keepest them beneath thy roof,
 safe from contentious men.
22) Blessed be Yahweh, who worked a miracle of unfailing love for
 me when I was (in a strong city).
23) In sudden alarm I said,
 "I am shut out from thy sight".
 But thou didst hear my cry for mercy
 when I called to thee for help.

Exhortation to Love and Loyalty
24) Love Yahweh, all you his loyal servants.
 Yahweh protects the faithful,
 but pays the arrogant in full.
 Be strong and take courage,
 all you whose hope is in Yahweh.

An urgent portrayal of Suffering
 In spite of a distance of more than two thousand years, the modern
reader of the Psalm could feel himself invited by the urgent and vivid
language of this poem to place himself immediately in the position of the
poet. We can have the impression that the Psalmist wishes to impart his
personal experience, his inner awareness of suffering and consolation.
The concrete and vivid nature of the pictures, metaphors and similes
elicits this effect.
 In addition to this the poet never satisfies himself with one apt word,
but employs a whole series of words of similar meaning. Thus the
translator can get into difficulties when he has to find two words for
"rock", and two for "strong place of refuge" (verses 3 and 4); none of
these words seems adequately to represent to the Psalmist the security
given by God's presence. He is clearly penetrated by trust that he no
longer *compares* "rock" and "stronghold" with his security with God in a
mood of cool calculation, but — in metaphorical language — immediately expresses his inner experience; God is my rock, my stronghold.[87]
 The subtlest application of this art is in the forcible concatenation of
words of like meaning in verse 13:
 I am forgotten, like a dead man out of mind,
 I have become like a pot that is thrown away.
A statement is made twice over with words of synonymous meaning

138

and exactly parallel sentence-forms. This type of language, the so-called parallelism of members, is a prevalent formal law of Hebrew poetry, and is also used in this Psalm; in verse 13 the poet, instead of speaking in general terms about his loneliness, represents its terrors vividly. The sufferer is useless and disregarded, a pot that is beyond repair; he is excluded from human society, a dead man in whose presence the Israelite can only feel horror and fear. This double comparison describes the uttermost extremity of the Psalmist's experience of suffering; the man who speaks thus of himself hardly dares to believe that there can be any recovery. Through the emphatic linguistic figure of parallelism of members this climax of the lament is expressed with immense urgency.

For the rest, the poet avoids stringing together a wearisome chain of artificial repetitions. Instead, he sets in contrast positive and negative statements (verse 9: antithetic parallelism); with a second statement he goes beyond the first (verse 15: synthetic parallelism); he only hints at the parallelism, omitting the expected repetition — that is, he allows himself so much freedom in relation to the formal law of Hebrew poetry, that the Psalm can follow all the stirrings of his heart, and all his experience.

The reader is drawn into all the experiences of the man who is at prayer. The picture of his suffering is put together in short sentences; people on the street flee from the sufferer; he hears how others whisper; he sees them before him, how they plan an attack on his life (verses 12 and 14). The reader can share in the bodily exhaustion of the Psalmist and his spiritual powerlessness; for years the petitioner has been able to do nothing but wail and groan (verses 10 and 11).

Inexact Description of the Situation
This vividness can still immediately appeal to the imagination of the modern reader. The striking linguistic form of parallelism, the impressive accumulation of similar words can impress him powerfully. But in spite of all it is not possible to reconstruct the situation in which this Psalm was created. Above all, it is impossible to understand the break between verse 9 and verse 10. Twice the petitioner traverses the way from prayer in deep distress to exultant thanksgiving (verses 1-9; 10-25). After rejoicing over the help which he received, there follows once again the petitioning cry of the man in misery.

Further, in spite of all the exact details, it is not clear what the particular distress of the petitioner is. Had he already been imprisoned (verse 4)? Or is he simply being persecuted (verse 14)? Who are his enemies? Are they people whose disdain and contempt he drew upon himself through long illness (verses 10, 12,19)? But why should these scoffers wish to remove him (verse 14)? When people persecute him, how can he say he is wholly forgotten (verse 13)?

It is still less clear what is the nature of the salvation, although the Psalmist describes it in many words of like meaning. It is deliverance from present affliction (to save, to set free, to deliver, to set in a broad

139

place, to snatch away), it bestows on the petitioner a home with God (protect, preserve, guard, lead, guide).

One third group of verbs particularly draws our attention, verbs which plead for rescue: God is to see and take heed of the Psalmist, not to let him come to disgrace, to cause his face to shine upon him. Has God perhaps not seen and heard the sufferer, has he let him come to disgrace, and left him in darkness? The Psalmist indicates in these petitions that the heart of his sufferings is his distance from God. The experience of persecution and contempt, illness, loneliness and deadly threat is for him only the occasion to press forward to the depth of his suffering, which for the faithful can lie behind every painful experience: God has forgotten me. What can at first appear as a vivid description of personal experience turns out to be an impressive picture of the suffering of the faithful in general.

Subject of the Psalm, a typical Fate

The first hearers of the Psalm certainly understood from the start that here it is not an individual who is speaking out of his unique situation, but, as it were, the typical sufferer. The phrases of the Psalmist are familiar to the Jew from the prayer-language and the tradition of his people. Even at the climax of his lament the poet takes from Jeremiah and Hosea[88] the simile of the broken vessel, he recalls the figure of Jeremiah who was threatened with death, and heard the mutterings of others: "Threats of terror let loose" were uttered by men full of loathing against the man who already had about him the smell of death.[89]

If what we have here in this Psalm is not a lyric expressing a religious experience and mood, it is only natural if the personal situation of the supplicant remains undefined. Yet if we are not to see the prayer against the background of the personal history of an individual, what is the context of its origin, what was its *Sitz im Leben*? The concluding verses give us a hint. The Psalmist addresses "all the faithful", he challenges them to love and loyalty in waiting upon God. The story of suffering and deliverance becomes an exhortation for all the faithful. The Psalm was recited to the congregation of the faithful; it was a part of their worship of God. In order to be intelligible to the many, the Psalm speaks in the familiar language of tradition. In order to make it possible to join in prayer, it avoids mentioning a unique situation. It bases itself not on personal experience but on the long stored experience of the people.

Yahweh protects the faithful,
but pays the arrogant in full.[90]

Reproduction of Personal Experience of God

And yet our first impression was not entirely wrong when it led us to see in the Psalm a personal prayer spoken in a moment of deep depression. In spite of everything the complaint retains its vividly nearness to real experience. True, the break in the structure of the

Psalm, the double transition from supplication to praise, teaches us that the author did not intend to picture his personal story of suffering and salvation. What he does in this Psalm is rather to picture his experience of prayer, and the development which he lived through in prayer.

The petitioner does not at first really venture to speak of his misery. Only requests and expressions of trust indicate in the first part (verses 1-3) that he is in distress. The Psalmist must first of all find his way by prayer to confidence, and reassure himself of his trust. He asks for security in God and he affirms to himself at the same time that he may already enjoy such security. "I seek refuge — my refuge art thou"; "Be my rock — my rock art thou!"

All the statements take the form of addresses to God; the Psalmist seeks to approach him with the whole urgency of his prayer.

In the second part, however, the brief invocation "Be gracious unto me" is followed by a long description of his distress. Suffering had at first too much oppressed the petitioner for him to be able to face it. Only after he has sought the way into the presence of God, has he the power even to confront the depth of his distress. Now he can support himself on the confidence that he won for himself in prayer at the beginning.[91]

So what we have in this Psalm is not a universally valid case of need and salvation constructed for the instruction and exhortation of the faithful; no vague pattern is put forward into which everyone might fit himself. Here, rather the Psalmist is bearing personal witness before the congregation how out of his experience of suffering and of salvation from distress, he came into the presence of God. This interpretation of the Psalm is contradicted neither by its conventional language, nor by its occasional references to the experiences of all the faithful. For the Psalmist the familiar phrases of the language of prayer are no mere colourless formulas. In a situation where his relationship to God has become questionable, he tries to find his way again with the help of old traditional words. He can fit in the story of his new-found trust with the story of many of the faithful. His own confidence is strengthened when he can first of all praise God for his loyalty in his dealings with the many (verses 20f), before he praises him for his own personal salvation (verses 22ff). In his suffering he was solitary, in praise he knows himself to be taken up into the communion of the saints.

The poet adapts the fixed formal elements of the Hebrew Psalm of lamentation to fit the inner story of his prayer: petition, complaint, declaration of trust, and narrative extolling God's intervention do not follow one another in order. In the first part (verses 1-9) the lament is missing; the supplicant seeks his way to God through prayer; he steadies himself also by brief declarations of trust, till at last he ventures unreservedly to give himself into God's hand (verses 6f) and thus first finds his way to the praise of God.

In the second part, on the other hand, the supplicant needs only a small introductory request to draw God's attention to himself. Now he knows himself near enough to God to lay his complaint fully before him, and by his assertion of trust, to point out to him how great a contradiction there is between his fate and his piety. Against this background then he directs his requests to God, which then pass over immediately into praise of God for his loyalty and his act of salvation. In this second part wider room is given for the individual formal elements. The prayer runs onward more smoothly, and the poet no longer swings hither and thither between them. It is all the more striking that in the midst of the narrative of praise a sentence of complaint should appear. If we pay attention only to the real complaint in verses 10-14, we might think that the poet wished only to *complain*, and to *accuse* his enemies before God. But in the supplications we found the real core of the complaint concealed; the *accusation* against God, who has forgotten the good man. Only when he looks back to praise the act of salvation, does the Psalmist venture to confess this fact to himself:

I am shut out of thy sight!

The Argument with God

This Psalm is an argument in prayer with God, who seems absent, but reveals his nearness to the supplicant. From this point of view also we can understand certain peculiarities which must strike us as odd: the seemingly unmotivated change of mood from supplication to praise, but also the bitter execration of the enemies, and the apparent self-righteousness of the supplicant. If the heart of the poem is God's distance, the real turning-point for the better lies in the new-born certainty of God's nearness; in contrast with this there is no longer need to speak expressly of a transformation in the external situation. Yet we ought not to overlook the fact that God's distance is outwardly experienced in sickness and persecution. In just as tangible a manner the supplicant would like to experience the nearness of God in the destruction of his enemies. God is for him a reality with which he would like to reckon in his outward fortunes also. God is not for him the Unapproachable who in any case knows everything already, so that one cannot win him over. Even when God has turned himself away, the supplicant can move him to intervene once more against the affliction. God has indeed himself given the best inducements when he made himself the God of Israel — now the man who remains loyal to him can appeal to his loyalty.[92] What the prayer is asking for is not salvation from one distress; the Psalmist would like to see himself restored into the lasting covenant of mutual loyalty between God and man.[93]

2. ISRAEL'S SONGS AND PRAYERS

Israel's Poetry and Music

In the Old Testament only a small section of the poetry of Israel has been preserved to us. Apart from the Psalms Israel possessed a wealth of songs of various kinds. In reference or quotations, in fragments or in entirety much of this has been preserved in the surviving documents of the Old Testament. People sang on the most varied occasions: at a wine festival (Isaiah 22,13) and at work — for example, in the joy of harvest (Isaiah 9,2) or at the building of a well (Numbers 21, 17f) — at a wedding (in the Song of Songs wedding-songs are collected) and at the funeral service for the dead (2 Samuel 1, 19-27); songs of scorn directed at the enemy served as political propaganda (Numbers 21, 27-30; Isaiah 37, 22-29; 2 Samuel 5,6); people struck up songs also after a victory (Exodus 15, 20f; 1 Samuel 18,7).

Nearly every section of the Old Testament bears witness to Israel's joy in song; between the song of the well of Numbers 21,17f and the song in praise of Judas Maccabaeus (1 Maccabees 3, 3-9), there is an interval of nearly a thousand years. People in foreign countries apparently thought highly of Israel's music. The Assyrian Sennacherib claims as tribute from Hezekiah of Jerusalem not only money and treasures, daughters and concubines of the king but also male and female musicians; the songs of the exiled Israelites were valued by the Babylonians.[94]

Great quantities of songs, prayers, and other forms of poetry of the peoples living in Israel's neighbourhood have become known through archaeology. Israel's poetry is of course closely related to the poetry of the ancient orient. But the Psalms of Israel make a stronger impression on us than the Accadian hymns and poetical works of Canaan. This is not only due to the fact that Christianity has to the present day preserved unbroken the link with the poetry of the Old Testament Psalms — while in the case of the Canaanite and Mesopotamian poetry we are immediately confronted with the strange forms of speech of a world of the distant past — Israel has left behind no evidence of special artistic talent, but in music and literary art it outstripped its neighbours.

We can, of course, form no conception of Israel's music; even the rhythm and metre of its music and poetry are almost unknown. The late Jewish transmitters of the Old Testament text unified the language of the Bible, and, above all, accommodated it by vocalization to a much later type of speech. For this reason unambiguous inferences about the peculiarities of Hebrew metrical art are not possible.

Parallelism

Metre and rhythm give pleasure to the hearer, in so far as through their repetition they awaken and satisfy the expectation of similar movements of speech. A similar role is played by the most striking characteristic of Hebrew poetry, the so-called parallelism of members (cf. above p. 48). A verse is divided into two parts of similar significance, which often correspond word for word, without simple repetition. Cf. Psalm 31,13: synonymous parallelism;

I am forgotten, out of mind/like a dead man
I have become/like a pot that is thrown away.

Joy in ornate speech and the artistic mastery of language has developed this play with synonymous words and speech-forms to a fine art. But Hebrew poetry gains even more in impressiveness by this formal element than in playful artistic accomplishment. Every statement has to impress the hearer once again, clad in a different form of language. The poets do not seek for one exact formulation; instead through duplication they gain greater inner amplitude of room for the imagination of the hearer. They delimit the field of utterance by contrasting an affirmative with a negative sentence. Psalm 31,9: antithetic parallelism:

Thou hast not abandoned me to the power of the enemy
but hast set me free to range at will.

With the second half they carry the reader a bit further than with the first. Psalm 31,18b: synthetic parallelism:

Let the wicked be ashamed,
let them sink into Sheol in silence.

Only very seldom do we meet with a comparable artistic dexterity and variety of forms in the use of parallelism in the poems of the neighbouring peoples. There the formal law of parallelism tempts the poet to bring together similar statements into wearisome sequences. The hymn can easily turn into a litany:

His word, that like a well-established storm, whose inner depths cannot be seen through,
The word of the great Anu, that like a storm . . . whose inner depths . . .
The word of Ellil, that like a storm . . .
whose inner depths . . .
The word of Ea . . . Marduk, etc.[95]

Repetitive parallelism is to be found not only in poems from Mesopotamia, but also in Israel's immediate neighbourhood, in Canaan. In many Psalms this archaic form recurs. Seven times Psalm 29 repeats "The voice of Yahweh" but with every repetition the power of the appearing God is differently and more forcibly represented. The poet also of Psalm 93 understands how to combine repetition with intensification:

Yahweh, the ocean lifts up
the ocean lifts up its clamour,
the ocean lifts up its pounding waves.

Metaphor

Such repetitive forms are, however, the exception; the rule in Old Testament poetry is parallelism, which pours the same content into another form. This formal law of poetry satisfies an inclination of the Hebrew mind which can be observed in many places in the Old Testament. In speaking it inclines less to outline exactly and name an object than to refer to a wider field of significance whose boundaries are indistinct. In Hebrew verse this peculiarity is especially prominent. Many words of closely related meaning are used to throw light one after another on new sides of a happening (synonyms). The poets love to use the different possibilities of replacing precise names by another word (synechdoche, metonymy).[96] In comparisons they open out new fields of experience. More frequently they do not hold apart the comparison and the reality (metaphor).[97]

The Hebrew language lends itself to such use of metaphor in any case: "Narrowness, constriction" is a subsidiary meaning of the word for "distress"; for a "snorting nose" and "anger", for "burning" and "being angry" there is always only one word.

The poets gladly take advantage of the possibilities thus given. If "narrowness" means distress, so "breadth" means salvation (cf. Psalm 31,8 and 9). God's wrath is described in visible terms:

Smoke arose from his nostrils,

devouring fire came out of his mouth,

glowing coals and searing heat. (Psalm 18,9).

What these poems lose in precision through their many synonyms, metaphors, and similes, they gain by their vividness and nearness to experience. At a distance of thousands of years they impart to us the intense emotion of those who first gave voice to them. We may indeed assume that the faith in Yahweh stimulated Israel's natural gift for language. The place of the polytheism of the neighbouring peoples was taken by the faithful response to the one personal God who claims man wholly for himself. All men's powers must serve him.[98]

Eloquence

Yet we should guard against interpreting the formal elements of the Hebrew poetic art as merely the almost unconscious means of expression of the emotion of the heart. The art of eloquent and ready speech was highly valued in Israel. In 1 Samuel 16,18, David is described as the ideal of a young man;

I know the son of Jesse from Bethlehem, who can play the zither well.

He is a hero, valiant in war, wise in speech and handsome, and Yahweh is with him.

The ideal young man must not only have courage and power, he must also have success ("Yahweh is with him"). Here we encounter the ideal figure in a hard world of peasants and warriors, in which the weak and the unlucky go to the wall. But even in this time proficiency in music and speech are regarded as worth striving for. Centuries later, in Daniel 1,4 we meet with an idealization in which other aspects are accentuated.

Young men of good looks and bodily without fault, at home in all branches of knowledge, well informed and intelligent.

It becomes clear that for Israel the world has changed. The place of the valiant warrior has been taken by the scholar. But external beauty is still among the advantages worth striving for, and with "wisdom" also the art of the right word.

Proof of such eloquence is not only linguistic dexterity, for which a large number of words, similes and metaphors are at disposal for an utterance, but also the capacity to create sound-harmonies between words (assonance, alliteration)[99] or even to follow the alphabet in the first letters of the lines of a poem (acrostic).[100]

The Cultus, the Home of the Psalms

Yet not merely the Hebrew joy in fine language should prevent us from explaining too quickly the formal elements of this poetry as the expression of the personal emotion of the poet. Since Gunkel's fundamental work it is an assured ground principle of exegesis that the Old Testament psalms have their home not so much in private piety as in the cultus. Many hymns expressly say that they were written for the ceremony of the public worship of the community. The worshippers are in the Temple, take part in the congregational music and in the festal procession, and are reminded of the prescription to celebrate the festival or pilgrimage.[101] Lamentations can also serve as prayer formulae for everyone who comes to ask Yahweh for help. Cf. the inscription which heads Psalm 102:

A prayer for the afflicted, when he is overwhelmed and pours out his complaint before Yahweh.

Popular Psalms are written down and preserved in the Temple for future use (Psalm 102, 19[18]). A worshipper can hand in his song in the Temple as a votive gift (Psalm 19,15[14] could be the votive formula for doing this).

Israel had many kinds of songs. If only the Psalms are preserved in such profusion, the reason is certainly that this category of songs was collected and preserved in the *Temple*. Psalms of longing for the Temple (cf. Psalms 42 and 43), written in distant lands are only preserved to us because they reached the Temple, and there continued to be handed down.

The hymns above all preserve liturgical form. They begin usually with imperatives, challenging men to praise; such verses may be thought of as sung by leading singers, to whom a choir then responds.

Another kind of liturgical dialogue is the basis of Psalms 81 and 95. A hymn of the congregation is replaced by a speech of exhortation from God. Psalm 50 also contains such a speech by God; it is even introduced with the traditional motifs from the description of the divine epiphany. As once he did on Sinai, God appears and confronts just men and the wicked with his claims.

Cult Prophets

Were there occasions in Israel's worship on which such divine speeches were recited? Who proclaimed these commandments and exhortations in the name of God? To transmit the word of God is in Israel the task of the prophets. Modern exegetes have assumed that in addition to the prophets whose books we know there were in Israel a fixed professional class of cult prophets who had regularly to recite God's utterances in public worship.

This institution of cult prophets is also thought to explain a peculiar phenomenon in many hymns of complaint; the sudden change of mood from bitter lament to rejoicing and praise. Prophets are thought to have answered the person in distress with a consolatory speech of God and the former responded to this with praise.

But since there is no direct evidence in the Old Testament for the institution of cult prophets, it must be asked if this hypothesis is at all necessary to understand the texts cited above. Certainly at times the great prophets regarded even divine worship as a fitting place in which to announce their message. The speeches of Amos 5,1ff and Isaiah 1,10ff gain at once a new intensity, when we consider that they were addressed to people attending divine worship. The prophets confronted the mere heaping up of sacrifice and thoughtless worship with the divine commandment which challenges man to right behaviour in relation to our fellow-men.

It is now to be noted that the Psalms in question, (50; 81; 95) in their divine speeches also take up themes of the tradition of law. Why should not Psalm writers and prophets in their divine speeches about the commandments have made use of the same procedures of worship? During the service priests proclaimed the divine commands in the name of God, so that there existed here also the speech-form of divine address, not only in the mouths of the prophets.[102] The three Psalms, as well as the prophetic texts mentioned above, could well reflect this practice.

The example of God's speech in the Psalms can show us what kind of connection there is between the Psalms and the cultus: the Psalms are not rituals which indicate the course of the service, but they speak in the language that was used in the service; they build upon the model of prayer in the cultus.

Dating of the Psalms

This explains also why it is very difficult to ascribe individual Psalms to definite historical epochs. There are absolutely no unmistakable references to historical events. It is true that in the superscriptions 73 Psalms are ascribed to David (in the Septuagint, indeed, 84), two to Solomon, Psalm 90 to Moses, other Psalms to singers of David's time, like Asaph, Heman and Ethan.[103] Sometimes the superscription sketches even the situation in David's life, which is supposed to have occasioned the Psalm. The authors of the historical books act in the same way when they make David, and Hezekiah and the mother of Samuel sing a Psalm in an important moment. Even Luke puts Psalms into the mouths of Mary and Zachariah.[104]

147

If one were to trust the information in the superscriptions, for many centuries in Israel and among the Jews new Psalms were continually being produced, though the most of them belonged to the time of David. However, none of the Psalms which are traditionally ascribed to one particular situation is unmistakably related to that special occasion. The hymn of praise of a victor for deliverance from distress in 2 Samuel 22 fits many other situations. The prayer of Jonah in the fish's belly could be spoken by anyone in deadly danger.

We may make the same observation in relation to the New Testament Psalms: at the birth of John, Zechariah sings a hymn about the liberation of Israel from the hand of its enemies (Luke 1,74).

Thus two things can be affirmed; we are not free to rely unconditionally on the superscriptions; definite references to historical events are not to be found in the Psalms. In consequence the only way left to date these poems is by inner criteria — language, type of thinking, etc. But their kinship with cultic language makes this work hard for us. Nowhere has the text and rite of an Israelite service been preserved for us. How are we to picture this cultus? After the model of the Roman Mass, which maintained its form unchanged for centuries? Or as we judge a modern service with its numerous changes, accommodations, experiments, local variations? Did the service remain unchanged from the time of the empire of David to the dissolution of the remnant state Judah, and up to the rebuilding of the Temple after the exile? Or does historical development influence the language of prayer and the cultus — as Christian worship of the first centuries accommodated itself to the development from a small community into a state church, and, for example, solemn language from Caesar's court ceremonial conjoined themselves with the original celebration of a feast among friends?

Psalms and Ancient Oriental Festivals

Since Gunkel pointed out the connection between the Psalms and the cultus, different groups of scholars have increasingly attempted to understand the Psalms as merely textual formularies of the official cult festival. The attempt was made to find a home for as many kinds of Psalm in one single kind of service. Mowinckel believed that he could find in the Old Testament evidence of a festival of God's enthronement; he ascribed about a third of all the Psalms to this festival. Other Scandinavian scholars fit the Psalms into a service in which the suffering and exalted, deified king played the chief part. They conceive of Israel's worship as being similar in pattern to the cultus of the surrounding peoples.

These hypotheses involve an early date for most of the Psalms — the superscriptions which indicate the time of David, would then be accurate! Hand in hand with this location in an early time goes the effort to interpret the Psalms exclusively in terms of the heathen mythological conceptions of the neighbouring peoples. It is claimed that Israel, took over, for example, almost unaltered hymns of the Jebusites, the original inhabitants of Jerusalem into the worship of the Temple.

When we consider the kinship of the motifs, thoughts, and figures of the Psalms with prophetic[105] and wisdom texts, it is however better to date a large number of Psalms in exilic and post-exilic times. Half-heathen festivals, the enthronement of a previously feeble Jahweh, the ritual of a suffering and resurrected king, cannot therefore be postulated as *Sitz im Leben* of the Psalms. The prophets very clearly show that people in Israel at this time had long been capable of using heathen mythology as mere illustrative material in the representation of faith in Yahweh, without taking over the mythical background of the images at the same time. In spite of individual borrowing from the colourful world of mythical ideas, Israel's own faith is in control.

Israel's Prayer

The Psalms not only resist being drawn into the cultus of the heathen ancient orient, they also resist attempts to understand them solely as a function of the cultus. We see clear differences between the private prayer of the individual and the official prayer of the cultus. Private prayer reflects the unique personal situation of the individual; in form and in content it accomodates itself subtly with the mood of the moment: the worshipper's power of expressing himself in words, his mental type and his piety. On the other hand, public prayer tends to use formal language, often of an old-fashioned character. The themes of public prayer can nearly always without difficulty be distinguished from the themes of private prayer. Admittedly we know one kind of personal prayer which uses stereotyped forms. For example, people pray the Lord's Prayer with a particular personal intention, such as deliverance from danger. This last kind of praying has a distant resemblance to the way in which an Israelite turned to God in personal prayer. It must not be forgotten that stereotyped phrases and formulae were characteristic of Hebrew speech in general, and especially of the language of prayer. Only with the support of the traditions of his people does the Israelite venture to turn to God. The personal concern of the worshipper appears only as one example of the long history of the relationships between God and his people. The themes and the linguistic forms of personal and public prayer thus overlap. Public prayer and personal prayer cannot be sharply distinguished from one another. The *Sitz im Leben* of the Psalms is thus less the cultus than Israel's prayer in general.

How different Israel's manner of praying is from ours may be seen by choosing as an example the earlier history of the word Eucharist (thanks-giving). From Jesus' thanksgiving spoken over the bread and the wine the name "Eucharist" has been transferred to the whole liturgical celebration of the Supper. In the primitive Jewish Christian Church such a prayer of thanksgiving was called *B^{e}rākāh* — Blessing. The Greek translation, Eucharist, is thus seen to be a change of meaning.

For the Hebrew word *b^{e}rākāh* is so full of meaning that it can hardly be translated, and must rather be interpreted. According to our way of thinking, "blessing" is something which only a person or a thing can receive from another human being or from God. But in the Old Testament the $b^e r\bar{a}k\bar{a}h$ which man returns to God corresponds to the $b^e r\bar{a}k\bar{a}h$ which God has bestowed on man. An example of this use of the word is to be found in Genesis 14,19f: in Abraham's victory over the kings God has shown his power; so in a first proclamation of blessing Mechizedek must first state that in Abraham God's power of blessing is at work. But in a second proclamation of blessing he gives God the honour for this victory: "Blessed be Abraham . . . Blessed be God" (Genesis 14,19f). In the $b^e r\bar{a}k\bar{a}h$ the man gives God the honour for the saving acts which he has experienced. When Abraham's servant learns that he has made the right contact with the distant relatives, when David receives supplies from clever Abigail, when he learns of Solomon's anointing, when the women hear of Naomi's good fortune, they bless God for these acts of his.[106]

Thus in the Old Testament the $b^e r\bar{a}k\bar{a}h$ did not originate purely in the sphere of the cultus. In contrast with this "Eucharist" from the beginning describes the Christian liturgy. Everywhere that the Old Testament believer traced the action of God's hand, he ascribed the power and the blessing which he had experienced to God. The mood of the worshipper is here less one of gratitude than of praise. In thanking, the worshipper has his eye still on himself, on the benefit which he has experienced. In praise he regards the greatness of the one who has given the benefit. There is in Hebrew no word for "thank".

A child will not say "thank you" unless he is reminded to do so, but he is quite able to praise, i.e. to acknowledge the excellence of a person or a thing. For the Israelite thanks is also included in praise. This is shown by the Hebrew description of the Psalms. The Hebrew $h\bar{o}dayy\bar{o}t$ = Praises corresponds to the Greek word Psalms = Hymns. To the Jewish transmitters of the tradition the praise of God appeared the principal characteristic of these prayers, taking no heed of the fact that we reckon by far the largest number of the Psalms to be "laments". The modern study of categories agrees with the judgement of these men who handed down the Psalms to us; in all the different genres — in laments as well as in the hymns of confidence or Psalms of instruction — it finds "Hymnic" elements. The characteristic mood of Israel's prayer is its spontaneous expression of faith as well as in the liturgical formula is praise.

If in our prayers thanks corresponds to petition, the contrast for the Hebrews was rather that between praise of God and lament. Abraham's word in Genesis 15,2f gives an example; to God's promise of a rich reward his answer is:

> Lord Yahweh, what canst thou give me? I have no standing among men, for the heir to my household is Eliezer. Thou hast given me no children, and so my heir must be a slave born in my house.

The man who asks has exact ideas of how the present lack should be made good, the man who laments lays his distress before God in order to remind him that he must interpose, the worshipper however leaves open the manner of the intervention.

Our last reflections have shown that for the interpretation of the Psalms it is not enough to ascribe a particular place to them in Israel's cultus. We must understand them against the background of Israel's prayer-life. We have just as little apprehended the essence of the Psalms by being able to order them in different categories as hymns, laments, etc. Hymn and lament are not only literary structures that are built up according to particular laws out of different elements; they are also modes of prayer.

3. LAMENTS

"To pray" and "to ask" are for us closely related activities. During the evangelizing of the Germans, the missionaries found there was no German word for prayer. They translated *orare* with words from the root *bitten* ("to ask") e.g. *beten, Gebet.*

Prayers of Supplication in the New Testament and in the Old Testament

Prayer of supplication has a particular meaning in the New Testament. The Lord's Prayer lists seven requests one after another. Jesus' words of exhortation and his parables represent the person praying in the role of a supplicant, as the importunate man who even in the middle of the night receives bread from his friend, as the child who asks good things from his father and receives them,[107] as the man who does not seek and knock in vain. This prayer of supplication is by no means an expression of anxiety. It is not meant to remind God of something which he might have forgotten; as a kind Father, God knows beforehand what we need, and gives it to us in any case (cf. Matthew 6,25 ff). In spite of this we are to make requests of God, even in matters that must lie near to God's heart (the first petitions of the Lord's Prayer; Matthew 9,38: God the Lord of the harvest is asked to send workers for the harvest). When people ask each other for things, it is when they want to have something from one another — according to the teaching of the Gospels requests to God have another meaning: in them man is to acknowledge God as the good Father, and to bring his own wishes into obedience to God's saving will.[108] In the New Testament teaching about prayer, the linguistic form of the "request" has radically changed in character. It is no longer the expression of the wishes of the man in need, who is anxious whether he will get what he needs; the man who prays as Jesus teaches us to pray, can be sure that his prayer will be answered.

The Old Testament form of prayer which we encounter in the Psalms is clearly different from this — but at the same time Jesus' teaching about requests from the kind Father develops a possibility which was already contained in them. A simple prayer of supplication is hardly to be found in the Psalter. A large amount of space is taken by laments, in which the supplicant lays his misery before God. Requests which accompany this complaint do not ask for particular things which the supplicant needs — as does for example the Bread Petition of the Lord's Prayer. The content of the petitions remains open; the supplicant would like to be freed from his present difficulty, but does not say how he pictures this liberation to himself.

Save me from my enemies (Psalm 59,2[1])

Help with thy right hand (Psalm 60,7[5])

Deliver me (Psalm 69,19[18])

He would like to know that God thinks of him, he would like to startle him from sleep, rest, deafness and blindness — but the manner and the way of this renewed movement of grace he leaves in God's hands.

Awake, arise, cast us not off for ever (Psalm 44,24[23])

Arise (44,27[26])

Hear my prayer (54,4[2])

Hide not thy face (69,18[17])

The supplicant cries out of particular situation of distress to God — only seldom do we find in the Psalter requests about the enduring concerns of God's people or mankind. The Lord's Prayer, on the other hand, contains only such requests. The Psalmists do not merely ask that there should be a turn for the better in their misfortunes, but above all that God should turn to them once more in grace. In their requests the supplicants are more concerned about God than about their own wishes. They leave to God the manner in which he is to fulfil their wishes. Almost their only positive wish is for continued assurance of God: Be to me a rock and a fortress (Psalm 31,3[2]; 71,3).[109] If this kind of supplication comes very close to the New Testament prayer of supplication — supplication being one way of seeking the nearness of God — the prayer of the Old Testament is essentially different in that complaint takes up a large place in it. In situations where we would utter a supplication to God, Israelites behave quite differently.[110] Faced by the oppression of Israel by Pharaoh, or the flight of the Israelites before the Canaanites, Moses and Joshua do not utter a supplication to God; they do not understand how God could treat his people in such a way; their lament draws God's attention to his extraordinary behaviour (Exodus 5,22; Joshua 7, 7-9).

Why, O Lord, hast thou brought misfortune on this people?

Here we are far removed from the boundless trust in the goodness of the Father which underlies the supplicatory prayer of the New Testament; the final ground of the lament is the accusation; the supplicant fears that it is God's intention to be untrue to the people, though he has chosen to be its deliverer.

Communal Laments

The "Communal Laments" of the Psalter[111] are profoundly marked by this attitude to prayer. The mighty God has joined himself to the people and promised to be loyal to it; every misfortune that comes upon the people appears therefore as a sign of God's absence, indeed of his disloyalty. God had had the power to prevent it. Joel 1,13 ff interprets a situation in which such a communal lament may have been sung. Locusts have devastated the land, Israel is summoned to penitence and fasting, and a public fast and day of lamentation is proclaimed. Such days of mourning there were certainly for other reasons, certainly on the occasion of a defeat of the army and a victory of the enemy.[112] No Old Testament writer has described the Order of Worship at this kind of service of lamentation. The communal laments however show clearly enough how these ceremonies were understood.

Apart from the lament these Psalms contain a series of other elements; the praise addressed to God, supplication, confident confession and expression of trust, here and there an adjuration to praise, yet all of these structural elements take their particular meaning from the lament.

The Praise of God only reveals more clearly how contradictory and unintelligible God's behaviour is in relation to his faithful people.

In God we have gloried all day long,

and we will praise thy name for ever.

But now hast thou rejected and humbled us

and dost no longer lead our armies into battle (Psalm 44,8f).

The *address* reminds God of his covenant promise, of his greatness and power which he is concealing.

Thou shepherd of Israel . . .

who leadest Joseph like a flock of sheep . . .

thou that art throned on the cherubim . . .

Lord of the heavenly hosts . . . (Psalm 80, 1-5)[113]

In the *affirmation of trust* is shown the kind of agitation to which the confident hope of the supplicant in God is exposed.

In these Psalms a part of the confession of trust is the *historical commemoration*. Its principal theme is the beginning of the history of the people: God delivered Israel from Egypt and bestowed the land upon it in Canaan.[114] The intention of the commemoration is not to strengthen the confidence of the supplicants that now also God will give his powerful aid. The prayer is not addressed to the people, but to God. A reproach underlies these portrayals of history. Why is God acting so differently in the present? This experience leads to the verge of doubt. Has God changed? Is he no longer powerfully active to help Israel as he was in the past?

This is what troubles me, that the mighty arm of the Lord is shortened (Psalm 77,11).

In troubled reflection about the contrast between the present and the past, the Psalmists learn to understand the unity of Israel's history. The

153

past is not gone for ever. In spite of all present distress the same God is still at work on his people's behalf. It is precisely the confidence that God cannot suddenly bring salvation history to an end, which gives them courage to make their lament and accusation.[115]

The appeal addressed to the strong God of the covenant, his praise, the expressions of trust, together with the commemoration of God's saving power in the past, all these elements of the lament, are marked by the endeavour to provide God with *motives for his intervention*. However cautious the singers may be about specifying for God any one particular kind of help, yet they urgently wish to know that God really does help. God's nearness to his people must become obvious and tangible. The Psalmists are concerned about the reality of God's power and loyalty. Since Israel did not know of another life, the faithful could not console themselves with a "hereafter". The present misfortune of the people therefore radically called that faith in question. Must it not be God's concern, too, to keep alive the trust he had himself awakened, and never ceased to require? Could it be a matter of indifference for him if doubts in his power and loyalty should arise?

Even the *complaint* itself bears signs repeatedly of the attempt to move God to intervene. Since God has bound himself so closely to Israel that he can say "my people" and Israel can say "my God", he is continually moved by the misery of the people. The frequent use of the possessive pronoun in the 2nd person in the complaint, reminds God of this covenant promise: "thy people", "thy name", "thy sanctuary", "thy servants" are under attack; "thine enemies" triumph; Israel's disgrace is God's defeat, its struggle is God's dispute.[116] We encounter here an Old Testament form of the faith in God's "incarnation". Even if in the misfortune of the people it may seem that God has withdrawn himself — the covenant is not annulled. Blows that strike the people strike at God. So the complaint does not merely have regard to the fate of the unhappy people; it is concerned rather with the disturbance which has entered into the relation between God and man, and men's relations with one another, and correspondingly, the complaint has three subjects: the sufferer, God, and the enemies; the unhappy man bewails his unhappy lot, he makes a charge against his enemies, he accuses God.

In the communal lament, the accusation is the dominating feature of the complaint, and can attain to an unprecedented intensity. But even here, the Psalmists do not cease to address God — they never pass from the accusation which is addressed to the party accused, to the judgement that condemns him. The accusation continues to seek God. In spite of God's apparent estrangement, the supplicants have not abandoned the hope of touching God's heart with their accusation. In the questions (why? how long still?[117]) the accusation is still not wholly explicit; at least formally the supplicants leave room for the possibility that God's unintelligible behaviour might be explained. But the accusation appears without ambiguity when the form used is the indicative. Like an enemy God has dealt with his people, he has broken his promise and rejected it, has made it drunken and deceived it.[118]

The Old Testament supplicant can only conceive of the experience of God's absence in the light of the gracious approach of the living God to his people. He cannot understand the misfortune of the people as a sign of God's indifference or powerlessness. Nor yet is God for him the Unapproachable with whom man cannot argue, so nothing remains for him but to charge God with unintelligible hostile behaviour.

In comparison with complaints against God the two other elements of complaint are less prominent. The *description of misery* in which the supplicant bemoans his fate is mostly included in the indictment against God; God himself has sent all the misfortune. The *charge against the enemy* speaks of the wicked deeds of the enemies and their contemptuous and blasphemous speeches; its purpose is to show God that he himself is under attack. God's self-contradictory behaviour is revealed, as in the indictment; he gives victory to people who do not honour him — while he leaves his supporters in the lurch.[119] The indictment of God falls silent in proportion as the connection between the sin of the people and its misfortune is developed. (Here there is a resemblance to the Deuteronomic interpretation of history.)[120] Confession of guilt takes the place of indictment.[121]

Individual Laments

Not only the misfortune of the people, but also the misery of every individual might be spread before God. Psalm 62,9[8] actually challenges the worshippers:

Pour out your hearts before him.

The so-called "individual laments" in the Psalter differ from the communal laments; even if only by reason of their number they are clearly predominant. There are reckoned to be about forty of this kind. This striking fact might be explained thus; that in the Temple a relatively large number of individuals wished to declare their need in a lament — a national misfortune, on the other hand, was a much rarer happening. It was therefore easier to gather in the Temple the individuals' laments, and thus many more forms and examples of prayers were available for these worshippers. 1 Samuel, 1, 9 ff tells of one such lament in the shrine. The childless Hannah, later Samuel's mother, is so engrossed in her prayer, that her strange behaviour gives offence.

Yet the "lament of the individual" is not only a prayer of the cultus, spoken in the Holy Place. The religious man can bemoan every misfortune to God. When Samson is thirsty, he brings this before God in the same form as that in which Moses and Joshua had spoken of the misfortune of the people. He reminds God in his lament of his self-contradictory way of acting.

Thou hast let me, thy servant, win this great victory, and must I now die of thirst? (Judges 15,18).

155

The lament of the individual can challenge God in exactly the same way as the communal lament. The persecuted Elijah declares, "It is enough, Lord". Jeremiah expresses his disappointment:

Thou art to me like a brook that is not to be trusted, whose waters fail.[122]

With unexampled bitterness Job seeks to compel God to justify himself.

In the individual laments contained in the Psalter, we meet the same forms of lament as in the communal laments, indictments of God, charges against enemies, descriptions of misery. The root of all misfortune which comes upon the individual, as in the people, is to be forsaken by God. Yet there is a difference from the communal laments, in that in the individual laments, the complaint against God is not ventured in so downright a fashion. Sometimes we meet the lament put in the form of a question, which still in a manner conceals the indictment:

My God, my God, why hast thou forsaken me? (Psalm 22,2[1])

How long, O Yahweh, wilt thou quite forget me? (Psalm 13,2[1])

Psalm 6,4[3] does not even quite ask the question:

And thou, O Yahweh, how long?

The lament is surrounded by expressions of trust;[123] sometimes it is even put in the mouth of the enemy (Psalm 71,11), or the lament is transformed into a petition:

Hide not thy countenance.

Do not reject me.

Finally, as in the communal, so also in the individual laments, the complaint falls silent, and is replaced by the thought of education through suffering.[124]

The *"description of misery"* and the *"charges against enemies"* take up a much greater space in the individual laments. In Babylonian laments, the singer often loses himself in long descriptions of the misfortune. In contrast with this, the descriptions of misery in Old Testament Psalms are still very short. The supplicants' own misfortune does not cause him to forget that he is standing before God, before whom he is privileged to declare his misery. The description of misery never loses its connection with words addressed to God in supplication, complaint, or expression of trust.

We must not expect to hear, in the individual laments, about all the forms of misfortune in the everyday life of the Israelites. But it may strike us as strange that laments for the dead do not find expression in prayer. Israel knows poetic forms of such laments; but they are not addressed to God but to the dead person.[125] According to the ideas of Israel, a man departs at death out of the sphere of the living God; therefore one cannot bring before God one's sorrow about a dead person.

In other respects too the individual laments by no means convey a picture of all the dark sides of life at that time. We meet again and again in stereotyped representation only three forms of misfortune, which in addition are seen to be closely interconnected; sickness, guilt, persecution. The modern reader notices above all how much space is occupied by the charges against those who persecute the supplicant. These enemies are not accused because they had caused the misfortune of the supplicant. The situation is different from that in the communal laments, which describe the wicked *deeds* of the enemies. In the individual laments we are concerned with the wicked *plans* and *talk* of the enemies. The freedom and life of the supplicant are threatened. The pictorial language of the laments does not permit of any clear inference as to how we may concretely envisage the execution of these designs. The supplicant has for the time being only learnt of the hostile attitude of his opponents through their scornful talk — they have not caused his misery, but they despise him for it and are glad of it.[126] His misfortune is an occasion for his enemies to accuse the supplicant; they mendaciously construct a connection between his sickness and his guilt.[126a]

What actual reality underlies these frequent laments? Are we to assume that malice and dislike, ridicule of the unfortunate and slander played such an exceptional role in Israel's everyday life?

The pious supplicant traces back the wickedness of his persecutors to their attitude to God, which is contrary to his. They abuse him because he hopes for deliverance from God;[127] they do not believe that God concerns himself about the doings of men; they think they can use violence without incurring punishment.[128] Here there are surely indications that Israel was split up into hostile factions. The cleavage was so deep, that people felt it divided them from those who were supposed to be their brothers and friends,[129] even in relation to their faith in God. More precise conclusions cannot be drawn from the vivid and formalized language of the Psalms. Even to this day no satisfying explanation has been found of the charges against enemies in the individual laments.

Strange though even the complaints against enemies may appear, this side of Old Testament prayer can become completely unintelligible to us when we think of the numerous vengeful wishes of the Psalmists.[130] When we think of the sublimity of the New Testament commandment to love our enemies, we may even look down contemptuously on this outgrown stage of Old Testament piety. But such an evaluation ought not to be our first reaction. We must first try to understand prayers of this kind in their temporal context. In the communal laments the worshippers' enemies were represented as God's enemies. Since God had joined himself to Israel by covenant, every attack on Israel meant at the same time an attack upon God. In the hymns of individual complaint, the enemies of the supplicant are described as despisers of God; they too stand on the side of the powers hostile to God. The charge against the enemy describes him as a typical evildoer. It leaves no room for the thought that enemies of the supplicant might in another respect deserve leniency, that they might reform and that the pious man cannot exclude them from the salvation for which he himself hopes. The Old Testament supplicant does not expect to be able to revenge himself personally; his point of departure is that God's opponents, (and he regards his enemies as such), must be made utterly powerless, if God's salvation is to win the day. Further, since the thought of a hereafter did not yet come in question for these supplicants, they expected that the decisive victory must come in this world. In confrontation with their enemies they counted on visible help from God. The enemies in the Old Testament are types, not individuals.

No more are we justified in seeing in the "I" of the individual laments a unique human being in his particular situation in life. We misunderstand the Psalms if we make the attempt to put ourselves in the spiritual situation and the external circumstances of the sufferer. Even the words which the supplicant uses to describe himself cannot be understood as the utterances of one individual about himself. Frequently the supplicant describes himself as poor and weak. Here "poor" is a religious, not a social concept. The poor man, who cannot help himself, is compelled to implore help from God. (Psalm 12,6[5]). The violent enemies on the other hand, rely upon their own power.[131] There is nothing left to the poor man, but to rely on God. This is no colourless consolation. On the contrary according to Israel's law God has guaranteed to the poor man a legal claim to aid. The man who describes himself as "poor" is reminding God of his promise.

The supplicants' description of himself as "poor" is therefore to be reckoned as one of the expressions of trust, which form a regular constituent of the individual complaints. The trust bases itself on God's actions in the past on behalf of his people and the supplicant himself.[132] References to concrete historical facts are almost entirely lacking in the individual complaints. In the communal laments the principal purpose of expressions of trust in God was to remind him of the contradiction between his past and his present behaviour. In the individual laments they achieve much greater importance of their own. In some Psalms, indeed, this element has made itself quite independent.[133]

The prayer is in essence a struggle of the supplicant for trust in God. When the supplicant has won the assurance that God is listening to him, then the burden of his distress has already been removed. The deepest cause of the suffering was separation from God. If God hears the prayer, then he is already near. Then an answer to it is already certain (Psalm 55,18f[17f]).

In many individual laments we are reminded of the certainty of our prayers being heard which Jesus promises to the supplicant. The man who prays to the Father in the sense that Jesus implies is heard and answered because this request is made according to the will of God. Similarly, in the Old Testament laments the aim is not this or that advantage for the supplicant, but communion with God.

Certain expressions of confidence seem to point to the fact that the supplicant has a particularly vivid experience of the presence of God in the life of the Temple.

Yahweh is the portion of my inheritance in the land, and my cup (Psalm 16,5).

Obviously we have here prayers of Levites who lived continually in God's presence. Their confidence that God will never be far from them gains such power over them that sometimes in prayer they transcend the barrier of death which according to Israel's thought inexorably separates man from God. The supplicants trust that God's presence can never forsake them even in the land far away from God, the land of death.

Though heart and body fail
yet God is my possession for ever (Psalm 73,26).

Israel believed that only in life could man experience God's grace; God no longer turns in grace to the dead.

(I am)
like the slain who sleep in the grave,
whom thou rememberest no more
because they are cut off from thy care (Psalm 88,6).

But in the Psalms of the Levites this limit is transcended, God's grace is worth more to these worshippers than life.[134]

Righteousness in the Psalms

Other utterances, on which the confidence of the Psalmist relies, surprise us on the other hand, because they make the supplicant appear extremely self-righteous.

Thou hast tested my heart and watched me all the night long;
thou hast assayed me
and found in me no mind to evil (Psalm 17,3).

Such words may remind us of the Pharisee in the New Testament parable, who in his confrontation with God appeals to his blameless life. Does not this parable require of the supplicant that he confesses his sinfulness (Luke 18,9-14)? It is true that certain individual laments describe the distress of the supplicant as consciousness of guilt,[135] but even in these Psalms persecution by enemies and sickness contribute to the unhappiness of the supplicant, indeed these two elements of the description of misery usually predominate. Beyond this a series of Psalms assert with an assurance incomprehensible to us, that the supplicant is righteous: God is at liberty to test the supplicant's heart; he may himself search through his thoughts by night; he will not find any unrighteousness.[136]

Whence do the Old Testament supplicants derive this certainty that they are righteous? In "the Rich Young Ruler" we meet, even in the New Testament a religious man of this kind, who in answer to Jesus' reminder about the Decalogue can answer "I have kept all these since I was a boy". And Jesus does not by any means turn this answer of his into a reproach, for we read further, "his heart warmed to him" (Mark 10,17-24 par).

The question about the "righteousness" of the Old Testament worshippers can only be satisfactorily answered when we again remember

159

that it is not merely individual experience that speaks out of the Psalms. People do not have the thought that it is possible for God's commands to be more or less well obeyed, that if conscience were examined usually a still better kind of behaviour could be thought of. For these worshippers there are not many gradations between "righteous" and "unrighteous". There is only the alternative: a man belongs to God and is righteous — or he has separated himself from fellowship with God and is unrighteous. Only the righteous man can come into the Temple and there take part in prayer. Psalm 15 and Psalm 24,3f reflect a liturgy which reminded the worshipper of this as he entered the Temple:

Yahweh, who may lodge in thy tabernacle? . . .

The man of blameless life, who does what is right . . .

But the concrete claims which the righteous man is to satisfy are quite possible to fulfil — like the commandments of the second table of the Decalogue, which Jesus enumerates to the young ruler. The question whether e.g. one has slandered another, or put out money to usury, is one which can be answered with a simple Yes or No. The statements in which the supplicant describes himself as "righteous" must not therefore be understood by us as "Pharisaic". The worshipper is not counting up his good deeds before God in order to exalt himself over other people. The self-description "righteous" is rather to be set beside the self-description "poor". By using both the worshipper declares that he belongs to God.

The pairs of contradictory terms "righteous-unrighteous", "Belonging to God-godless", "poor-violent" have yet to be considered from another viewpoint.

Wisdom Psalms

In a series of Psalms the complaint about the persecution of the supplicant by ruthless enemies fades into the background. The very fact of the existence of evildoers is an offence which he does not find it easy to accept.[137]

My feet had almost slipped . . .

when I saw the good fortune of the godless.

These prayers are not concerned with the personal misfortunes of an individual, but with reflections about fundamental principles — they come from the tradition of Israel's wisdom. Trust in God has here an equally hard test to undergo. God's salvation could only be real for the Old Testament worshipper when he had a vital experience of it — but does not the mere existence of godless men (who in addition continue to prosper) contradict the fact that life and divine grace are closely interconnected?

Generalizing thought, which leads to the antithesis righteous man - evil-doer, penetrates from the genuine wisdom Psalms into other Psalms also. The expressions of confidence in Psalm 25 speak, for example, not of historical or personal experiences, but express profound reflections on

160

God's dealings in relation to the godless and the faithful. Also new forms of supplication appear. No longer is prayer made for God's nearness and protection, but for the power to live according to God's demands (Psalm 85,11).

It was indeed teachers of wisdom who placed Psalm 1 at the beginning of the whole Psalter as its introduction. This Psalm draws the ideal picture of the man who meditates by day and by night on God's law. That is not the ideal of the scribe, but of the man whose aim is to direct his life wholly by God's will, and seeks for the way to this in meditation.[138] These followers of wisdom obviously did not understand the Psalter to which they gave this introduction as a collection of official prayers of the cultus of the society. They did not in the first place think of the use of these hymns in the Temple, but saw in them an invitation to personal prayer, texts about which they could meditate. Appendices and insertions have been preserved in particular Psalms as signs of these meditations.

From the individual laments particular elements have found individual expression and attained further independent development in the songs of trust, the wisdom Psalms, and Psalms of the law. From the communal laments the meditations on history detached themselves, and the didactic historical Psalm took its origin. The true laments distinguish themselves from these special forms through the rich variety of the elements employed in their construction. The movement of the Psalms often rises and sinks unsteadily in violently contrasted moods.

Praise in Individual Laments

The most striking thing in the individual complaints is the *swing of mood* away from complaint about adversity to praise.[139] What appears particularly strange to us is that no event is mentioned that forms a link between the two contrary forms of prayer. Persecution and sickness have not suddenly and miraculously ceased. More than elsewhere it becomes clear at this point that the laments do not set out to be the story of an unfortunate man and his salvation. They are, on the contrary, to be understood as products of the experience of the presence of God in the sanctuary. If his misery counted for the supplicant as a sign of his God-forsakenness, then in prayer in the sanctuary he may be certain of the nearness of God.[140] This means that the true root of all unhappiness is already eradicated.

In view of the fact that a great part of the Psalms are individual laments, Gunkel has said that the human heart is indeed more ready to ask and to lament than to praise. But it ought not to be overlooked that a considerable proportion of these individual complaints are *declarations of praise*.[141] The movement of these Psalms passes from complaint through supplication and expression of trust to praise. In individual cases indeed there is great freedom in the sequence of these elements.

The individual has brought his personal unhappiness before God, and

161

has been assured that God has heard him — he does not wish to keep this fact to himself, but to pass it on to the congregation.[142] This vow is fulfilled in the Psalms of individual praise, which are to be seen in close connection with the individual laments.

4. SONGS OF PRAISE

Individual Songs of Praise

The individual laments lead immediately to the individual songs of praise.[143] The Psalms of lament do not content themselves with lament and supplication. God hears the lament, and that already means deliverance; so the supplication is only the first step towards praise of God for the deliverance. Correspondingly in the individual songs of praise the praise is relative to the misfortune which has just been experienced.

Thou hast turned my laments into dancing (Psalm 30,12[11]).

The vow of praise in the individual lament, with its reasons adduced, is paralleled by the introduction of the individual hymn of praise with the proclamation "I will praise" and the accompanying summary concerning God's act of deliverance.[144] It is his deliverance out of distress which the complainant plans to celebrate before the whole congregation — in the individual hymns of praise he fulfils his vow (Psalm 116,14).

The use of the word "praise" at this place may attract attention. We would be more inclined to describe the answer to help in need as "thanks".[145] I can thank my deliverer where only he and I are present — an essential part of the individual hymns of praise is proclamations of the act of deliverance in the presence of the congregation. In thanking, the man who has been delivered speaks of the feeling that fills *him* — the songs of praise sing of *God's* action. The man who has been delivered does not wish merely to respond to God's action with feelings of gratitude, but with an action, with a thank offering and the public praise of God (Psalm 116,7f). By reporting his suffering and his deliverance to the congregation, he wishes to bear witness to the power and greatness of God. In this report, which is the central part of the individual songs of praise, there are no individual biographical details — for it is not the supplicant's experience, but the act of God which is in the foreground. But formality and stiffness are also absent, for the supplicant is bearing witness to a concrete experience.

In generalizing figures the distress is pictured retrospectively as imprisonment in the realm of death.[146] In every misfortune it is the absence of God that hits man, and in this degree death, the final banishment from God also invades our life already. In the Psalms every suffering is traced back to God-forsakenness as its fundamental form. Correspondingly deliverance is understood as God's turning to us, and as liberation from death.

For thou hast rescued me from death

to walk in thy presence, in the light of life. (Psalm 56,14[13]).

The individual songs of praise often close with a new promise of praise (Psalm 18,50[49]; 30,13[12]). The fulfilment of the first vow of praise, the song of praise, is not to end the story of the communion between God and the one whom he has delivered. The newly-won life has its meaning in everlasting praise.

The individual hymns of praise proclaim before the assembled congregation the praise of God — in this category of hymns of praise the cultic context is clearly visible. Yet in Israel the praise of God is by no means confined to public worship. In the Song of Deborah, the oldest piece in the Old Testament, all the riders, wayfarers, and people sitting at rest are challenged to come to the well in order to praise God's saving act on the people's behalf (Judges 5,10).

The original *Sitz im Leben* for praise is not the cultus, but the experience of divine help. People who have been delivered do not wait until the official public service. In Exodus 15, 19-21 the story is told how Israel passed dry-shod through the sea. Then Miriam struck up a song of praise:

Sing to Yahweh, for he has risen up in triumph;
the horse and his rider he has hurled into the sea.

Communal Songs of Praise

The song of Miriam, like the song of Deborah, is an example of "communal songs of praise" which respond to God's action in delivering the whole people. The principal part of both these national songs and the individual ones is the report of God's action.[147]

The Psalter contains only two communal songs of praise, Psalm 124 and Psalm 129; one might add Psalm 67, a song of thanks for the harvest. This is perhaps to be explained by the fact that post-exilic times, in which the collection of the Psalter took place, hardly provided an opportunity to experience God's saving power on behalf of the whole people in a historical event.

It was different in the times of the Judges, in which the Song of Deborah (Judges 5) was created. The wars which Israel waged in this time had a sacral character. Yahweh was the true hero of the "holy war" of the tribal confederation. So the song of victory is a song of praise to him. The vivid description of the battle is an essential component of the praise of God; all who fight on Israel's side "come to the help of Yahweh" (Judges 5,23).

God is present at that point where Israel's fate is being decided. The description of the epiphany of God at the beginning of the song (Judges 5,4f) makes this divine presence visible. Long ago the people entered into the land of Canaan from the desert in the south. Along this road God still comes repeatedly after his people in order to be with them at the turning-points of their history.

In the Song of Deborah the warriors of Israel fight for Yahweh — only

163

in 5,20 f is a cooperation of cosmic powers indicated. But later songs of praise, which pick up motifs of the song of victory,[148] emphasize alone and praise the miraculous intervention of Yahweh the warrior hero. If the poet who composed Judges 5 still stands under the impression of the historical event that he has experienced, these Psalms are testimonies of late reflection concerning the great deeds of God in the past.

Hymns

Individual and communal hymns of praise originated from the experience of the divine help. A chief constituent of these hymns was the account of the deliverance. Beside the narrative of praise was the descriptive praise, the hymn. The praise is not kindled from an immediate experience, but from reflection on who God is, and how he has acted hitherto.

God is to be praised because he is great, but above all, because he causes man to experience his greatness. This holds good even for the song of the Seraphim in Isaiah 6,3, probably the oldest hymn in the Old Testament. The song praises not only the holiness of God, but also the fact that God's glory irradiates heaven and earth. At the same time the song of the Seraphim is an example of how much nearer the hymn, which has lost its connection with immediate experience, is to the cultus than are the songs of individual and communal praise.

This is also to be seen in the structure of the hymn. The central portion is surrounded by imperatives, which call for the praise of God. The hymn in Nehemiah 9,6-31 shows where these imperatives have their *Sitz im Leben*. The Levites summon the congregation to praise God, and the congregation answers with a hymn on the greatness of God. In some of the latest Psalms, the imperatives more and more clutter up the real hymn, the praise becomes frigid, and the justifications for praise become more and more meaningless.[149]

In most of the hymns, however, the imperatives are only a framework, enclosing the real heart of the Psalm.[149a] Here statements about God's action predominate over the descriptions of God's being. People in Israel know who God is only from his historical actions. So even the descriptive praise is still held captive in the narrative form. Yet it is a narrative composed upon reflection from a distance, which seeks to apprehend the fundamental characteristics of divine action. God is praised because he sets at nought all human standards, exalts the poor, but humbles the rich.[150] The singers endeavour to give us a general view of God's action in history. The events surrounding the exodus from Egypt and the entry into Canaan, the time of Israel's birth as a nation, seem to them appropriate to show God's power and goodness as pivotal forces in history.[151]

To this is added the praise of God the creator; in the creation — as in history — is revealed not only the power but also the goodness of God. From the very beginning God has worked for the salvation of men.[152]

From the classical categories, individual and communal laments, individual and communal songs of praise, and from the hymns, there develop some late categories of Psalms, which can mostly be described no longer formally, but merely on the strength of their content, as special forms of psalmody. The study of sacred history for didactic purposes, the Psalms of the law, and Psalms with wisdom-themes, could be regarded as akin to certain formal elements of the lament.[153]

Prophetic eschatological Psalms

Other minor categories of Psalms of later times are akin to the hymn. Themes, principally of the wisdom poetry connected themselves with elements of the lament; the hymn and the speech of the prophets coalesce in different hybrid forms. G. von Rad has described the Psalms as "Israel's answer" to the experiences of history. But the prophetic eschatological Psalms do not only reflect past experiences, they do not only reflect on historical events and God's mighty acts in the creation. From faith in God's greatness, which was proved by his action in the world, and on behalf of God's people, they develop new insights into the purposes of his divine activity.

These Psalms have three central themes: God's kingship, the rule of the king anointed by God, and Zion, which God has chosen.[154] In the present state of research there is no agreement as to the date to which these Psalms are to be ascribed, whether to the early time of the monarchy, or after Israel's return home from exile. The interpretation of these Psalms will vary considerably according to the dating. Essential utterances in all three groups are impossible to place in any period of Israel's real history. The nations unite themselves with Israel to praise Yahweh, the king of the world. The kingdoms are brought into subjection to Yahweh's anointed king. On the hill of Zion, which towers high above all mountains, there breaks the assault of all hostile powers. In the early times of the kings one would have to understand such utterances mythologically. The Psalms about God's kingship, if the early dating be presupposed, are interpreted as songs for the festival of God's enthronement. It is claimed that every year Yahweh — like the gods of the peoples surrounding Israel — ascended the throne of his world-domination. The Messianic Psalms are understood as royal songs which ideologically ascribe divine honours to the ruler on David's throne, like the kings of Babylon and Egypt: as the son of God, the invincible eternal ruler. In the praise of the city of God it is claimed that there survive traditions of the pre-Israelite inhabitants of Jerusalem, the Jebusites. As the Babylonians saw their earthly shrine as a reflection of the heavenly dwelling of the god, as a heavenly mountain, so too, the faithful Israelites of David's and Solomon's time exalted the hill of Zion.

But there are weighty arguments that suggest a late date for these Psalms. These songs were created on a basis of prophetic promises. The cry "God is king" was taken into the Psalms from Deutero-Isaiah

(Isaiah 52, 7ff). The prophet places it in a coherent description of his vision of the return from the Exile. The call concerning the king is a message which has been long expected by the watchers on Zion, and is greeted with joy. A short hymn is attached, a summons to praise, with a reason for it.

> Break forth together in shouts of triumph, you ruins of Jerusalem; for
> Yahweh has ransomed his people.

In the hymns, experiences of the past constitute the reasons for praise of God. Here, in contrast, the ruined Jerusalem is to rejoice over its restoration, now already the answer to the coming act of deliverance is to be given. With this, Deutero-Isaiah has created a new form of the hymn, the "eschatological song of praise".[155]

This was the literary form to which the Psalms about Yahweh's kingship had recourse. In these Psalms the cry of acclamation to the king no longer needed to be explained as in Deutero-Isaiah (as a message to the watchers of Zion): the hearers of these Psalms already understood its context. Thus the Psalms are dependent on Deutero-Isaiah, not the other way round. In comparison with the prophets they have further developed the conception of God's kingship. God rules not only over Zion, but over the world, the peoples, and the gods.

The songs in honour of the anointed king also (Messiah) can only be fully understood against the background of prophetic texts. From Nathan's prophecy to David (I Samuel 7), the prophets in the time of national disaster had developed the conception of the true king according to God's will, for whom Israel may hope. The Messianic Psalms show how lively that hope continued to be. Even formally the connection of this group of Psalms with the sayings of the prophets is palpable. Important statements are made in the form of divine utterances, often in connection with the promise of Nathan.[156]

For the songs of Zion too, the comparison with the related prophetic texts is instructive. The pre-exilic prophets rejected together with trust in human power all security that sought to rely upon the presence of God in Zion.

> Therefore, on your account, Zion shall become a ploughed field,
> Jerusalem a heap of ruins, and the temple hill rough heath.[157]

Only after the destruction of the temple do the prophets depict in figures that are borrowed from myth the hope of the continuing and blessed presence of God in his city.

> In days to come the mountain of Yahweh's house shall be set over all
> other mountains, lifted high above the hills (Micah 4,1).

It is here that we have to place the songs of Zion.[158]

None of these groups of songs speaks any longer in mythical language which exaggerates the present earthly experience and immediately transfers us to the divine sphere. What they do is rather to use figures borrowed from myth in order to be able to speak of the consummation of

God's work of salvation, which immeasurably excels all present human experience.

Summary of Categories of the Psalms
I. Laments
(a) Individual lament.
(b) Communal lament.
Further developments on the basis of parts of the individual lament.
aa) Songs of trust.
ab) Wisdom Psalms.
aba) Contemplation of the fate of the evildoer and the righteous man.
abb) Psalms of the law.
Further developed from the Communal lament:
Didactic historical Psalms.

II. Songs of Praise
a) Narrative praise (songs of thanksgiving).
aa) Individual songs of praise.
ab) Songs of communal praise, e.g. songs of victory, songs of harvest.
b) Descriptive praise (Hymn)
(Themes: history, creation, destiny of men, divine epiphany).
Further development on the basis of the hymns.
c) Prophetic and eschatological Psalms.
ca) Songs of God's kingship.
cb) Songs of Zion of the last times.
cc) Songs of the Messianic king.

5. WISDOM SAYINGS

Israel's Wisdom and the Wisdom of the Peoples
"Wisdom" is an intellectual movement that flourished for centuries throughout the ancient orient. We know it also from Egyptian, Sumerian, Accadian and Aramaic texts. In many points Yahwistic faith deliberately rejected the intellectual and religious inheritance of other peoples, but this was not the case with "wisdom". Israel was conscious that she had this in common with other peoples. Solomon's wisdom is compared with that of the east and of Egypt; in wisdom the king enters into competition with the Queen of Sheba (1 Kings 5,10 f; 10,1 ff). The wisdom of the Edomites was renowned in Israel; the Old Testament Book of Proverbs quotes words of wise men of Edom.[159] Without declaring the source of the quotations Proverbs 22,17 — 23,11 takes over an excerpt from the Egyptian teaching of Amenemope; Proverbs 23,13 ff writes proverbs from the book of the wise man Ahikar, which was widely known and translated in the east; Tobit is even reckoned to be a kinsman

167

of Ahikar (Tobit 1,21). For those who are familiar with the historical traditions of Israel, the wisdom teaching must seem a foreign body in the Old Testament. The covenant of God with the people, the election of Israel, are hardly mentioned, there is no concern for God's dealings with his people. The teaching is meant for every individual, the Israelite and the foreigner alike.

And yet the Old Testament recognizes no contradiction between wisdom and faith in Yahweh. Yahweh is the Lord of wisdom. When Solomon asked him, he gave to the king the wisdom that Solomon needed to govern justly; and conversely the wise man directs his whole life according to the word of God (cf 1 Kings 3,4 ff; Psalm 1). The Old Testament wisdom can appear as an intellectual inheritance of other peoples, which Israel has appropriated to itself, but also it can be seen as instruction in the ways of Yahweh.

Israel's wisdom is marked by another pair of antithetical concepts.

Wisdom of the People and of the Learned

On the one hand we encounter it as wisdom of the people, and on the other as wisdom for the aristocratic and learned. For centuries the *sōd* was a feature of the everyday life of the people of Israel. It was the assembly of grown men that used to meet on festal evenings. It was taken for granted that one would attend. Jeremiah is depressed because his calling as a prophet excluded him from this circle.[160] Here was the place where the concerns of the day could be discussed, where judgement was passed on injustice done; here people entertained each other with stories and songs.[161] Here however also people exchanged their life-experiences, and took pleasure when such experiences found fitting expression in sayings, similes, riddles, jests and mockery. Much of all this has been handed down in the Old Testament wisdom writings; yet these forms of popular eloquence were only thought worthy of collection and written tradition because they had been adopted into another, aristocratic environment, into a kind of wisdom teaching which people in Israel first learned from other peoples.

The time of the first adoption can be determined: the time of Solomon. While Saul's style of government still corresponded to the forms that were in use in the time of the free tribal confederation, and David's government was still largely stamped by the warlike time of his ascent to power, Solomon was the first to create a court according to the pattern of the courts of foreign kings. Holders of office, scribes, and chroniclers[162] had to be trained for their office. As in Egypt, Phoenicia, and Babylonia, teachers of wisdom introduced them to the courtly life-style, suggested to them modesty in their dealings with the ruler, gave example of courtly table-manners, instructed them in the art of timely speech and appropriate silence, showed the value of self-control and level-headedness — in a word, wisdom was introduction to well-bred life at court.[163]

Another, third antithesis can characterize the Old Testament wisdom.

It stood on the one hand in close relation to the practical experience of life, yet on the other was reckoned as a privilege of the learned. Originally gifted woodcarvers, artists, and even experienced sailors and oarsmen were called "wise". But later Ben Sirach on the other hand denied "wisdom" to all who work with their hands; yet he draws a splendid picture of the learned and wise counsellor.[164] Gradually there was formed a special class of wise men; as people are proud of the priests who transmit God's instructions, the law, and proud of the prophets who proclaim God's word, so also the wise who give counsel are reckoned as leaders and pillars of the people.[165]

The Book of Proverbs
Through the interplay of these different influences the Old Testament wisdom texts were created. The Book of Proverbs bears clear traces of this origin. Wise men in Israel from the 10th to the 4th centuries left their mark on this compendium of different, originally independent collections.[166] The oldest pieces are also the most "worldly" (above all 25-27). They merely set in order detached proverbs; Proverbs 10,1 - 22,16 contains for example 375 independent units. This material has been ordered only superficially, sentences of a similar form are placed together, e.g. proverbs beginning with b, proverbs in antithetic or parabolic parallelism;[167] sometimes the content decides — 16,12-15, e.g., contains words about the king. For the most part there is no recognizable order. The varied accumulation of many single sayings may indicate that the old collectors possessed neither a clear idea of the different forms of the wisdom proverbs, nor a system of the contents of wisdom teaching. Thus even the chief Hebrew concept for the wisdom sayings, *māšāl*, is used in the most different contexts. It can mean a popular saying, and the use of a simile in speech, a satire, or saying of God, a historical memory;[168] yet does it not for that very reason correspond to the manifold influences that are at work in the wisdom of Israel?

Popular Forms of Proverbs
In the popular sayings Israel created forms like those that grew up in our cultural milieu. Truths which we have ourselves experienced, are retained. Often only two phenomena whose kinship we have not only experienced, but can also recognize, are put together ("early to bed and early to rise, makes Jack happy and healthy and wise").[169] Riddles in which it is necessary to discover what is really meant by a comparison or a general description, were obviously just as much treasured by Israel as by our ancestors.[170] The proverbs using similes in Proverbs 25,11 ff must be understood as each divided between two speakers; riddle questions and answers stand in contrast with one another.

A peculiar form of competition underlies the number-proverbs. One person names a remarkable property that he has observed in a number of things — another names these things, indeed he perhaps knows how to add yet another to this series.

> Three things there are which will never be satisfied, four which never say "Enough!" The grave and a barren womb, a land thirsty for water, and fire that never says, "Enough!"[171]

This play too has a serious intention. In the confusing wealth of appearances which encounter man, the wise man looks for order. The search for this is in the first instance even more important than instruction and exhortation. Indicative statements outnumber imperatives.

The "Counsel" of Wise Men

In Israel people spoke of the "instruction" (*Tōrāh*) of the priests. Everyone who desires access to the worshipping congregation has an obligation to keep the *Tōrāh*. In contrast with the *Tōrāh*, the word of the wise men was called "counsel". A counsel differs from the *Tōrāh* in that its usefulness must first be tested; the question must be asked if the maxims of the wise man are applicable in the changing circumstances. It is far from the purpose of the wise man to give fixed rules of behaviour. His concern is to find the right word at the right time (cf. Proverbs 15,23). He is just as little concerned merely to satisfy his inquisitive understanding, when he seeks to know the ordinances of the world; his purpose is rather to make right action in the world easier — correspondingly "foolishness" is not the want of intelligence, but a behaviour that misunderstands the given order.

How far the teacher of wisdom is from the ethical preacher, is shown by the many proverbs which refrain from all value judgements, they simply state the success of evil behaviour;

> He who offers a bribe finds it works like a charm, he prospers in all he undertakes.[172]

The foundation of wisdom teaching is observation. It is therefore impossible for a system to take shape; on the contrary the wise man sees himself sometimes compelled to allow contradictions which intellectually are mutually exclusive to stand beside each other.

> Experience uses few words; discernment keeps a cool head. Even a fool, if he holds his peace, is thought wise, and as sensible if he keeps his lips shut. (Proverbs 17,27f, cf 26, 4f).

In the living world of men paradoxes confront the ordering intellect — but precisely through his naming of these paradoxes the wise man helps himself to find his way in the chaotic profusion of appearances.

> A man may spend freely and grow richer . . . (Proverbs 11,24).

> A soft tongue may break down solid bone (Proverbs 25,15).[173]

It is only against this background that we have to understand the numerous proverbs which declare that there is a connection between man's action and his fortunes.[174] The wise men did not think here in the categories of reward and punishment, right behaviour is not only praised because it brings happiness. As the wicked deed bears disaster within itself, so the good deed bears salvation. The statements about the connection between action and results are an outcome of the observation of the right ordering of the world. Sometimes, however, Yahweh is named: he rewards people according to their deeds. From proverbs of this kind which name Yahweh, we must not infer that there was a special Israelite form of wisdom. The fact is rather that the Israelite wise men here took over an essential concern of their Egyptian models.[175] There Ra stands in the place of Yahweh, in Mesopotamia it is Shamash.

On the other hand, a peculiar characteristic of Israelite wisdom is to be found in the contrast made between the righteous man and the evildoer, the fool and the wise man.[176] The Egyptian wisdom preferred not to start from the fundamental behaviour of a man, but from particular situations. This kind of contrasts between human types indicates that the Israelite wisdom is a late form, which more and more breaks free from close linkage with the observation of the particular case, which abstracts and systematizes. One says, "So it is ever with a righteous man, or with an evildoer", instead of saying, "This is the result of a righteous deed, and this the result of a deed which disregards the order of things". Instead of making us capable of doing the righteous thing in a unique situation, the Old Testament wisdom asks more and more the fundamental question "How can the life of man best succeed?"

Yet it is never forgotten that life according to the given order can never be absolutely sure of success, even for the wise man. True, the doctrine of the connection between action on the one hand and bearing the consequences on the other, proclaims riches for the industrious man, and poverty for the idler — but not with full assurance. The ordering of the world is not wholly transparent. Modesty belongs to the wise man; he can never say that in everything his actions have corresponded with the right order (Proverbs 20,9). Therefore protection is given to the poor, from a person's fortunes the wise man can make no inference to his actions.[177]

This consciousness of the limits of human wisdom is powerfully reinforced by faith in Yahweh. Strewn among the earlier and later Wisdom proverbs are sentences that call in question the whole of the wisdom thinking. Yahweh's will transcends every order that can be perceived by earthly powers. He works as he will, independently of human action.

A horse may be made ready for the day of battle,
    but victory comes from Yahweh.[178]
God's will breaks the sequence of action and results:
    The blessing of Yahweh brings riches,
    and he sends no sorrow with them (Proverbs 10,22).
Wisdom endeavoured to find a way for men through the confused multitude of appearances, and even to throw light upon the inscrutable;
    The glory of God is to keep things hidden
    but the glory of kings is to fathom them (Proverbs 25,2).

171

But in face of the world-transcending freedom of God's will such an endeavour is questionable;
Face to face with Yahweh
wisdom, understanding, counsel go for nothing.[179]

Summary of the Kinds of Wisdom Proverbs
We may distinguish
I according to the *Sitz im Leben*
  a) popular sayings
  b) maxims for a man educated at court
II according to formal peculiarities
  a) riddles
  b) proverbs of comparison
  c) proverbs of number
III according to the intention of the speaker
  a) words in the indicative
  b) words in the imperative
IV according to the kind of world outlook
  a) observation of human life (without value judgements), e.g. also in antinomies and paradoxical statements
  b) investigation of the connection between action and consequences
  c) reflections concerning the "righteous man" and the "evildoer"
  d) experience of the nothingness of wisdom in confrontation with Yahweh.

REFERENCES
1 The term "the descent of God" acquires theological importance in the Old Testament. The description of a particular place is never conjoined with it, in order to indicate God's complete freedom; cf outside Genesis 11,5 also Micah 1,3; Exodus 19,11. 18.20; 34,5.

2 Cf von Rad; *Das erste Buch Mose*, p. 124, Eng. tr. *Genesis*, p. 147. Von Rad indicates the irony of this text: "The Lord who sits enthroned in heaven laughs them to scorn" (Psalm 2,4).

3 Cf the use of the word in Deuteronomy 1,28.

4 Falkenstein/von Soden. *Sumerische und akkadische Hymnen und Gebete*, Stuttgart 1953, p. 182. When the gods built for the victorious Marduk his tower in Babylon, they raise him "high as Apsu", the immeasurable deep of ocean. (*Enuma elish* VI 61)

5 The plural indicates the conception of God as a great King, who is surrounded by his court, cf Genesis 1, 26; 3,22.

6 Genesis 15; 18. In other narratives the word of promise is subsequently added; only in Genesis 15 and 18 is the promise as goal of the narrative inextricably connected with the narrative.

7 The oak of Mamre, Genesis 18; the spring of Lahai-roi, Genesis 16,14; Genesis 21,19; the burning thorn-bush of Exodus 3; the ford of Jabbok of Genesis 32; the Dead Sea, which floods Sodom, in Genesis 19, etc.

8 The report of 1 Samuel 17 is different from that of 2 Samuel 21,19 which tells us that Elhanan killed Goliath. This contiguity of different traditions bears impressive witness to the difference from our historical thinking. Other fairytale motifs are to be found in 2 Kings 4,1 ff (the pot that is not emptied), Numbers 22,22 ff (the speaking ass).

9 Cf on this Chapter I,4.

10 It is different with the Song of Deborah (Judges 5). Here we are simply not told in what relation the rain and the manifestation of the God stand to one another, both merely happen at the same time. In Genesis 6, 1-4 there seems indeed not to be merely one single motif, but a whole mythological narrative underlying the biblical text. And yet it is consciously broken up, only the fragments, which can no longer be clearly explained, are given to us. (Mortal women together with divine beings produce the giants of early times. But why are not the seducers, but the mortals punished?)

11 Cf Genesis 2; 8 with 2,10 and 4,16

12 *Enuma Elish* VI. To connect contemporary political events and conditions prevailing since immemorial times is even in our day still a widely distributed characteristic of human thought. Rome understood itself as successor of the famous Troy. The case was similar when many Frenchmen still understood the first world war as a continuation of the age-long conflict between Latin culture and Germanic barbarism. It was, of course, the same way of thinking which was used by the Germans who saw in Herrmann the Cheruscan their ancestor who proved German superiority to cowardly Romans — it is all the more surprising that the Israelites told themselves no sagas about the glorious beginnings of their people, that they remained conscious of their descent from other peoples.

13 Only with the account of the fall of man does this account of creation take on the full character of a narrative. Here too the creator has no partner: only when man comes on the scene are the presuppositions of a narrative (at least two persons) given.

14 Cf Genesis 2,6; 3,19; Beside the word "ground" we find on both occasions (dealing with the creation of man), the word "dust", a word symbolizing death. Man was from the beginning created mortal.

15 "To know good and evil" is a synonym for knowing everything. The serpent and even God in the narrative call this knowledge divine (3, 4.22). But this statement is neither meant to distinguish the first human beings as specially wise people, nor is it intended to say that men have appropriated something for themselves that God wished to retain for himself. It is man's task to reach this knowledge in obedience to God (1 Kings 3,9).

16 A later version of the story of the Flood has been worked into the old saga. There once more are to be found signs of mythical exaggeration; the flood of chaos, otherwise confined under the firmament, breaks forth again.

17 Cf J. Wellhausen, *Prolegomena zur Geschichte Israels*, Berlin, 1927, p. 316 Eng. tr. *Prolegomena to the History of Israel*, 1885.

18 A. Alt: "Der Gott der Väter" in *Kleine Schriften*, 1959 Eng. tr. *Essays on Old Testament History and Religion*, 1967, p. 1ff. For the names of God, cf Genesis 31,42; 49,24.

19 Thus the name of the place Mahanaim (double camp) is explained. A second derivation of the name stands immediately beside it. Jacob meets messengers of God, and infers from this that a camp of God's army was near his camping place. We have here an example of the way the biblical writers thought. To them unambiguity and logic was less important than the faithful reproduction of tradition.

20 Of him it was also told that he used in sleep one of the great fragments of rock which lie around Bethel as a cushion for his head in sleep (Genesis 28,18).

21 Cf 1 Samuel 28,13; Isaiah 8,19 (Spirits of the dead); Joshua 23,7.16; 24,2.14-16.20; Deuteronomy 3,24 etc. (strange gods); Hosea 12,4; Judges 13,22 etc. (God's messengers).

22 Cf Ezekiel 18,7 Isaiah 58,7 etc.: the poor and helpless man is naked; Deuteronomy 28,48; to be naked is a punishment; Job 1,21; Ecclesiastes 5,14-15); nakedness belongs to death.

23 Cf Genesis 16,7.14., Ezekiel 16,39.

24 Cf Genesis 12,6.

25 Cf Genesis 32,23 ff.

26 Cf Genesis 28,10 ff.

27 Cf Exodus 13,21 f; 14, 19.24; Numbers 14,14; Numbers 9,15 ff; 10,11 ff; Leviticus 16,2; 1 Kings 8,10 f.

28 Exodus 26,1; 29,44 ff; 40,34.

29 1 Samuel 4,7; Numbers 10,35 f; Jeremiah 3,16.

30 Cf Genesis 12,7; 17,1.9.15; 26,1.24; 35,1.9.

31 Genesis 28,10 ff; 1 Kings 22, 19 ff; Isaiah 6; Ezekiel 1; Daniel 7,9 ff.

32 Genesis 11, 5,7; Exodus 3,8; Isaiah 31,4; Exodus 19, 11.18.20; 34,5; Nehemiah 9, 13; Micah 1,3; Numbers 11,7.25; 12,5; cf also 1 Kings 8,27; Isaiah 66,1.

33 Ezekiel 1,4; Isaiah 63,19; Psalm 18,10.

34 Judges 5,4 f; Deuteronomy 33,2 f; Psalm 68; Hebrews 3,3.

35 Exodus 19; Judges 5; Ezekiel 1.

36 Exodus 15; Psalm 18; 29; Habbakuk 3 etc.

37 Exodus 12,12 f; Amos 5,17; Hosea 10,10; Deuteronomy 9,3; 31,3.

38 Many of these motifs, which the Old Testament uses to describe God's presence, have been taken up by New Testament authors;

Mark 6,48 represents Jesus, walking upon the lake, as passing by the disciples — Mark represents Jesus' manifestation by using the theophany motif. Cf also Luke 24,29 (The Emmaus story).

When Jesus proves his power over storm and water, he is represented as the one in whom God appears.

The motif of the opening of the heavens is met with in the narrative of the baptism of Jesus, the motif of the cloud in the pericope about the transfiguration on the mountain.

39 Deuteronomy 26,8; Joshua 24,17; Daniel 9,15; Nehemiah 1,10.

40 Joshua 24,17; Exodus 32,11; Deuteronomy 5,15; 6,21; 7,8; 9,26; 26,8.

41 Cf also Isaiah 7,4; 30,15.

42 Exodus 16,20. A similar confidence is seen in the petition for "daily bread" in the Lord's Prayer; we ask only for bread to meet the needs of the current day.

43 Genesis 49,24; Isaiah 1,24; 49,26; 60,16; Psalm 132, 2.5.

44 Saul's messengers and finally Saul himself are smitten by prophetic ecstasy — so David is saved (1 Samuel 19, 18 ff). The information of the priestly oracle points out to David the right way (1 Samuel 23;11). Neither report intends to tell of a miraculous rescue of David; anyone can inquire of the priestly oracle; prophetic utterance was at the time a well-known phenomenon.

45 1 Kings 11,41; 14,19.

46 2 Samuel 8,16 ff; 20, 23 ff; 23, 8-39; 1 Kings 4,7-19; 5,7 f.

47 An example of such a text: Shalmaneser III, Battle against the Aramean coalition (722 B.C.): "I set out from Argana and came to Karkara. I destroyed Karkara, pulled it down and thus burned its royal residences. I set fire to its palaces. He brought to his aid 1200 chariots, 1200 horsemen, 20,000 infantry of Hadadezer of Damascus (cf 2 Samuel 8,3) . . . 2000 chariots, 10,000 infantry of Ahab, the Israelite (1 Kings 16,29) . . . There were, altogether 12 kings. They revolted against me and challenged me to a decisive battle. I fought against them

with the mighty power of Ashur, which my lord Ashur (a god) had given to me, and the strong weapons which my leader Nergal (the god of war) had delivered to me. I inflicted a defeat on them between Karkara and Gilzau. I put 14,000 of their soldiers to the sword. I came upon them like Adad (the storm-god) when he sends down a storm (Pritchard, cf ANET pp 278-90).

48 Exodus 17,8 ff; Yahweh fights for Israel: Joshua 10, 14.42; Judges 20,35. He brings elements of nature to help: Joshua 10,11; 24,7; Judges 5,20; 1 Samuel 7,10. He confuses the enemy and strikes them with the "terror of God": Judges 4,15; 7,22; 1 Samuel 7,10; 14, 15.20.

49 Judges 3,10; 6,34; 11,29. In the Samson stories we are often told of the descent of the Spirit, but even Samson is thus only empowered each time to one mighty deed. In Saul the Spirit of God is at work before the only battle which this king in alliance with God brings to a victorious conclusion (1 Samuel 11,6).

50 Judges 6,15 ff; Exodus 3, 11 ff; Jeremiah 1,6; Ezekiel 2; Luke 1,34 ff; "God is with you" is said to Moses, to Gideon, and to Mary; cf also 1 Samuel 10,7.

51 This motif also recurs in similar contexts in other narratives, and is thus not a communication about the person of Isaiah, but a statement about the position of man before God. When Samson's parents saw the angel, they feared that they must die (Judges 13,22). When, through a miracle, Peter recognizes divine power in Jesus, he reacts in just the same way (Luke 5,8f).

52 2 Kings, 2,15. The gospels picture the beginning of Jesus' ministry according to the pattern of the call of Ezekiel. Like Ezekiel, Jesus too sees the heavens open (Ezekiel 1,4; Mark 1,10 par); like Ezekiel Jesus too is filled with the Spirit.

53 Judges 6,11 ff; 1 Samuel 11,5 ff; cf the call of the disciples of Jesus.

54 Elijah; men from Jabesh for Saul; an angel; Jesus in the call of the Apostles.

55 Cf also 1 Kings 19,16: Elisha is anointed by Elijah. In the Old Testament there are three traditions telling of the call of Elisha: 1 Kings 19,1; 2 Kings 19,16; 2 Kings 2,15.

56 Exodus 2,1-10; Judges 13,2 ff; I Samuel 1,5.

57 The stories of the miracles of Jesus in the New Testament are more akin to the miracle stories of the Old Testament, which deal with the deliverance of the people, than the legendary miracle stories from the Elisha tradition. Jesus helps with his miracles all the needy among the people; the miracles are not for his own glory, but for God's. So praise and thanks for the miracle are often given in the New Testament narratives to God, not to the miracle worker. In this respect these miracle stories recall Old Testament miracle stories like, for example, the narrative of the crossing of the sea, which also concludes with the praise of almighty God.

58 Cf 2 Samuel 8,16 ff; 20,23 ff; 23,8 ff; 1 Kings 4,7 ff; 5,7 f.

59 The text as we have it bears most visibly the traces of revision and ordering of the world of nations according to the ideas of the priestly document. Remains of an older list of people composed by the Yahwist have been worked into it.

60 For example, all the Anglo-Saxon kingdoms had divine genealogies, and called Wotan their kingly ancestor.

61 Cf Gressmann, AOT p. 147; Pritchard, ANET p. 265.

62 Genesis 2 4a; 5,1; 6,9; 10,1; 11,10; 11,27; 25, 12.19; 36.1; (36,9); 37,2; Numbers 3,1. On this cf Eisfeldt βίβλος γενεσεως, in *Kleine Schriften* II.

63 The author of the Priestly Writing reveals himself as the composer of this reason for the Commandment. He refers back to the beginning of his work, the story of Creation, in Genesis 1. In his time, after the exile, the celebration of the Sabbath was an important sign by which the Jews declared their loyalty to Yahweh. For this reason P lays great emphasis on the Sabbath: God instituted the Sabbath at the very creation; in the time in the desert he caused Israel to discover

175

the Sabbath (Exodus, 16, 22-26). Deuteronomy repeats the Decalogue. It is striking that here the Sabbath commandment is given another explanation. It is given a social justification; in other respects also Deuteronomy gives special emphasis to the social aspect of Israel's lawgiving.

64 The prohibition of images is to be distinguished from the prohibition of strange gods. It places the creation of images of Yahweh also under God's threat. In the ancient orient images served the purpose of magical adjuration of the person represented; every attempt to control God is forbidden to Israel.

65 Since Christian catechisms often grouped together the prohibition of strange gods and the prohibition of images as one commandment, they divided this last commandment in two, in order to recover ten.

66 We find negative formulations of the Commandment concerning parents in Exodus 21,15,17. The Sabbath Commandment is still read aloud in Nehemiah 13,17f, in its negative form "Do not desecrate the Sabbath".

67 Exodus 19,3. 7 f. 14; already in the preparation for the Theophany, Moses goes repeatedly from God to the people and back again.

68 Deuteronomy 5 knows of an independent Sinai narrative. But the Decalogue there is to a large extent the same as in Exodus 20. (On the difference cf note 63.) Thus the history preceding the Decalogue was complete when it was inserted in these two Sinai narratives.

69 On the following matter, cf A. Alt, *Ursprünge des israelitischen Rechts'*, 1934, in *Kleine Schriften* I, 1959 p. 278-332.

70 In the casuistically formulated law concerning the treatment of a "rebellious son" in Deuteronomy 21, 18-21 the significance of the judgement of the gathering of heads of local families at the gate of the town is disclosed.

71 Cf also Exodus 22,17. 27; 23, 1-3. 6-9.

72 Cf Deuteronomy 27: The Document of the Twelve Curses is read aloud by priests in an act of worship, and answered at each pause by the people's "Amen".

73 Cf Exodus 34, 6 f; Numbers 14, 18; Deuteronomy 7,9 f.

74 Cf Ezekiel 18, especially verse 4.

75 This and other texts of the ancient orient important for research into this theme, and the literature relevant to it, are most easily to be found by consulting the report on investigations by D.J. McCarthy, *The Old Testament Covenant*, 1972.

76 Cf also Amos 7,7 f. The law appears to the prophet as a plumb-line in God's hand, by which the people are measured as a mason tests walls for stability.

77 Cf Leviticus 19; Exodus 34, 10-28.

78 Cf Proverbs 3, 27-31. The RSV shows the linguistic structure of the Hebrew text. Every sentence begins with a verb in the negative imperative. There is a difference from the apodeictic formulations of law, in that every individual command, is briefly brought into the contemporary life-context.

The 25th chapter from the Teaching of Amenope cited above, is to be found in James B. Pritchard's *Ancient Near Eastern Texts*, p. 242. The connection between "Apodeictic Formulations of Law" in the Old Testament and forms of Wisdom language has been treated in detail by Erhard S. Gerstenberger, *Wesen und Herkunft des apodiktischen Rechles*, 1965.

79 Proverbs 1,4.8; 2, 1; 3, 1.11.21; 4, 1.10.20 etc.

80 Exodus 24,7; 34,28; further Psalm 50,16; Deuteronomy 33,9.

81 Zechariah 7, 1ff; 8, 18 f; Psalm 15; 24, 3 ff; Micah 6, 6-8; Deuteronomy 21, 5, Malachi 2, 6 f.

82 The same attitude of Israel in relation to the law is expressed in its description as "the way"; Psalm 18, 31[30]; 119, 27 even call the entire body of ordinances "the way".

83 Alfons Deissler uses the same comparison in his book of meditations on the Ten Commandments: *Ich bin der Herr, dein Gott, der dich befreit,* 1977.

84 Psalm 119, 11. 16 f. 25. 43. 49 etc.

85 Cf Jeremiah 18, 18.

86 Cf 1 Kings 21, 13.

87 Further metaphors: verse 5; his enemies lay a net. Verse 9; his feet are set in a broad place — this metaphor corresponds to the metaphors of distress-constriction and abandon-deliver in verse 8 and 11. Cf also the figures of speech concerning God's ear, hand, and face which make God's nearness vivid.

88 Hosea, 8,8; Jeremiah 22,28; 48,38.

89 Jeremiah 20, 3 ff.10; cf also Jeremiah 6,25; 46,5; 49,29. Further borrowings from familiar phrases: with verse 15b cf Hosea 2,25; with 16b — Jeremiah 15,21: with 17a — Numbers 6,25; with 7a-Jonah 2,9.

90 Verse 24, cf 7a and 20.

91 Cf verse 6 and verse 16; verse 2 and verse 20; we might perhaps think that the double transition from supplication to praise results from the juxtaposition of two originally independent Psalms. Yet relationships of this kind between the two parts show clearly the unity of the Psalm.

92 Compare the motives for intervention in verse 4b,6: to vindicate God's loyalty; verse 7: for the sake of the trustful supplicant; verse 2: for the sake of God's righteousness; verse 19: for the sake of the innocence (blamelessness) of the supplicant.

93 Cf verse 2: "for ever"; verse 6 "God of truth".

94 Prism of Sennacherib in ANET p. 287f — cf 2 Kings 18,15; Psalm 137,3.

95 From Grether, *Name und Wort Gottes,* p. 140.

96 Synecdoche: a part stands for the whole; bolt for door; hand or face for the whole person. Metonymy: a thing from the immediate context is named in place of what is actually meant; cup for wine, fire and sword for war.

97 "Rock" for God, "Net" for ambush.

98 Deissler, *Literarische Gattungen,* p. 454: The divine is "not broken in the prism of polytheism, but streams with intense brilliance and warmth as it were from one point as *mysterium tremendum et fascinosum* into the "heart".

99 Assonance: similarity in sound of vowels, Alliteration: similarity in sound of consonants.

100 Acrostic: the letters which begin the verses constitute a meaningful series. cf Psalm 9/10; 25; 34; 37; 111; 112; 119; 145; Lamentations 1-4; Proverbs 31, 10-31.

101 Psalm 33, 2f; 68,26f[25f]; 81 2ff[1ff]; 96,8; 98,4ff; 100,4; 118,20.27; 122,1ff; 150.

102 In Nehemiah 8,18 we have evidence that in a late period the law was read in public worship. Even to explain the change of mood in the laments, cult prophets are not absolutely necessary. On this point cf the following section on the laments.

103 Cf 1 Chronicles 6, 18.24.29.

104 2 Samuel 22,1-51 = Psalm 18; Isaiah 38, 10-20; 1 Samuel 2,1-10; Luke 1, 46-55; 1,68-79; cf further the Psalm of Jonah in Jonah 2, 3-10; the hymn of lamentation of Habbakuk in Habakkuk 3; the prayer of Azariah and the three young men in the fiery furnace in Daniel 3, 25-45; 3,51-90 (= the Song of the Three in the Apocrypha).

105 For the dependence of the composition of the Psalms on the prophets, cf textual example Psalm 31, note 4. Cf further in the section "Hymns of Praise" the investigation of the connection of the "Hymns of Enthronement" with Deutero-Isaiah.

106 Genesis 24,26f; 1 Samuel 25,32; 1 Kings 1,48; Ruth 4,14.

107 Luke 11,5 ff; 11,11 ff; Matthew 7,9 ff.

108 Mark 14,36; Matthew 6,10; 26,53 f.

109 Beyond this the Old Testament laments express only two concrete wishes: 1. The request for revenge on one's enemies had indeed from early times an established place in prayers of supplication (cf Judges 16,28). 2. The prayer to be given the power to hear God aright, to serve him rightly, comes from the Wisdom School (cf 1 Kings 3,9).

110 Simple prayers of supplication are rare in the Old Testament, and of late origin. The eloquent prayer of supplication on the occasion of the dedication of the Temple in 1 Kings 8,23ff is shown by precisely this copiousness, to be a late formation.

111 Psalm 44; 60; 74; 79; 80; 83; 89.

112 According to 1 Kings 21,9 ff the elders of the town are ordered by the king to proclaim a trumped-up fast and lamentation. On this occasion Naboth is to be got rid of.

113 Cf also Lamentations 5,19.

114 Psalm 44, 2-4[1-3]; 74,2; 77, 16-22[14-20]; 80, 9-12[8-11]; 83, 10-12.

115 The contradiction between the fortunate past and the misfortunes of the present is not transcended in the communal laments. Here there is another view of history from that taught by the Deuteronomic school. Here the history of Israel was seen as determined from the very start by stubbornness and revolt of the people against God. Misfortune should have taught the people repeatedly to repent and return to God. God never tired of giving his ungrateful people new proofs of his kindness. There is no place here for complaint. This kind of view is not to be found in the communal laments, but in the psalms which give historical instruction, cf. Psalm 78.

116 Psalm 44,13[12]; 74, 10.19.23; 83,3.4[2.3].

117 Psalm 74,10f; 79, 5.10; 80,13[12].

118 Psalm 44,11f[10f]; 60,3, 12[1,10]; Lamentations 3,42f; Jeremiah 4,10. Psalm 90 does not touch the fate of the people of God, but that of human life in general. It is to be understood as a product of the late wisdom tradition (Koheleth). It has taken over from the communal laments the accusation of God. Here it appears in the sharp form of the call to repentance: "Repent, O Lord" (Psalm 90,13).

119 Psalm 44, 18-23[17-22]; 74, 18f.

120 Cf Note 115.

121 Cf Judges 10, 10.15; Daniel 9, 4-19. In Lamentations 5, 6 f. 16b and Psalm 79, 8f of the confession of sin has also found its way into the communal lament and yet in addition, the accusation is left standing in the form of a question, Lamentations 5,20; Psalm 79, 5-10.

122 1 Kings 19,4; Jeremiah 15,18.

123 Psalm 42,10[9]; 43,2 etc.

124 Psalm 66,10; 118,18; 119,67.77; cf Job 33, 12-33.

125 Cf 2 Samuel 1,17ff; David's lament for Saul and Jonathan. The following elements belong to a lament for the dead; invocation of the dead man, summons to lamentation, description of the sorrow for the dead.

126 Psalm 22,8[7]; 35,21.

126a Psalm 31,19[18]; 38,13[12].

127 Psalm 22,9[8]; 71,11.

128 Psalm 10,4 ff; 64,6[5].

129 Psalm 28,3; Psalm 35,12-14; 55,13f[12f].

130 Psalm 9,18[17]; 35,4ff; 55,16[15]; 58,7-10[6-9]; 64,10[9]; 69,24-29 etc.

131 Psalm 140,13[12]; cf also Psalm 18,28[23-28]; 35,10[9]; 116,6; 146,7; 149,4.

This interpretation of poverty had its locus in the prophetic preaching against the social abuses of their time. In God's name they took the poor, the socially underprivileged, under their protection. Certainly the large part of the people belonged to this needy class; in their confrontation with the leading classes they had nothing in their favour but the fact that they belonged to the same chosen people of God. "Poor — bowed down — humble — righteous" are closely interconnected.

132 Psalm 22,5 f.11[4f.10].

133 In Psalms 16;23;63;131 there is no lament at all; in Psalms 4;11;27;62;121 the lament stands in the background; Psalm 91 has the form of instruction and address to men, which comes out of the wisdom literature.

134 Psalm 16,5f.10 f; 27,4; 63,4[3]; 73,23 ff.

135 The so-called penitential Psalms, cf Psalms 25,7.11; 32,2-5[1-4]; 38,5[4].19; 40,13[12]. In Psalm 51 the motif of guilt even predominates. In the communal laments the confession of sin appears in connection with the later Deuteronomic outlook on history which makes a connection between the people's suffering and its sin. Cf Note 115. Further on this subject see Lamentations 5,6 f. 16b.

136 Psalm 17,2 ff; 26,1-6; 66,18; in the hymns of the communal lament 44,18f.21 f [17f.20f] etc.

137 Psalm 10; 13; 36; 37; 49; 52; 73.

138 Psalms 19 and 119 also give a central place to the theme of the law.

139 Psalm 6,8[7]-6,9[8]; 28,5-28, 6; 56,8[7]-10[9]; 69,30[29]-69, 31[30].

140 Psalm 57,6[5].12[11].

141 Psalm 35,9f ; 56,13[12] etc.

142 Psalm 22,23[22],26[25]; 30,13[12]; 35,18.

143 Psalms 9; 18; 30; 66, 13 ff; 116; 138; in Psalm 107 every strophe is concerned with a different group of people who have been delivered.

144 Psalm 30,2[1] (individual song of Praise) "I will exalt thee, Yahweh, thou hast lifted me up" — Psalm 56,13 f [12f] (Individual lament) "I have bound myself with vows to thee, O God, for thou hast rescued me from death".

145 Correspondingly Gunkel too spoke of the "Songs of thanks of the individual". Westermann pointed out that this response to a deliverance was something different from thanks; it was praise.

146 Similar pictures are of course to be found in individual laments: bondage: 18,5-6[4-5]; 116,3. pictures of death: 36,4.10; 40,3[2]; 56,14[13]; 69,2ff[1ff].

147 In the Song of Miriam a short sentence contains this report; the national hymn of praise which is quoted in Psalm 118,15 f is just as short. Judges 16,23 f even contains a hymn of praise of the Philistines to their god for the capture of Samson. Again the hymn consists of only one brief sentence.

148 Exodus 15 in verses 1-12; Psalm 68 in verses 2f[1f]; 12f(11f). 18f(17). In Psalm 18,38-46[37-45] motifs of the song of victory have been incorporated in an individual hymn of praise. In other cases the enemies of the individual are hostile members of the community — here they are foreign peoples. The speaker of such verses can only be a king.

149 Psalms 100; 148; 150; Daniel 2,19 ff.

149a In hymns from the ancient East that we have discovered requests are a normal part of the prayer. Such requests hardly occur in Old Testament hymns.

150 I Samuel 2,1-10; Psalm 113; Psalm 147,6.10; Luke 1,46 ff.

151 Psalm 135,8-12; 136,10-24; Psalm 105 is the only one which goes further back into history, to Abraham.

152 Psalm 19 and Psalm 104 are pure hymns of creation: motifs of creation are added to other motifs of praise of God in Psalms 33,6 ff; 95,4 f; 135,7; 136,5-9; 147,8 f.14-18.

179

153 Didactic historical Psalms: Psalm 78; 105; 106. Psalms of the law: 1,19; 119. Psalms with the theme of the doctrine of retribution (wisdom): 34; 37; 49; 73; 91. Psalms with the theme of human existence: 8; 90; 139.

154 Psalms about God's kingship: 47; 93; 96-99; individual motifs on the same theme in Psalms 95; 24. Psalms about the Messiah-King 2;45; 72; 89; 110; 132. Songs of Zion; Psalm 46; 48; 76; 87.

155 Cf further Isaiah 42,10-13; 44,23; 49,13; a song of this kind has also been taken up into the book of the first Isaiah, Isaiah 12,4-6.

156 Songs of the kings, which can be imagined in the mouth of one of the historical kings of Israel, are clearly distinguishable from the Messianic Psalms, Psalms 20;21; the second part of Psalm 18.

157 Micah 3,12; Jeremiah 7;26.

158 Songs of the pilgrimage to Jerusalem, songs of longing for the holy city show how differently the contemporary Jerusalem is regarded: Psalms 84; 122.

159 Cf Jeremiah 49,7; Obadiah 8; Proverbs 30, 1-14; 31,1-9.

160 Jeremiah 15,17.

161 Here is the *Sitz im Leben* of statements about law, sagas, songs, and proverbs.

162 Cf 1 Kings 4; here lists originated which provide a seedbed for historiography.

163 Modesty in the ruler's presence: Proverbs 25,6 f; at the royal table: 21,1 ff; speech and silence: 15,23; 17,27; 21,23. Level-headed calculation: 20,18; self-control: 16,23. Further references to life at court and the ruler: 14,28.35; 16,10 ff; 20,26; 21.1; 23,1; 24,21; 25.2 ff; 28,3; 31 ff. etc.

164 Ecclesiasticus 38,24 ff — cf on the other side Ezekiel 27,8; Isaiah 3,3; Jeremiah 10.9.

165 Jeremiah 18,18, cf 4,9; 8,9; Ezekiel 7,26.

166 According to the superscriptions in 1,1; 10,1; 22, 17; 24,23; 25,1; 30,1; 31,1; 31,10 we can distinguish eight parts of which the book was composed. In 10,1-22,17 additional collections of different origin have been worked in, as many doublets prove. In 22,17-24,22 Egyptian and eastern wisdom teachings have been included; 25-29; 22,17-24,22 seem to belong to the oldest parts.

167 11,9-12: four proverbs which begin with b: 10-15; 25-29; proverbs in antithetic parallelism; 25-27: proverbs in parabolic parallelism. In parabolic parallelism in both halves of the proverb the comparison and the thing with which it is compared stand over against each other.

168 *Māšāl* means a proverbial saying in 1 Samuel 10,12; 24,14; Ezekiel 12,22; 18,2 f; a comparison in Ezekiel 17,2; 21,5; 24,3; a satire in Isaiah 14,4; Micah 2,4; an oracle (utterance of God) in Numbers 23, 7.18; a historical memory in Numbers 21,27 ff; Psalm 49,5[4]; 78,2.

169 Cf Proverbs 11,2; *zādōn* and *qālōn*, presumption and disgrace, answer to each other.

170 Cf Judges 14,12 ff; "Out of the eater came something to eat, Out of the strong came something sweet".

171 Proverbs 30,15; cf 30,17; Ecclesiasticus 25,1 ff. The proverb that builds up to a climax is related: cf Proverbs 27,3 f.

172 Proverbs 17,8 — but compare 17,23. Observation without evaluation is further noticeable in Proverbs 13,7.23; 14,10.14.20; 16,30; 18,11.16; 19,4.6.7; 20,14 etc.

173 Cf further Proverbs 22,16; 29,23.

174 Cf 11,3f. 6.17; 12,24; 19,17; 20,13; 21,5.7.17; 25; 28,19f. Sometimes it is Yahweh who sets in train this course of events: 25,21 f; 24,12.

175 The originally independent collection, Proverbs 22,17-24, 22 contains 29-30

proverb poems, which in two or three verses apiece connect a warning or exhortation with a statement of the consequences of the action. Here the model is the wisdom poetry of Amenemope. 10 of the 12 proverbs have been excerpted almost verbatim from this work.

176 Righteous man — evildoer: Proverbs 10; 15,29; 18,10; 28.1. Fool — wise man: 10,22; 17,12; 26,7-12; 27,22.

177 Proverbs 14,31; 17,5; 19,17; 21,13; 22,22; 28,11; 31,8 f etc.

178 Proverbs 21,31; cf further: 16,1 f, 9; 19,21; 20,24; 21,2.

179 Proverbs 21,30; cf Jeremiah 9,22.

CHAPTER III

CHAPTER III

THE INDIVIDUAL PERSONALITY AND THE TRADITION OF THE PEOPLE

MOSES AND THE TRADITIONS OF THE PENTATEUCH

1. TEXTUAL EXAMPLE: THE DEUTERONOMIC "TODAY"

The Greek Bible gave to the last book of the Pentateuch the name of Deuteronomy (second law), because it represents itself in the context of the five books of Moses as a recapitulation of the law. Under the leadership of Moses Israel has reached the territory of Moab, has conquered land there, and stands ready to enter into the promised land. There Moses calls the whole people together in order to impress on it once again the divine commands (Deuteronomy 4,44-5,1). The situation in which the whole law, beginning with the ten commandments (Deuteronomy 5,6-21), is again recited, appears thus to be clearly defined.

The Recapitulation of the Sinai Convenant in Moab
But on a closer examination a number of questions arise. What is the need for such a recapitulation of the law? Has not Israel, according to the tradition of Exodus 19 ff already received at Sinai all God's instructions?
Deuteronomy 1,18 itself refers back to this first instruction in the law:
At the same time I instructed you in all these duties.
The situation in the life of Moses could give us the explanation of this. According to the will of God Moses is not to cross the Jordan. In four great farewell speeches he hands over his bequest to the people. But in his last words Moses is not only reminding the people of the past, of Sinai, he is claiming their obedience to what he has to proclaim to them "today".
Listen, O Israel, to the statues and the laws which I proclaim in your

hearing today. Learn them and be careful to observe them (Deuteronomy 5,1).

The law is here recited with all the solemnity of the first hour. The thought that we have here only a *reminder* of Sinai is expressly rejected:

Yahweh our God made a covenant with us at Horeb. It was not with our forefathers that Yahweh made this covenant, but with us, all of us who are alive and here this day (Deuteronomy 5,2f).

The line of thought of these verses may seem hard for us to follow. Moses recalls the past, the covenant made at Sinai, but only to insist that this covenant, entered into in past years at Sinai, is now "today" being made for the first time in the land of Moab. The term "recapitulation of the law" does not do justice to this strange telescoping of the times. What is recited "today" is not the old law of past times, but the law through which Israel at the present moment of time is being placed under God's will.

Back-dating of Laws to Moses

Thus "today" in Deuteronomy means, on the one hand, the point in time at which all Israel, gathered together in the land of Moab before entering the promised land, hears the speech of Moses. But at the same time "today" the covenant made forty years before at Sinai becomes contemporary reality.

There is still a third plane of time to be added to this. The speech of Moses, which begins in Deuteronomy 5 with the recapitulation of the decalogue, does not end until Deuteronomy 26,19. This great complex includes two parts of different kinds; one long speech of exhortation (Deuteronomy 5-11) and a recitation of laws. In the laws Moses gives instructions which must have remained unintelligible in their detailed character to the wandering Israelites. The people, who for forty years had been moved from place to place in the desert, are exhorted to worship God at one place only (Deuteronomy 12,1 ff); Israelites who had not yet learnt agriculture, hear about the payment of tithes from the harvest, of the dedication of the first fruits, of the right of the poor and hungry to glean and "pick" in vineyard and field, of the veto on taking a millstone or a mill in pledge. They are warned not to remove boundary-stones secretly.[1] The association of the twelve tribes is to accept laws that regulate the duties of the king — who did not exist in Israel until centuries later (Deuteronomy 17,14ff); Israel is to agree to the setting up of towns of refuge, which in cases of unintentional killing guarantee protection to the killer (Deuteronomy 19,1ff).

Could Moses have prophetically foreseen all this, and laid these injunctions on the people? Ordinarily laws are enacted to regulate already existing conditions. Are the laws in Deuteronomy to be understood differently?

The regulations for the most part take for granted that Israel already possesses the land. Deuteronomy "recapitulates" the commandments of Sinai for the *settled* people of farmers, for those living in towns, for the kingdom of Israel.

At Sinai a people received God's law who had forsaken the fleshpots of Egypt. In the Deuteronomic sermons the people who have already grown rich must be reminded of this time in the desert.

> When you have plenty to eat and live in fine houses of your own building, when your flocks and herds increase, and your silver and gold and all your possessions increase too, do not become proud and forget Yahweh your God who brought you out of Egypt, out of the land of slavery (Deuteronomy 8,12-14).

With this we have found a third time-plane which overlies the making of the covenant and the convocation before the entry into the promised land. According to our modern thinking Deuteronomy was really only justified in calling this time "today", the two other times would have to be characterized as the past.

> Moses summoned all Israel and spoke to them (Deuteronomy 5,1).

In this introductory sentence two things must appear as mere fiction. Neither can Moses have recited the laws of Deuteronomy as we have them, nor can he have had "all Israel" in front of him before the entry into the promised land. Modern critical investigation has shown that it is improbable that all Israel advanced at once into Canaan; that there were several waves of immigration of different tribes which only united to form the tribal union after arriving in the land, and only under David formed a society under a single political leadership.

What intention underlies the fiction "all Israel"? This question can be subdivided into three questions. Why did the authors put laws and introductory speeches of exhortation into the mouth of Moses? Why did they choose the point of time before the entry into the promised land centuries earlier? Why did "all Israel" have to be the recipient of the proclamation of the law?

All Israel as Covenant Partner

We can find the answer to these questions if we try to understand the remarkable Deuteronomic "today", which draws together the proclamation at Sinai and in the land of Moab.[2] By "today" Deuteronomy describes principally the time at which God makes the covenant with Israel through the mediation of Moses. It is not any part of the people but its totality that is God's covenant partner.

> You all stand here today before Yahweh your God, tribal chiefs, elders, and officers, all the men of Israel, with your dependants, your wives, the aliens who live in your camp — all of them, from those who chop wood to those who draw water. You are to enter into the covenant which Yahweh your God is making (Deuteronomy 29,9f (10f)).

187

All ranks and groups in the people are addressed as a single person: you. This one totality of Israel embraces at the same time also all the generations of history:

> It is not with you alone that I am making this covenant and this oath, but with all those who stand here with us today, before Yahweh our God and also with those who are not here with us today (Deuteronomy 29,13f [14f]).

Even we can follow the thought that "all Israel" is to obey God's law; but in so doing we think historically, we survey the whole history of the people. Deuteronomy has another way of thinking, as its word "today" shows. The hearers of the preaching of the law are aware today of themselves as Israel. The covenant made with Israel is always a contemporary challenge. It is not the man who looks back that hears the covenant challenges of God, but the man who remembers God's continuing loyalty to his covenant and his nearness.

The principal occasion for this act of remembrance is the celebration of divine worship. Here God is near to the celebrants, the representatives of all Israel. Here all the challenges that arise from the covenant with God are heard ever and again with the vividness of the first beginnings. "Today" Moses lays the law before the people;[3] "today" the people must decide for God.[4]

What is proclaimed in the cultus is always to remain present to Israel. Israel's whole life is to be enacted in this presence.

> These commandments which I give you this day are to be kept in your heart; you shall repeat them to your sons, and speak of them indoors and out of doors, when you lie down and when you rise (Deuteronomy 6,6ff).

We have now defined more exactly the situation of the recital of the law in Deuteronomy. For centuries the ever new proclamation of God's covenant and his claims stood in the forefront of Israel's worship. It is this continual presence of the Sinai covenant which gives the text of Deuteronomy its peculiar impressiveness. The exhortations and claims never belong to the past; they are in all times issued to the hearer who desires to enter into the covenant with God. Now also we can understand why Deuteronomy represents itself as "recapitulation", as making present the covenant of Sinai before the entry into the land. The law book thus shows by means of an example how the historical distance is transcended when God's demands are issued to the people.

Promise and Possession of the Land

This example is not, however, chosen capriciously. The authors of Deuteronomy might not just as well have chosen any other situation as the situation of the entry into the promised land. For them possession of the land and covenant with God were closely connected. The land is a pledge of the covenant, God's beautiful gift to the people:

> When now Yahweh your God will bring you into the land . . . with

great and fine cities which you did not build, houses full of good
things which you did not provide, rock-hewn cisterns which you did
not hew, and vineyards and olive-groves which you did not plant, and
    when you eat your fill there . . . (Deuteronomy 6,10-11)
all this God has first bestowed upon the people — only then is the people
to think of its covenant obligations:
    . . . then be careful not to forget Yahweh (Deuteronomy 6,12).

But Deuteronomy knows also the converse implications: possession of
the land is not only God's act of grace, to which the fulfilment of the law is
an answer; the fulfilment of the law is also a presupposition of the
possession of the land:
    You must conform to all Yahweh your God commands you, if you
    would live and prosper and remain long in the land you are to occupy
    (Deuteronomy 5,33).
Israel may never look on the land as its unquestionable property; it is
God's gift for the man who keeps the covenant. Thus the people really
remains always standing on the threshold of the land. For every generation must first in its turn fulfil the presupposition of the possession of the
land. By transferring the proclamation of the law into the situation
immediately before the entry into the land, Deuteronomy's purpose is to
show the hearers that they possess the land, and yet do not have it as their
property. If the covenant is broken, Israel can again lose the land, and
will receive it again as a gift every time it fulfils the covenant.

Moses, the one Mediator
    The third question still remains to be answered. With what justifica-
tion is Moses represented as the speaker of the law in the presence of all
Israel? Why do the authors of Deuteronomy remain anonymous? Basically this question has already been answered. The proclamation of the
law in Deuteronomy draws all its solemnity from the proclamation of the
law which has continued for centuries in public worship. The man who
recites the law in worship does not speak his own words, he merely fulfils
the role allotted to him in the service. The authors of Deuteronomy feel
themselves to be such speakers. They are not expressing their own
thoughts. They have collected ordinances and laws which already existed. They explain these and urge the people to take them to heart.

It never occurs to them to regard the multiplicity of laws as the result of
a long historical development. They regard these ordinances in another
light. All the commandments and laws that regulate the life of the people
can have only one source, the covenant with God. If a commandment has
another origin, Israel must not obey it. Just as the many historical
generations of Israel are seen collectively as *one* Israel, and as God's
covenant partner, so the many rules of life which originated under
different historical circumstances are seen as the *one* commandment of
God.

Only if we exactly obey this whole commandment in the sight of

Yahweh our God, as he has bidden us, can we be counted as righteous (Deuteronomy 6,25).

The question of the modern reader — Why do the authors of later times put these laws into the mouth of Moses? — would have hardly been understood at that time. To be sure even Deuteronomy must itself give a reason why it chooses the form of a speech by Moses; not because the form of proclamation of the law by the authors of Deuteronomy might also have been chosen, but because in public worship *God's* commandments are proclaimed. As a matter of fact God himself should pronounce the commandments. Why does Moses speak, and not God? At Sinai at first the people still heard God's voice as he himself out of the fire proclaimed the commandments. Stricken by deadly fear, the people asked Moses to listen to God's word, and to transmit it to them. God grants this request (Deuteronomy 5,24-30). Since the people cannot hear God himself, God appoints Moses as mediator of the covenant.

You yourself stand here beside me. I will set forth to you all the commandments, the statutes and laws which you shall teach them. (Deuteronomy 5,30-31).

Thus according to the conception of Deuteronomy Moses already heard "the whole commandment" from God. He is the *one* mediator of the *one* covenant. Only those who stand on the foundation that Moses transmitted to the people, can remain in the covenant with God. The man who declares the law in public worship stands in the place of Moses. Thus even the authors of Deuteronomy have no other desire than that people in their times should learn to hear anew the one true mediator of the covenant. They retain the linguistic form of a speech of Moses for their collection of laws and sermons on the law which stems from the liturgical tradition of Israel. Thus they bear witness to the unchanged power of the Mosaic covenant with God.

2. THE WORK OF MOSES

The investigations of recent decades have taught us to see how great was the power of custom and habit in the ancient world. The individual could hardly speak and act differently from those in his environment. Still less did people venture to deviate in matters of faith and religious life from old tradition. The contribution of individual personalities to the religious literature of ancient Israel can only be understood in the context of received forms of language and speech. Thus form-critical studies inquire in what society and what situation the individual linguistic categories were created and handed down. This type of interpretation of literature gives special attention to the contribution of the society.

The Pentateuch a Work of Israel and a Work of Moses

We can rarely recognize particular characteristics of individual authors of the Old Testament texts; the individual is overshadowed by the people. The decisive factor is not the special endowment of a single individual, but the election of the whole people to be God's covenant partner. For the truth of revelation it is therefore not decisive whether we are able to ascribe individual parts of the Bible to a particular author or not.[5]

Yet the peculiar character of the Old Testament cannot be judged solely according to the categories which stamped the language of religious association. In spite of all that modern historical science has taught us about the gradual coalescence of the tribes to form the people of Israel, we cannot understand Israel's origins without the personality of Moses. The faith of Israel is so clearly different from the religion of the surrounding peoples, that its beginnings must remain unintelligible without the figure of this great founder of religion.

In spite of all insights concerning the manifold forms of popular tradition, even the origin of the Pentateuch is therefore inexplicable if we do not trace it back to the work of this man. The Pentateuch is Israel's basic document and Moses' work, many hands in Israel had a part in it, but Moses had given them a stimulus and a purpose. Early Judaism saw in the Pentateuch a writing of Moses. Even in the Pentateuch itself individual sections are ascribed to Moses as the author. But this just as little describes the peculiar characteristics of this great literary work as do the modern hypotheses which not only deny Moses authorship of the Pentateuch, but even express a doubt whether Moses played any part in Israel's original tradition of the exodus from Egypt, the revelation at Sinai, and the desert wanderings.[6]

What influence had Moses on the formation of the Pentateuch? It is impossible to find texts that Moses might have formulated himself in their present form. In the second chapter we showed that there is no individual author behind the narratives and laws in the Pentateuch. These texts originated among the people, and were formed in a long oral tradition.

The Origin of the Materials of the Pentateuch

When we wish to trace the influence of Moses, we must not ask about the individual literary forms, but about the origin of the materials. How was the knowledge of the times of the fathers, the exodus and the desert wanderings transmitted? The second chapter indeed gave a first answer to this question; in the oral tradition. But when we consider the peculiar character of the Pentateuch, we cannot find this answer wholly satisfactory. It was shown that the oral tradition employs short units of material. A self-contained series of actions form the kernel of each of its sagas and narratives. But the Pentateuch cannot be understood as a mere collection of short units of this kind. Such a way of regarding it would fail to take account of precisely that characteristic which distinguishes Israel's retrospect on the past from the historical representations of other

191

peoples in the ancient east. Israel alone was able to give an account of
wide-ranging historical contexts which far transcended individual series
of actions; the transmission of divine promise and divine blessing in the
generations of the fathers, the creation of the people of Israel through
the deliverance out of Egypt and the making of the covenant at Sinai, and
the entry into the land. Such a historical representation could not have
come into being through the mere gathering of old popular traditions.
What was the origin of the great pattern of the course of history? A
modern hypothesis gives an illuminating answer. Even before people in
Israel began to collect the individual sagas, they knew the course of
history in its great stages: the time of the fathers, Egypt, the exodus,
Sinai, the time in the desert, the taking possession of the land. Every
Israelite knew from his confession of faith in what manner Israel had
come into the land. Before the collectors began their work, they already
confessed themselves to be descendants of the fathers of Israel, they
gratefully acknowledged the existence of their people to the mighty
saving acts of God, who had freed them from Egypt, led them in the
desert, and bestowed the land upon them; they placed their whole life
under the commandments of the divine covenant. They neither desired
to collect national antiquities, nor to "represent how things had happened" (Ranke); their intention was rather to represent the vital foundation of the faith of Israel. The great pattern of the course of Israel's
history served them as a framework into which they fitted the many
different individual pieces of material.

Where could the collectors find this framework? In the life of Israel
there were various situations in which people reflected together on the
history of the people and the basis of their faith.

Deuteronomy 26,5-9 shows that a kind of "Credo" formed part of
Israel's public worship. The literary form "Credo" can be described as
follows: the individual confesses his faith; he does not, however, trace it
back to personal experience of God, but to the acts of God on behalf of
the whole fellowship to which he belongs. Gerhard von Rad makes the
hypothesis that the Pentateuch grew out of a Credo of this type into its
present baroque final form. Yet surely in this final form the literary
structure of a Credo is hardly recognizable. The Pentateuch is no longer
the individual's witness to the historical foundations of the faith of the
fellowship.

In the Psalms we become acquainted with a second liturgical situation
in which the historical origins were spoken of; in times of distress the
believer reminds God of his mighty acts in the past, in order to impel him
to intervene. But the origin of the great literary structure of the Pentateuch is not to be found in the historical retrospect of the lament either,
nor yet in the historical hymn.

The Pentateuch has neither the form of a confession of faith nor that of
a prayer, but to a great extent the form of a report. Teaching, rather than
confession or prayer seems to be the fundamental form of the Pen-

tateuch. This is borne out by the fact that later the Jews called the whole Pentateuch *Tōrāh* — i.e. instruction. The collections of laws, too, which claim a large space in this work, fit best into this fundamental category of teaching.

The transmission of the fundamentals of faith in the form of teaching lived on in the instruction of children and in family worship.[7] But this instruction belonged also to the official life of the religious community of Israel. Two biblical passages refer to this; Joshua and Samuel give to the assembled people a survey of the course of their historical experience of God (Joshua 24,2ff; 1 Samuel 12,6ff). An Israelite custom will be reflected in these reports. It is probable that the people regularly received such religious instruction in the course of worship. The prophet Ezekiel may be appealing to this when he depicts the history of Israel as a history of the continual sin of the people (Ezekiel 20,5ff).

In the passages cited the historical instruction is not merely a renewal of the confession of faith, but a challenge to serve Yahweh. In this point also these texts will reflect the custom in public worship; the people is challenged to answer with its own loyalty the loyalty of God which is demonstrated in history. Psalm 78,2-8, a text from the time of the later Kings, reflects upon this meaning of the historical traditions of Israel.

It is however not enough for historical and critical thinking to know that the fundamental plan of the Pentateuch was already present in the religious tradition. The modern reader of scripture would wish to know beyond this whether we have here a sketch of history "as it was". He will be all the more inclined to doubt the historical reliability of this fundamental plan of Israel's history, because it stems from traditions which are not dealing with historical knowledge, but with the confession of living faith (creed), with comfort in distress (lament), with praise (hymns of praise), with exhortation to loyalty in relation to God's kindness (teaching). "People speak of Gods's acting in history, [but] nothing more tangible is ultimately there than an Israelite way of thought for which divine action in history is central."[8]

This judgement proves to be premature. On the basis of the fact that in the last resort we encounter traditions of faith behind the great historical work of the Pentateuch, we cannot reject the proposition of the historicity of the Old Testament revelation and substitute for it merely the thesis of its origination in the thought of Israel. We ought to keep before us two sides of the history of Israel. This history takes place on the one side in external events: the exodus, the conquest of the land, and so on — but on the other side at many levels of inner experience, in which the things externally experienced are handed down, interpreted, and become the foundation of the faith of Israel. The "passion of transmission awakened by the event" (Buber) distinguishes Israel's religion from the religions of the neighbouring peoples. What the people has experienced in its history must never wholly belong to the past and to forgetfulness. It is handed on, and lives on with the following generations. This tradition originates in historical happenings; it only comes into existence because the historical happening was so impressive. But it does not remain stationary. The past is not only conserved, but remains the centre of contemporary life. The tradition, Israel's inner history, is at the same time the history of the beginning of the Old Testament.

The history of the origins of the Old Testament has the most intimate connection with the development of Israel. The developing Old Testament and the developing people of God influence and stimulate one another mutually. (In the same way the origin of the New Testament and that of the church are partial aspects of the same happening.)

Themes of the Tradition
We find the tradition grouped around five main themes:

1) Election of the fathers   4) Preservation in the desert
2) Exodus from Egypt   5) Conquest of the land.
3) Revelation at Sinai

All these themes stand in relation to the external history of Israel. The history of the tradition shows how these themes, each one at first independently handed down at different shrines, are fitted together to form one historical picture, as the tribes of Israel grow together to form one people of God.

However, these themes are not only placed side by side and given equal emphasis, they group themselves round a central point which gives them significance. Since Yahweh led Israel out of Egypt, he remains with the people, and it must remain with him. The conquest of the land is the goal of the liberation. The land is not Israel's absolute property, it is Yahweh's gift to those who will remain with him. The tradition of guidance in the desert links together the tradition of the Exodus and the tradition of entry into the land. The tradition of the fathers had been kept alive at various shrines in Palestine. By recognizing that the centre of gravity of these traditions was in the still unfulfilled promise of possession of the land and a numerous progeny, people were able to make it the prelude of the history of Israel. So all the happenings gain their meaning from the fact that Yahweh freed his people from Egypt, and thus became their God.

It was possible to describe the origin of the Pentateuch without mentioning Moses: in many individual self-contained narratives the meaning of the past lived on. Further, in public worship and instruction the themes of the historical tradition were interpreted as the foundations of the faith of Israel. It is possible that one theme or another had its own special centre where the tradition was preserved. In proportion as Israel grew together into unity they grouped themselves around the one centre that gave them significance, the theme of deliverance from Egypt. It was this outline that collectors of popular narratives shaped into great historical works, from which at last the Pentateuch took its origin.

To be sure Moses, the leader in the deliverance from Egypt, belongs immediately to the core of the Pentateuch — but it is impossible to separate his personal work from the work of those who built upon it. In the generations of Israelites who collaborated in the history of traditions that constitutes the Pentateuch, no one thought of separating a "genuine" piece of Mosaic tradition from later additions and reinterpretations. This is not merely due to the fact that these people did not think historically. Their attitude is also determined by the fact that what stood in the centre of their tradition was not the founding of a religion, not the birth of a new conception of God which we would have to attribute to Moses. The centre of the Pentateuch is rather an event between God and people: Israel is saved by Yahweh out of its extremity. So we do not need to wonder at the fact that, outside of the Pentateuch and independently of its tradition the Bible so rarely mentions Moses.[9] It is not Moses that stands in the centre of the Pentateuch, but God. Moses is only the tool that God uses in the liberation from Egypt, through whom he gives himself to be known to Israel as the liberator. Thus even the Pentateuch does not represent Moses as a man who has significance because of his own capabilities. Moses is neither warrior nor guide in the desert, nor sacrificial expert,[10] he is above all the man who can approach the presence of God, hear God's word, and pass it on to the people.

Should we then look for "genuine" words of Moses in the tradition of the law? For example we might ask whether the decalogue was not for the first time transmitted to Israel by the mouth of Moses?

The Tradition of the Covenant

Up to this point only three themes of the religious tradition have in this section been linked with the exodus from Egypt, the centre of the pentateuch. We have not mentioned the theme of the revelation at Sinai. But this theme is especially important if we wish to understand the fundamental form of the pentateuch. What is notable in this great literary structure is the connection of historical memory and law. Judaism finally laid greater weight on the law; it named the whole Pentateuch after its legal parts, *Tōrāh* = guidance.

The theme "revelation at Sinai", "the giving of the law" is notably absent in all the summaries of sacred history which the Old Testament provides for us; in the "credo" of Deuteronomy 26, as well as in the instructions given to the people in Joshua 24 and I Samuel 12, even in the late Psalms.[11] It may be inferred from this that this theme was the subject of an independent tradition longer than the others, before it received its secure place in the outline of sacred history. But it did not, for this reason, have a less significant place in Israel's life of faith. On the contrary, it belongs to the very centre of the religious tradition.

This centre, as we have seen, was constituted by the tradition of the liberation from Egypt, to which the people owed its existence. Like this, the other traditions associated with it show that the life and happiness of the people are to be traced back to God's intervention. With the Sinai tradition, it is otherwise. Here the consequences are drawn which result from the great act of God on the people's behalf. Yahweh is Israel's God, its Lord, who gives it commands. His basic commandment is "I am Yahweh, thy God." This orientation of the Sinai tradition explains why it was handed down at another place in Israel's religious life from the tradition of God's mighty acts for his people. Historical instruction and the preaching of the law probably ran for a long time in parallel courses. Yet through Israel's fundamental commandment the connection with the other themes of the tradition is established. Even Israel's law is derived from the liberation from Egypt:

> I am Yahweh your God, who brought you out of Egypt, out of the
> land of slavery.

All the laws and ordinances according to which Israel lived in the course of its changing history have been made subordinate to the basic commandment, beginning with the apodeictic legal ordinances which bear witness to the sense of justice of nomadic desert tribes, down to the casuistic laws belonging to the legal practice of the settled society and to the cultic priestly regulations. All of them have only authority in so far as they are dovetailed into Israel's basic commandment. The origin of many principles of law can without hesitation be ascribed to the general legal traditions of the orient. And yet the Israelites were right when they placed these in the context of the divine law mediated through Moses at Sinai. For they were only binding on Israel when it recognized in them the expression of the divine will. Principles of law taken over from other peoples could not have authority for Israel, only the word of its God.

When the Babylonian lawgiver Hammurabi received his law direct from the sun god, that was regarded merely as a natural fact, which did not require any further justification. For who was a better judge and lawgiver than the sun god, who shone into every corner of the world? But it was by no means to be taken for granted that Israel should receive through Moses the commandments of Yahweh. Yahweh was not "by nature" a lawgiver, but had only made himself sovereign through the deliverance of Israel. Thus history and law belong together. This is what distinguishes Israel from all the surrounding peoples. It was to this close connection between God's act of deliverance and God's commandment, the mutual connection between the continually antecedent divine act of salvation and the obedience of the people that Israel referred when it called its law "the covenant". A covenant unites partners who were not previously bound together; a covenant has always a history preceding it. The confirmation of the covenant is made by means of visible signs. In the case of covenants between peoples this sign is usually a written treaty. There was probably a document of the covenant also in the case of the covenant between God and Israel. The story of the two tablets could be a reference to this.

Usually every partner to a treaty receives a copy of the treaty. At Sinai both copies were stored up together in the shrine, as befits the special circumstances of this treaty. The antiquity of this tradition could be confirmed by the memory of "stone" tablets. In this original document we might see the foundation of the tradition of the Pentateuch. It is clearly useless to try at this date to extricate its text — it probably contained both the memory of the deliverance from Egypt and the "fundamental declaration" in which Yahweh represented himself as Israel's God, together with individual commandments.

We may be surprised at the fact that a document, a form of words, which to us seems a sober dry matter of paper-and-ink, should constitute the heart of Israel's religious tradition. It perhaps repels us to find evidence of legal thinking at the centre of Old Testament faith. But it was just this that protected Israel from the mythical thinking of the environing religions, that its God encountered it as saviour in a historical extremity, that Yahweh, in order to make an everlasting bond with the people, chose forms which have parallels in the historical intercourse of the peoples.

The written treaty sealing an alliance can be stowed away and forgotten in archives. This was not the case with the document of the covenant with God. It was regularly proclaimed to the people in public worship. In the long periods of cultic use, new situations in Israel's life made additions and changes necessary. In spite of this growth it always remained the same official document of the covenant between God and the people. Through it God manifested himself as ruler of the people, as he had done by means of its original essential form mediated by Moses.

The work of Moses is the seed from which Israel's tradition grows; it is no longer possible for us to separate it from this tradition. Both the ground-plan of history and the revelation of the law are grouped around the one centre, the deliverance from Egypt, Moses, the mediator of the act of God and the commandment of God, stands always at the beginning. But the further development of this seed is most intimately connected with the further development of the people of Israel, and is at the same time its expressions and its dynamic. The work of the great personality and the work of the people cannot be separated from one another — for the believer both of them are reckoned to be the one work of God.

THE PROPHETS

1. TEXTUAL EXAMPLE: EZEKIEL'S VISION AND CALL (EZEKIEL 1,1-28)

(Superscription of the Book)
(1,3a) The word of Yahweh came to Ezekiel, the son of Buzi the priest, in the land of the Chaldaeans, by the river Chebar.

(The Introduction)

(1,1)   It came in the thirtieth year, in the fourth month, on the fifth day of the month, when I was in the midst of the exiles by the river Chebar. Then the heavens opened and I saw a vision of God.

(1,2)   (On the fifth of the month, that is, in the fifth year of the exile of Jehoiachin).[12]

(1,3b)   The hand of Yahweh came upon me.

(The Penomenon of the Thunderstorm)

(4)   I looked, and behold, a storm wind, coming from the north, vast clouds and flashing fire and surrounding radiance, and, coming from the midst of it, something that looked like brass glowing in the fire.

(The Four Living Creatures)

(5)   In the midst of it a form like that of four living creatures. This is what they resembled: they had the form of men. (6)   Each of them had four faces, and every one of them had four wings. (7)   Their legs: their legs were straight; the soles of their feet were like a calf's hoof, shining like polished bronze. (8)   Human hands under their wings. (9)   To the four sides were turned the faces and the wings of all four of them. (10)   The form of their faces: a human face and a lion's face to the right, all four of them. A bull's face to the left, all four of them, and an eagle's face. (11)   Their wings were outstretched upwards. Two were connected with each other, and two covered their bodies. (12)   They went, each one of them, straight forward. They went where the spirit caused them to go. They did not swerve in their course.

(The Fire)

(13)   In the midst of the living creatures something like torches. That moved hither and thither between the living creatures. The fire was shining, and out of the fire darted lightning.

(The Wheels)

(15)   I looked, and behold: a wheel on the ground beside each of the four living creatures. (16)   The wheels looked like topaz. All the four had the same shape, so built as if one wheel were in another. (17)   They ran in the four directions, without turning as they ran. (18)   They had hubs. I noticed this in them: in every case their hubs were full of eyes all round. (19)   If the living creatures moved, the wheels moved beside them. If the living creatures raised themselves from the ground, the wheels rose also, (20)   for the spirit of the living creatures was in the wheels.

(The Platform of the Throne Chariot)

(22)   The structure above the heads of the living creatures was a vault like ice-crystal, stretched over their heads. (23)   Beneath the vault their wings, stretched out towards each other. In each case two covered their bodies. (24)   I heard the noise of their wings, like the rushing of many waters, like Shaddai's voice. When they moved there was a sound like the noise of an armed camp; when they halted, their wings drooped down.

(God Enthroned)
(26)   Above the vault, that was above their heads, there appeared, as it were of sapphire stone, something in the shape of a throne. Above, on the likeness of the throne was a form that had the appearance of a man. (27)   I saw something that looked like brass — a structure surrounded it of a fiery appearance — it reached upwards from what looked like the waist. From that which looked like the waist downwards I saw what looked like fire, and there was an encircling radiance. (28)   Like a rainbow in the clouds on a rainy day so was the sight of that encircling radiance. This was the appearance of the glory of the Lord.

Introduction
    Among the prophetic figures of the Old Testament Ezekiel is one of the most inaccessible. From the very first verses of his book, his contradictory character is evident; his intense exuberance and dry learning, courageous innovation and sober explanation, revolutionary personal experience clothed in conventional forms of language. The account of the vision begins with a precise date, but it contributes nothing to the understanding of the vision that follows: it even seems like a foreign body — for the mysteries disclosed transcend time. Has Ezekiel, himself the son of a priest, been unable to discard the habit of priestly precision? More is here at stake for him. This date changed his life; this day made him a prophet. Since this day his words have the character of the divine message to Israel. That is why Ezekiel must give the exact date; from now onwards he is called to this appointment of the prophetic office. The heavenly vision does not lead away out of the world and out of time, but gives him the authority to work there.
    Just as important as the time of the vision is the place! Ezekiel is at the river Chebar, perhaps at the exiles' place of prayer.[13] If this were the case, then we are reminded of the vision and call of Isaiah. Isaiah's call took place in the temple at Jerusalem. It was there that the glory of Yahweh dwelt; it was there that Israel celebrated public worship. But the exiles asked themselves if their prayers from the unclean land of the Gentiles could reach God at all.[14] Ezekiel experiences something overwhelmingly new for a Jew of that day; God does not come from Jerusalem, but from heaven, he himself apppears at the river Chebar in Babylon; it is not the prayers of men, but a divine event that brings God near. But this advance into new territory is at the same time secured by tradition; the call of Ezekiel and that of Isaiah ran a similar course. Ezekiel knows that his call does not belong to him alone, it is only a part of God's history with Israel.
    On the occasion of his vision Ezekiel was alone — why does he then speak expressly of the exiles? The prophet does not wish to separate himself from the sinful and severely punished people: the man chosen by God stands in the midst of the sinners. Yet how can such a man ever receive God's commission? The prophets before Ezekiel could simply

199

state the fact: "I saw Yahweh". Ezekiel needs an explanation for the manner in which the vision became possible.

The heavens were opened, and I saw a vision of God.

This explanation must have been just as surprising for Ezekiel's hearers as the fact it was meant to explain. It was a new thought, that God should reveal himself in a strange land — it is a new conception, that he opens the heavens to do so. The heavens were then considered to be the wall of division, behind which God is remote from men; dwellers on the earth are for him as grasshoppers; indeed, the scoffer will say that from there he sees nothing and cannot judge.[15] Ezekiel experiences the improbable; the wall of division is broken through. He omits to say who brings about this event — only after the long introduction, which continues to 1,27, will he speak of God, the centre of the vision. Before Ezekiel can speak the word of the visionaries "I saw", an inexplicable miracle must happen.

As if he had entered too boldly into new realms with the motif of the opening of the heavens, Ezekiel at once indicates in addition that his vision is a continuation of the experiences of other elect spirits in Israel. He employs at the same time two different formulas of the technical language of the prophets. In both cases he links up with the oldest prophetic traditions. With the expression "vision of God" Ezekiel places himself on a level with Samuel, to whom God called in the night, and with Jacob, to whom also God spoke in the night (1 Samuel, 3,15; Genesis 46,2). To this prophet also a realm of experience has been opened that transcends day-to-day experience. But as if he feared to claim too exalted powers for himself by doing so, he adds the second sentence which depicts him as a mere tool in God's hand:

There the hand of Yahweh came upon me.

In the narratives about Elijah and Elisha we meet the identical expression used by Ezekiel. When Yahweh's hand comes upon Elijah, he is given power to run very far ahead of the king's chariot; Elisha gets a lyre player to play before him, till Yahweh's hand comes upon him. The classical prophets wished to distance themselves from this older type of prophets who could fall into prophetic ecstasy (cf Amos 7,14). But Ezekiel does not hesitate to link up with these traditions. They permit him to say that he is nothing but a tool that God uses to do extraordinary things.

The Phenomenon of the Thunderstorm

With verse 4 of the actual description of the vision begins. The literary style changes. Hitherto finite verbs in narrative form spoke of the new experience of the prophet. The last verb in this series stands at the beginning of verse 4: "I saw". In 1,1 it was connected with the indefinite object "divine visions". In 1,4.15. 28 it is repeated without object; the very fact that he sees at all is for Ezekiel sufficiently remarkable to be emphasized.[16]

In the visions of Amos in 7,1 and Jacob in Genesis 28,12 we meet a similar figure of speech as here: a finite verb in the indicative tense speaks of the experience of the visionary, the interjection "behold" follows, and then phrases consisting of a noun and a participle follow, describing the vision:

So Yahweh caused me to see, and behold, locusts flying
He dreamt,   and behold, a ladder standing
I looked,   and behold, storm-wind coming.

Certainly Ezekiel did not choose this honoured rather circumlocutory figure of speech by accident. Even the detail of his description is meant to show that he does not wish to base his prophetic claim on his own new insight, but on the traditions of the seers of Israel.

The question as to how God's appearing to the exiles is at all possible, obviously oppresses him so much that in 1,4 he recurs to it. Surprisingly, however, he now answers it differently. In 1,1 he spoke of the heavens opening, now he speaks of the phenomenon of a storm that comes from the north.

Here too again Ezekiel uses traditions which were already familiar in Israel before the time of the prophets. The motif of the heavens opening might have suggested conceptions similar to those to be found in Isaiah 6: Isaiah is granted access to the divine realm; he sees God, enthroned and at rest, surrounded by his servants. Ezekiel counts man to be too insignifcant to be able to approach God; God must come to man.

The motif of the coming God is very ancient in Israel. Judges 5,4 and Deuteronomy 33,2 sing of God's approach from the south. It was in the south that God first met his people in the desert; from there he follows them in their journeys. But still more often the motif of God's coming is linked with the thought that the direction of his coming cannot be known.[17] The motif of the coming God time and again reminded Israel that God is completely free to be present with his people.

By taking up this thought, Ezekiel gives it a new aspect; the freedom of God is proved in a new way. He does not indeed require to warn the exiles not to be all too certain of the presence of God; on the contrary, they believed that God was unattainably distant. But it is Ezekiel's experience that God himself can come to them.

Externally also, the old motif of God's coming is decisively changed. The epiphany comes from the north. For the Babylonians, that is the place, on the summit of the world-mountain, where the Gods have their dwelling-place. Has not Ezekiel, with this mythological reference, not falsified the old motif, limited God's freedom? The dwelling-place of the gods is part of this world; when the gods fled from the Flood, they were forced to fear for their safety even at the northernmost point of the heavens. Yet Ezekiel's intention is not to connect with this one word "north" *all* the conceptions which a Babylonian entertains in this context. Yahweh has here chosen a form to represent him that is appropriate to the strange land. The approach from the north does not refer to the divine reality, but is only a representation of it. This Ezekiel makes clear by his juxtaposition of "opening of the heavens" and "approach from the north", without harmonizing them; no representation can fully correspond to the reality.

At the first glance Ezekiel sees the divine epiphany as formless natural phenomena: storm, cloud, fire. Only in a few, though important, passages before him did the Old Testament make use of this possibility of describing the presence of God.[18] Through his exceptional situation as the prophet of God in a land far distant from God, Ezekiel saw himself occasioned to rely on traditions which hitherto hardly anyone had touched upon. The exiled Jews heard of gods that appear in the storm, who thunder in the storm cloud, who cast the thunderbolt. Such gods could show their power everywhere that storm and thunder raged. In the face of this, how must Yahweh appear to the Jews? Yahweh dwelt with his people — but this dwelling-place was in the utmost danger. Faced by such doubts, Ezekiel can counter with the old tradition of the theophany in the thunder cloud. Yahweh had already at his disposal the signs of power of which the strange gods can boast. So here Ezekiel mingles Israelite and foreign images, traditional and new material. By so doing he opens up new possibilities for religious language, that retain their vitality.

But Ezekiel's hearers could hear something different in the motifs of storm, fire and thunder. In the reports about the holy wars from the time of the conquest of the land and the judges, the tale had been told of Yahweh's unleashing against Israel's enemies the powers of nature, earthquake and storm. The prophets turned this motif upside down; God will send all these powers against sinful Israel.[19] Even Ezekiel indicates with these motifs that the coming of God bodes no good for Israel. The exiles had thought that God was far from them. Ezekiel teaches them that the exile does not mean God's absence but is a sign of the nearness of the angry God. Even in exile God has not ceased to be Israel's Lord.

> I will reign over you with a strong hand, with arm outstretched and with wrath outpoured (Ezekiel 20,32ff).

The description of the thunderstorm phenomenon closes surprisingly with the words which seem to be taken out of Ezekiel 1,27:

> And brilliant light about it, and within was a radiance like brass in the heart of the flames.

In 1,27 these words have their meaning; the divine form is surrounded by a radiance like brass, a shining envelope encircles it, God himself is concealed even in the moment of revelation.[20] But in 1,4 Ezekiel, by using the same words, forsakes the realm of what can be envisaged. The terrible natural phenomenon of thundercloud, lightning and storm is surrounded by a mild radiance, conceals in itself a centre of coloured light. The word "radiance" stirs to life memories of salvation and happiness, it recalls resplendent visions of God.[21] Again, as at the beginning, with the association of the "opened heavens" and "the north", mutually contradictory ideas are brought together. Ezekiel must repeatedly surpass the limits of human imagination. The heathens may experience their gods in thunder and storm, the greatness of Yahweh cannot be fittingly described by means of these signs. At the same time the though of the nearness of the terrible God is given a surprising turn; the nearness of God, is, in spite of everything a splendid experience that brings happiness. The suffering of the exiles receives a meaning, when God comes; the punishment is then no longer a cause for despair, for it is not abandonment by God.

The Four Living Creatures

The description of the theophany by means of formless natural phenomena is an old tradition in Israel. From verse 5 onwards Ezekiel departs from this tradition in a hitherto unprecedented manner. The phenomenon of the thunderstorm turns out on closer examination to be an elaborate structure of heavenly figures. Four strange living creatures that carry a platform, which is recognizable by its wheels as a chariot, above this a throne, and on it the figure of God. But this general picture the reader must first put together laboriously for himself; in a prosaic and circumstantial manner a bold symbolization of the presence of God is here set before us. For the sake of accuracy the prophet is not unwilling to repeat himself. In spite of this, no exact description is forthcoming. Has each living creature one leg or several (1,7)? If their faces point to the four corners of heaven, what then does "straight forward" mean? (1,12, Hebrew: "over against their face")? According to 11a their wings are stretched upwards, but according to 11b two are lowered, in order to cover the body. Why then so many details? This question arises above all for the reason that this description of the vision differs very much by reason of its length from the reticence of earlier models. If Ezekiel's intention was to prove by enumeration of many details the authenticity and probability of his vision, such ineptitudes as those mentioned above would be very damaging to him.

Yet nothing is further from the prophet's intention than to demonstrate the originality of his vision. Even in portraying the heavenly figures, he uses elements of a world of images that was familiar to his contemporaries, while fitting them into a new general picture. The tradition of Israel had for long spoken of heavenly beings in human form.[22] Ezekiel appeals to this, but he contradicts it in the same breath — every attempt of man to penetrate the heavenly reality must miscarry.

These "beings in human form" round about Yahweh he calls "living creatures"; in other contexts this word describes untamed animals. To be sure, they have a human face, but in addition they have three more animal faces; human hands are to be seen under their wings. The Babylonian temple guardians, beings that are a cross between a man and a beast, have probably been their models.

But Ezekiel can call upon the tradition of Israel even in the case of these composite beings. Isaiah had already pictured in like manner the six-winged seraphs in his vision (Isaiah 6). The conception of bearers of the divine throne in the form of beasts, or in the mixed forms of the Babylonian temple guardian was widely current in the ancient orient. Israel must have taken it over early, in the time when "the name of Yahweh, who is enthroned upon the cherubim, was mentioned over the ark" (2 Samuel 6,2). The statuesque rest, in which the living creatures hold their wings stretched upwards, remind us of the statuary in the temple at Jerusalem.[23]

Although the living creatures are described fully, they have no independent function. In the vision of Micaiah in 1 Kings 22, the heavenly host are taking counsel with one another; the seraphs in Isaiah 6 are calling to one another the praise of God — but the living creatures are joined together in rigid order. They are not even in themselves capable of bearing the throne. The whole apparatus, that is to move the throne of God — the living creatures with legs and wings, and the wheels to boot — is nothing but stiff imagery, only the one power of the spirit gives life to all the four creatures and the wheels.

Thus the living creatures are not portrayed for their own sake. In dealing with the subordinate throne bearers Ezekiel is rather venturing to image forth the experiences which were imparted to him by God himself. The four, the number of the points of the compass, determines the description: Yahweh is Lord of the world. For his throne-bearers the way in all four directions goes straight forward, for they have a face and wings on every side, their foot is circular: Yahweh can without effort appear everywhere that he wills. In the description of the wheels Ezekiel himself settles for lack of clarity in order to depict this mobility, even these do not need to turn when they move to the four points of the compass — are perhaps the four wheels telescoped into a spherical wheel? Not only in freedom of movement, but also in power, Yahweh excels all the gods. For even his servants describe him as possessing at the same time attributes which the gods each use only singly to demonstrate their powers.

The Fire

At a first glance it may appear as if Ezekiel was describing the divine phenomenon on the basis of a more exact "knowledge", as if he were more inquisitive than his Old Testament models. The traditional language of theophanies spoke of Yahweh's appearing *in* fire; Ezekiel "knows" that this fire is situated between the living creatures. But Ezekiel makes it unmistakably clear that even he cannot give a better picture of the divine mystery. He piles one simile upon another; the phenomenon between the living creatures is *like* a fire of coals and *like* torches; it moves flickering hither and thither and is for that very reason not to be clearly perceived. Then at first he definitely describes it as "fire", but at once calls this clarity in question; for the "fire" is described not only as a flash of lightning that rouses fear, but also as "splendour" a word that suggests salvation and happiness. Even the word "fire" is a way of describing God's activity, his angry and destroying will, and the salvation that his presence brings.

The Wheels

The wheels of which Ezekiel speaks evoke the picture of the chariot throne, and tempt us to compare Yahweh with the powerful gods of Mesopotamia; Yahweh drives in his chariot like the great sun-god, like the victorious Marduk in his struggle against the goddess of chaos. But fundamentally Yahweh is beyond comparison, since for him the chariot is an unnecessary accessory — the wheels are moved by "the spirit". For this reason, in spite of all his circumstantial details, Ezekiel is not at pains to depict clearly the function of the wheels; it remains completely obscure how they are connected with the chariot throne. It is more important for him to describe, in the image of its jewelled splendour and its adornment with eyes, something of the beauty of God, and to show that nothing can remain concealed from him.

The Platform

Neither is the depiction of the platform clearly outlined. Where is it attached? To the wheels. To the heads of the living creatures? Or to their outstretched wings? Again, it is more important to know what this figure tells us about God. The platform is called a "vault", as the firmament of heaven is also named; it is compared with a sheet of ice — people thought of the heavens as frozen water; it is outstretched as the heavens are above the earth.[24] Here the mighty Lord of heaven appears; the platform separates him from the living creatures; he is concealed even from the heavenly beings. In this vision God reveals himself as the distant and concealed God.

Even mighty thunderstorms, in which the heathen gods manifest themselves, reveal little of the power of this God. Even the wings of the lesser living creatures, which cannot even see Yahweh, move with a sound of thunder. And how are we to understand the thunder? For Ezekiel it is unimportant whether it is the voice of God, or the voice of the heavenly waters which the God of storm attacks, or the floods of chaos, which prepare to do battle against God.

God Enthroned

Long and carefully the prophet has prepared for his climax, the picture of the enthroned God. Even now his words approach the divine mystery with the greatest caution. Even with the living creatures, the fire, the wheels, the platform, Ezekiel had repeatedly emphasized that he could only describe the outer appearance, and even this only by means of similes. When he comes to describe God, he does not any the more leave the language of simile. The older prophets could say "I saw Yahweh".

Ezekiel sees only what Yahweh allows to be seen of him, and even that he can only reproduce approximately. Surrounded by fire and splendour, itself shining with metallic light and fire, the outlines of the divine figure can only be divined.

But such caution is united also to a boldness, which dares to say unprecedented new things about God. Yahweh remains concealed from the heavenly beings that bear the throne; even the seraphim in Isaiah 6 veil their faces before God; far less could the men to whom he appeared behold his form.[25] But Ezekiel at least sees so much that he can compare it with the human form. Here Ezekiel goes beyond all limits previously set. "Man" in Israel's thought is actually the antithesis of "God".[26] Ezekiel was quite aware of this. He himself was always addressed by God as "man" — not, as were other prophets, by his name. He was, as it were, overwhelmed by his god-given task and forced to give up all his individuality: in the presence of God he is nothing but "man", a weak creature. In spite of this Ezekiel ventures to speak of God's human form. He who is concealed in the depths of heaven, the overwhelmingly powerful and dreadful One, the Lord whose freedom cannot be comprehended, allows himself to be apprehended by puny man. The exiles could believe that they had lost everything that could bring them near to God: the land, the kingdom, Jerusalem and the temple. Then God himself comes to them along a road where there can no longer be any obstruction; he is no longer near to his own, as the chosen people, on whom he has bestowed the land, the king, and the temple; he is near to them as weak men.

In spite of such insight Ezekiel speaks even here not as a man who is carried away by his bold thoughts, he remains even here true to his circumstantial learned style. He closes the vision like a lecture with a summary; as scholars do, he seeks a new definition for the newly discovered phenomenon:

This was the appearance of the form of Yahweh.

It is of a piece with this sobriety that even here he does not behave like the discoverer of a new reality; that he remains the loyal interpreter of the tradition. The enthroned God appeared also to Isaiah and Micaiah ben Imlah; above the sapphire-like firmament, according to Exodus 24,10, the elders were permitted to see Yahweh; by ancient tradition the narrative of a call was not thinkable without an encounter with God.

It is striking how lengthy the description of this encounter is. How are we to understand this explicitness? The prophet who is to be called plays no part in the circumstantial description of the vision; it is not until the short continuation in Ezekiel 1,28b-3,15 that the other elements of the narrative concerning the call are taken up.

In the case of the earlier calls the description of the encounter with God served as accreditation before the people, but in Ezekiel's case it contains over and above this the message that he has to deliver: God is near even to the exiles. Another, second reason can be found for the increased importance of the divine epiphany: in this vision and call the foundation is laid for the thought of the holiness of God which permeates Ezekiel's preaching! Yahweh acts above all for his own sake; he wishes once more to vindicate the honour of his holy name, which was stained by the disgrace of his people. Further, the length of the description is an expression of the mentality of the priest's son: God's epiphany in the unclean land of the Gentiles must seem to Ezekiel himself as wholly unfitting to the holiness of God — the secrecy of the inmost temple would hardly have been the right place for it. Because Israel has sinned and has been punished by exile, Yahweh is compelled to reveal his holiness at such a place. Indeed he must emerge so far from his concealment, that Ezekiel can compare his form with that of humble men.

I became to them only in small measure a sanctuary in the lands to which they came (Ezekiel 11,16).

2. THE COMMISSION OF THE PROPHETS

The prophets, whose words the Old Testament hands down to us, were all active in the relatively short period of time in which the people of Israel saw itself caught up in the movement of world history (*circa* 800-450). The threat of the great powers of Egypt and the East, the end of the states of Israel and Judah, their absorption by the great powers, and finally the gathering together of the repatriated Jews, are the historical background of their activity. Their proclamation falls silent as soon as Judaism has consolidated itself and is able to lead its own life apart from the mainstream of history.

The Origin of Prophetism

In spite of this temporal contiguity it appears almost impossible to apprehend Israel's prophetism as a single movement, and to describe the literary forms peculiar to it. Even early Old Testament records show a great variety of forms of the prophetic phenomenon. We hear of bands of prophets who together fell into rapture, and could infect others (1 Samuel 10,5; 19,20ff); of the solitary wanderer Elijah, who appears everywhere that the cause of Yahweh is called in question (1 Kings 17ff); or the sons of the prophets who gather around their master Elisha (2 Kings 4ff); or the man of God or the seer, of whom inquiry may be made where to discover lost property (I Samuel 9); of prophets, whose task is to give information about the outcome of military issues (1 Kings 22); of the prophet Nathan, who lives permanently at the royal court (2 Samual 7; 1 Kings 1).

Further, from the point of view of the history of religion it is impossible to find one single source of the prophetism of Israel in the scanty tradition of other lands than Israel. The investigation of predictive signs and the consultation of divine utterances (oracles) with a view to understanding the future, may stand at the beginning of prophetism, but cannot explain its origin. The prophets carry out God's commission uninvited, often even against the will of the hearer. According to the Egyptian narrative of the journey of Wen Amon to Palestine, a young Canaanite discovered in a state of trance that Wen Amon was carrying about with him in concealment the statue of a god, and demanded that it should be worshipped. There are four letters, found in Mari (in Mesopotamia) and dating from the 18th century BC, which speak of official prophets, who on their own initiative exhort the king, and complain of defects in the observation of the cultus and in the administration of government. Such interest in political action is evident in Isaiah, Micaiah ben Imlah (1 Kings 22) Elijah and Jeremiah — but not in Amos. The aim of the political utterances of Old Testament prophets is, moreover, not human action, the correction of omissions — they announce God's action; they are not concerned with everyday events, nor individual cultic and religious acts, but with life and death, with the existence of the whole people.

Transformation of Linguistic Forms and Traditions

Just as we are unable to find any common origin of Old Testament prophecy, since there were from early times different forms of the prophetic phenomenon, so it is impossible to discover any fundamental form of prophetic language. The prophets took over existing linguistic forms, detached them from their actual *Sitz im Leben*, and made them serve new purposes. According to its form, Amos 5,1-3 is a funeral lament — but the speaker's intention is to threaten and exhort. Prophets develop the paradoxical form of a satirical funeral lament.[27] Ezekiel harks back to folk-tales, though he was anything but a narrator of folk-lore.[28] Isaiah uses the form of a love-song (Isaiah 5,1-7) or of the wisdom-teaching (Isaiah 28,23ff), but in so doing has nothing in common with a minstrel or a teacher of wisdom. Even categories of religious speech are given a new function. Amos 1,3-2,16 may resemble the structure of Egyptian comminations whose aim is to call down curses on one's enemies; Jeremiah (chapter 19) may imitate the ritual action of banishment, the breaking of a clay vessel — but the prophets are by no means cult-functionaries of the ritual transaction of outlawry. On entrance into the temple the worthiness of the participant in public worship was ascertained in question and answer:

Who may dwell in the holy mountain?[29]

But in Isaiah 33,14 this question is only asked rhetorically — no one is worthy to approach this God:

Who may live with a devouring fire?

Even satirical distortion of religious categories is not alien to the prophets. In Israel's tradition there was the so-called cultic decree, the priestly information (*tōrāh*) concerning how the sacrifice and prayer pleasing to God must appear. Amos 4,4f imitates this *tōrāh*, but in irony he challenges men to a worship of idols that is pleasing to men.

What the prophets had to impart could not be fitted into any form, so far did it transcend what Israel had hitherto known of Yahweh. No new, specifically prophetic form was found to contain this content. The prophets announce judgement in forms that are borrowed from secular procedures, in order to communicate God's words they make use of the originally secular language concerning messengers. Exegesis must do justice to this tension between content and form. It must not only exactly distinguish between the original function of a literary form and the intention of the prophetic speech, it must also each time determine the relation between the two.

Stable categories of speech are created above all in a society of people that know common experiences and anxieties and have developed stable forms of communal life. The outsider often does not know what the speaker means. Form criticism investigates such forms of language. It seeks to know and to understand the connection of each text considered with the life and institutions of such a society (*Sitz im Leben!*) When it investigates prophetic texts, form-critical inquiry soon comes up against its limitations. The prophets cannot be fully fitted into any of the institutions and social groupings of Israel. They are individuals.

The Yahweh similes of the prophets give a clear indication of this. Through a long period of time Israel had created for itself a cultic language in which people could speak of God and speak to him — a language which in all reverence could still reflect even the personal experiences of the individual in relation to God, including disappointments and reproach (cf the language of the psalms). The prophets forsake these linguistic conventions and use "hair-raising similes without dignity and respectability"[30] Yahweh, the rock in whom the worshippers in the Psalms put their trust, has become "the stone of stumbling" (Isaiah 8,14); God has wearied himself to no avail with heavy labour in the vineyard (Isaiah 5,1ff); he is the disappointed loving adoptive father of a foundling child that grows up to be a harlot (Ezekiel 16,4ff); he seeks the sinners in the streets of Jerusalem with a lantern in the hand (Zephaniah 1,12); he is a festering sore in the body of the people (Hosea 5,12); he is a barber shaving head and body with a hired razor (Isaiah 7,20).

Nineteenth century exegesis discovered prophecy as an independent phenomenon. Wellhausen, Duhm, and others saw in the prophets the great lonely summits in the landscape of the Old Testament. They opposed the prophets' message to "the law", to the traditions of the Pentateuch. This legal tradition was more and more levelled down and accommodated to the general study of religion. They held that the prophecy of Israel had raised itself above this in a towering religious achievement.

Today we can no longer look upon the unique greatness of the prophets of Israel as men did in the first enthusiasm of discovery. To be sure the prophets cannot be fitted into any fellowship and order of Israel,

209

but they remain within the traditions of their people. Their message does indeed rupture all familiar literary forms, but they remain in constant contact with the old faith of Israel. They come from the same traditions from which the pentateuch took shape: Yahweh has chosen Israel; he has bestowed life upon the people and continually preserved it; he requires that Israel should acknowledge this fact by obedience to the commandment. It is only because they hold fast to this faith that their own experiences — the threat to Israel and its end — become a problem. They are lonely among their people, but not as revolutionaries who explode old traditions. Still less are they reformers, who only seek to bring to honour the faith of the past, the original loyalty, that had been forgotten. The fact is rather, that they have learnt from the standpoint of the present, to see the old traditions of election in a new light. A foundation of Israel's faith is, for example, the confession concerning the deliverance from Egypt — Amos 9,7 places this event in a fundamentally new context.

Did I not bring Israel up from Egypt,
the Philistines from Caphtor, the Aramaeans from Kir?

The Prophets as Individuals

What was it that gave the prophets such freedom in relation to the language-forms and traditions of their people? What made them such unforgettable figures in the ancient world that was so ruled by conventions?

Even their environment obviously valued the prophets as unique personalities. Their sayings, speeches and their stories were collected and handed down under their names. It is only natural that we should not know any of the names of the people who handed down the sagas of the fathers, that the traditions of the pentateuch were handed on anonymously — for many individuals and many generations formed them. But it must appear strange to us that even the author of the famous "History of David's Succession to the Throne" remains unknown to us. Although it was unquestionably a genius who shaped this work, which leaves far behind it the historical representations of the ancient orient, the work was regarded by the tradition as of more importance than the author. But the message of the prophets, in the eyes of the tradition, obviously could not be abstracted from their persons.[31]

We must, however, take care not to regard the prophets as personalities in the modern sense, as distinguished, perhaps, by free originality or a wholly independent creativity. They are made unique figures by the revelation which each one of them has received for himself, through obedient hearing of a word that is directed to every individual among them. They know themselves to be different from their contemporaries, not by reason of their own reflections, but by reason of the word of God that is embedded in them, which they must speak forth, and from which they cannot escape.

The lion has roared; who is not terrified?
The Lord Yahweh has spoken; who will not prophesy?[32]
They understand themselves as the mouth, through which God speaks.[33] They have not at all times free power of disposal over their prophetic word; they must rather wait until God causes his word to come to them. When the false prophet Hananiah contradicts Jeremiah, the latter must at first go his way in silence until he receives a new commission from God.[34] They are individuals, but not independent. In obedience to the divine commission the prophets see themselves in a manner hitherto unprecedented brought into the midst of things with their responsibility. For this reason the prophetic commission is continually changing, always according to the personality of the prophet and the historical hour.

Isaiah is aware of the freedom of his obedience from the hour of his call. He hears Yahweh ask in the heavenly assembly, "Whom shall I send?" and, without waiting for the answer of the heavenly beings, he places himself at God's disposal (Isaiah 6,8).

Ezekiel's case is quite different. By his own power he is not capable of standing in God's presence and hearing God's word; God's spirit must first give him the power to accept the divine commission (Ezekiel 2,1f). Yet even he is more than a mere speaking-trumpet and inert vessel for the word of God. He knows himself to be compelled, by the threat of the loss of his own life, to go after all those who are his fellow-exiles, one by one, and to exhort them to return to God. He is appointed by Yahweh as a watcher, in order to warn of the deadly danger which Yahweh himself constitutes for sinful Israel. With his responsibility he stands as final protection between the people and God (Ezekiel 33).

The second Isaiah, the other great prophet of the exile, understands his office in a similar manner, he seeks to converse with the faint-hearted and the weary.[35]

The pre-exilic prophets spoke in another tone to the Israelites, who, in proud confidence in their election or in forgetfulness of God still felt themselves secure in the land; they confronted the whole public with the sentence of judgement, exhorted and warned the people in general.

In contrast with this, *Nahum*, in a particular historical situation, appears as a bearer of good tidings, not as a warning and threatening herald of judgement to come upon Israel. He celebrates the overthrow of Assyria (612 B.C.); his message could have been pronounced within public worship, at a joyful festival. On the other hand it is unthinkable that other prophets performed their task as cult-functionaries. An official of the cultus had no need to authenticate himself by reference to a special call from God. The message of a final judgement of God upon Israel could hardly have found its place in the cultus. People celebrate public worship in order to find there new access to salvation, but the prophets proclaim the certainty of judgement.

An end is come upon Israel (Amos 8,2).

211

If the prophets for the most part feel themselves compelled to deliver the divine message of judgement, with Habakkuk the rôles are reversed: Yahweh is the one who is challenged; the prophet presses for an answer that explains the delay of the long-awaited salvation.

So in the case of each of the prophets we must in each case ask afresh for the nature of his commission — even the changing linguistic forms which the prophets use to deliver their message, are to be explained in the context of this continually changing task.

Even in the duration of their public ministry the individual prophets differ: Amos probably had an activity of only a few months, until he was expelled from the state of Israel as an alien Judaean. Isaiah knew himself to be commissioned to prophetic activity at determinate times — at other times he regarded himself as discharged from the prophetic office.[36] Jeremiah's call was for lifelong service. His prophetic calling did not only include the proclamation of the message of judgement, but also compassion with his people in an increasingly sombre destiny. Finally, the servant of God, whose coming Deutero-Isaiah proclaims, stands in unbroken communion with Yahweh; he does not need to wait for the word of God in continually changing situations (Isaiah 50,4).

Many special characteristics of these great individuals must therefore be taken into account, when we attempt to describe the linguistic forms used by the prophets. Yet there are also elements of continuity. Jeremiah, for example, harks back to his predecessors. In the first proclamations of his youth he imitates Hosea; when brought to court he appeals to the prophet Micah (Jeremiah 26,18). A common prophetic tradition was formed. The prophets included themselves as members in the historical fellowship of prophetism, they did not regard themselves as individuals. Above all, two things are common to them: each knows himself called in a special manner, and responsible for the people among whom he lives. They worked in public and for the public, and for their contemporaries. This is connected with the fact that they were not writers, but speakers. Their language is expressive of the intention of exercising an immediate influence upon their hearers.

Interpretation of the Present

They wish to interpret to their hearers the events of contemporary history in the light of faith in Yahweh. Yahweh has not only guided history in the past, when he led Israel out of Egypt into the land, when he chose David — he is also active in the historical events of the present. The mightiest kings of the great empires are only his tools. Never hitherto had anyone observed the historical transformations of the present so watchfully as did the prophets. They see themselves at the beginning of a new hour in history which Yahweh will inaugurate for his people. Their message is elicited by the expectation of something to come that is immediately imminent. God has something hitherto unprecedented in store for his people. Yahweh is bringing Israel to an end

(Amos 8,2). The prophets are compelled to announce this divine plan.[37]

But neither their threat of judgement nor their expectation of salvation can be described as prediction. The prophets do not wish to foretell the future course of history. They do not wish to force their hearers to consider in future whether history follows the course that they predicted. Therefore we are not being just to them if we expect such a kind of fulfilment. To the prophets it seems to be almost a matter of indifference what the future course of events looks like in concrete details. Hosea can just as much threaten banishment to Egypt as to Assyria.[38]

In Aeschylus the Trojan king's daughter Cassandra can predict the future because she has prophetic insight into the inevitable events predetermined by the ancient curse. The prophets are different; they know that what is to come is not inevitably determined. Both men and God can still freely influence it. The prophetic proclamation of immediately impending judgement is intended to give last-minute warning; the hearers have still just time to align themselves with the will of God. By proclaiming disaster before it comes, the prophets are teaching Israel not to look on the coming events as the anonymous decrees of fate, not merely as the consequence of political inferiority to the great powers — but to see in them the free decision of God.

The announcement of what is to come can have a further significance. According to ancient conceptions, the word that has once been spoken has a continuing influence. The prophets see themselves compelled to hasten by their threatening words the evil that God is bringing upon Israel. This is what is to be understood when Isaiah receives the commission to speak to Israel and thereby to lead the people into disaster and godforsakenness (Isaiah 6,9f). The word of God which the prophets transmit does not only proclaim the coming event, disaster or salvation, but also causes it. This is how the hearers of the prophets also understand it. Elijah has to fear for his life and to flee, Amos is expelled because "the country cannot tolerate what he is saying" (Amos 7,10). Jeremiah has the fear of death put on him when he proclaims God's word to the king (Jeremiah 38,15). The Israelites were convinced that if they got rid of the messenger who proclaimed disaster, they could also get rid of the disaster itself.

In Israel there were special "categorial descriptions" for each type of utterance, of the prophets, the priests, and the wise men respectively. The giving of "instruction" was in Israel the task of the priest; he had to keep before the eyes of the people their permanent obligation to keep God's commandments. The wise men gave "counsel"; their task was to enable men to do the right thing through free consideration and decision in the changing situations of life. But the "word" belonged to the prophets; they proclaimed was was to happen, and by so doing they brought about the event (Jeremiah 18,18). "The word of Yahweh" is really to be regarded as a prophetic technical term. O. Grether has reckoned that this expression occurs 241 times in the Old Testament, and that among these 225 instances refer to the word of God which has been given to the prophets. In the law also, which the priests proclaimed, God spoke. But the word of God in the law was meant to be valid for all times, it must be passed down word for word, fixed as far as possible in writing. Israel expected another kind of word of God from the prophets.[39] Its purpose was to intervene in determinate historical situations, to proclaim an event, and thereby bring it to pass. As the king Ahijah is worshipping the idol Beelzebub, the prophet Elijah proclaims to him such a word of God;

This is the word of Yahweh; you shall not rise from the bed where you are lying, you will die (2 Kings 1,4).

This word is extremely important — until it has been fulfilled.

The word of Yahweh which Elijah had spoken was fulfilled, and Ahijah died (2 Kings 1,17).

Israel could trace the whole divine law back to the one mediator Moses, but it needed many prophets who ever and again intervened in changing historical situations with the power of the word of God. For this reason Israel did not think of retaining the prophetic word, so long as it could always count on new prophetic revelation.

3. CATEGORIES OF PROPHETIC LANGUAGE

Messenger Sayings

It is not easy, beginning with the linguistic categories, to learn anything about the specific self-understanding of the prophets: the prophets imitate other categories and modify them to suit their own use. An exception is the speech of the messenger sent by God. We encounter this form of speech exclusively in the prophetic literature. The messenger's formula "Thus Yahweh has spoken" or "Utterance of Yahweh" strikes every reader of the prophetic books. Where it is missing it can be heard as an undertone originating in the superscription of the prophetic book. It is improbable that the prophets ever announced a speech of God without using this formula.

But even this category of the messenger's speech — it connects the messenger formula with the speech of the sender of the messenger — was not created by the prophets themselves. The secular messenger's speech has the same form.[40]

Like this, the speech of the prophetic messenger is an oral category. The prophets only used written proclamations in cases of necessity. God's word is meant to be heard in the immediate contact of person with person.

What does this prophetic category tell us about the self-understanding of the prophets?

Israel shared with other peoples the conception that God sends messengers who carry out his commissions. Heavenly beings from his court mediate between God and the world, deliver in his name the word to men.[41] The prophets refrain from calling themselves "messengers" like these beings.[42] In the vision which constituted his call, Isaiah stands together with the heavenly beings before the throne of the Lord. But it is not the heavenly ones that are commissioned, it is the man. Even here the word "messenger" is avoided. "Whom shall I send? Who will go for us?" asks God. The prophets felt that man cannot in the full sense be God's messenger; they know themselves to be transmitters of Yahweh's threats and promises, not representatives in whom Yahweh himself is present.[43]

We must not see them in the role of mere speaking-tubes, but rather in that of translators who must deliver the message of God intelligibly to those who receive it. This, among other things, can be seen by the fact that they also make use of traditional literary forms familiar to their hearers, for the utterances of God, whose content is usually threat or promise.

Forms of Divine Speech

Three such forms will be described here. (1) Deutero-Isaiah puts "I-am" statements in Yahweh's mouth, which are formed after the model of *self-praise of the gods*. (In Babylonian hymns the gods boast in the presence of their rivals.)[44] Deutero-Isaiah carries this boasting of the gods *ad absurdum*, for beside Yahweh there is no god (Isaiah 45,5). (2) Early prophets encouraged Israel's kings before battle with divine utterances in the form of so-called *divine self-manifestations*.

I give you the rabble of your enemies today into your hand, that you may know that I am Yahweh (1 Kings 20,13.28).

Ezekiel harks back to this saying: through the predicted deeds of God "Israel and the Gentile peoples shall know that I am Yahweh".[45] This formula shows that Israel's wellbeing is not the final goal of divine action, but the acknowledgement of God. (3) A third form of the divine utterance gives us at the same time insight concerning the relationship of the prophets to public worship. According to a number of texts which cover the whole period of prophecy, Yahweh repudiates Israel's cultus. People have seen in such passages a conflict between cultus and God's moral commandments. The prophets, it is claimed, had required "know-ledge of God" instead of "sacrifice".[46] This is in the first place a misunderstanding of Israel's public worship, in which the preaching of obedience to God's commandments played an important part. In the second place, the message of the prophets is also misinterpreted. They do not speak about the cultus from outside; they deliver their judgement in words that come from the cultus itself. God does not "accept with good pleasure" the sacrifice, he does not "hear" the prayers. In these terms God was asked to accept the sacrifice and the prayer.[47] God did not hear and answer automatically. The Israelite had usually to wait for a *cultic decision* which probably priests gave in the name of Yahweh. The

215

prophets use this form. Yahweh's proclamations of judgements which they announce, do not repudiate the whole cultus; what they do is rather to give a negative cultic decision, because the participants in the cultus are guilty.

Forms of the Prophetic Word

The prophets saw themselves not merely commissioned as messengers to transmit God's word. They justify God's judgement with their own words. The connection of God's word and the justifying prophetic word is a characteristic form of speech of the Old Testament prophets. Here two different sides of the prophetic commission find expression. By their public utterance of the divine decision the prophets play their part in the realization of the judgement which they proclaim; once spoken, the word has become a fact whose influence continues, which is to be reckoned with. But by seeking to justify this word of God they prove that they are educators of the people. Their first aim is to challenge the people to acknowledge their own guilt, so that it cannot avoid acknowledging that the consequent decree of judgement is justified.

Often they choose the form of personal address to the guilty parties. Here they quote their own words, in order to allow them no loophole of escape. Time and again they seek to alarm the guilty by denunciations of woe; the subsequent threat is already an undertone in the introductory "Woe!"[48] The recipient of the threatening message must see that in punishing, Yahweh is only returning on his own head the evil that he himself has done. Therefore punishment often exactly fits the crime: the man who trusted in swift horses rather than in God will be compelled to flee swiftly (Isaiah 30,16); the man who oppressed others, is himself oppressed (Habakkuk 2,6ff); the man who unjustly took possession of the land, is dispossessed (Micah 2,1-5).[49]

Such prophetic *invectives* are to be understood as *speeches of warning*. Their aim is to let Israel know that it still has time to prepare for the coming fate, which Yahweh has prepared for it. The connection of word of God and prophetic justification is so characteristic of the prophets, that the exegetes have coined for it the term *"prophetic saying"*.

Changes of Forms in the Later Period

After the time of Jeremiah the "prophetic sayings" are less in evidence. *Prophetic lament* and *lament to Yahweh* may take the place of the invective. Both are distinguished by their broad expansive form from the curt brevity of the messenger sayings. With this the boundary between the speech of God and the speech of the prophet becomes indistinct (cf Jeremiah 2ff).

The speeches of God in the older prophecy are short, and most of them have a striking rhythmical form; the language, breaking into stately verse, shows that a judgement from the celestial realm of God is breaking into Israel's day to day life. In contrast thereto, for example in Jeremiah

7,1-15, a whole *sermon* is stylized as God's word. The aim of a sermon is to convince rather than to overwhelm — the prose form corresponds to this.

The climax of the speech in Jeremiah 7 is God's threat to destroy the temple:

Therefore what I did to Shiloh I will do to this house which bears my name, the house in which you put your trust, the place I gave to you and your forefathers (Jeremiah 7,14).[50]

Compare with this the threat uttered in Micah 3,12:

Therefore, on your account
Zion shall become a ploughed field,
Jerusalem a heap of ruins,
and the temple hill a rough heath.

In the threefold parallelism of Micah only the one inexorable fact is stated; God has spoken over the temple the decree of destruction. The three-fold repetition of the verdict makes its fulfilment all the more inevitable. The threat expressed in Jeremiah 7 makes a different impression. Here it is not left to the hearer to elaborate in any way the horror about the threatened destruction of the temple. Rather, the prose form permits their possible objections to be included in the threat. The destruction of the temple is placed within the context of Israel's religious traditions: God knows that he is acting in glaring contradiction to the election traditions of the people. He sets against this contradiction the contradiction of the people to its duties under the covenant. If the purpose of the poetic form of threat is to make the occurrence of judgement inevitable, the purpose of the prose form is to make it impossible for the hearers to avoid the word of disaster. The prophetic sermons which are only to be found in the later prophetic books, (especially Jeremiah and Ezekiel), are marked by the efforts of the prophets to convince their hearers. The principal purpose of the prophetic sayings on the other hand is to shake the hearers, by confronting them with facts, with their guilt, and its consequence, the divine judgement.

Disputation

Even though the accents of the individual prophets are laid on different points, they always pay attention to both sides of their commission, to deliver God's message, and to touch men in their particular situation. They are not content to be messengers of God's word. They defend and explain this word against objections, doubts, and arguments of the hearers. Polemical disputes as we know them from the tradition about Jesus are not to be found in the prophetic books, but the answers to words of opponents (words of disputation).[51]

Thus, for example, we note that Isaiah in the parable of the farmer defends Yahweh's action before sceptics: the many activities of the farmer can appear senseless to the uninitiated — and just so it may happen to the ignorant layman when he sees the divine activity (Isaiah

28,23-29). It is notable that Isaiah himself has to assure us that this kind of apologetic speech is a part of his commission:
This message, too, comes from the LORD of hosts.[52]

Linguistic Forms taken from Judicial Life
In our earlier description of prophetic forms of speech, in addition to the wider concepts of invective and threat, the terms "accusation" and "judgement" were also used, which both, strictly speaking, describe speech-forms of judicial life. The prophets often made their utterances similar to this special form of invective and threat. It is even conceivable that the accusation was the original form of speech from which the invective developed.

Israel's religious traditions saw the relation of Yahweh to the people in judicial categories. Yahweh had bestowed the covenant on the people. The covenant treaty was based on the protection and deliverance that God of his free-will gave to the people. This treaty laid covenant obligations on the people, but not on the sovereign Lord who granted the covenant. It is here, indeed, that we must see the centre of Israel's judicial thinking. All the tradition of the law attaches itself to the traditions of the making of the covenant. So there was really no secular judicial life. All the ordinances according to which Israel lived, had their origin in the last resort in its obligation to the God of the covenant. The prophet Elijah does not only confront Ahijah, who has sought an oracle from Baal, he confronts also Ahab who has illegally appropriated Naboth's vineyard. Both of them hear words from the prophet which might be taken from an action at law before Yahweh the judge. The accusation by the prophet is followed in the messenger's speech by the divine judgement (1 Kings 21,17ff; 2 Kings, 1,3).

Anyone who reads the prophetic judicial speeches from a modern standpoint may be surprised that Yahweh is at once accuser and judge. He is accuser in his own case and gives judgement (Hosea 4,1-3; Jeremiah 2,10-12). A glance at the legal system of Israel will serve to explain. Even in the customary processes of law, the hearers of the prophets were not acquainted with any fixed delimitation of roles. There was no public prosecutor, charges were normally brought by the injured party. This is not contradicted by the fact that in Isaiah 3,13-15 Yahweh makes accusation on behalf of the poor of his nation against those in Israel who in fact should have defended the rights of these poor people — but even here he is himself an interested party, what is at stake is the survival of his people.

In the administration of public justice in Israel the accuser may propose a sentence, the judge can be a witness to the crime that has been committed; Saul can act in relation to Ahimelech as at the same time accuser and judge (1 Samuel 22,6ff). So we do not need to be surprised when Yahweh the judge himself brings forward evidence in Israel's favour (Jeremiah 2.1-3; cf also Leviticus 26,45).

Occasionally, however forms of speech are also to be found in the prophets that must have shocked Israel's feeling for justice. Yahweh defends himself, or challenges Israel to go to law with him.[53] In this case who would be judge?

These prophetic texts are understandable, when we think that already in the tradition of the covenant treaty between God and the people the secular form of justice was modified. The guardians of a covenant which a sovereign granted to his vassal were the gods — they are, for example called upon in Hittite treaties to punish breakers of the covenant. But Yahweh's covenant with Israel could not be protected by any authority except him — he himself keeps watch over his covenant.

The people that accused this Lord of the covenant is doubly lacking in understanding. It should surely have known that Yahweh, whom it compels to defend himself, will himself as judge utter the verdict. The reproach of breaking the covenant which Israel directs against Yahweh is really directed at itself. For the sovereign Lord of the covenant has no duties that can become the grounds of an accusation. If the people still accuses him, it has already silently transformed the covenant of a sovereign into a covenant between equals, in which both parties give each other rights and duties. Thus Israel has broken the covenant — this fact underlies the speech-form of the judge's self-defence, and his challenge to a settlement at law of outstanding questions. These really senseless forms of speech are intended to bring drastically before the eyes of the hearers the senselessness of their behaviour.

Parable

Isaiah 5,1ff marks a culminating point in this art of the prophets in surprising their hearers with paradoxes. The text begins like a love song: "I will sing for my beloved". It continues by describing the wearisome labour which is entailed by the laying-out of a new vineyard. Inexplicably, all the labour turns out to be in vain. Here already the attentive hearer would realize that Isaiah was not concerned to display his knowledge of viticulture. The vineyard is a parable, the failure of the vinedresser is only intelligible when the figure is interpreted, when it is understood what is meant by the vineyard.

Jesus frequently used the prophetic speech-form of the parable. The most of his parables require the same method of interpretation. The place in the parable narrative is to be sought which at the level of the figure is paradoxical. Here the interpretation engages with the figure; this is the point of the parable. The interpretation of a parable does not require all the particulars of the figure to be transferred. What it must do is to start from the main statement, from the "point of departure" at which the parable passes into the interpretation. This change over from the figure to the interpretation in Isaiah's vineyard song is to be found at the point where it speaks of the fruitlessness of the vinedresser's work.

A second surprising turning-point is characteristic of the parabolic style. The interpretation appears at first to be a purely intellectual task; the hearers think that they can keep their distance from the story. Isaiah actually challenges his hearers to keep their distance. He appeals to them as impartial judges between vineyard and vinedresser. (So David at first had contemplated from a distance the parable of the prophet Nathan, and, full of scorn, had spoken his judgement about the shameless rich man (2 Samuel 12).) Yet God takes from them their judicial office and himself delivers the verdict — they are the accused.

The vineyard of the LORD of Hosts is the house of Israel.

The parable cannot be interpreted by the hearers in the cool light of reason, for in the interpretation their own fate is disclosed. (So David too, who imagined that he was the judge, becomes the accused: "You are the man!")

If we compare Ezekiel's *figurative language*[54] with Isaiah's song of the vineyard, a similar change is evident to that which underlay the transition from the prophetic saying to the prophetic sermon. As a judge compels the accused man to confess his guilt by suddenly producing before him the *corpus delicti*, so the intention of the parable is suddenly to unmask the guilty parties and startle them out of their security. Ezekiel's figurative speeches on the other hand are meant to be taken as artistic literary productions; he gives his utterances a stylized expansive baroque poetic form.

Speech-forms in Deutero-Isaiah

It is not possible within a restricted space to give an account of all the literary forms of prophetic speech. Above all, it is difficult to describe clearly the forms of the exilic and post-exilic periods. Here the place of the short saying is taken by longer linguistic units which cannot always be clearly defined. If in the case of the pre-exilic prophets it was nearly always possible to recognize the model which they were imitating, when, for example they chose forms of speech from judicial life or from the cultus, it is not always possible in the case of the later prophets to connect the linguistic forms with definitive situations.

The form of *dispute with the gods* which Deutero-Isaiah uses probably comes from the judicial sphere. Here the situation is different from that envisaged God's dispute with Israel. Here we are not concerned with the rectification of a crime. What is at stake is rather the decision between two claims at law. Who has the right to say that he guides the destinies of the peoples? The situation is not quite clear: Yahweh is a claimant, but at the same time he is in charge of the process of arbitration. Thus from the beginning he is the dominant figure. Yet for all that the gods are so far acknowledged that Yahweh will hear them and test their arguments.[55]

In the *dispute with Israel*[56] the people is the accuser. In a kind of disputation before the court God opposes the accusations of the people. By so doing he allows the people more than it has a right to expect. In reality the people had only deserved condemnation; for it has no right to accuse the Lord of the covenant. But God does not reject it; he takes its standpoint seriously and gives a reason to Israel for his behaviour.

It is not only in passages of dialogue which are dependent on the speech-forms of the courts that accusation is made against God in Deutero-Isaiah. Many words of God in this prophet can be understood as answers to questions of the people. Why have you forsaken us? Why are you silent? Why do you conceal yourself? How long are you going to abandon us, to hide your face, to make us drink the cup of your anger?[57]

This kind of accusation of God has its origin in the communal laments. Other prophets before him had already used the form of the communal lament, in order to pronounce their message.[58] Yet Deutero-Isaiah uses the model differently from his predecessors. Formally it is not left unchanged, the questions mentioned above are not quoted. They are only to be inferred from the *divine answer* that is given to them.

The form is not only filled with new meaning, but is itself recast. Even in content the answer leads beyond the circle of ideas handled in the communal lament. The authors of the lament had only paid attention to their own fate, here they are made aware of the vastness of creation. They have no reason to complain. The God whom they reproach for not helping them has in truth willed their salvation from the very beginning, from the creation.[59]

With a like freedom Deutero-Isaiah adopts the language-forms of the hymns. He creates the new form of *the eschatological hymn of praise*. After the introductory summons to praise, the report about God's deeds only appear to look backwards. In reality this report announces God's impending action. Through its announcement God's salvation becomes so much a present reality, that the prophet already challenges men to answer him with praise.[60]

The faith and trust of Israel must vindicate itself by the fact that God's future saving action finds an echo now, already. Thus the liturgical language of the Psalms characterizes the promise that this prophet makes to the exiles. Even where he indicates or quotes the thoughts of his hearers, he uses the style of public prayer. He sees his audience as a praying congregation. His language might therefore be described as a *sermon suited for pubic worship*, as exhortation.

4. CATEGORIES OF REPORTS ABOUT THE PROPHETS

Reports in the First Person

In contrast with the speeches of the prophets, reports about them take up only a small space in the prophetic books. Beside the reports which speak of the prophets in the third person (cf Isaiah 7), *the reports of the prophets concerning themselves* attract attention. Their first personal character is unusual in the literature of the ancient east. To be sure an "I" speaks also in the laments and hymns of gratitude, but the experiences of

221

the worshipper can just as well be those of others, his words hold good for many. In contrast with this the prophets see themselves called out from the instutitional life of their times. What they report about themselves to their contemporaries opens new fields to the latter. Yet we must not understand these accounts as autobiographical in the sense that here a man wished to depict his life as exemplary or as interesting and unique. This can be seen already from the fact that these reports are indeed stamped with the patterns of categories of a universal interest.

A number of *reports concerning symbolic actions of the prophets* have been handed down to us, mostly in the form of first-person reports. To us it may seem remarkable that a prophet went about barefoot for three years and half-naked (Isaiah 20,1ff) and that another wore a wooden and then an iron yoke on his neck (Jeremiah 28), but their contemporaries were familiar with symbolic actions.[61] And yet the thing that the prophets intended to express by their symbolic actions must have caused surprise. The reports regularly begin with the command of God to perform a symbolic action — the report of its execution can understandably be omitted; the latter was taken for granted. Nearly always eyewitnesses of this action are mentioned, the meaning of the procedure is always interpreted. The priests of heathen oracles might announce in ecstasy and in confused speech the words of the gods — Israel's prophets pass on intelligible news of God's intentions, not only in their utterances as messengers, but also in their symbolic actions.

But their commission includes still more than this. The symbolic actions are not meant merely to illustrate the message. If that were the case, what would be the meaning of the commission to perform an action being given, long before Yahweh gives the interpretation (Jeremiah 8,1ff; 20,1ff)? The man commissioned by Jeremiah sinks the documents containing the curse in the Euphrates without anyone being there to see (Jeremiah 51,59-64); in the report of Ezekiel 4,4-8 it appears unnecessary that anyone should see how for days he lies still first on his left, and then on his right side. We might be tempted by such passages to give a magical interpretation to the prophetic symbolic actions: that their aim was not to communicate God's will to the faithful, but purely through their performance to effect what they represent. There might be memories of a kind of analogy-magic underlying the prophetic symbolic actions, but the prophets gave them another meaning. They do indeed look on their action as efficacious, it brings about what it represents, but they ascribe such power, not to themselves, but to God who gave them their commission. God's will speaks in these actions, and it will prevail.

They do not, however allow a separation to be made between their person and their office; with their whole being they are committed to the divine will. This becomes particularly clear in situations where they have to perform actions involving themselves. The prophets are compelled to marry (Hosea 1) or remain celibate (Jeremiah 16); Ezekiel is not permitted to mourn the death of his wife (Ezekiel 24,15ff); the names of the prophet's children are determined by God (Isaiah 8,1ff; Hosea 1). The form of the first-person narrative is here given its special significance. The prophet's being is wholly engaged by God's commission. But with all this the prophets do not wish to sever themselves from the mass of the people. They experience first in their own persons the reality of the word of God, which determines the fate of the whole people. When Ezekiel lies down for a long time as if in chains, he feels in his own body what it means to bear Israel's and Judah's guilt. Hosea expresses his solidarity with the sinful people when he lives with a wife who has stained her virginity through cultic surrender to the idols. When Jeremiah may not share in the mourning and festivals of his fellow-countrymen, he anticipates in his loneliness the destiny of the people.

Still more clearly is the category of the *report concerning the prophetic call* stamped by both the fundamental characteristics of the prophetic commission. The person of the prophet in its absolute uniqueness is involved in his vocation, but through his vocation the individual only carries out what many others before and after him received as God's commission. In the first-personal reports of their call the prophets bear witness to a personal experience that changed their whole life — but they thoroughly formalize these reports according to the same model. They are not diary-entries concerning an overwhelming mystical experience, but products of a later reflexion about this experience. These reports are public proclamations of the prophetic claim and are constructed out of the following elements:

1) Encounter with God.   4) Objection of the prophet.
2) Preparation of the prophet.   5) Assurance of divine help.
3) Commissioning   6) Accrediting sign.

Clearly the prophets did not themselves create this form of narrative relating to their call; a messenger commissioned by men reports in a similar way concerning his mission. When Abraham's servant, who went to ask for the hand of a bride, wishes to accredit himself to the Mesopotamian relatives as a genuine messenger of Abraham, he follows in his speech a similar order. The prophets seize upon these forms lying ready to their hand in order to accredit themselves to the people in the reports of their call as messengers of God.

At the same time they imitate the narratives of the commissioning of Moses and Gideon.[62] By so doing they represent themselves as mediators of the divine activity, just as Moses and Gideon were. Like Moses and Gideon they would contribute to the fulfilment of God's work.

In the call reports the prophets also are correspondingly not only commissioned to *say* something to the people, but also to *work* among the people.

> This day I give you authority over nations and over kingdoms, to pull down and to uproot, to destroy and to demolish, to build and to plant (Jeremiah 1,10).

The prophets are more than messengers, in addition they are active to bring about the end of the people.[63] Thus the hopelessness of Isaiah's and Ezekiel's service as messengers is brought before our eyes. The people will not listen to Isaiah's words. Because it has received God's message through the prophets it will sink still further into its disobedience.

The description of the encounter with God is a part of the report concerning the call. It is striking how strictly the prophets refrain from any speculation. Amos sees Yahweh, who holds a plumb-line. To the question "What do you see?" he answers "A plumb-line" (Amos 7,7). In the report of Jeremiah it only subsequently becomes clear, that he not only heard God, but also saw him. For as he speaks of the sign of accreditation, we read:

Yahweh stretched out his hand and touched my mouth (Jeremiah 1,9).

Only when we bring Jeremiah 23, 18.22 into consideration are we able to assume that Jeremiah saw God surrounded by the heavenly council in session.[64]

In contrast with this Isaiah and Ezekiel picture vividly the presence of God in the midst of his heavenly court. Yet they appeal to no ecstatic experiences of their own, but to an old tradition of the representation of the theophany. When Jacob saw God, messengers who came forth from God and returned to him were part of the vision of his dream (Genesis 28). For Jacob who saw them himself these messengers had no significance. Obviously even here a traditional picture is utilized, which represents God as the great ruler who has to regulate many things through his messengers. In 1 Kings 22 Yahweh the king appears on this throne; he commissions heavenly messengers. Isaiah 6 agrees with this report, in part in verbal detail. Ezekiel transforms the traditional picture: Yahweh has to come of his own initiative into a foreign land, the throne becomes a chariot-throne, the messengers of the heavenly court become throne-bearers (Ezekiel 1).

Thus according to the call narratives the prophet has access to the heavenly assembly, but not in an ecstatic experience, in which the self is no longer conscious of itself. (See in contrast Genesis 15: Abraham's vision of God comes to him in a "deep sleep"; his waking consciousness is put out of action.) But the prophets are different, in sending them God speaks to them as men who can react in full awareness. Ezekiel, in particular, is set on his feet again; he is to hear his commission standing upright (Ezekiel 2,1f). The divine will does not simply overwhelm the messengers. What happens is that God prepares them for their commission, and indeed each one in an individual manner that corresponds to his personality and his commission. Jeremiah is informed that he has been destined since birth to be a prophet to the nations; he will always have to suffer from his inability to escape from his commission (Jeremiah 1,5a). Isaiah learns, in deadly terror, that together with the sinful people, he cannot face God's presence; his mouth is purified, so that he can himself offer to accept God's commission (Isaiah 6,5-7).

The prophets raise their objections to the divine commission. We must not regard this as a sign of their modesty, which finds God's commission too great. In fact the objections arise from the tension between their personal ideas and the will of God; they do not submit listlessly to the divine decree. Isaiah's cry "how long?" has even the note of indignation and accusation.[65] According to the report of Ezekiel the ego of the prophet has to be almost violently repressed (cf Ezekiel 2, 6 and 8).

But each time God confronts the objection with the renewed, urgent bestowal of the commission, but at the same time with an encouragement for the weak human being who has been chosen as a mediator.[66]

Evidence from the Life of Jeremiah

Probably nowhere in the Old Testament and in the whole ancient East does the unique personality of the individual shine so clearly through the well-defined patterns of linguistic categories as in the case of the prophets. Some particular forms can confirm to us yet again the fact that the prophets look on themselves as committed with their whole lives to their service. The principal evidence for this are the confessions of Jeremiah. The prophet represents to God the distress which his commission brought upon him, and God answers. Here Jeremiah is following the traditions of the laments which lay before God the misery of the man, his God-forsakenness. But here the confessions break away from the tradition; the suffering of the prophet cannot be presented in the traditional form. A part of the laments was the change of mood to praise of God; the worshipper learned that God had not forsaken him. This change is still indicated in Jeremiah 11,18ff. But in 15,10ff, instead of the passage speaking of an encouraging experience of God's presence, there stands a bitter reproach against God. In the end Jeremiah utters his reproaches into the darkness, he no longer experiences any answer from Yahweh. We may ask, how did these confessions ever get into the book of Jeremiah? Jeremiah is here wrestling with God about the meaning of his commission — why has he communicated this personal experience to others? Jeremiah probably saw in his fate a mirror of the destiny of his people. As God was leading him into the darkness, so was he dealing with the whole of Israel.

We know also approximately what external experiences form the background of the inner history of Jeremiah, which finds expression in the confessions. Baruch, the friend and amanuensis of Jeremiah has depicted in Jeremiah 37-45 the prophet's way of suffering. Even in these narratives concerning the prophet we can observe once more the peculiar confluence of two really contradictory tendencies. The individual fate of one particular man is reported — but not in order to praise the prophet and glorify his suffering. It is unprecedented for an ancient writer that the "hero" should disappear in ignominy and suffering as here, without a

225

sudden change of fortune and without a tragic climax. Baruch explains this course of events with a word of God. God is destroying everything in world history that he has built up; how may then an individual expect great things for himself (Jeremiah 45,3-5)?

Like the confessions of Jeremiah, the servant songs of Deutero-Isaiah break all the traditional categories. They stand nearest to the prophetic autobiographical accounts, and the confessions of Jeremiah. The prophet of the exile pictures a figure who unites in himself all the prophetic tasks, but who at the same time is taken by God into his service in a hitherto unprecedented fashion. He is the messenger of God, and represents the Lord of the covenant before Israel, but in so doing becomes himself a "covenant". In his fate, as in the case of the prophets, is reflected the fate of the people, but in addition he "bears the sin of many".

It repeatedly becomes evident how little the category-question can contribute to the understanding of prophetic literature, if this question does not allow itself to be controlled by the effort to understand these men themselves, who with their whole unmistakable individuality had to be witnesses for God, not only with their speeches and reports, but with their whole life.

5. THE PROPHETS AND THE RELIGIOUS TRADITION OF ISRAEL

The prophets trace their activity to the immediate action of Yahweh. Every single one of them was called in a special manner; their task varies according to the situation of each. For this reason they cannot be fitted into traditional patterns. Yet they are not revolutionary innovators who derive hitherto unprecedented truths from their encounter with God. They all wish to preserve the old religious traditions in their purity. Their experience of God's call draws them out of the mass of the people, but refers them back again to the foundation of this people's existence, the covenant with God, of whom the people have grown forgetful. The people owes its existence to Yahweh; it ought to be obedient to the commandments of the God who gave it life by delivering it from Egypt and who maintains it by his guidance and the gift of the land.

The Tradition of the Covenant

The prophets wished to acknowledge no other foundation of faith than this old traditional one:

> God has told you what is good; and what is it that Yahweh asks of you? Only to act justly, to love loyalty to the covenant, to walk wisely before your God (Micah 6,8).

How faithfully the prophets guided themselves by the old law of the covenant is also made clear from the way in which their reproaches correspond, even in details, with traditional statements of the law. They do not attack the social injustice of their time because they regard themselves as the heralds of a new and better morality, but because Israel has incurred guilt in relation to the old divine commandment. Solidarity with the poor, the widows and the orphans is enjoined upon every Israelite, for these also are members of the same divinely chosen people, loved by Yahweh and protected by him just as much as all the rest. The land is God's gift to the people; for that reason it is not just that individuals should snatch it for themselves at the cost of others.[68]

The prophets refer repeatedly to the limits that God's commandment has set for Israel. In their time these must have felt as troublesome restrictions. Economic life has developed, in the towns riches were being amassed. The old solidarity of the village community law was disappearing more and more. Some people were dependent, others were independent. In this situation the prophets did not wish to turn back the wheel of history, still less did they wish to create a new social order. They are compelled to expose many different crimes, but their challenges are simple and fundamental.

Do right!

Cease from evil, do good![69]

Instead of preaching many laws, they grasp the kernel of their legal tradition, and interpret it for the new age: the man who is not concerned to maintain the fundamental stance of justice and love to his fellow-citizens among God's chosen people under new circumstances, despises God's covenant with his people.

The old traditions spoke of Israel's election. Is not the message of the prophets concerning the imminent end of the people in flat contradiction to this. They proclaim not salvation and gracious protection from destruction, but punishment and annihilation:

For you alone have I cared among all the nations of the world; therefore will I punish you for all your iniquities (Amos 3,2).

The prophets did not themselves invent the message of God's judgement upon Israel, they could derive it from the old tradition. The God who comes to punish is only protecting his ancient rights. He himself had taken the poor of his people under his protection: "I will hear their cry" (Exodus 22, 22.26). According to the tradition Israel had only become a people through the covenant with God. When the people no longer reverences commandments entailed by the covenant, it surrenders the basis of its existence. In the election there lay from the beginning the possibility of the rejection of the man who was not willing to affirm the bond with Yahweh.

The contemporaries of the prophets had forgotten this side of their faith; the prophets reawaken it and give it fresh life. This does not, however, mean that they merely remain with what, for good or ill, has been handed down; that would mean a second extinction of the tradition. The tradition is given a further interpretation. Ezekiel gives examples of this. Himself the descendent of a priestly family, he likes to use the style of priestly instruction, and can thus even become for modern research a witness to very old legal tradition.[70] He has an exact knowledge of the tradition, and above and beyond this he knows the way that his predecessors in the prophetic office interpreted the tradition, and himself goes yet another step beyond both. According to the old tradition of Israel, the covenant with God guaranteed life to the whole obedient people; the prophets had inferred from this that disaster was threatening the whole recreant people, if it did not "do good". Ezekiel sees himself authorized to apply to every individual this exhortation directed to the whole people. It is indeed further true that salvation and damnation are offered to the whole people — but God makes every individual responsible for his action, ever and again he gives to every individual new freedom to turn away from his sin. Everyone has at any time the possibility to lay hold of salvation for himself (Ezekiel 18 and 33).

Historical Tradition

Even where the prophets appeal to old traditions it is more important for them to waken them to new life than to conserve them. They look more to the present than to the past. For the "average" religious man in Israel, it might perhaps be the case that everything of importance for his faith had happened in the past. It was then that Israel was chosen, that the land had been given. But the prophets see that what began in the past is continuing in the present; the encounter of Yahweh with his people. This encounter is actually taking place again in their own words. The imminent disastrous end however gives a new aspect to this encounter. From the election, the deliverance from Egypt, Israel can count on no special advantage for itself:

Did I not bring Israel up from Egypt, the Philistines from Caphtor, the Aramaeans from Kir (Amos 9,7)?

The formula of the covenant "You are my people" can be annulled: "You are not my people".[71] The luxuriant vineyard, Israel, protected by God, is worth nothing. Planted as a noble vine, the vine has become a wild-vine. Ezekiel estimates quite satirically the use of the vine merely as a function of the value of the wood.[72] The meaning of the words in which Israel sought to express its special nearness to God, is consequently turned into its opposite.

The threatening approach of disaster teaches the prophets to survey the entire course of the history of Israel hitherto. Isaiah pictures it as the laborious and carefully-planned cultivation by Yahweh of his vinyard (Isaiah 5), Hosea as the loving and patient education of a child (Hosea 11 — cf also Isaiah 1,2), Ezekiel as Yahweh's care of a foundling child (Ezekiel 16). According to all these texts Yahweh's century-long concern for Israel turned out to have been a failure.

For the prophets Israel's history is to be reckoned as a history of disaster. According to Hosea, Jacob, the great ancestor of the people, was nothing but a deceiver and a rebel against God (Hosea 12,3 ff); the taking possession of the land is not a confirmation of God's good-will to the prople, but rather the beginning of the prople's apostasy from God (Hosea 9,10;6,7). The enumeration of the catastrophes which Yahweh, according to Amos 4,6 ff brings successively upon Israel sounds like a parody of sacred history. Ezekiel sees the four stages of the history of Israel — the leading out of Egypt, the giving of the law, the guidance in the desert, the capture of the land — simply as a chain or miscarriages and divine punishments (Ezekiel 20).

By their use of this kind of representation of history the prophets show that they are very far from merely handing on the historical traditions as loyal traditionists. They accuse all Israel, and their apostate contemporaries are representatives of the whole people since its beginnings. Their references to past history serve often as justification for judgement, which is followed by the announcement of impending punishment.[73] Seldom is the past seen in untroubled light. Only in Jeremiah 2,2 and Hosea 2,17 is the retrospect of the time in the desert meant to call back the people to the first love of Israel's early days. Yet such a simple return to the past is not possible for the people. Since the beginning of history it has been incapable of obeying God (Ezekiel 20); no punishment can move it to repentance (Amos 4,6ff); its present life has closed every path leading thither (Hosea 5,14):

Can the Nubian change his skin, or the leopard its spots (Jeremiah 13,23)?

In their historical reflections the prophets realize that for Israel there is no way back. The gifts of Yahweh's election have been squandered beyond repair by its own guilt.

The Significance of the Present

But this by no means implies that they are merely mourning for a better past. Quite the contrary; their keenest attention is directed to the present. The old salvation history miscarried; now a new hour must dawn for Israel. For this reason they attentively observe the political changes of the present. They await an immediately imminent turn in affairs, which Yahweh in his freedom has planned. Exegetes use the technical expression "eschatology" to describe this stance in relation to history.

The eschatological expectation, the heart of the prophetic message, marks the beginning of something completely new in Israel's religious history. The present comes to have for the faithful a significance such as hitherto was possessed only by past history, from the deliverance out of Egypt to the conquest of the land and the election of David. Contemporary events also take place according to Yahweh's plan. But God does not miraculously interpose in the course of events, as once he did at the Red Sea, in the desert, at the Jordan, at Jericho and in the war when the land was conquered. Israel's enemies do not know that they are mere tools in Yahweh's hand.[74] So even Israel can only learn through the interpretation of the prophets that in the disastrous events of the present Yahweh is

229

at work. The eschatology of the prophets is not the "Doctrine of the Last Things", of the end of the world and the end of history that are accompanied by miraculous events. The fundamental characteristic of the eschatological expectations consists in this, that the present day is seen as the end of the old epoch and the threshold of a new age in history.

In order to represent this new thought, the prophets have recourse to old traditions. In the time of the conquest of the land, Israel had fought for its own existence in "holy wars". These wars were not counted holy because Israel was fighting for its faith or for Yahweh; but because it was believed that God was fighting for his people. Israel's army relied on God's action; they waged war according to almost liturgical rules.[75]

When, in face of all threats, Isaiah exhorts his contemporaries to maintain peace and quietness, he awakens, by so doing, memories of the times of the wars of Yahweh (Numbers 21,14). At that time Israel was fundamentally only an observer of the actions of God, who took the part of his people; contemporary political events also take place according to his will.[76] But the elements of nature, which at that time Yahweh unleashed against Israel's enemies, are now sent by him against apostate Israel.[77] Today also a "day of Yahweh" is to be expected, in which God's power is revealed — but it will be a day of disaster for Israel.[78]

So the familiar motifs from the tradition of the holy wars provide only the material which is used to represent a new content, the background against which the terrifying changes of the present stand forth in full clarity. Yet the old expectation of salvation for Israel and disaster for Israel's enemies is not simply turned into its opposite. The catastrophe that looms over Israel is not inevitable. The threat of annihilation is meant to place before Israel the alternative of salvation or destruction (Isaiah 1,19f). The eschatological time is the time of decision. Its events take the course that God wills, but God reserves his full freedom even in relation to his word proclaimed by the prophets.

Expectation of Salvation

This freedom of God to take different action from that which he justly threatened and actually took in the exile, is the only thing on which Israel can now place its hopes. Only a new initiative of God can lead beyond the end. The memory of God's former savings acts, the exodus from Egypt, his covenant with his people, the election of David and of Jerusalem, does not only lead to the realization that all God's gifts have been squandered by the people. God's choice of Israel in former days was completely undeserved; with David he made the least of the family of Jesse his holy king; the heathen town of Jerusalem became the place of his presence. May he not in future bring to pass other similarly unexpected events? Isaiah sees the possibility that even the enfeebled Jerusalem and the almost extinguished family of David may still be able to provide a point of contact for Yahweh's saving will.[79]

Many believed during the exile that Yahweh had finally forsaken his people.[80] The prophets come to another conclusion. They do indeed believe that it is impossible for Israel by its own efforts to become again obedient to God. But God can "heal their apostasy" (Hosea 14,2ff). A new covenant (Jeremiah 31), a new exodus (Deutero-Isaiah)[81] are possible for it. It does not need to follow out consistently the lines of the bankrupt old history (cf Isaiah 43,16ff). Already, in earlier days God gave salvation to Israel for nothing in return. His new saving action is just as surprising, indeed, it surpasses the old; for now all risk incurred through human disobedience is to be excluded. For this reason God gives to his people a new spirit (Ezekiel 36,16ff;37), his law is set within their hearts from the beginning (Jeremiah 31), so that they can no more depart from him.

Thus even the themes of the eschatological expectation stem from the tradition. Like the traditions of justice, covenant, law, and of God's help in battle, so neither are the traditions of Israel's election taken up because the prophets believe that there is a way leading back into the old time, but because from them the immediately imminent, unexpected new action of God can at least approximately be understood.

The prophetic word of promise builds a bridge between God's saving action in the past and the new salvation of the future. Such speech about the future cannot be called "prediction", much less can it be called "soothsaying". In their promises the prophets bear witness to their faith in God's will to save, which they have come to know in Israel's historical traditions. Thus the messianic prophecies in Isaiah 7;9;11 and in Jeremiah 23 go back to the promise made to David.[82] The purpose of these texts is not to picture future events before they happen. The expectations that God's promise to David were bound to raise, had hitherto been fulfilled only in part, but beyond all expectation God will redeem his promise. The prophetic words of salvation do not indicate one point in the future at which they will be fulfilled. The messianic promises would therefore be misunderstood if we were to regard them as outdated by the coming of Jesus. The fact is rather that with the uttering of the word of salvation, a history of God's gracious activity begins. It starts as soon as the word is spoken. Deutero-Isaiah can summon his hearers to give thanks for future saving events; for in the word of the prophet these have already become real and effectual. The prophets do not think of an end to this history.

TEACHERS OF WISDOM AND THEOLOGIANS

1. TEXTUAL EXAMPLE: THE REVELATION OF THE MYSTERY OF WISDOM (PROVERBS 8)

I. *Wisdom as a Speaker in Public*
(1) Is it not Wisdom that calls here, is it not understanding that cries out?

231

(2)   She stands at the cross-roads, by the wayside, at the top of the hill;
(3)   beside the gate, at the entrance to the city, at the entry by the open gate she calls aloud:

Her Invitation to all Men
(4)   "Men, it is to you I call, I appeal to every man:
(5)   understand, you simple fools, what it is to be shrewd; you stupid people, understand what sense means.
(6)   Listen! For I will speak clearly, you will have plain speech from me;
(7)   For I speak nothing but truth and my lips detest wicked talk.
(8)   All that I say is right, not a word is twisted or crooked.
(9)   All is straightforward to him who can understand, all is plain to the man who has knowledge.

The Value of Wisdom
(10)   Accept instruction and not silver, knowledge rather than pure gold;
(11)   for wisdom is better than red coral, no jewels can match her.

II.   *Wisdom introduces Herself*
(12)   I am Wisdom, I bestow shrewdness and show the way to knowledge and prudence.
(13)   The fear of Yahweh is to hate evil. Pride, presumption, evil courses, subversive talk, all these I hate.
(14)   I have force, I also have ability; understanding and power are mine.

The Power of Wisdom
(15)   Through me kings are sovereign and governors make just laws.
(16)   Through me princes act like princes, from me all rulers on earth derive their nobility.

The Profit of Wisdom
(17)   Those who love me I love, those who search for me find me.
(18)   In my hands are riches and honour, boundless wealth and the rewards of virtue.
(19)   My harvest is better than gold, fine gold, and my revenue better than pure silver.
(20)   I follow the course of virtue, my path is the path of justice;
(21)   I endow with riches those who love me and I will fill their treasuries.

III.   *The Mystery of Wisdom*
(22)   The Lord possessed me as the firstborn of his works, before all else that he made, long ago.
(23)   Alone, I was fashioned in times long past, at the beginning, long before earth itself.

232

Wisdom, older than Earth and Sea

(24) When there was yet no ocean I was born, no springs brimming with water.

(25) Before the mountains were settled in their place, long before the hills I was born.

(26) When as yet he had made neither land nor lake nor the first clod of earth.

Wisdom, present at the Creation

(27) When he set the heavens in their place I was there, when he girdled the earth with the horizon,

(28) when he fixed the canopy of clouds overhead and set the springs of ocean firm in their place.

(29) when he prescribed its limits for the sea and knit together earth's foundations.

(30) Then I was at his side each day a master-craftsman

God's Joy and the Joy of Wisdom

and his delight, playing in his presence continually,

(31) playing on the earth, while my delight was in mankind.

IV. Concluding Exhortation

(32) "Now, my sons, listen to me: happy is the man who keeps to my ways!

(33) Listen to instruction, and grow wise, do not reject it.

(34) Happy is the man who listens to me, watching daily at my threshold with his eyes on the doorway,

(35) for he who finds me finds life and wins favour with Yahweh.

(36) while he who finds me not, hurts himself, and all who hate me are in love with death.

The Summons of Wisdom to all Men

Israel's teachers of wisdom never regarded themselves as the guardians of a secret knowledge or as an educated élite, to whose information the common people had no access. The collected life-experience of the people, coined in proverbs, was in their eyes just as valuable as internationally known maxims and precepts for the life-style of the court and the good administration of government. The same outlook also underlies Proverbs 8. Wisdom introduces herself in this poem, and reveals her ancient and noble origin, her exceptional position in the world, her special mission — one would think that such a poem was only meant for a select few. But it is expressly stated that not only a few chosen spirits are permitted to hear the speech of wisdom. It is not in public worship or in a lecture hall that wisdom proclaims her mystery, but in the streets and squares. She addresses all men, without requiring from them any preparation, education, or piety. It is precisely the foolish and those without insight that are to hear her words (8,1-6).

The urgent summons to hear has always been a part of the wisdom teaching,[83] it is an expression of the strongly didactic ethos of the wisdom teacher. But the traditional form of the summons is here surprisingly transformed: it is not a teacher, but wisdom herself that exhorts and calls: "Is it not wisdom that calls here?" the writer asks almost in surprise at the beginning of his poem. Nor could this poem be put in the mouth of any wisdom teacher; for no one could know what is imparted in it. Wisdom has her origin in God, no human being was present at her origin — therefore wisdom must herself disclose her mystery to the public. The models for such public proclamation of what was concealed were the prophets. They had made known in the streets and squares the hidden counsel of God.[84]

Elaboration of traditional Motifs.

This poem addresses itself without distinction to all men, but it does not speak in colloquial language. Its peculiarity reveals itself only to those who are at home in the old traditions, and know how to observe their transformations. It is the work of a scribe who forms his expressions in dependence on the sacred traditions of Israel. This scholar of the fifth century B.C. had collected old wisdom proverbs and published them. His work is known to us as the Book of Sayings, Proverbs. He himself is the composer of the introduction to this collection (Proverbs 1-9). The loyalty to the tradition which finds expression in his editorial work, marks also his introduction. But he does not take over the traditional material without reflection; he makes it the means to express more widely ranging thoughts.

He does not only use the stylistic forms and maxims of his predecessors, but is aware also of his obligations to the prophetic and legal traditions of Israel. Not only the summons to listen,[85] but also the theme of the preciousness of wisdom[86] and of wisdom as kingly teaching[87] was found by him in the older proverbs which he had collected. From these he could also take over the description of his hearer as "son".[88] At the same time the learned poet refers with this word to Deuteronomic sermons; there too, the hearers were named "sons" — but sons of God; Israel was there regarded as a child whom God is educating.[89]

The author will have been aware that he is here transferring to wisdom a term traditionally applied to God; for after this he piles up further similar allusions. According to Job 12,13 God possesses the gifts of counsel and strength, of insight and success; according to Isaiah 11,2, the coming king of salvation is to receive these gifts from God's spirit — but here wisdom ascribes to herself these properties (Proverbs 8,14). As God turns in grace to those who seek him, so wisdom lets herself be found by those who concern themselves with her, and loves in return those who love her.[90] In the older wisdom sayings which he collected the poet found already the topic of wisdom as the way to life and the source of life.[91] He takes it up, but recalls at the same time kindred prophetic texts and thus gives it a new dimension. The prophets promised life to those who find God[92] — here wisdom promises life to her dependents. The traditional wisdom promised guidance in the practical management of everyday life — here wisdom promises much more: life from the authentic source of life, from God.[93] The teacher of wisdom becomes the theologian, who reflects on the connection between life and wisdom. The man who attaches himself to wisdom, wins God's approval and thus finds life.

The Divine Origin of Wisdom

The harmony of wisdom and theological speculation stamps above all the best-known strophes of this poem, in which wisdom reveals her mystery, her origin at the beginning of creation (Proverbs 8,22-31). According to the ancient wisdom teaching everyone could gain wisdom, and was, indeed, obliged to do so, if he wished to succeed in his life. Wisdom helped him to find his way in every contingency that he encountered in every day affairs; it taught him the right behaviour in the world. Thus this poem too seems to regard wisdom as indeed a lofty value, but one that can be attained by all men; the call of wisdom sounds in full publicity, she herself says her speeches are easy to understand and clear (Proverbs 8,9); she challenges men to seek her and to find her. Proverbs 8,22ff, however, gives a different picture of wisdom. It is anything but natural that access to wisdom should be open to men. Another poem written in the same time asks itself the question, "Where is wisdom to be found?" without knowing an answer (Job 28). In Proverbs 8 an answer is given — but not by a man, by wisdom herself. Man could not give this answer, because he has not wisdom — God's wisdom — at his disposal.

Yahweh possessed me as the firstborn of his works. (Proverbs 8).

Even the older wisdom teaching had known that the true wisdom is God's alone. Wisdom is a gift of God to man.[94] But here wisdom enters into a closer relation to God than any teacher of wisdom had hitherto surmised. From her very origin she has been in the immediate presence of God.[95] The still vigorous original power of the creator brought her into existence. Her nobility is incomparable, no thing or person in the creation can point to a more ancient source. No creature perceived her origin; therefore none can know her nature, unless wisdom herself should give up her mystery. But wisdom knows everything; for she was there when all things came to be.

Who has gauged the waters in the palm of his hand,
or with its span set limits to the heavens?
Who has held all the soil of earth in a bushel,
or weighed the mountains on a balance
and the hills on a pair of scales?
Who has set limits to the spirit of Yahweh?
What counsellor stood at his side to instruct him? (Isaiah 40,12f)

235

Deutero-Isaiah gives no answer to these questions. How could such a man be able to give them an answer? The author of Proverbs 8 ventures an answer because he lets wisdom herself speak. Wisdom stood by God's side at the creation. The prophet's question was intended to glorify the greatness of the creator, who needed no help of any kind — but here, with the same motive, wisdom is glorified.

Personification of Wisdom

Wisdom in this poem is more than a divine property, more than God's fairest gift to men. The poet's imagination represents it as a person. In this way the poet makes it clear that wisdom can never be produced by human efforts. It was there before men were, before anything in the world happened. This personification of wisdom, who speaks to men and herself reveals her origin, is without precedent in the tradition. One might think that since statements about God were transferred to wisdom, the first personal form of this speech of wisdom corresponded to utterances of Yahweh about himself, which are known in the Old Testament. That is not the case. While Yahweh refers to his acts in history in order to elicit trust in further help,[96] wisdom speaks of her origin before history, and of her activity effectual at all times in the world. The speeches of Egyptian gods are more akin to this text. Inscriptions, rituals, and myths tell of a goddess Maat ("wisdom") who was there even before the creation, who is the bestower of life, and has her sphere of activity in the royal administration of government. When the author of Proverbs 8 expresses his joy in the perfected creation of God in the picture of wisdom playing in the presence of God in the world, he can appeal for precedent to Egyptian utterances about Maat, the playful child of the gods.

Even these references to non-Israelite myths and rituals are only intended to make men take to heart the exhortation to a life with wisdom. For this reason the poet who wrote Proverbs 8 does not get lost in speculation about the unfathomable nature of wisdom and its relation to God that surpasses human understanding. The strophe in which wisdom speaks of her origin at the beginning of creation appears at a first glance like a foreign body in the unity of the poem. In 8,32ff the author returns to the exhortations and instructions of the beginning. Their connection with the reflections concerning the relations between God and wisdom is not at first clear. Only when the connection with traditional motifs is noted, does it become plain that in all parts of the speech of wisdom the theme is the nearness of wisdom to God. Statements about God have become statements about wisdom.

Even from of old, in Israel the exhortation to be wise was an exhortation to hearken to God's word and his law. It had always been known that the man who forgets God's word, then only possesses his own wisdom, which is then useless.[97] This close connection between the faithful acceptance of the word of God and a wise life-style, is what the poet wishes to establish on a theological basis. God possesses wisdom from the beginning and rejoices in her — wisdom rejoices in man and — although in her being she is unfathomable — allows herself to be found by them (Proverbs 8,31). She mediates between God and man. The way to wisdom is the way to life with God.

2. DIDACTIC POEMS CONCERNING THE DIVINE WISDOM

The Wisdom of the Post-exilic Age

Since the time of Solomon, the 10th century, wisdom teaching was at home in Israel, and in succeeding times had never entirely lost its influence there. It received a strong impulse at the time of the return from exile (538) Yet its form had changed. The writers, the royal officials who educated their successors with the help of the wisdom doctrines no longer exist. Now priests and scholars gather the old traditions of Israel, and give them new life in order to link up again with the great past of the people. They are men of kindred spirit, who create a new edition of old wisdom sayings (the Book of Proverbs), and put together a codex of the prophetic books.[98] But new wisdom texts also came into being in these circles of tradition-conscious scholars, who not only developed further in their poems the thoughts of the older wisdom, but conjoined with them conceptions and ideas from the whole of the older literature and tradition of Israel. The exile was a deep incision in the course of the history of Israel; after the return the Jews could no longer take up again where they had left off. Thus even the oral tradition lost its significance, the threads had been cut. The men of the restoration group appeal to sacred *texts* of the old time; the group of Jewish scholars of the *scriptures* comes into being.

The old wisdom teachers wished to give an intelligible conspectus of the rich variety of phenomena. This effort is given a new stimulus, but the goal has changed. The aim of wisdom is to explain the universal coherence of the world.

She is but one, yet can do everything.

Thus the latest of these scriptural scholars and wisdom poets describes wisdom.[99]

In order to do justice to this task, wisdom must penetrate the whole religious tradition of Israel: prophetic revelation and wisdom, divine law and wisdom are for these thinkers just as closely connected as is the divine order of creation with wisdom. The old teachers of wisdom only wished to give counsel for right behaviour — each individual had to look to it how he applied it in a way suitable to his own situation. In contrast with this, the younger teachers of wisdom wish to establish the nature of wisdom; they are theologians who believe that they can only teach the right behaviour of man in the world when they have made visible its final foundation in the divine plan.

Adoption of Prophetic and Legal Tradition

As an example of the adoption of prophetic traditions we may take Proverbs 1, 20-23. Wisdom herself speaks. She speaks in public, in places where many people gather, as the prophets had done.[100] The prophets spoke to sinners, to renegades. Wisdom calls fools and the wicked.[101] Like the prophets she exhorts to repentance,[102] indeed the wisdom poet puts words in her mouth such as God once himself spoke in the words of the prophetic messengers. In Joel 3,1ff God promises that he will pour out his spirit on all men, and thus make them prophets — in Proverbs 1,23 wisdom announces the outpouring of *her* spirit, the revelation of *her* word to men. Wisdom takes on the role of a prophet. In Proverbs 1,24ff her language is in the style of a prophet's threatening speech, prefaced and justified by the accusation of the sinners; in the matter of content motifs of the prophetic preaching of repentance are set out: the accusation of the reprobates, who are not willing to hear,[103] threats of the day of vengeance of wisdom, who, like Yahweh, has been forgotten, and who, like him, will have this day of vengeance.[104] As once the prophets threatened that men will seek God but will not find him, so on that day men will also seek wisdom in vain.[105] It is a day of terror, thunder, and stormy wind, like the day of Yahweh that the prophets announced to the faithless people.[106] Then Wisdom will laugh the unfortunates to scorn as the Lord of heaven does when the peoples revolt.[107]

There is hardly a word in this learned poem which does not have a deep significance in the context of the sacred tradition. This link with the holy scriptures of the people gives to the wisdom teaching, which in its older form in Israel had almost the same appearance as that of the surrounding peoples, specifically Jewish characteristics. Wisdom is so closely related to God, that statements about God, and forms of speech in which he had spoken through the mouth of the prophets, can be transferred to her.

Like the prophetic tradition, the tradition of the law is incorporated in the wisdom teaching. At a first glance this may not appear as a specifically Jewish trait; for elsewhere in the ancient orient the wisdom of the lawgiver is praised, on the famous stele of Hammurabi we can read:

> Hammurabi, the king of righteousness is my name. To me (the sun god) Shamash transmitted the law. My words are precious . . . Only to fools have they nothing to say — but to the wise they give food for amazement.[108]

In Israel too it is held to be the mark of a wise man that he fulfils the divine law and rejoices in it;[109] yet here men know that God's law distinguishes them from the other peoples:

> When the other people hear about these statutes, they will say, "What a wise and understanding people this great nation is!" What great nation has a god close at hand as Yahweh our God is close to us? . . . (Deuteronomy 4,6-8).

This thought is brought to its climax in Ecclesiasticus 24: Wisdom, created before all the world, sought in vain her home among men —

finally, as the divine law she was able to find in Israel a permanent resting-place. The old wisdom thinking is here given a peculiar twist — if originally men count as wise, because they have received God's law and fulfil it, here wisdom is identified with the law and at the same time personified as a superhuman being of mysterious origin.

Personification of Wisdom

A like transformation is to be observed in the wisdom literature's reflections concerning the creation. On the one hand, God is praised as the cunning architect of the world, who has measured it, and given it order and secure foundations.[110] God reveals his wisdom in the creation of the world (Proverbs 3,19). But on the other hand, a personified wisdom is the witness of God's creative activity at the beginning of the world (Proverbs 8,22ff); in the Wisdom of Solomon 7,2 wisdom herself is even called the "creator of all things."

The older teachers of wisdom named "wisdom" either right behaviour in the world, or counsels leading to such behaviour. But now wisdom appears as a person who addresses man,[111] who wishes to meet man as a familiar friend, as sister and bride.[112] This particular development also is specifically Jewish; it has no parallels in any wisdom literature except that of Israel.[113]

The Hiddenness of Wisdom

Even the older wisdom teaching was aware that wisdom can only be striven after, that there are no sure instructions as to how she may be found. The invention by later successors of the figure of wisdom as a person makes it possible for them to show that wisdom, from its very nature, does not lie within the range of man's capacities; she is a heavenly power, created before all the world; she stands at God's side in the act of creation, and she is at last even called the "sharer of God's throne" (Wisdom of Solomon 9,4).

The wisdom poem in Job 28[114] has chosen the inaccessibility of wisdom as its principle theme. The poet asks himself vainly "Where is wisdom to be found?" He plays with the theme of the wisdom poetry, which compares the search for wisdom with the profitable search for noble metals (Proverbs 2,4), and inverts its meaning: man is indeed capable of finding silver and gold in mines, but he cannot discover wisdom. The poet praises the technical capacities of man, which in earlier days were regarded as proof of wisdom,[115] but contrasts them with the incapacity of man to achieve wisdom. Only God knows where wisdom is to be found, and uses it in guiding the world.

Thus this poem seems to contradict not only traditional conceptions of wisdom, but also later ones. Repeatedly indeed the wisdom poets of later times teach that man is quite able to find wisdom (Proverbs 3,13), wisdom herself invites men (Proverbs 2,20ff; 9,1ff), she even seeks her adherents on the street (Wisdom of Solomon 6,16). And yet the two apparently contradictory lines of thought can be harmonized. The wisdom, who invites men to herself, is indeed a figure of very ancient, mysterious origin. Instead of breaking with tradition, Job 28 rethinks it. Even the old wisdom was characterized by a similar contradiction: It could not be comprehended in any system, could not be formulated in ready-made regulations for behaviour — and yet its intention was to guide man in his daily behaviour. Job 28 thinks through the peculiarity of wisdom, and discloses its ultimate principle — wisdom is not to be found, and yet is full of significance for human life.

The last verse of this poem has often been regarded as the moralizing appendix of a redactor, who was not satisfied by the statement that wisdom could not be discovered. Yet why should not the poet of Job 28, like other wisdom thinkers of his time, hold in high regard the theme of the fear of God as the true wisdom? Even in the older sayings the fear of God was reckoned to be a constituent part of the wise life.[116] But now it becomes the foundation on which the whole of wisdom is based.[117] The man who fears God takes wisdom, which he has not in fact at his disposal, as a gift from God's hand. According to the teaching of this poet, man, if he is wise, can solve the problems and questions of the world and of his life in right behaviour and action, but only if he does not think that he has wisdom in himself, or possess it as his property.

3. THE BOOK OF JOB

Anyone who concerns himself with Old Testament literature, must above all relinquish one idea, which seems to him self-evident in his dealings with modern books: he must not read these writings as the work of individual authors. Long intervals of time, widely ranging social circumstances have given to the linguistic forms and themes of the Old Testament texts so firm a form that the share of individual authors can only seldom be distinguished, and their influence on the main thesis and fundamental form is often very small. In the late period of the Old Testament we meet with another kind of book: Daniel, Job, and Koheleth are, in their general plan and purpose to be regarded as the works of individual authors. It is indeed true that we do not even know the names of these men. We cannot interpret these books in the light of the personality of an author, or even of his biography, both are completely unknown to us, nor is it possible to infer them from the works. The author conceals himself behind his work. However unmistakable the characteristics of these books, yet at every turn we encounter traditional utterances and forms. These authors form their own new thoughts in conversation with existing traditions.

Unique in Form and in Theme

Two things distinguish the Book of Job from all the other books of the

Old Testament. Its dialogue form, and its restriction to one single theme, the question of the sufferings of the just man.[118] Parallel forms have been sought for in the environment of Israel in the ancient east, but in vain. The poet of the book of Job may indeed be to some degree dependent on certain writings from the Mesopotamian and Egyptian areas. The problem of the injustice of man's fate and the injustice of the world order has found expression in different poems, and we also find the dialogue form in such writings.[119] When there the evil lot of men is made the theme of lament, the intention is that deliverance from the suffering imposed by the god shall be found. The poet of the book of Job seeks more than this. It is not enough for him, that Job should be set free from his suffering; it is not sufficient for him to discover the meaning of the suffering.[120] Job seeks for a confrontation at law with the personal God, or, if he does not achieve this, he would rather have death and complete annihilation.[121] In respect of this conception, the book of Job remains without a parallel.

The central theme is the search for the personal God, on whose faithfulness reliance is to be placed, however terrible and incomprehensible he may be (16,18ff). This means that the Book of Job is much more deeply rooted in traditions of the Old Testament faith than in the wisdom literature of the ancient orient. In individual details also much of the material, many of the motifs and forms of speech stem from the tradition of Israel and are transformed to suit the new intention of the poet. The orthodox faith, which sees a connection between what men do and what they suffer, is shaken. Human insight can no longer discover that God still remains true to the fellowship with man, which he entered upon, that he is still righteous. And yet the poet has no intention of giving up the old faith in the faithfulness of God. He seeks a new foundation for it. This intention finds expression also in the language-forms of the composition and in its way of dealing with traditional material: old material appears with a new function and a new meaning. A new literary genus arises from the mingling of different categories, the debate and didactic language of the wise, pre-judicial and judicial forms of speech of the people of Israel, and the lament of the God-forsaken, as we find it in the Psalms. The poet writes for readers who can detect identities or similarities with older texts of the Old Testament, and can grasp and interpret the deviations. He expects them to have the scientific knowledge of his time as well as an acquaintance with the mythological material of the world literature of his day.

Narrative Framework and Dialogue

The author is but little concerned that people should credit him with unprecedented new insights. The starting point of his reflections is an exemplary tale, long familiar among the people, concerning the proving of a religious man whom God puts to the test, a narrative from distant times and lands — Job is supposed to have lived in the age of the Patriarchs in a foreign land. The author uses this narrative as the framework of his book (chapters 1 and 2;42,7-10). It has so artistic a form, that we may ask if the old folk-narrative remained wholly unchanged. The regular change of scenes in heaven and scenes on earth is striking. A remodelling could have also included the statements of the framework narrative. For even here the old doctrine of the connection between action and consequences is called in question; Job "fears God for nought" (1,9f), remains pious even in misery.

However the aim of the remodelling is not to smooth out unevennesses in comparison with the dialogue poem. Inconsistencies between the two parts are evidence of the loyalty of this poet to the current tradition. In the dialogue the loss of honour is added to the loss of wealth (chapter 30), spiritual suffering to physical illness (7,1.11). For the Job of the dialogue not only the misery that he suffers in his own body becomes a temptation, but also the unlucky fate of all men, their laborious life (7,1), their transiency (7,6.9 etc.), their lack of justice (12,6). Hopelessness is his own real temptation.[123] Has God the right so to put man to the test? This question the dialogue puts in all its sharpness, in the framework it does not arise. And yet the poet of the dialogue repeatedly uses the framework as presupposition: in order that the question concerning the justice of the trial which God requires may be clearly developed, it is important for the author of the dialogue that in the framework God should acknowledge Job's behaviour as right; Job's misfortune is not punishment (42,7ff). On the other hand, however, the composer of the dialogue can release himself from this problem posed by the framework narrative. In order to illuminate on all sides the question of the justice of the trials sent by God, he reflects not only on the suffering of the righteous — not even the sinner should be so hard hit by God. He has himself made man small and weak. Is it right that he then so inexorably holds judgement concerning every misdeed?[124]

Thus the dialogue is in part independent of the framework, and in part unintelligible without it. Not only the conception of "righteous Job" comes from the framework narrative, but also the thought that distress and suffering have no other origin than the will of God. Starting with this presupposition the question in the dialogue concerning suffering becomes a controversy with God. Even for the judgement of the participants in the dialogue the framework must play its part: Job, the accuser of God, is justified, his friends, the defenders of God are put in the wrong (42,7ff). But with this the friends are not simply condemned, their humane bearing is acknowledged (2,11ff). The reader of this work is not permitted to think in the stock categories of pious people, contradictions and striking judgements repeatedly make him realize that he must leave familiar lines of thought.

The author uses the existent narrative framework, without binding himself to it. Loyalty to the tradition is conjoined with freedom; that holds good also in relation to other themes, motifs, and linguistic forms that he adopts. People have tried to place his work as belonging to the wisdom literature, to understand it in the light of the linguistic forms of judicial life, or to interpret it as a dramatization of the lament,[125] but with all this each of them has only illuminated individual pages of the book, which develops a new literary form of its own out of the categories handed down traditionally.

Job as a Wisdom Book

The book of Job differs from the historical and prophetic books of the Old Testament, and from the Book of Proverbs, in that it centres round one single theme, the question concerning the suffering of the righteous man. By so doing it opens up a question that has great significance in the wisdom doctrine. What connection is there between the action of a man and his condition? Christian popular wisdom has coined the saying "Where the need is greatest, God's help is nearest". The wise men of the Old Testament come to an almost contrary conception. Manifold experience teaches that bad seed bears bad fruit, evil deeds have evil consequences. Eliphaz teaches:

Mischief does not grow out of the soil nor trouble spring from the earth, but man begets trouble (5,6f).

Where unhappiness reigns God is far off, for sin brings forth disaster.[126] This traditional wisdom teaching is acknowledged by Job, just as by his friends: only for this reason can he, an innocent man, experience unhappiness as infuriating injustice on God's part (Job 27,5).

Thus in Job's revolt there is at first no expression of scepticism in relation to the traditional wisdom doctrine. This had always been marked by a refusal to preach rigid fundamental principles, but challenged men to test the doctrines of wisdom as the times demanded in each new situation of life. The doctrine of requital taught by wisdom does not touch Job's particular fate. It is characteristic of true wisdom that it knows its limits. For this reason the friends of Job remind him of God's unfathomable mystery (11,7), and remind him that man, "the maggot" is small and impure in his sight (4,17; 252ff).

In this also, Job agrees with his friends. It belongs to the peculiar characters of this dialogue, that great parts of the discussion are thinkable in the mouth of Job as well as in those of his friends. The book is not constructed like a polemical discussion, that leads step by step to a definite conclusion. The same doctrines are the subject of reflection from different viewpoints for both parties, without an approximation of opposed conceptions, or a decision between alternatives being always reached as a result. Like his friends, Job also acknowledges the indisputable pre-eminence of God. Yet he does not stop there. Does not God use his pre-eminence to put men, who are weaker, in the wrong in every case (9,17ff)? Job also sees how insignificant man is; but ought not God to be generous to him just because of his littleness, and overlook his failings (7,17.21)?

It may surprise us that Job indulges in such reflections at all. They do

243

not in fact fit his case, for he can with great certainty maintain his innocence. Yet the poet did not intend to represent in the figure of Job the singular fate of an individual. For this reason we must not see in the declarations of innocence any expression of self-righteousness. Just like the statements about the weakness and impurity of man before God, they serve to give expression to the indignation of this poet at the disproportionate sternness with which God inflicts evil upon men.

Job goes on undeterred to inquire for the reason of suffering, even after he has been reminded that before God all questioning must fall silent. With this he passes beyond the limits of wisdom, which indeed teaches man to be modest. A later reviser of the book of Job wished to show that even when confronted by such stubbornness, wisdom is not put to silence. He inserts the Elihu-speeches (32-37) which offer a solution to the question about the meaning of suffering. The man who insists on learning the reason for his suffering for that very reason deserves his suffering. The right question in the tradition of Wisdom is not "Why does suffering afflict me?" but "For what purpose does suffering afflict me?"

For those whom he loves Yahweh reproves (Proverbs 3,11).

The Dialogue as a Case at Law

The purpose of suffering is to teach men the right bearing in relation to the God of unfathomable mystery. Yet Elihu has misunderstood Job's obstinacy. Job does not seek to find the solution of an intellectual problem. He seeks his own justification. The poet uses forms of language taken from the judicial field, in order to show that what is at stake is the establishment of justice and injustice. There is a double dispute at law, between Job and his friends, and between Job and God. The aim of a judicial proceeding in Isreal was not in every case to establish certain facts beyond cavil. It was enough if the disturbed conditions of peace and justice could be restored. In the dispute between Job and his friends Job had disturbed this peace. It was not the friends, but he himself who had broken the long shared silence, had made an accusation, and called in question the judicial order. The issue in the controversy is now that the one party should bring the other to silence. The friends attempt at first to settle the quarrel in a kindly way (chapters 4-14), but soon words become bitter, and the parties address one another as if they were making accusations against one another before a court at law.[127] In the end Job is confronted by a whole catalogue of sins, crimes against justice of a religious and social character (22,5ff). But Job silences the friends by making use of the purification oath. In cases at law this can serve as complete exoneration of the accused, when a human court cannot investigate the credibility of the case. The oath includes the request to God that he may be pleased to investigate the case himself.[128]

The case at law against the friends is from the first intermingled with the case at law against God. Accusations of the friends in Job's speeches pass over time and again into accusations of God.[129] But this form of the case at law means that the poet thrusts beyond the limits of what was thinkable in the judicial practice of Israel. There God could only be introduced in the procedure of seeking a divine judgement, perhaps in the form of a decision by means of the lot. Here God's will could only be learnt with the help of an impersonal device. But Job seeks the personal God, who not only somehow communicates his will, but declares it and justifies it in man's presence. For this reason the poet can only use the judicial forms of speech in a non-literal manner to describe the case against God. This already shown by the fact that for Job God is not only the accused, but also the partner whom he challenges to a case at law concerning a disputed matter; the arbiter and advocate at law, even the judge who is to hear the cry of the man who is unjustly put to death.[130]

Imitation of the Laments

A model for this way of speaking to God could be found by the writer of the Book of Job in the prayer laments of Israel. Job calls God's righteousness in question (13,23f), and also his grace (7,17ff); he traces back the bad experiences of men, the injustice and distress of life, to God;[131] he represents God as the hostile assailant[132] — but with all this he does not turn away from God, but seeks answer and help from him.[133] Just in the same way the worshippers of the lament-psalms stood in God's presence.

The attempt has sometimes been made to cut out the hymnic passages, the praise of God's greatness[134] out of Job's speeches as later additions. But precisely these passages have an important function. They are evidence that at heart Job considered a dispute with God impossible. Job knows that he cannot appeal to an order of justice that stands above him and God; what he seeks is not the verdict of a court, but speech with the personal God.

This expectation of Job's is not disappointed. God speaks to him and thus proves to him that he wishes to maintain fellowship with man. It was this fellowship that Job had stubbornly sought for, precisely through his accusations. God shows that he is near to man even when the latter dreams himself in misfortune to be abandoned by God. On the other hand the near God remains the unfathomable God. This fact the poet represents by two methods. (a) He chooses the old motif of the divine epiphany in a thunderstorm, God does not bind himself to one place. (b) He gives the speech of God in the form of a list of questions. The questions make it clear that the ordinances of nature are unfathomable to man — and yet he lives daily among them. How then should he not be able to live in fellowship with the unfathomable God? Even this "solution" is not given by the poet as his own invention — Deutero-Isaiah too had represented the superiority of God in the form of lists of questions concerning natural phenomena — in this form people had represented also the inaccessibility of wisdom and the fruitlessness of all endeavours to fathom God.[135]

Job's friends had been silenced by him in the dispute at law; before God he himself falls silent — this means that the dispute at law is settled in God's favour. And yet Job hears God's confirmation that he had rightly spoken. Job was in the right, inasmuch as he had held on to God, even with his sharpest accusations he had sought God. But the friends had not sought God; they had sought the solution of the problem that the case of Job represents for the wise man.

Freedom and Loyalty to the Tradition

The author of the Book of Job uses traditional genres in a free manner. We would misunderstand him, if we were to consider only the form-critical aspect of his work, and content ourselves with discovering the original *Sitz im Leben* of the forms of speech used by him. Originally, we may say, the silence of one party in a legal case, is the sign that it is in the wrong — but God expressly declares Job to have been right. The infringement of the social commandments is reckoned properly as the mark of the evildoer (cf 22,5ff) — but for Job the fact of social injustice becomes the proof of the injustice of God's government of the world (24,2ff). The list of questions contained in God's speech is based on the so-called science of lists; lists of the things to be found in the world are meant to help men to apprehend the order of the world — but the divine speech shows that the world order cannot be apprehended. The traditional encomium on the happiness of the just man is turned in parody into a song about the happiness of the evildoer (21,7ff). The laments in general look for salvation from distress — in Job they become an expression[136] of hopelessness. In Psalm 8,5 and in Psalm 144,3 the contemplation of the littleness of man leads to wonder at God's great care for him — in Job it leads to the request that God should not concern himself about man (7,17f). A hymn in 3,17ff does not celebrate God, but praises the underworld that is far from God. Without letting the connection with tradition be broken, here an individual has ventured in all freedom to win new utterances from it.

4. THE BOOK KOHELETH

The External Form

The conversations in the Book of Job are not severely logical, but a general conceptual structure can be found. Above all the final climax of the book in the speech of God gives a definite purpose to the whole. The Book Koheleth has no unifying thought-structure running through it. But neither does it represent itself as an unordered collection of individual sayings and groups of sayings like the Book of Proverbs. A *leitmotif* ("All is vanity") holds shorter and longer proverbs and poems in the Book Koheleth loosely together.

The author gives to himself the pseudonym "Koheleth", which is usually translated by "preacher". This rendering could awaken false expectations. Here an orator is speaking not to a congregation attending public worship, but to a gathering of the wise. This man is a master of the traditional forms of speech of the wisdom school. The publisher of his book, who composed an epilogue, describes the linguistic category which koheleth used, as *māšāl* (Ecclesiastes 12,9). The boundaries of this category cannot be clearly defined; short sayings and similes are so named, but also longer processes of thought. The Book Koheleth was not written before the 3rd century, but we find there speech-forms of the old wisdom, such as we know from the Book of Proverbs. Proverbs are often employed;[137] comparisons are borrowed from popular word-play and riddles;[138] doctrines that contradict one another (antinomies) warn the reader not to take a maxim of the author as a ready-made recipe for structuring one's life;[139] we find there encomiums and laments, illustrations and pedagogical speeches.[140] These traditional linguistic forms of the wisdom doctrine are handled in a masterly manner — but at the same time koheleth understands how to give an individual stamp to his work.

In this two characteristics of style are of use to him. (a) He represents himself to us as the wise king Koheleth, who can trace back all his teachings to his own observation and reflection. Even before this, it occasionally happened that the teacher of wisdom spoke on one occasion of himself in the first person,[141] but nowhere else except here is a whole work stylized in this fashion in the first person, nowhere else has personal contemplation and experience of the world become the point of departure of the teaching. (b) A second device is the stereotyped repetition of the same sentences. Above all the recurring judgement "This too is vanity"[142] makes the whole book the expression of a single mood.

The Destabilization of Wisdom

Although this man is equipped with all the armoury of Wisdom, he does not contribute to the spread of the wisdom teachings; what he does is to disturb its foundations. The antinomies, by means of which the other wisdom teachers disclosed contradictions in human life, in order to lead men to test the actual situations in which they found themselves, are turned by him against wisdom itself. Wisdom is valuable for man, can protect him from loss, can secure power and riches for him[143] — but what man can attain to it? Koheleth understands "wisdom" not as right human behaviour in the changing situations of life, but as the capacity to explain "all that is".[144] (Here he picks up the traditions from the didactic poems about the divine wisdom.) Such a wisdom is divine, inaccessible to men.

But even an order of human life cannot be discovered by Koheleth; long life is bestowed on the evildoer, the righteous man is struck by misfortune, and no wisdom can name the reason why things happen to them thus.[145] Not even the man who is concerned about wisdom, can say with certainty whether he is not a fool (2,19). Poverty, human weakness and failures, and evil times hinder man from being wise.[146] In the face of such facts, what is the profit of doctrines of wisdom? In this way, by pushing the wisdom thinking in antinomies to extremes, and by applying them to wisdom itself, he completely removes the foundations of the wisdom teaching.

Topics

Koheleth's manner of writing is strange to us. He does not express his thoughts in his own words, but in *topoi*, i.e. in phrases, motifs and ideas that as an educated man he selects from the literature of his time. He is not careful to use a *topos* in exactly the same sense that it had in his literary models. An approximate allusion is enough. Often the use of *topoi* gets its singular charm precisely because it contradicts a familiar *topos*. For example, Koheleth was already familiar with the creation story of Genesis 1-3 in the form which we possess today. Jesus Sirach also knows it and takes from it proofs of the greatness of the creator.[147] But Koheleth draws from it his fundamental insight: everything in the world is in vain, all things and all human activity are transient. According to Genesis 2, 7.19 man and beast are formed from the soil of the field, man is given life by the breath of God — for Koheleth that is an occasion to equate man and beast are touched by the same fate of death (3,19). What is left of man when the dust returns to the earth and the breath of life to God. (12,7b)? Yet Koheleth praises God's work as perfect (3,11) — a memory of the fact that the priestly account of creation had called it "very good".

Alongside of such allusions to biblical writings there stand topics from the literature of the ancient East. The ancient peoples, above all the Semites, for whom after death there was only a shadowy existence, reckoned the name, the fame, and the great achievement that outlast the man, as one of the highest goods. Only at this point can the grim law of transience be transcended.[148] Koheleth too joins in the praise of man's achievement and the famous name.[149] But he makes an important reservation; men forget so quickly. Ever and again they marvel at something new, but they only do that because they have forgotten that something like it has long existed (1,9ff). Name and fame are worthless and transient, like everything in the world.[150]

How can man find satisfaction? Koheleth again gives the answer with the help of allusions to literary models. The Egyptian Song of the Harper, the Semitic wisdom doctrine of Ahikar challenge men to enjoyment of life against the sombre background of inevitable death. Thus even Koheleth praises the joy of life as the best that man can strive for.[152] But he does not even let the exhortation to enjoy life pass without qualification; even pleasure and joy in one's own work and possessions are as transitory as a breath of wind (2,1-11). In Isaiah 22,13 the prophet quotes people who in sinful carelessness despise the coming judgement of God: "Let us eat and drink, for tomorrow we die". Koheleth does not only reject such frivolous pleasure in life, but even the joy that does not forget a wise moderation:

"So I grew greater and richer . . . and my wisdom remained with me . . . and behold, everything was emptiness and chasing the wind" (2,9).

The Limit of Scepticism

Nietzsche called the Book of Ecclesiastes "the Song of Songs of Scepticism". And yet Koheleth does not call everything in question. At one point he ceases making reservations; on the question of faith in God's sovereignty over the world. It is he who bestows the joy of life,[153] but who also can take away from men the enjoyment of the good things of this world. Vain are man's efforts to understand God's works, and vain would be the attempt to assess God's righteousness or unrighteousness.[154] Even if God's work is inscrutable — Koheleth does not cease to maintain that it is perfect (3,10-14). It is not scepticism, nor fundamental doubt as to the existence of anything of value, that Koheleth questions everything that hitherto had been highly treasured: the ancient thought of the worth of a famous name, a great achievement, a heroic deed, the traditional exhortation to rejoice in life. The limited value which he ascribes to these things, was not intended to destroy ancient insights, but to interpret them from another angle; that of the ancient traditional faith in God's incomparability, with which no rival can be compared. Everything is in God's hand, even wisdom has only value, insofar as it comes from God (Ecclesiastes 9.1).

THE APOCALYPTIC WRITERS

Modern literature can often be interpreted by our asking for the intention of the author in question. The greater part of Old Testament literature cannot be questioned in this manner. The written version that we possess is very different from its original form. Sagas, songs and sayings, even the tradition of Israel's history and the laws were first handed down from mouth to mouth. The history of the text down to its final fixed form must be taken into account, oral tradition has stamped it, in each case in a manner corresponding to its nature and duration. For this reason we are not at liberty to ask for the intention of a single author, but must try to see it in connection with the groups and societies in which it originated.

The Book of Daniel, the Work of a Single Author

This changes in the later age of Old Testament literature. Works are created which we can ascribe to a single author. The only book of Jewish apocalyptic, which was included in the canon of Holy Scripture, the

Book of Daniel, has one individual author, it was composed and written down at once. (It is followed by a series of other apocalyptic books, which were however only handed down extra-canonically.)

The prophetic books contain for the most part several collections of utterances of each prophet in question, which were put together by pupils. Only in exceptional cases do the prophets themselves write down their words; their intention was to speak directly to their contemporaries; the word was meant to have an influence on the present — they seldom thought of the future.

In contrast with this the peculiar form of the apocalyptic books requires from the first to be set down in writing; they usually purport to be the book of a great man of the past. To him the future has disclosed itself in visions, (*apokalyptein* — Greek for 'to disclose'); these visions were written down for the coming generations, who are to experience this future. Thus Daniel, who according to the fiction of the biblical Book himself was alive to experience the capture of Jerusalem in 587, foresees the future course of history — up to the time after Antiochus IV (175-164 B.C.).

But even at this early point we must let ourselves be warned not to put without more ado to the biblical book the modern question concerning the intention of the author. For under the pseudonym of that Daniel from the sixth century an author of the second century B.C. is concealed. He betrays himself by the fact that he possesses first-hand knowledge of the Hellenistic time, the last epoch of those foreseen by Daniel. With the help of this criterion even the date of the composition of this book can be exactly determined. From Daniel 11,40 onwards the author can no longer describe events of the past. He is really looking into the future, and immediately becomes more inexact. His prophecy of the death of the enemy of God in the holy land by the hand of a hostile king was not fulfilled — unlike the "prophecies" by means of which he described events which really belonged to the past.

Thus the author in a great part of his book is looking back on past events, but describes them as if he were prophesying events of the future. What is the meaning of this strange form? Is the pseudonym "Daniel" meant to deceive the reader to give a contemporary work the higher sanctity of past times? That cannot have been the intention of the author; he lets himself be quickly recognized by everyone who looks more carefully into the matter. His contemporaries must have found it easy from 11,2 onwards to substitute the names of kings and great men known to them for the disguised descriptions; it was possible to see through the "prophecy" as a description of the very recent past.

Further, pseudonymity in Israel was nothing new. Under the name of "Moses" many later traditions of the law were united, under that of David, the father of the Psalmists, many later Psalms; wisdom writings are named after Solomon, who could not have written them. Without special indication words of the prophets Deutero- and Trito-Isaiah were added to the book of the first Isaiah. People in Israel had a conception of authorship and spiritual fatherhood that seems strange to us. The origin of a category has more attention paid to it than later formulations. The man who created a form of expression made its later use possible. Therefore, as "author" he is more important than his pupils and imitators.

Considerations like these may have moved the author of the Book of Daniel to choose a pseudonym out of the times of the exile. In his day faithful Jews saw their chief task as the preservation of the holy traditions unchanged. "The law and the prophets" contained for them the full revelation of the divine will, beyond which it was forbidden to trespass. They only required further interpretation. Using the fiction of composition in the exilic times, when there was still new revelation through the Prophets — a fiction easily seen through by contemporary readers — the author proposes to represent effectively his dependance upon his revelation of the past.

At the same time he can speak with less danger when he conceals his own name and in the disguised form of prophecy attacks the rule of the unbelieving Antiochus.

Interpretation of History

Finally the form of a prophecy of past events helps him to place vividly before the eyes of the reader examples of the divine control of history. For — according to the fiction of the authorship of Daniel — God imparted beforehand to the visionary the course of events, and thus proved himself the Lord of history. Deutero-Isaiah had proclaimed in similar form this faith in the power of Yahweh over history: because Yahweh knows history beforehand, he is superior to all the gods (Isaiah 41,21ff; 45,19ff). The prophets wish, through the utterance of their words, to influence the course of history: the apocalyptic writers wish to interpret history in their written book. The Book of Daniel teaches trust in the mighty Lord of history. Under the oppression of the powers of the present who are God's enemies, it is a consolation for the reader that the overthrow of the rulers of the world and the end of the world are immediately imminent. The man who lives in this time no longer needs to fear any persecutions; for him it is only important to prepare himself for the advent of the Kingdom of God.

Legends and Visions in the Book of Daniel

The theory of the composition of the whole book as a unit by one single author seems at a first glance to contradict the form of the book. It is divided into two clearly separate halves: chapters 1-6 contain a cycle of legends about Daniel and his friends, chapters 7-12 on the other hand contain the descriptions of visions narrated in the first person singular.[155]

According to the legend Daniel held high office in the Babylonian, Median, and Persian courts (for fifty-seven years!). Various inconsistencies,[156] the change of the central figures in the different narratives (sometimes it is Daniel who stands in the centre, sometimes his friends) indicate that the author has collected, connected,[157] and made serviceable to a single purpose legends that were originally independent; they challenge the faithful to stand fast in the persecution. It is not possible to disentangle genuine historical tradition of events in the time of the exile. These legends are exemplary tales, to be compared with wisdom narratives, which represent how the wise man should behave, by using as illustration an ideal figure, for example that of Tobit.[158]

The legends are in several ways connected with the formally quite different descriptions of visions. Chapter 2, a legend, is closely akin to the visions; it deals with a dream and its interpretation, with the transformation and end of world history. The doctrine of God's care of the righteous finds expression not only in the legends, but we find it also in chapter 12, at the climax and conclusion of the second part. Both parts throw light upon the relation of the earthly world-powers to God, the Lord of history.

Thus we may really ascribe this writing to one author, but cannot apply to him the criterion of originality. He has put together legends already familiar, and in the visions of the second part he has used, enriched and developed materials lying ready to hand (e.g. in chapter 7 the mythological picture of the ocean of chaos and the older theophany-language of Israel, in chapter 2, the myth of the world's body). When he ascribes his work to a figure from the time of the exile, that is essentially consistent, for even in the essential thesis of his book he does not appeal to a new revelation of God — as the prophets did — still less to his own insight. The heart of his book, the foundation of his interpretation of scripture, is a word of Jeremiah. He has searched the scriptures to get an answer to his questions (chapter 9).

Interpretation of Jeremiah 25,11

Jeremiah had spoken of seventy years of exile (Jeremiah 25,11; 29,10). For the imaginary author Daniel, these seventy years had not yet passed, but the author of the second century is confused about this assertion. The final restoration of Israel at his time is still to be expected, the faithful are persecuted by a godless ruler, the temple is desecrated. A divine message declares to Daniel the real meaning of Jeremiah's words. The author of the book recognizes the exceptional significance of this place in scripture for his particular time. Jeremiah spoke of seventy year-weeks, i.e. seventy times seven years. Thus the author of the book estimates that at his time the half of the last year-week had already past, the end was immediately imminent.[159] Such speculations and calculations may shock us. Should they not be left to sectarian enthusiasts? For the author of the Book of Daniel they are not more than a means of linking beyond any possiblity of cavil his interpretation of history with the prophetic view of history, the sacred tradition.[160]

The interpretation of this word of Jeremiah is a point of central importance in the book. The period in chapter 9 defined as seventy year-weeks is repeatedly the object of consideration. Every vision looks back on the entire period, interprets it, and casts a new light upon it. In this outlook on history the Book of Daniel takes much from the heritage of the prophets. Like the prophets, the author of this work also knows that history has come to its end; a new beginning can only happen if a completely new start is made. Only God, who up till now has guided history can through a new intervention lead it out of the dead-end which it has reached.

Interpretation of World History
And yet since the time of the prophets, the life of Israel had completely changed. The exile brought to an end the period of Israel's independence; this epoch — from the creation to the destruction of Jerusalem — had been described and interpreted long before the creation of the book of Daniel. The author has no wish to add anything to this sanctioned interpretation. His sole concern is with the subsequent epoch of history. In this time the centre of history does not lie in Jerusalem, but in Babylon. And yet even in this time Israel's God remains the Lord of history. By means of the four successive world kingdoms he is extending his rule over all nations.

The prophets too saw the foreign peoples and their rulers as tools in God's hand; but their interpretation of the history of the times left untouched the immanent causal sequence of the world. In contrast with this, the apocalyptic writers see the real decisions as being made in the "beyond". Normally an insight into the true background of history is not possible; the apocalyptic writer must disclose it. Even the favoured seer has no access of his own to it; dreams and visions, sent by God and interpreted by God, bestow insight upon him. The prophets could expect every believer to recognize the signs of divine activity in the events of temporal history; but the apocalyptic represents himself as the only enlightened one, on whom the knowledge was bestowed how God controls world history.

According to the picture of history outlined by the apocalyptics the present stands under the sign of world history — God works in the whole world, in all the world kingdoms. This was preceded by the epoch of Israel's history — God worked only among his people. The epochs of world history are divided by the author into four kingdoms, following each other in succession.[161] It ends in the godless arrogance of the last kingdom. With the help of dreams and visions Daniel the man of God had led the kings of the Babylonian, Median and Persian kingdoms, and they had acknowledged the power of the God of Israel.[162] In contrast with this the rulers of the Macedonian-Hellenistic kingdom are known to Daniel from his vision of the future, but he is no longer able to give them counsel. With the last of these rulers, his contemporary Antiochus IV,

253

the apocalyptist deals in special detail. With this overweening opponent of God[162a] the second period of world history will end. God will destroy all that has hitherto existed, and create a new world without human aid. According to the vision in chapter 2 the stone detaches itself, which shatters the fourfold statue, without the cooperation of men.

The prophets also spoke of an immediately imminent turning-point; they exhorted men to repent now, before the end, and awakened the hope of the transformation of the human heart, so that it might be able to obey God. According to the prophets man must cooperate, in order that time's turning-point should come; but for the faithful who listen to the apocalyptic, nothing is left but to wait in the present evil time for the coming of the era, which is sent from above.

In contrast with the description of world history the depiction of the new indestructible Kingdom of God occupies but little space in chapters 7 and 12. The apocalyptic writer no more loses himself in speculations about the beyond than do the prophets.

Peculiarities of Style

The modern reader may at first be struck by the mysterious character of this writing. The disguise of historical events and personal names with the aid of figures, symbols and concealing names, may appear to him as deliberate obfuscation, whose intention is to make difficult for the uninitiated the understanding of the book.[163] Even to contemporaries the book seemed dark, but certainly less than it does to us. Its peculiarities of style were familiar to them. Reports of visions in the first-person, the basic form of the apocalyptic writings, were already known to the prophetic tradition.[164] Similarly they knew how to record the rapture of the prophets in order to beheld divine mysteries.[165]

Above all, Ezekiel is a model to the apocalyptic writer. The circumlocutory mode of speech is taken from him, which has the appearance of an extremely exact description, but in reality confines itself to the mere outward appearance, and is silent about what is essential, indeed often confuses the context with a plethora of details.[166] Even the concept on of heavenly messengers, who mediate between the incomparably distant God and man, was ready to hand contained in the tradition and is only much expanded in apocalyptic.[167] Further, the representation of the fate of great kingdoms in the fate of their kings as their representatives was customary.[168] Even individual symbolic pictures for the kings of the world empires could be recognized by the educated reader.[169]

The Book of Daniel is made very difficult for us by the fact that the author takes no trouble to be unambiguous and logical. He repeatedly attempts to say the same thing with many circumlocutions and approximations. This manner of speech was known to his comtemporaries from the prophets. As Hosea without concern can place side by side the punishment of returning to Egypt with exile to Assyria, so can Daniel 7,11 prophesy the death of Antiochus in a giant conflagration; according to Daniel 11,45 he dies in an invasion of Palestine. The Book of Daniel is distinguished from older writings of the Old Testament, not by a completely new manner of speech, but by the fact that it exaggerates already familiar peculiarities of style. Even the prophets can say the same thing in many ways, but here prolixity become a structural principle. All the visions from start to finish represent the same period of time — only the pictures vary each time. This exaggeration of the figurative, prolix and alogical method of expression required even from the ancient reader an unusual degree of attention, and was very well suited to serve as a secret language for the persecuted Jewish community.

FOOTNOTES
1 Deuteronomy 14,22; 19,14; 23,25f; 24,6.19ff; 25,4; 26,1ff.12ff.
2 Cf not only 5,2f but also 26,17; 27,9.
3 Deuteronomy 4,40; 5,1; 15,15.
4 Deuteronomy 5,39; 30,15,19.
5 Exodus 20,2; Deuteronomy 5,6. Cf A. Deissler, *Das Alte Testament und die Neuere Exegese* p.22f.
6 Josephus, *Jewish Antiquities* IV, 8,48, for example exemplifies the late Jewish conception of Moses as the author of the whole Pentateuch. M. Noth, *Überlieferungsgeschichte des Pentateuch* thinks that possibly Moses originally had a place on the Israel's tradition of the sojourn in the land east of Jordan, and was subsequently transferred from there into other traditional themes. In the Pentateuch itself the following texts are traced back to Moses; the Book of the Covenant (Exodus 24,4.7); the report about the war with the Amalekites (Exodus 17,14); the words of the covenant (Exodus 34,27f); a list of camps (Numbers 33,2). Deuteronomy ascribes the whole of Israel's law to Moses (Deuteronomy 31,24 etc.); similar statements in Joshua 1,8; 23,6; I Kings 2,3 etc., are dependent on Deuteronomy. The history of the Chronicler takes up the same idea (2 Chronicles 23,18; 25,4; Ezra 3,2; 7,6). See further Daniel 9,11; 9,14; Malachi 3,22.
7 Exodus 12,26; 13,14; Psalm 78,5.
8 Barr *Old and New in Interpretation*, p.67.
9 The only old reference is Hosea 12,14. Hosea does not even once mention the name of Moses, but speaks of "the prophet".
10 Exodus 17,8ff; Numbers 10,29ff; Exodus 18,12; 24,5.
11 Psalm 136; Exodus 15.
12 Ezekiel himself had retained the date in I,1. But it had soon become unintelligible — either Ezekiel himself had already omitted the reference to the thirtieth year, or a word had got lost. So a student of Ezekiel added a date attached to a word of the master. This date could be right.
13 According to Psalm 137 the exiles came to "the rivers of Babylon" for their laments.
14 According to Psalm 137 the prayers of the exiles, the "songs of Zion" were directed in longing back to Jerusalem, from there one can pray to God.

15 Isaiah 40,22; Job 22,13f; Lamentations 3,44; Job 35,5.
16 Ezekiel 3,11 is another example of the great importance for Ezekiel already of the current prophetic formulae. The formula of the messenger had hitherto for the prophets been the introduction to the actual word of God "Thus saith Yahweh . . ." Ezekiel wishes to impart nothing to his life-companions but this formula alone. For them it is of essential importance that God should send a messenger at all.
17 Genesis 11,5.7; Exodus 3,8; Isaiah 31,4; Exodus 19,11.18.20; Micah 1,3; Numbers 11,25; 12,5.
18 Only 1 Kings 19,11 spoke of the storm; only Exodus 19 of the mighty cloud and the lightning. Cf also Judges 5,4; Genesis 15,7.
19 Cf Joshua 10,11; 24,7; 1 Samuel 7,10; 12,17f; 21,14; Isaiah 28,2; 29,6; Hosea 4,19; Jeremiah 4,11 (the enemies' armies come like storm); Amos 2,5; Hosea 8,14; Jeremiah 17,27; 21,14; (the war burns like fire).
20 With this Ezekiel associates himself with the description of the Sinai theophany; God appeared *in* fire, thunder, and cloud, in signs that at the same time conceal him.
21 Cf Amos 5,20; Isaiah 9,1; Exodus 24,9ff; Deuteronomy 33,2.
22 Cf Judges 13,6ff; Genesis 18f; Joshua 5,13.
23 Ezekiel 1, 11.23; Exodus 25,50; 37,9; 1 Kings 6,25.
24 "Vault" = heaven: Genesis 1,6ff; 1,14f; 17.20; Psalm 19,2,150,1; solidification of the water: Job 37,18; Proverbs 8,27; the outstretched heaven: Isaiah 40,22; 42,5; 44,24; Jeremiah 10,12.
25 According to Exodus 24,9ff the elders beheld only the blue heaven beneath his feet; according to Isaiah 6 even the skirts of his garment filled the temple; according to Exodus 33,22f Moses does not see Yahweh until he has passed by.
26 Isaiah 31,3; Ezekiel 28,2.
27 Nahum 2,12; 3,7.18f; Ezekiel 32,1ff; Isaiah 14,4ff.
28 Ezekiel 14,12-23; 16,1-43; 17,1-10; 19,1-14 etc.
29 Cf Psalms 15,24.
30 G. von Rad, *Theologie des Alten Testaments*, p.188, Eng. tr. *Old Testament Theology*.
31 We must of course not be surprised that there are also anonymous prophetic texts. The disregard for the author in comparison with the work and its effect remained even in this sphere so dominating, that people had no hesitation in inserting prophetic texts into an existing tradition, or in appending it thereto, when their content fitted.
32 Amos 3,8; also Jeremiah 6,11; 20,7ff speak of this element of compulsion in the prophetic experience.
33 Jeremiah 15,19; Isaiah 30,2, cf. also Exodus 7,1; Haggai 1,13 the prophet represents himself as a messenger, who carries out God's commission.
34 Jeremiah 28,11ff; cf Jeremiah 42,7; Habakkuk 2,1.
35 Isaiah 40,27; 41,10; 49,14-16a; 54,7.10.
36 Isaiah 8,16ff; 29,11: the prophet does not preach any more, but continues his work only by writing.
37 Amos 3,7; Jeremiah 1,12; Ezekiel 12,25,28.
38 Hosea 9,3.6-10,6.
39 Cf 1 Kings 14,5; 22,5f.13; Jeremiah 37,17; 38,14; 42,3f.
40 Cf Genesis 32,4ff; 45,9; Numbers 22,16; 1 Kings 2,30; Isaiah 37,3; To the formula "Thus NN has spoken" belongs a short speech, which is easy to remember. The purely religious form of divine utterance, already long familiar in Israel, the oracle, was not used by the prophets. People could approach God with definite questions, mostly to be answered with "Yes" or "No". The answer was

received through the casting of lots, and was given by the mediating party, usually probably a priest, in the form of an oracle from God. In the case of an oracle God's word is perceptibly given by the means of an inanimate instrument; in the case of the prophets through the mouth of living men. People inquire of an oracle; the hearers of the prophet only rarely sought this word of God.

41 Transmitter of God's words: Judges 13,1; 1 Kings 19,5ff; 2 Kings 1,3.15; mediator of God's judgement; 2 Samuel 24; 2 Kings 19,3; mediator between God and the world: Genesis 28,12.

42 Not until late times are priests and prophets as mediators of the word of God also called God's messengers: Haggai 1,13; 2 Chronicles 36,15; Malachi 2,7; cf also Zechariah 12,8. The Hebrew word for "messenger", *mal'āk* becomes *angelos* in the Greek Bible, and then in English "angel".

43 The heavenly messenger on the other hand appeared so much the representative of Yahweh, that in some narratives in Genesis "messenger of Yahweh" can be replaced by "Yahweh": Genesis 16,7.9.11 — 16,13; Genesis 22,11 — 22,14; Genesis 31,11 — 31,13; Exodus 3,2f; 6,7; Judges 6,11ff — 6.14.16.

44 Cf Isaiah 44,24; 45,5; 45,7. Falkenstein von Soden, *Akkadische Hymnen* 67.115.

45 Ezekiel 37,13f; 37,28; etc; cf also Joel 2,27.

46 Cf e.g. Balla, *Botschaft der Propheten*, 91 — Amos 5,21ff; Hosea 6,6; 8,13; Isaiah 1,10-17; Jeremiah 6,19-21; 14,11f; Malachi 1,10.

47 Deuteronomy 33,11; 2 Samuel 24,23; Psalm 17,1; 27,7; 23,1 etc.

48 Isaiah 5,8ff; 28,1; Amos 5,18; 6,1; Habakkuk 2,6ff.

49 By so doing the prophets take up an important theme of wisdom-thinking; they exhibit the connection between man's action and its consequences.

50 Shiloh was a famous Israelite shrine, the place where the ark was kept. As excavations confirm, it was destroyed about 1050, in the times of the Philistines. Jeremiah's threat uttered against the temple led to a tumult and the accusation of the prophet. The latter defended himself by referring to the older word of Micah, cf Jeremiah 26.

51 Amos 8,3-6; 3,7f; Jeremiah 8,8.

52 In the case of the pre-exilic prophets the delivery of the divine message stands in the foreground. Later the prophets assumed it to be part of their task to take up the objections of their hearers. Deutero-Isaiah opposes the laments of Jerusalem with his prophecies of salvation (Isaiah 40,12-31; 49,11-26). Ezekiel teaches the doubting exiles in the style of the priestly instruction (*tōrāh*) how even they can live according to the divine covenant (Ezekiel 33,10-20). In Malachi, lastly, the apologetic discussion wholly predominates.

53 Jeremiah 2,4-13; 2,29-37; Micah 6,3-5; Isaiah 1,18.

54 Ezekiel 15,1ff; 17,1ff; 19,1-9; 19,10-14; 21,2ff; 24,9ff.

55 Isaiah 41,1-5. 21-29; 43,8-15; 44,6-8; 45,20-25.

56 Isaiah 43,22-28; 50,1-3.

57 Isaiah 49,14; 40,27; 42,14; 45,15ff; 42,24f; 51,17.20b; 54,7ff.

58 Hosea 6,1ff; Jeremiah 3,21-4,2; Hosea 14,3ff; cf also from a later time Isaiah 63,7-64,11.

59 Many announcements of salvation by these prophets begin with a reference to the preceding lament; then follows the actual word of salvation, which promises God's new gracious approach, and a statement about the purpose of the divine action: Isaiah 41,17-20; 42,14-17; 43,16-21; 45,14-17; 49,7-10. The two great poems in 49,14-20.21-23.24-26; and in 51,9-16.17-23; 52,1-6 both repeat this pattern three times. Even in the announcement of the new time of salvation in Isaiah 54f there are to be found echoes of the lament.

60 In Isaiah 44,23; 48,20f; 52,9f these eschatological hymns of praise conclude

parts of the book. Further examples: Isaiah 42,10-13; 45,8; Deuteronomy 32,43; Psalm 9,12f[11f]; Isaiah 12,4-6.

61 People knew, for example, the gesture of taking off ones shoes in a holy place (Exodus 3,5; Joshua 5,15); it was regarded as an insult to take off a person's shoes (Deuteronomy 25,9f); but the same sign could serve as the ratification of an agreement (Ruth 4,7).

62				
1) Encounter with God:	Judges 6, 11b-12a	Exodus 3, 1-3.4a 4b-9	Genesis 24, (34-36	Intro-duction
2) Preparation:	12a-13	10		of the
3) Commissioning:	14	11	37-38	sender)
4) Objection:	15	12a	39	
5) Promise of help:	16	12	40-41	
6) Sign:	17		42-48	

63 Isaiah 6,8-10; Ezekiel 2,3-5.

64 Elements of the category "report concerning a call" are also contained by Isaiah 40,1-11. The encounter with God is here only indicated by the voices, which the prophet hears sounding ever nearer and more urgently.

65 Isaiah 6,11a; cf Exodus 10,3.7; Numbers 14,27 and the reproach against God in the laments. Jeremiah 1,2 and Isaiah 40,6f contain the element of objection to the commission. (Isaiah 40,3-5.6a reproduces this commission).

66 This encouragement consists in the assurance of the divine help, but in Isaiah 6,11-13 in the promise that a remnant will be saved.

67 The probability is that they were written by the author himself, but that they were only subsequently inserted into his book at different places, cf the bridge-passages in 43,22-8; 45,20-25.

68 According to old oriental tradition the protection of the poor was the noblest task of the kings; in Israel it is the duty of every man, cf Isaiah 1,23; 10,1f; Exodus 22,20-26; 23,6-9; Amos 2,6-8; 5,10-15; Isaiah 5,8.

69 Micah 6,8; Isaiah 1,16b-17; Hosea 6,6.

70 Ezekiel 18,5ff quotes, for example, old lists of commandments.

71 Hosea 1,8; cf Isaiah 6,9 "this people here" — on the other hand see Exodus 19,4ff.

72 Ezekiel 15; Jeremiah 2,21 — on the other hand see Hosea 10,1; Isaiah 3,14.

73 Hosea 11,1ff; 11,5; 13,4ff.7; Ezekiel 36,16ff.22.

74 Isaiah 7,18; 8,7 etc.

75 Memories of these wars are reflected in Exodus 14; 17; Joshua 6; 8; Judges 4; 5; 7; 20; 1 Samuel 30; 2 Samuel 5.

76 Exodus 14,13f; Isaiah 7,9; 5,12; 22,11; 31,1.

77 Joshua 10,11; 24,7; 1 Samuel 7,10 — cf Isaiah 28,2; 29.6.

78 Amos 5,18ff; Isaiah 2,12ff.

79 Isaiah 1,26; 11,1.

80 Isaiah 49,14; Ezekiel 20,32.

81 Isaiah 52,11f; 55,12f.

82 2 Samuel 7. If one judges according to their genre, the messianic promises cannot be so easily placed. They have neither the form of a messenger's utterance, nor do they bear any traces at all of a proclamation to the public like the rest of the prophetic speeches. Were they from the first only formulated for a smaller circle?

83 Proverbs 22,17; 23,12.

84 Jeremiah 7,2; 11,6; 17,19f; 22,2ff; 26,2.

85 With Proverbs 8,16 cf Proverbs 22,17.

86 With Proverbs 8,19 cf Proverbs 16,16.

87 With Proverbs 8,15 cf Proverbs 29,4.14.

88 Tournay has counteu in Proverbs 10-27 ten instances of the vocative "son" in Proverbs 1-9, fifteen.
89 With Proverbs 8,32f cf Deuteronomy 8,5; 1,31; Hosea 11,1ff.
90 With Proverbs 8,17 cf Deuteronomy 4,19; Jeremiah 29,13.
91 With Proverbs 8,35 cf Amos 5,4-6.
92 Proverbs 10,17; 13,14; 16,22 etc.
93 Cf Jeremiah 2,13; Psalm 36,10[9]; 43,2f; 63,2[1].
94 Cf 2 Samuel 14,20; 1 Kings 3,28; 5,9,26.
95 It has been thought that the origin of wisdom should in this place be understood rather as begetting and issuing forth from God rather than as creation. Yet it is hardly possible to render the verb in 8,22 as "beget"; according to Old Testament parallels it must mean "possess", according to Ugaritic parallels, "create". This interpretation is supported also by the verb in v.23, which can be rendered by "form", "shape" and frequently describes the creation of earthly things. Verse 24 speaks indeed of the "birth" of Wisdom, yet this term can be used to describe the origin of mountains, earth and sea (Psalm 90,2; Job 38,8), without involving the notion of a begetting God. The passages influenced by Proverbs 8, Wisdom 9,9; Ecclesiasticus 1,4; 24,9, understand the origin of Wisdom as parallel to the creation of the rest of the world.
96 Isaiah 46,3-13.
97 Deuteronomy 4,6; Hosea 4,6; Jeremiah 8,9; 9,22f.
98 Zechariah 1,4; 7,7.12 appeals to "earlier prophets", this suggests that at his time a beginning was made to the collection of their books in a corpus.
99 Wisdom 7,27; dating from the first century B.C.
100 With Proverbs 1,20f; 8,1-6; 9,1ff cf Jeremiah 11,6; 26,2.
101 A comparison between Proverbs 1,16 and Isaiah 59,7, which have approximately the same date, shows how wisdom teachers and prophets of the later age fought side by side against the corrupt social conditions of their time.
102 With Proverbs 1,23 cf Hosea 3,5; Jeremiah 3,14; Isaiah 3,14; Isaiah 44,21f; Jeremiah 25,5; 35,15; 36,3.7; Zechariah 1,4; Malachi 3,7.
103 With Proverbs 1,24 cf Jeremiah 7,24-29; 11,8; 17,23; Isaiah 65,1f; 66,3f.
104 Cf Jeremiah 30.7; 50,27.31.
105 With Proverbs 1,28 cf Hosea 5,6; Micah 1,3; Jeremiah 11,11.
106 With Proverbs 1,26 cf Isaiah 26,2.17; 30,30.
107 Cf Psalm 2,4; 59,9.
108 Stele of Hammurabi 25,95-26,1.
109 Cf Psalm 1; 19,8[7]; 37,30; 119,97ff; Ecclesiasticus 1,26a; 6,37; 15,1b; 33,2 etc.
110 Psalm 104,2; Job 28,25ff; 38,4-6; Isaiah 40,12; Proverbs 8,29; Psalms 104,5; 75,4[3].
111 Proverbs 1,20.33; 8,4ff; 9,1ff; Ecclesiasticus 24.
112 Proverbs 7,4; Wisdom of Solomon 8.
113 We do not meet with the goddess Maat ("wisdom", "world order") in wisdom texts, but in myths and rituals of the Egyptians.
114 Job 28 is an independent poem, inserted later into the book.
115 Isaiah 3,3; Jeremiah 9,16; 10,9; Ezekiel 27,8.
116 Proverbs 15,33; 14,27.
117 Proverbs 1,7; 9,10; Job 28,28; Psalm 111,10; Ecclesiasticus 1,14.20.
118 In its present form the book is no longer a complete unity; there were later additions to it: chapter 28, the speeches of Elihu and the speech of God about Behemoth and Leviathan seem not quite to fit into the context.
119 Cf: 1. The Sumerian poem in ANET Suppl., 589ff: a wise, just and fortunate man is stricken with disease and misfortune, but he does not rebel, but makes a

lament to his divinity. The latter is pleased, and frees him.

2. The Accadian poem in ANET Suppl. 596ff: A man in high office falls into distress, though innocent. He is, however conscious that the god might have been offended at something, though he did not himself feel that he had erred. The god makes things wonderfully change for the better, and completely restores him.

3. A pessimistic Accadian dialogue between master and servant in ANET Suppl. 600f: if the master gives a task to his servant, the latter knows how to find a reason for it — but if the master cancels the task, the servant knows just as good arguments for his doing so. Only one proposal of the master's causes a different reaction in the servant: The master plans to kill him: "Then my master will not survive me by three days."

4. An Accadian conversation in ANET Suppl, 601ff: a sufferer asks his friend what use is there in honouring the gods. In reply the friend points out to him, that men do not understand the gods, but should concern themselves about this difficult question. In conclusion, the sufferer asks the god for help.

5. An Egyptian conversation about suicide, ANET, 405ff. A man speaks to his soul, he wishes for death, since he finds life intolerable. At first the soul agrees with this, but then counsels him to enjoy life, then declares that in any case it will stay with this man.

120 Cf Job 23,13ff: God stands above every order of which we can have experience.

121 Cf 31,35ff.

122 Cf Job 3,8; 10,8-11; 15,7f etc.

123 Cf Job 14,7ff; 17,13.

124 Job 7,17.21.

125 For these different attempts, cf the books of Schmid, Richter and Westermann.

126 Job 8,8ff; 15,17ff.

127 Job 15,4-6; 16,1-4; 19,1-6; 19,21f.28f; 20,1-3 etc.

128 Job 31; cf Joshua 22,22ff.

129 Job 9,2f.14-16.19-21.22.24.28b; 10,4-7.14f.17 etc.

130 Job 13,13ff; 16,19ff; 19,25; 16,18.

131 Job 9,24; 10,18f.

132 Job 6,4; 7,14; 16,9.12f; 19,18ff.

133 Job 16,18ff; 19,23ff; 23,3ff — cf with this attitude that of the lament prayers, see p.138ff.

134 Job 9,5ff; 12,7ff.

135 Isaiah 40,12ff; Job 28; Ecclesiasticus 1,2-4; Proverbs 30,1-4.

136 Job 3,11ff; 6,8ff; 7,15.

137 Ecclesiastes 1,15; 2,14a; 9,4b.16a etc.

138 Ecclesiastes 10.1.

139 Ecclesiastes 4,5f; 8,1; 10,16-19.

140 Ecclesiastes 10,16; 9,13ff; 9,7ff.

141 Proverbs 7,6ff; Psalm 73; Proverbs 24,30-34; Psalm 37,25.35f.

142 The translation of *hebel* by "vanity" contains a value-judgement that does not reproduce the Hebrew equivalent. This word is meant to describe valuelessness, transiency. A parallel expression of Koheleth's is "Hunting after the wind".

143 Ecclesiastes 7,5.11f.19; 10,2ff; 10,12ff.

144 Ecclesiastes 3,11; 7,23f; 8,17.

145 Ecclesiastes 8,12ff.

146 Ecclesiastes 7,7; 9,11f.16.

147 Ecclesiasticus 16,24ff; 33,7ff.

148 Loretz reminds us of the speech of the Mesopotamian hero Gilgamesh to his

friend Enkidu, who fears the struggle with the monster Chumumba (Loretz, *Koheleth* 126):
"Only the gods sit for ever on their thrones with Shamash (the sun),
Men's days are numbered.
Whatever they do, is only a breath (cf Ecclesiastes!)
But you here are still afraid of death!
So I will have the advantage of you . . .
Were I to fall, I would make my name memorable;
(people will say) Gilgamesh fell in battle with the warlike Chumumba."
On the subject of the famous name in the Old Testament see Proverbs 10,7; Psalm 112,6; Ecclesiasticus 41,11ff; 44,6ff; Job 18,16ff; 30,8.
The praise of subsequent fame is a theme that we often encounter in ancient times. We may compare how Horace himself boasts of his poetry: "Exegi monumentum aere perennius . . . I have erected a monument more enduring than bronze."
149 Ecclesiastes 7,2; 3,22.
150 Ecclesiastes 2,16; 6,4; 9,5.
151 Cf ANET, 467 and ANET, 427ff, Ahiqar VI, 92. A similar challenge is to be heard in the Gilgamesh Epic. It is given to Gilgamesh who has set out on the search for eternal life:
"Gilgamesh, whither are you hurrying?
You will not find the life that you are seeking!
When the gods created mankind
they gave death to mankind as its lot,
they kept life in their own hands.
You, Gilgamesh, fill your stomach,
rejoice night and day,
give a feast of joy every day,
dance and play day and night,
keep your clothes spotless,
your head washed, bathe yourself with water,
look at your children at your side,
may your wife rejoice in your bosom."
On this theme in the Old Testament, cf Proverbs 5,18f; Ecclesiasticus 14,11-19.
152 Ecclesiastes 2,10.24f; 3,12f; 8.15.
153 Ecclesiastes 3,13; 5,18.
154 Ecclesiastes 2,26; 6,2.
155 1,1-2,4a has been handed down in Hebrew, 2,4b — 7,28 in Aramaic, and the conclusion again in Hebrew. The changes of language, understandable when we think of the late date, a time when Aramaic was ousting Hebrew — do not correspond to the formal structure of the book. We agree with Bentzen (*Daniel*, HAT 1952,p.8) that it can perhaps be explained by the conjecture that in the confusion of the times of persecution the book was circulating in fragments in various languages, and was subsequently reconstructed from these.
156 The date of 2,1 and the date recorded in 1,18 do not agree.
157 5,20 looks back to chapter 4; in chapter 2 Daniel is the only actor, but the friends are mentioned.
158 An older, but widely known ideal example of this genre is the narrative of the wise Ahikar.
159 From the destruction of the temple to its rebuilding: 7 × 7 years.
From its rebuilding to the murder of the legitimate high priest: 62 × 7 years.
From the death of Onias to the final restoration: 1 × 7 years.
The half of this is past. Cf also Daniel 7,25; 8,14; 12,7. In Daniel 12,11d the period

of time to the end is lengthened — the writer of the book found from experience that his reckoning did not add up.

160 Insofar the Jews who still honoured his work long after this calculation had proved wrong understood his intention rightly, and inserted it in the last part of their collection of the holy scriptures (the $k^e\underline{t}\bar{u}\underline{b}\hat{\imath}m$, i.e. writings). In the Christian canon it belongs to the prophetic books, on which the author chiefly bases himself.

161 This first comprehensive sketch of a systematic world history is still influential in the mediaeval historians, more than a thousand years later.

162 Daniel 3,28f; 4,22.31.

162a Daniel 7,25; 8,10f.

163 In Daniel 8,26; 12,9 the visionary is instructed to keep the vision secret.

164 Amos 7; Isaiah 6; Ezekiel 1.

165 Ezekiel 3,12; 8,3; 11,1; 11,24; 43,5; 1 Kings 18,12.

166 Cf Daniel 7,12f with Ezekiel 1,26f.

167 Ezekiel 8,2; 40,3; Zechariah 1,9.13.14; 2,2; 4,1.4f; etc.

168 Ezekiel 19; 28; 31.

169 Daniel 4,7ff; the ruler as tree, cf Ezekiel 31. Daniel 8, the rulers as wild animals, cf Ezekiel 19. In the ancient star-maps the constellation of the Ram belonged to the king of the Persians. The Hellenistic Seleucids had themselves depicted on coins as bedecked with horns.

CHAPTER IV

THE COMPOSITE WORKS

THE EARLIER LITERARY HISTORY OF THE PENTATEUCH

1. TEXTUAL EXAMPLE: THE PROGRAMME OF THE YAHWISTIC HISTORICAL
WORK (GENESIS 12,1-4A)

Yahweh said to Abram,
"Go out
from your own country,
from your kinsmen,
and from your father's house,
and go to a country that I will show you.
(2) I will make you into a great nation,
I will *bless* you and make your name great;
be a *blessing*.
(3) Those that *bless* you I will *bless*,
those that curse you I will execrate.
All the families in the earth are *blessed* in you.
(4a) And so Abram set out as Yahweh had bidden him, and Lot went
with him.

Position in the Pentateuch
   This text is a cardinal point in the Pentateuch. The preceding chapters
are planned to lead up to it, and the succeeding ones develop out of it.
The reader was previously led through the generations of mankind,
which lived on the earth since the creation. From these various tribes
one, the tribe of Terah, had been selected. The selection goes further;
God turns in a special way to a man from this family. This election of
Abram, of which Genesis 12,1ff speaks, stands at the point of intersec-
tion of human history: from mankind the lines of descent led to this man
chosen by God; from him the people of Israel proceeds, and thus once
again the blessing is to be bestowed on mankind.

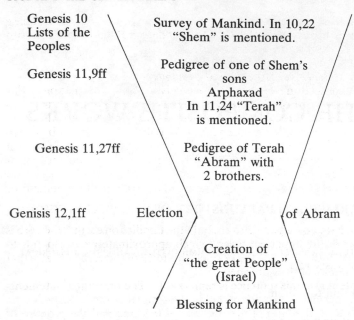

Genesis 10
Lists of the
Peoples

Survey of Mankind. In 10,22
"Shem" is mentioned.

Genesis 11,9ff

Pedigree of one of Shem's
sons
Arphaxad
In 11,24 "Terah"
is mentioned.

Genesis 11,27ff

Pedigree of Terah
"Abram" with
2 brothers.

Genisis 12,1ff   Election   of Abram

Creation of
"the great People"
(Israel)

Blessing for Mankind

Genesis 12,1ff is a key passage in the structure of the Pentateuch and therefore deserves special attention.

This text is not one of the numerous old popular sagas which have been built into the Pentateuch, for it lacks the element of increase and relaxation of tension, which is central to a narrative. God utters a command, and Abraham carries it out, apparently without contradiction. Nor can this section be understood as the fragment or the summary of a complete narrative, nor yet as the bare communication of facts which the collector might have taken from ancient narratives;[1] for the chief interest is centred not on what happened, the departure from Mesopotamia, but on God's word.

The man who formed this text, was well aware of the significance of this passage; his purpose is to underline it as the beginning of the history of Israel. This story is for him more than a succession of events. He begins it with the sentence "Yahweh said." The history of Israel in his eyes is a conversation of Yahweh with his people. This conversation began when God spoke to Abram; from that moment he did not let it be broken off. Thus it can be said that here it is not a narrator, but a theologian who is speaking.

In the interpretation of Genesis 12,1ff a modern reader might ask himself, how indeed Abraham, the citizen of a heathen land could have been able to hear God's command. The author of this text never put himself this question. He is not offering to us a story that explains the figure of Abram to us; he wants to make clear what is the determining factor in the history of his people. The foundation of this history is a word of God.

Analysis of Sentence Structure and Content
Careful reflection has obviously been given to the formulation of this fundamental word of God[2] It begins with a command to Abram "Go out!" Then — in three parallel sentences — God describes to Abram all that he must leave behind;[3] and just as important is the subsequent promise — in five parallel sentences: Abram is told how Yahweh will deal with him subsequently. This promise is not linked to the condition of Abram's obedience; it is offered as a gift. The word of God leaves no room for the question whether Abram will carry out the command or not.

A sixth sentence of promise (v.3b) is given special emphasis. The subject is here no longer Yahweh, but "the families on earth"; the verb is no longer in the imperfect tense (which approximately corresponds to the English future), but in the perfect (this form of the verb indicates that a fact is immovably established).

In content also this sentence is remarkable. The preceding statements in God's speech can be understood in the context of the tradition of the fathers, i.e. in the light of the promise of the land and the promise of descendants. The fundamental meaning of the promise of the land was the capture of Canaan by the tribes of Israel. These had seen in the shrines of the cultivated land which they conquered places that were made sacred by experiences of their ancestors.[4] They had told how the whole land into which they had penetrated had long ago been promised to their ancestors. In Genesis 12,1ff this theme of the promise of the land is indicated. Yahweh will "show" Abram the land; there is still no word of "giving" it (in contrast with this cf 12,7).

In what follows, the theme of the promise to the descendants is introduced quite explicitly. This promise had already its place in the family sagas, in which anxiety concerning successors plays a great part; the continuance or extinction of the family depends upon it.[5] Further, the fame, the praise and the blessing of the ancestor fits into this context.

The theme of the sixth, formally distinguished consequential clause in Genesis 12,3b, stands on a different footing:
All the families of the earth are blessed in you.
The men in whose circle the narratives of the fathers were created, were still living in a prehistorical world. They certainly never reflected on the relation of Abram to the peoples; their interest was focussed on the family and the clan. Just as little did the Israelite tribes who occupied Canaan think of looking on Abram as a blessing for the peoples. They had to defend their lives against the peoples.

This sentence leads us into another period of Israel's history. Such a thought could have originated in Solomon's time, in which the kingdom conquered by David was consolidated. In this age people could speak of Israel as the "great people" and of the "great name" of its ancestor (12,2). Israel could feel itself superior in contrast with the peoples. In Genesis 12,1-4a there speaks a man of this high summer of the time of Solomon. It is the so-called Yahwist, who at that time created his historical work out of the old traditions of Israel. He takes over from the tradition the promise of descendants, of the land, and of blessing, but he gives to these traditional conceptions a new interpretation in the light of the "modern" thought, that Israel is a blessing for the people. With this intention God blessed the ancestor, with this intention he gave Israel and the land and made it great: it was to bring blessing to the peoples.

Relation to Prehistory and to Israel's History

Thus the Yahwist sets out in Genesis 12,1ff the programme of his work. The most important word of his programme, underlined by fivefold repetition, is "blessing". Anyone who knows the beginning of the Yahwist's work, must pay attention to the word "blessing". As a prelude to the history of Israel the Yahwist has put together a series of sagas dealing with mankind, which tell of the curse that lies on men.[6]

To be sure, this curse was never quite absolute, God's solicitude always kept a way open for the following generations.[7] Only the story of the Tower of Babel ended without a sign of the kindness of God. The report of the election of Abram fills in this gap. Genesis 12,1ff offers the answer to the question that the story of the Tower of Babel had left open. For the Yahwist the history of Israel is an answer to the problem that mankind cannot solve. How is it to be understood that a curse lies on the world created by God? In Genesis 12,1ff, a bridge-passage of his work formulated by himself, the Yahwist declares that not a curse, but blessing is to be mankind's destiny. After mankind has failed, Israel is to confer the blessing.

But these crucially important verses of the Yahwist's historical work do not only look back to prehistory. The Yahwist also builds bridges to the stories taken from the history of Israel. Parts of God's speech are later repeated in new contexts, Genesis 12,2 is twice repeated in the last sections of the Yahwist's work:

Those that bless you I will bless, those that curse you, I will execrate, says Balaam concerning Israel (Numbers 22,6; 24,9). The saying about "blessing" occurs five times more in the story of the fathers. It reminds us what is at stake when the promise of descendants begins to find fulfilment in the family history of the fathers.[8]

Also the most important sentence of the "programme" which the Yahwist underlined by its position, the form of verbs and sentences, and expression, the sentence about the blessing for the peoples, recurs twice more almost word for word (Genesis 18,18; 28,14).

In addition to this the Yahwist bestows special attention to the theme we are here discussing even in his reworking of older traditional sagas. He finds examples of the way in which Israel can become a blessing for the peoples. Abraham generously hands over to his nephew Lot (the ancestor of a foreign people), a better piece of land (Genesis 13); he prays to God unweariedly for the Sodomites (Genesis 18,17ff); the blessed Isaac makes peace with the prince of the foreign people by a treaty (Genesis 26,1-31); Laban, the Aramaean, finds that through Jacob his property increases (Genesis 30,27.30); Joseph brings blessing into the house of the Egyptian Potiphar.[9]

In the story of the exodus from Egypt the catchword occurs again in a striking position. According to Exodus 10,28f Pharaoh wished to break off relations with Moses completely; the death of all the firstborn compels him to call Moses again, and to ask him to intercede with God (Exodus 12,29ff). Israel shall entreat with God even for Egypt, which has held Israel in slavery, The Sinai tradition is only briefly represented by the Yahwist, since it remains unproductive for his theme concerning Israel's position among the peoples. But in the report concerning Israel's sojourning in Moab at the beginning of the capture of the land, we immediately find again the familiar theme: the king of the Moabites calls Balaam, in order that he may curse Israel — and yet he blesses it!

It is not a matter for surprise that the question of the relation of Israel to the peoples is of such great interest to the Yahwist. In his time Israel lived in active intercourse with the peoples. Many surrounding peoples were subject to the king of Israel.[10] Yet it is astonishing that the Yahwist conceives of Israel's relation to the peoples in terms of "blessing". By so doing he not only reminds Israel of its responsibility for the others, but in this splendid time remains conscious of the possibility of failure. To be sure, Israel as the people of the blessing is pre-eminent among the peoples, but that makes her transgressions all the more grievous. It is certainly no accident that at the beginning and end of the Yahwist's work blessing and disobedience follow one another closely. Yahweh has no sooner promised the blessing to Abram, than the ancestor through his lie becomes a disaster for Pharaoh rather than a blessing. Shortly after the blessing of Balaam has been proclaimed upon Israel, the people begins to fall away from Yahweh.[11] This warning report is probably the last piece that we know of the Yahwist's historical writing. The Yahwist is not only conscious of the greatness of his people; he knows too of its weakness.

Genesis 12,1ff is a text which the Yahwist, the collector of old folk-narratives and other traditions, has formulated himself. The inter-pretation of this text and the definition of its place in the historical work of the Yahwist, have shown that he is more than a collector. He has a clearly defined conception of the meaning of Israel's history; he is a theologian who sets himself to make clear to his contemporaries their position in relation to God.

2. THE BASIC WRITINGS OF THE PENTATEUCH

At a time when the romantic movement in Germany had awakened an interest in the past of the peoples, the brothers Grimm collected German fairy tales which they had got old people in the villages to tell them. There was also a desire to preserve the songs which had been sung from ancient times among the people, before they had been forgotten (*Des Knaben Wunderhorn*). The great collection of "German Legal Anti-quities" was created at the same time. In Israel too there were collections of old tales, songs, and laws. There too people were interested in their own people's traditions of the past. The Yahwist (J) wrote about 900; about a century later the Elohistic Work (E) came into being; in the last quarter of the eighth century the basic document of the later Deuter-onomy was found during work on the temple, and lastly, in post-exilic times the priestly document (P) gave yet another new comprehensive fomulation of the old traditions. Can these works perhaps be compared with the productions of the German romantics?

The compilations of German romanticism are evidence to us of the longing to look back at past times; they were created by the wish to protect precious antiquities from oblivion, and by the desire to become acquainted with the roots from which contemporary life and thought had developed. Anyone who with such intentions confronts the testimonies of the past, will above all endeavour to restore and preserve them with the greatest possible accuracy — especially in their idiosyncrasies. The collectors in Israel did not let such considerations trouble them much. They did indeed have an understandable reverence for everything of honourable antiquity, which was a motive for them to leave it unim-paried as far as possible. Thus often they preferred to accept roughnes-ses, rather than to smooth them out and harmonize them at the cost of the material before them. (It is just these inconsistencies that enable us now to rediscover the original units from which they put together their work.) But they had but little interest in everything in the ancient material received by them, which was typical of the distinctively different life and thought of the past.

Before the composite works set down in writing the traditional mate-rial, it had been orally transmitted in two principal ways; in the instruc-tion of the priests, and in the story-telling of the people. The aim of these was to give pleasure to the hearers, to inform them about contemporary conditions, to instruct them concerning their religious duties or to encourage them to piety. As in the priestly instruction the various groups of traditions (the traditions of the fathers, of the exodus, of Sinai and of the conquest of the land) grew together into an ordered whole; the living faith of the present was the chief goal of all endeavours; Israel must know that it owed its life to the guidance of Yahweh, and must respond thereto with trust and obedience. Both among the people and in the official priestly tradition the motive for handing down memories of the past was interest in the present. The motivation of the authors of the basic writings of the pentateuch was precisely the same. Their composite works are not intended merely to give due place to the old material, but also to vindicate their own conception of the history of Israel. But this understanding of history in each case is rooted in the times in which the works were created.

For various reasons, however, it is not easy to discover these basic ideas. In the first place the original writings have not come down to us intact; they were gradually put together by later redactors to form the one great work of the pentateuch. It is certain that a series of parallel traditions have been sacrificed to this work of redaction, since the redactors did not wish to produce two or three accounts.

But neither do the authors of the sources themselves make it easy for us to discover the particular character of each of their books. They were more interested in reproducing faithfully the material lying before them than in underlining their own achievement.

3. THE WORK OF THE YAHWIST

The Yahwist's Sources

The first person who put together the old traditions in a composite work, was the so-called Yahwist. We should not underestimate his achievement. He had at his disposal, on the one hand, individual sagas that were in circulation in different places in Israel, each of them self-contained and complete. On the other hand the outline of the priestly tradition was available to him, which sketched in bold outline the course of the sacred history of the people. He harmonized these two different sources of the tradition. By finding a place for the manifold narratives and accounts in the official priestly scheme of the history of Israel, he filled the latter with vivid life. The Yahwist above all produces narratives whose scene is laid at places in the southern kingdom — it was probably here too that the Yahwist's document originated. But there is not yet any trace to be found of hostility to the north. The passage of Abram sanctifies the cult-centres of the north, Shechem and Bethel (Genesis 12,6-9); but the chief memory of the patriarchs is attached to Mamre in the south. Observation of this kind cause us to infer that the Yahwist must have created his work some time before the division of the kingdoms.

It is possible that he was able to base himself on predecessors who had already compiled similar composite works. We might so far agree with the hypothesis that would suggest that the sign J denoted rather a "school" than an individual man. But there are important grounds which suggest that the Yahwist was an individual author.

Individual Traits

Among the main written sources of the pentateuch, the Yahwistic work bears the most deeply the imprint of an author who was a personality with a will of his own. It is above all in his introductory study of prehistory that J distinguishes himself from the earlier religious tradition and from the religious outlook of the subsequent centuries. Faith in God as the creator played only a small part in Israel till long after J's time. This doctrine only attained a greater significance three hundred years later, in Deutero-Isaiah, at the time of the exile. There is originality in the thought of the Yahwist that the destiny of all mankind is linked with the history of Israel; this thought was hardly ever again so prominent in the religious outlook of Israel as in this early work.

Such an emancipated vision of humanity had been made possible by the unusual conditions of his time. The two great powers of the ancient eastern world, Egypt and Babylon, were then experiencing a time of decline. J speaks in slightly scornful tones about Babylon in the story of the building of the tower (Genesis 17,7ff), and of the strong Egyptian task-force he can say

"So you will never see the Egyptians again" (Exodus 14,13).

In this breathing-space in the history of the ancient east the insignificant people of Israel was able to bring the empire of David and Solomon to a brief flowering, and to bring other peoples into subjection. This experience might have led to contempt for foreigners, but it leads the Yahwist to the faith that Yahwist Israel's God, is the Lord of the whole world, the God whom long ago Enosh worshipped,[12] who holds the destiny of all mankind in his hand. Foreigners are to have a share in Israel's blessing. Foreigners go out of Egypt with Israel;[13] Hobab, the Midianite joins himself to the journeying people of Yahweh.[14] The Yahwist above all proves his self-willed outlook on history by prefacing Israel's history with prehistory. According to all that research has hitherto discovered about the development of the faith of Israel, the Yahwist was the first man who held it necessary to find a place for the history of Israel in the history of mankind. The integration of prehistory and the history of the people is his work.

But the prehistory itself is by no means the product of his creative imagination. He built it up out of narratives which were current among the people. The "mankind sagas" were familiar before his day; he only discovered their value in expressing his conception of Israel's mission.

A further important fact is to be traced back to the Yahwist: the mankind sagas were current among the people as individual self-contained pieces. The Yahwist ordered them, placing them in a series. In spite of failure and punishment, the life of mankind continues to move towards a goal. He makes out of individual self-contained sagas a *prehistory*, which in spite of the curse that mankind brings upon itself, always leaves open the way for the mercy of God.

Texts formulated by the Yahwist
There are only a few sentences that can with some certainty be regarded as formulations of his own. We must study them with all the more attention, for they disclose the conception of this work. We encounter two such passages in the prehistory, Genesis 6,5-8 and 8,21. In both cases the author makes Yahweh speak to himself. He interprets the events which he reports to us, by means of the word of God.

In Genesis 6,5ff God perceives the complete corruption of man. This interpretation gives theological meaning to the narrative of the Flood. The whole creation is not worthy to exist in the sight of God; in reality God ought to rescind it.

In spite of this God has not given man up. Through Noah the history of mankind continues. Once more this fact is interpreted by a word of God. God guarantees continued stability in the course of nature (Genesis 8,21):

While the earth lasts seedtime and harvest, cold and heat, summer and winter, day and night, shall never cease.

In heathen myths and festivals, which are meant to secure the return of the rainy season, the continued existence of the creation, the fear of the ancient people in the presence of uncomprehended powers of nature finds expression. The Yahwist knows that he is freed from this uncertainty. The heathen lived in fear and uncertainty, because they could not trust the caprice of their gods. But in contrast with this the Yahwist had stated in Genesis 6,5ff that not God, but the wickedness of men endangers the secure existence of the creation. Here in Genesis 8,21 he takes a further step. He believes that in spite of all human wickedness there is no danger for the creation; God's word gives him grounds for this confidence. God has promised to preserve the creation, although it does not deserve this.

These two passages, which the Yahwist himself formulated, are clearly related to one another; they develop one coherent theological thought. Further they prepare us for the central passage of the Yahwistic work, for Genesis 12,1ff. Here the Yahwist shows — once again in a word of God — what God's intention is: continuing to ensure the existence of the creation. His purpose is to send his blessing to mankind in this world through Israel.[15]

In Genesis 12,1 the Yahwist has linked together two different groups of tradition; the history of mankind and the history of Israel belong together, in Israel the salvation of mankind is decided. What he has practised in that text on a large scale, he continues in Genesis 18,17ff on a small scale. The conversation of God with Abraham is a bridge-passage between the report of the visit of the three men to Abraham and the tradition of the overthrow of Sodom. In the bold intercession of Abraham with Yahweh, the ancestor executes the commission which he received in Genesis 12,1ff: to be a blessing for the kindred of the earth. In the ancient world the fate of the individual counts for but little in comparison with the fate of the society to which he belongs — all the more surprising in this dialogue is Abraham's urgent request in spite of this to save the whole city for the sake of a few righteous men. But does not the idea of the Yahwist stand in the background, that the *one* Israel is destined to be a blessing for all?

It is certainly no accident that in all the texts which the Yahwist inserts in his compilation in order to interpret history, God himself speaks. In the prehistorical part he twice uses God's *monologue*, in order to underline the meaning of the narrative; at the beginning of the history of Israel stands God's *word spoken to* Abram, after the call of Abraham Jahweh carries on a *dialogue* with Abram. The Yahwist has obviously chosen the form of speech of the bridge passages with great deliberation. What his purposes with the whole of mankind are, Yahweh decides for himself; but as soon as he has chosen Abraham, he gives to the latter an insight into his deliberations, and calls for his active response.

With the conversation of Genesis 18,17ff the Yahwist has fused two different sagas into a unity. He had succeeded in binding the mankind sagas together to form *one* prehistory; in the same way his work also binds together the hitherto isolated traditions from the past of Israel to form the picture of *one* goal-directed history of Israel.

The Promise as a Connecting Link

An important instrument for the Yahwist in his task of giving unity to all the traditional material contained in the narratives from the call of Abraham down to the story of Joseph, is the theme of the promise made to the ancestors. The promise of descedants,[16] and the promise of the land, which were given to the fathers, point to the time in which Israel as a great people entered Canaan. With the help of these promises the Yahwist spans the arc from the beginning of Israel's history to the end of his work.

Representation of Events in the World

The historical work of the Yahwist can in many respects be compared with the history of David's succession to the throne, the other great work of Solomon's time.[17] The Yahwist knew how to underline and fill out the features in the narrative presented to him, which were valued in his time. For him there is no question that God is at work in everything that happens. But this is not visible in spectacular events. The great destructive Flood is caused by forty days' rain, the Red Sea is dried up by the east wind.[18] And it is not only to the powers of nature that God has given free scope. Man too is not immediately controlled by God in his decisions, his heart is open to many other influences, and it is free to direct itself according to its own impressions. So the Yahwist's narrative of the Fall represents with great artistry the psychological processes in the hearts of the characters of the characters.[19]

It is hard for us to imagine in what way God operates in the world. For this reason it may please us when the Yahwist conceals the divine intervention under the depiction of natural happenings. Yet when he does so, he is answering problems quite different from ours. That gods are active in the world of men and the world of nature was taken for granted throughout the ancient world. Man felt himself to be the plaything of forces he could not understand, which were at work in nature and even in politics. He understood these to be divine powers, and tried to influence them in his favour by mythical and magical devices. In contrast with this, the Yahwist asserts that God gives free rein to the powers of nature and the instincts of the human heart; God stands so far above these powers of nature that he is not to be influenced.

Anthropomorphisms

Much though the Yahwist's style of narrative may attract us, with its sober interest in all natural happenings, another feature of the style of this work must seem strange to us, its anthropomorphisms when it speaks about God. Seldom elsewhere in the Bible are human characteristics so boldly transferred to God. God repents of having created man, he is troubled for this reason; he closes the ark upon Noah; he deliberates with himself whether he should not reveal his plans to Abraham.[20] We should not understand such passages as evidence of a primitive conception of God. This author living in the period of "Enlightenment" in the time of Solomon is anything but primitive. He contrasts his anthropomorphism with the current representations of the gods in his environment. El, to whom belongs the symbol of the bull, had superhuman fertility, Baal, who casts thunderbolts and drives above the clouds, has superhuman power; far away from men, the gods determine the fate that men must accept. Israel's God is indeed superior to all human powers, but he encounters man not as a frightening and capricious power, but as a God with whom man can speak face to face.

4. THE WORK OF THE ELOHIST

It is now hardly possible to know the fundamental theme of the work of the Elohist. The redactor who put together J and E used J as a foundation. E was only used where according to the opinion of the redactor it offered special traditions. So this work has been preserved for us only in fragments. Yet, judged by literary style and ideas, and also by the place of origin of the traditions, sections of E can be clearly distinguished from those of J.

It is clear that E has preserved a larger proportion of traditions of the tribes who settled in the northern kingdom than J — narratives from the northern shrines of Bethel and Shechem, narratives about Joseph, the ancestor of Ephraim and Manasseh, the great northern tribes.[21] Thus the place of E's origin also is probably the north. Yet the author does not think in particularistic terms; he, like J, has the whole of Israel in view.

Theological Elaboration of the Material

In J doctrines of the faith which were the foundation of his life remain implicit in the background of his narratives — in E the urge to exact expression comes more clearly in evidence. Some examples may clarify this.

The work of the Elohist differs from that of the Yahwist; it only begins with the stories about Abraham. The first passage that a great many scholars ascribe to him is Genesis 15,1-6. Here his purpose is to mediate theological insight with the help of a story; the heart of the passage is the conversation between God and Abraham. In this the text distinguishes itself clearly from the old sagas, which draw their interest from concrete incidents. Theological terms interpret Abraham's behaviour.

Abraham *puts his faith* in the Lord, and the Lord *counted* that faith to him as *righteousness*.

The motifs applied in Genesis 15,1-6 also serve for theological discussion. In various narratives for example a sign gives help to man — here it makes faith even harder: Abraham is to look up to the starry heavens — how can a childless man have so many descendants? The Elohist does not tell a story here, he illustrates a theological thought; the fulfilment of the promise transcends all human possibilities.

The saga of the sacrifice of Issac probably originally explained the replacement of child sacrifice by the sacrifice of animals. It interests the Elohist for another reason. His intention is to explain how God could ever require from Abraham the sacrifice of his son. This question had not been raised at all by the original narrators of the Abraham saga. For to them it was natural that a God who bestowed fruitfulness and children might require a child for himself. Sacrifice of the first born was familiar to them from their surroundings. The Elohist will have only known of the sacrifice of the first-born as an abominable heathen custom. For him there was no longer any proof needed that Yahweh did *not* require the death of the eldest child. On the contrary, to him this narrative seemed to besmirch the conception of Yahweh. Was Yahweh to treat Abraham like a heathen child-devouring Moloch? He could not reconcile this narrative with this theology. Therefore he prefaced it with a sentence: God was testing Abraham. He converted the aetiology of a custom (animal sacrifice instead of child-sacrifice; into a theological parable: God can impose so hard a test on the believer.

Thus he gives a new appearance to an old form of this narrative. This saga of the offering of Isaac had not only been told with an aetiological intention, in order to explain the Israelites' custom of animal sacrifice. It was also a family-saga; what was at stake was the rescue of a single descendant, the continuation of the family. To this memory the Elohistic theology can look back. God requires from Abraham the sacrifice of

Isaac, the surrender of the only pledge for the fulfilment of the promise. To so hard a test can God expose his own people, that he refuses to let them have any security for their faith.

In comparison with the Yahwist, theological earnestness becomes even more marked in the Elohist's elaboration of the old sagas. According to J God left free scope to the evil urges of the human heart even in the case of his chosen one — for example, Abraham lies to Pharaoh, saying that Sarah is his sister (Genesis 12,10ff). The Elohist cannot let such errors of the ancestor pass without commentary; Abraham did not lie, since Sarah was not only his wife, but also his half-sister (Genesis 20,1ff). According to J the sly herdsman Jacob outwits his father-in-law Laban — according to E God increases Jacob's wealth in order to make good to him what Laban had withheld from his daughters. The Elohist demands that the whole of life should be permeated with obedience to God's command. He hands down the well-known decalogue of Exodus 20, which shows what limits God imposes on his people in everyday life. Always and everywhere the man who belongs to God must prove himself. J on the other hand transmits the so-called cultic decalogue. Israel is to acknowledge the leadership of God by keeping the prescribed festivals (Exodus 34).

Kinship with the Prophets

In the earnestness of his insistence that Israel should prove its loyalty to God in everyday life, he is related to the prophets. These too see in right behaviour to our fellow-men, as is required by the second table of the decalogue, a test of the right relationship to God.

The narratives included in the work of the Elohist dealing with the disobedience of the people in the desert also recall the preaching of the earlier prophets. To God's benefits Israel responded with murmuring and rebellion. While Moses is receiving God's gift of the commandments, Israel is already rejecting the divine offer and dancing round the calf. (Like Hosea, E too speaks, not of the bull, the symbol of divine strength and fertility, but scornfully and contemptuously of the calf.)[22] Like the early prophets he is anxious about the danger of empty formalism which is implicit in the cultus: Aaron, the ancestor of the priestly race, is the instigator of the worship of the calf.

When Moses intercedes for the sinful people, God answers with a speech of judgement which in its relentlessness recalls the prophetic message of judgement.

A day will come when I shall punish them for their sin (Exodus 32,34).

God does not threaten some kind of transitory judgement, but the day of catastrophe for all Israel. So also Amos was compelled to speak:

The time is ripe for my people Israel. Never again will I pass them by (Amos 8,2).

From such characteristics it may be inferred that E was probably written in the north, in the time of the early prophets (about 800). The author or authors belonged to circles that were in opposition to a government that tried, through the adoption of heathen elements — like the worship of the statue of a bull (1 Kings 12,25ff) — to do justice to the fact that the population of its territory followed different cults. E has become mistrustful of the ability of man to remain true to Yahweh. Even Aaron could see Yahweh in the figure of Baal, the bull (calf).

A Greater Distance from God

In the narratives of J, Yahweh dealt with man face to face; the three men allowed themselves to be Abraham's guests; the elders sat at God's table and beheld his throne.[23] In E narratives man must first enter into the strange realm of dreams or even the mysterious deep sleep in order to hear God speaking to them.[24] The distance between God and man is emphasized. To be sure, God has not departed from man — but man must know that he cannot take God's presence for granted.

We are no longer able to discover the general theme of this work, but at least it can be said that here deep faith and the capacity for perspective in theological and moral judgement were held together. The old narrative material is sifted and elaborated with theological seriousness. His main empahsis is on loyalty to God expressed in our daily actions, and reverance for God's greatness.

5. DEUTERONOMY

Comparison with J, E, and P

Among the four sources of the Pentateuch, Deuteronomy occupies a special position. The authors of the other basic writings collected traditions which to a large extent had already taken an established form. Their contribution to the works they published consisted primarily in the selection and arrangement of this material that lay before them, in a way corresponding to their conception of the history of Israel. In the passages they took over they emphasized the traits which fitted into their general picture, perhaps they suppressed others, and here and there added words of their own. Finally, some bridge-passages received a new formulation. In this way their works (J, E, and P) each received a characteristic form and an unmistakable identity. But in their fundamental character as compilations they remained so like one another that later redactors were able to fit them together to form one single work. This harmonization was so successful that for many centuries the pentateuch could be regarded as the work of a single author (Moses). Even we, for example, in reading the story of Joseph, can completely forget the complicated history of its origin — so little has the process of fusion deprived the story of its tension and its power to surprise us.

It was not possible for the redactors to treat Deuteronomy in the same way. It was not mixed with the other written sources, but placed in its entirety at the end of the Pentateuch. The mode of speech, the linguistic categories, the teaching and purposes of this book are in the first place so much of a unity, and in the second, so different from the other written sources, that its text could not be broken up into shorter units and inserted piece by piece into the suitable contexts in the other books.

Special Characteristics of the Style

The greatest part of this book purports to be addressed to Israel in the singular (thou) or in the plural (you). All Israel is to hear what is said here. In this style the priests spoke to the assembled congregation when they passed on the tradition of the law.

Deuteronomy contains examples of the different categories of laws and commandments; for example, a series of similarly phrased curses relating to secret crimes (27,15 ff), brief, apodeictic "you shall" commands (16,21 ff), precise and specifically formulated casuistic laws (17,2 ff).[25] Yet it is clearly distinguished from other Old Testament collections of laws. Explanations of the laws, exhortations to keep the commandments, promises for the obedient, and threats for the rebellious, permeate the law-book of Deuteronomy.

In addition the same words and sentences are continually repeated. The characteristic Deuteronomic description of God is "Yahweh, thy God". It recalls the covenant formula (your God, my people), and its purpose is to exhort Israel to love all the commandments as signs of the covenant: in the commandments God is near to the people. Further typical phrases of Deuteronomy are: Israel is Yahweh's "special people", therefore they must "put away the evil thing from among them". They have already in anticipation received as a gift "the land that Yahweh your God giveth to you".

In these and other, continually recurring and varied words the law of God is not only proclaimed, but warmly recommended to Israel. Israel's tradition of the law,[26] is here passed on by preachers, whose purpose is to touch the heart of the people and rouse its understanding. Continual repetitions serve to make easy the learning of the law.

These preachers of the law had an ear open to all expressions of living faith in their time. But at the same time they drew life from their historical roots. Repeatedly they appeal to the experience of the exodus and the time in the desert.

> You shall rejoice before Yahweh, your God, with your sons and daughters, your male and female slaves . . . the aliens, orphans, and widows among you . . . Remember that you have been a slave in Egypt and reverence these statutes, and act accordingly (Deuteronomy 16,11 ff).

While the law is being read, the history of the people in the present and in the past is held vividly before them. In this is shown their understanding of the law; for them Israel's law is not a guide to a higher morality, it is not intended to create eternally valid ordering of human society and in communion with God. On the contrary the law is the gift of the God who leads Israel in history. Israel must be obedient to the law, because it knows the lawgiver from its history, and knows his goodwill towards the people.

Now and again the Deuteronomic preachers do not scorn to appeal to the universal insights of men. Even the wisdom traditions must serve to make the law intelligible.[28]

But above all it is the prophetic preaching of the eighth century that is reflected in Deuteronomy. Like the prophets the publishers of these laws wish to try once more to make the rich upper classes obedient to their faith. The poor and the unprivileged are to be respected as members of the same people of God. A strong urge for social renewal, and a continuing exhortation to reverence our fellowmen are characteristic of the whole work,[29]

When one of your fellow-countrymen becomes poor . . .,
do not be hard or close-fisted . . .
Be open-handed towards him,
and when you give, do not begrudge him your bounty. (Deuteronomy 15,7.10).

We find also in Deuteronomy other themes of prophetic preaching. Like Hosea, Deuteronomy speaks of Israel as a child of God[30] and sees that the good gift of the land is also a danger, a "snare" for the faith of Israel.[31]

Origin Shortly before 721

Some signs in Deuteronomy indicate that its editors lived in the second half of the eighth century in the northern kingdom. One of these is its kinship with the work of the Elohist, which had also originated in the northern kingdom. Like E, Deuteronomy represents the making of the covenant at Sinai as the central point in the history of Israel, and the taking possession of the land as the goal of the divine guidance. He pursues aims like those of his precedents, the prophets Elijah and Hosea, who wished to save the northern kingdom from an adulteration of the faith in Yahweh with the religion of Baal.

The creation of Deuteronomy falls in the time immediately before or after the fall of the northern kingdom (721). Its authors know the danger which threatens Israel from Assyria; they know that Assyria takes from the victims their homeland, and deports them.[32]

This throws a new light on the theme of the possession of the land. The land is the fair gift of Yahweh; in the land Yahweh places at his people's disposal in profusion everything that it needs for life (Deuteronomy 7,10 ff; 11,9 ff). That means, however, that Israel can only keep the land if it accepts this gift in obedience and joy from Yahweh's hand. It must never look upon it as the gift of the gods of the land, it must not go into the snare of the Canaanite religions; if it does, the land is lost.

280

According to the fiction that underlies the book of the law, Israel hears these commandments before its entry into the land — according to the time of its origin, it hears them in the moment of its history when it loses the land. So we are confronted by the remarkable fact that in Deuteronomy a gift is promised, which through its falling away from Yahweh it has long since forfeited, perhaps even already lost. What is the significance of this strange interchange of the times? Did the authors mean to say that God still holds open the possibility of a new beginning for his people if it will only accept his commandment?

The Eternally Valid Law

However, the origin of the book cannot be pinned down to one single moment in time. Nor can its literary form be decisively determined. A preliminary interpretation sees in Deuteronomy the eternally valid law. The laws, which it sets before Israel had been current in Israel for centuries previously, and had been continually reinterpreted. Additions, new interpretations and modifications were taken up into the book even after the redaction at the end of the eighth century. From this viewpoint we can understand how the chapters 12-26, the actual body of the law are, even by standards of the ancient east, very lacking in order. Further, it is not possible to discover any homogeneous original draft by excluding additions, or making changes in the order, or suchlike devices.

In its first edition this law-book was surrounded by a framework: Deuteronomy 5-11 and 27f. The introduction to the collection of laws was to provde an instructive retrospect on the history, the conclusion was to be formed of benedictions and maledictions. G. von Rad has suggested that the model of this sequence of historical introduction, proclamation of the law, blessings and curses was to be found in the liturgical use of public readings of the law,[33] yet the pattern here is freely applied and there is no connection with liturgical use.

This work was brought by Levite refugees from the northern kingdom to Jerusalem, was lost and forgotten, and, according to the report of 2 Kings 22 discovered in the year 621 in the temple. King Josiah made it the basis of a religious reformation, whose principal aim was to implement the command to centralize the cultus (Deuteronomy 12). Further additions were included in a new edition at this time, its relationship to the preaching of Jeremiah indicates mutual influence. The book was enclosed in a further framework, which is principally and most clearly recognizable in the introduction (chapters 1-4).

From now on Deuteronomy was binding law in Israel; supplements and adaptions from the time of the exile are evidence of its effectiveness. For the faithful of Israel, the commandments of God continued to be an ever-contemporary challenge, which no historical development could outdate. The Deuteronomic "today"[34] was still in force.

The Witness to Israel's Bright Past

To this interpretation of Deuteronomy as an ever-living law there was soon added a second one, which we owe to the so-called deuteronomic school. Here too Deuteronomy continued to be a vital guiding principle of faith. It formed the beginning of a historical work, which reached from the time of Moses to the most recent past, the end of the southern kingdom and the exile of the Davidic king. This means a changed understanding of the law. No longer does the eternal "today" of the divine commandment stand in the foreground; the Deuteronomists see in it above all the clear light of the beginning. In those days Israel still stood ready to receive the promise, which in the end it had flung away.[35]

The Crowning of Moses' Work

The post-exilic age added to this a third plane of interpretation. At that time the law of Moses moved into the centre of religious life. It was the foundation for a new orientation of the people of the return. The Deuteronomic preaching of the law was united with the writings which tell the story of Israel from its beginnings and was placed at the end of the pentateuch. Deuteronomy now appeared as Moses' farewell speech to Israel, it received the solemnity and sacredness of the last hour of the great lawgiver. The message of Deuteronomy — the exhortation to heartfelt surrender to God, to joy over the promised gift, the reminder that God had first loved his people — was understood as the crowning work of Moses and as the heart of the religion of the law. Thus the modern reader can define the genre of Deuteronomy three ways, in the light of its history.

1. as the ever-living commandment of God.
2. as a reminder of the beginning of the covenant between God and Israel.
3. as the farewell speech of Moses and the crown of his work.

6. THE PRIESTLY DOCUMENT

The Role of P in the Pentateuch

The Pentateuch is a work of almost unimaginable richness. Different styles of speech, a variety of literary forms, traditions of manifold origins out of several centuries are united — and yet the five books of Moses unmistakably form one work. This unity they owe essentially to the redactor, who is unknown to us, who in the post-exilic age united the written sources J, E and D with the priestly document (P), and chose P as the foundation of his work. The first and last verses of the pentateuch, Genesis 1 and Deuteronomy 34,7-8 stem from P. P determines the framework of this principal work of Israel: in union with P the priestly document the pentateuch covers the period from the creation to the death of Moses. (In J probably the occupation of the land was the climax of the historical account.) P contributed also the plan of construction — the other written sources were only inserted where they contributed divergent material. Further, the redactors consider even slight variants as divergent traditions, so they only abbreviated slightly, and for the most part contented themselves with inserting the text of the other basic documents at suitable places in P. This procedure allows us to a large extent to reconstruct the fundamental documents.

In the pentateuch P plays a double role: it gives us the fundamental design of the whole structure, and is one of the sources elaborated therein. Thus we must consider three levels of interpretation of the pentateuch.

1. The stratum of the individual narratives: popular forms of speech were created when the knowledge of the ancestors of Israel, from Moses and the time in the desert, was transmitted orally.

2. The stratum of the historical tradition: the great plan of the course of Israel's history was gradually built up, through the coagulation of the traditions of different shrines. In the cultus knowledge of the history of Israel was given an "official" form.

3. A third area comes under inspection when the original documents are investigated. The collectors fitted together the material before them according to their theological viewpoints.

The Prosaic Style of P

The priestly document left a much stronger impression than did the older written sources on everything that it incorporated. And yet the "theology" of this work is not easy to recognize. The reason for this lies in the prosaic style of the priestly document. It reports facts and gives very little interpretation.

This can be shown by a comparison with Deuteronomy. The laws and commandments of Deuteronomy bear the stamp of centuries of proclamation of the law to the people in public worship. The collections of laws which were incorporated in P grew through long periods of priestly (levitical) use. If the aim of Deuteronomy is to impress urgently God's command on the hearts of the people of Israel, the priestly document only reproduces soberly what pertains to the professional knowledge of the priests. For example, it shows the criteria by means of which the priests should determine the cleanness or uncleanness of a person or an object.[36] But it leaves us with the unanswered question, what does it mean that people and the world were divided for the Israelite into these two sharply separated realms "clean" and "unclean". The priestly document contains many individual regulations about the ritual of the different sacrifices, but no theology of sacrifice. We find in it a detailed description of the construction and equipment of the shrine but no theological interpretation of the meaning of all these details. Here more forcibly than in any of the other Old Testament texts the modern reader feels the interval of thousands of years as a gulf of separation. For this reason, the archaeologist, who studies the life-style of old times, can in many fields contribute more than the theologian to the explanation of the priestly document.

The sober and prosaic character of P may be less attractive to us than the earnest preaching of Deuteronomy, but it is not fitting for us to despise the style of the priestly document for that reason. The priestly document expresses reverence for all the details in which Israel's religion can be concretely apprehended. Thus in its own way it gives expression to the faith of Israel, faith in the God who wills to the present among men, and to be experienced by them.

Preference for Lists

Even the narrative material, which P incorporated, is unmistakably reproduced in this prosaic style. In this the priestly document is clearly distinguished from the older historical books. P was completed in the time of the exile, J and E were probably known to its authors. Yet they completely renounced the vividness of their models. In P the figures of the past do not become living persons that awaken human sympathy. The backbone of the historical writing of the priestly document is characteristically the so-called "Book of the Toledoth", a work that enumerated in eleven genealogies the successive generations from Adam down to Aaron and Moses.[37] The lists of names are only filled out by a few dry observations, for example about the dates of births and deaths. Sober dates and numbers show what is the real historical basis of faith in the living God.

The style which uses enumerations of lists and repetitions of formulas can, however, at times still be impressive even to the modern reader. The priestly account of creation in Genesis 1 is an example of this.

Genesis 1

The theological labour of many generations has left its traces in this text. Like many Old Testament texts Genesis 1 cannot be interpreted from one angle, but only in the perspective of a long process of development.

In the remote background the creation myth of the world's origin from the watery chaos can still be recognized — but Tiamat, the mythical goddess of chaos, has meantime become an impersonal component of the cosmos, *t^ehōm* the primaeval watery flood. The reader of this account of creation can now only guess at the mythical origin of *t^ehōm*; a sign thereof is that even the last reviser does not succeed in including the watery chaos in the divine works of creation.

There are further indications that the passage did not come into being at once, but through repeated revision of older versions. The conception of the working creator God is overlaid by the thought of creation through the word, a scheme of eight works has been fitted into a six-day scheme.[38]

This report of creation was given a last new interpretation when it was placed at the beginning of the priestly document. There was also an account of creation at the beginning of the Yahwist's work (Genesis 2 f), which was given a special function within the framework of the whole work. The Yahwistic account of prehistory showed how much the whole of humanity needed the salvation that Israel was to bring to it; the Yahwist points out to Israel, that it is chosen for the sake of all mankind.

The creation story in P has another significance; one might say that according to P the whole creation is there for Israel's sake. The climax of the account is the seventh day, the day of God's Sabbath rest. According to P the Sabbath existed from the beginning of creation. Yet it had not yet been discovered by men; this discovery was reserved for Israel. In the time of Moses the people discovered that God had ordained the seven-day rhythm for man's sake.[39]

The Making of Covenants

The covenant makes the encounter with God possible. The making of covenants constitutes for the priestly document important turning points in the course of history. The covenant with Noah includes the whole of mankind, and all living creatures on the earth (Genesis 9,1-17): God guarantees the continued existence of the world. The authors of the priestly document thus answer the question how a world in which murder and violence reign, can continue to exist. God has patience, even with such a corrupted world; his word of blessing holds good even for this humanity. "Be fruitful, and multiply!" Mankind does not need to be petrified by the fear of possible destruction. God has bestowed on it a security that liberates it from fear, and gives it the possibility of seeking God.

This first covenant is far transcended by the covenant with Abraham; God himself here approaches man. He puts himself on the side of Abraham and his descendants (Genesis 17,1f). More than himself Yahweh cannot give. So no further covenant is any longer necessary. This explains the first remarkable fact, that while J and E mention the Sinai covenant, P does not.[40]

And yet the time of Moses is for P the centre of the history of Israel, and gives it meaning. According to P, the decisive new thing which this time brought is the cultus. Israel learns to make the fitting answer to God's gracious approach to it. According to P, it is only now that Israel learns with what name it can appeal to God.[41] Only from this moment can it speak to God in the right manner, that is well-pleasing to God, and praise him for his gracious approach. For P it is public worship, the celebration of the God of the covenant, that is the meaning of the existence of Israel.

For this reason P can conclude its work with the death of Moses. There is no account of the conquest of the land. P has indeed taken up the old theme of the promise of the land to the fathers, but it unconcernedly leaves this promise open. The contemporaries of P, who were living in exile, might infer from this that the possession of the land was not unconditionally necessary for standing in covenant with God. It was more necessary to worship God, and to acknowledge him in cultus and observance of the law as Israel's Lord.

THE HISTORICAL WORKS

1. THE HISTORICAL WRITING OF THE DEUTERONOMIST

The Unity of the Books of Joshua to 2 Kings

Six Old Testament books describe the history of Israel from the entry into the land down to the end of the kingdoms of Israel and Judah: the Book of Joshua and the Book of Judges, the two Books of Samuel, and the two Books of Kings. But this division is not original, as anyone can perceive who compares the ends and the beginnings of the books. In part, coherent unities are torn asunder,[42] in part the same information is given at the end of one book and repeated again at the beginning of the next.[43]

Old Testament exegesis has made the hypothesis that these books, together with Deuteronomy, once formed a single coherent book; in the rich variety of different language-forms of different kinds which they contain, individual pieces strike us, which all have the same modest style of language, and which all equally concern themselves with the interpretation of history.

Sometimes these historical interpretations are put in the mouths of figures of the past,[44] at times at a crucial turning-point in events the author himself also speaks.[45] His simple style is so characteristic that even his shorter additions are easily recognizable.[46] He repeatedly bases his interpretation and judgement of past facts on thoughts out of Deuteronomy, and uses Deuteronomic turns of speech.[47] For the men who created this historical work the Deuteronomic law is a secure standard of judgement. For that reason it is called the "Deuteronomistic historical work".

Unhistorical Ways of Study

We might think that it would be enough to consider the shorter language-forms, e.g. deliverance sagas, sagas about the prophets, lists, the history of David's succession to the throne, etc. These are indeed older than the Deuteronomistic historical work which incorporated them. They will also — we might think — give a better picture of Israel's historical tradition than that inclusive work. A superficial observer might quickly seek to prove that this composite work deserved no particular attention. The pattern which the Deuteronomists impose upon the information concerning the kings of Israel and Judah appears to be not merely tedious, but in addition inaccurate. What we learn of the kings are mostly nothing more than a few dry data like name and length of reign. The Deuteronomists seem to find their judgements about the kings more important than a lifelike picture of these figures; time and again they censure the kings in identical word about their attitude in relation to worship of idols and sacrificial cultus outside of the temple.[48]

This information of the Deuteronomists must seem wholly inadequate in the case of so distinguished a man as King Omri of Israel, who raised his state to such greatness, that for a long time after, Israel was called the "House of Omri" in Assyrian inscriptions. This king and his son Ahab tried to be just also to the Canaanite, heathen part of their subjects. For such a politically astute behaviour we can find no understanding in the Deuteronomists' allocation of censure — every form of turning to heathenism is there most sharply repudiated.[49]

Thinking in rigid categories cannot apprehend living history. A further example of this is given by the Deuteronomistic treatment of the times of the judges. The individual narratives about this time bear witness how insecure the ordinances of Israel still were in this early time. All cooperation of the tribes is sporadic, only thinkable in special circumstances. But these narratives are forced into a framework, according to which the same processes repeated themselves in a stereotyped manner. Israel "does what displeases Yahweh"; the Lord in punishment sends enemies; on the cry of the oppressed people he awakens a deliverer, who sets the people free. But after a period of rest lasting forty years this deliverance is forgotten. Israel "does again what displeases Yahweh" and the circle turns again.[50]

Thus it is not the historically unique that interests the Deuteronomists; their intention is rather to illustrate through the material of this time what according to their opinion is typical of Israel, a continual breach of loyalty. But in contrast with this, what we expect from the historian is that in addition to the typical and universally valid he should also grasp what is special, and unique in a time. We regard it as valueless to place on one level documents from different tiimes and different fields; but that is precisely what the Deuteronomists do. In the Book of Joshua descriptions of tribal boundaries and lists of places which stem from different centuries — from the times of the tribal confederation as well as from the first times of the Kings — as evidence for the occupation of the land.

Another example: in addition to the sagas of the deliverers, the Deuteronomists still had a list from the time of the Judges which did not contain much more than the names and times of office of the so-called "minor judges".[51] To this day we have no exact idea of the task of these judges — was it to make judicial decisions for the tribal league? was it to possess exact knowledge and to give regular exposition of the law? The deliverers, on the other hand were warrior heroes who were called to perform one great single act of deliverance and not to an enduring office. The deliverance sagas still show that these men did not originally liberate the whole of Israel but only individual tribes from hostile oppression. These two different traditions are fused together in the Deuteronomistic historiography: the deliverers become "judges" and are included in the series of "minor judges". The deliverance sagas originally told of single episodes from the time of the judges; the question of the temporal sequence was not raised. Now these narratives are put together, and the picture emerges of a continuous history of the whole of Israel in which the times of office of "judges" succeed one another.

According to modern ideas the Deuteronomists' way of writing history by such methods has falsified the historical report of the individual texts. Would it not then be better today to disregard this composite work, and merely try to recover as far as possible the individual texts which it has elaborated?

Our judgement about the Deuteronomic historical work can be even more critical, when we reflect that much earlier a quite different kind of representation of historical events had been developed in Israel. The Deuteronomistic historians themselves incorporated the history of David's succession to the throne (2 Samuel 7-1 Kings 2) into their work. The author of this famous passage succeeds in grasping the variety of secular influences and the complex interplay of motives in human decisions, and also the varied consequences of human action, while almost entirely refraining from making judgements upon them. How simple, in contrast, do the Deuteronomists appear to make things for themselves; to put it too forcibly, they see everywhere only the same thing: apostasy from God and consequent disaster. They feel themselves competent to pass detailed judgement on what pleases Yahweh and what does not. The Deuteronomic law is for them the standard by which all historical events can be judged. In the face of such behaviour can we still really speak of historical writing?

Historical Thinking

And yet the Deuteronomists have not lost sight of the diverse witnesses of the past. They believe that they can only rightly describe the relation between Israel and God when they allow all the sources out of Israel's past to speak: stories of miracles from the time of the conquest of the land as well as lists of places, prose narratives no less than songs, sagas about deliverers and historical representations from the early times of the kings, extracts from chronicles of the royal bureaucracy as well as narratives and legends about the prophets, short isolated traditional fragments and compilations or greater writings dealing with one theme. We must not undervalue the achievements of the Deuteronomists, who recognized in many different speech-forms witnesses that spoke powerfully of Israel's past. Even modern historical investigation must sometimes discover for the first time the historical and informative value of an old linguistic form.[52]

Further, the Deuteronomists show themselves concerned to provide for their readers information as complete and accurate as possible about the past. Twice reference is made to the fact that a poem is to be found in the "Book of the Upright"; in the history of the Kings the readers are expressly informed that better information about the actions of the kings is to be found in the "Book of Annals" and in the "Book of the deeds of Solomon."[53]

We have seen that in this composite work the sources are forced to comply with a rigidly conceived picture of the relation between Israel and God. On the other hand they are respected for their individual value. They are allowed to speak of happenings and circumstances, which according to the rigid standards of the Deuteronomists could not really have existed, as, for example the appearance of the dead Samuel whom Saul causes to be conjured up (1 Samuel 28). Contradictions between the sources are not artificially smoothed out. This loyalty to the material given in the sources enabled modern research to discover in the double series of accounts in 1 Samuel two traditions of the rise of David.[54]

Strange Character of Historical Thinking

And yet it is precisely the loyalty to the sources which shows how little this way of writing corresponds to modern ideas. Critical judgement of the given material which we require of a modern historian is alien to these men. One might be inclined to regard the Deuteronomists as mere compilers who without reflection pile up old material as mere redactors who only here and there venture to throw a little light.

However, disparaging comparisons of this kind with modern historical writing can give but little insight into the peculiar character of the Deuteronomists' work. In dealing with the ancient world we must reckon with other presuppositions and goals of historiography.

The fact of the double accounts can give us a first insight into the strange character of ancient historical thinking. No offence was taken at the contradiction between narratives, that, for example Saul asks the conqueror of Goliath for his name and lineage, although according to the preceding narrative he had long ago brought him to his court (1 Samuel 16,22f; 17,55ff). This carelessness in relation to the question whether such an incident could really have happened in this manner, must be kept in mind when we interpret the passage. We can, of course ask the question whether something can really have happened, but we must know that in doing so we do not touch the intention of the ancient writer. For a long time the only possible criterion for a believing exegesis of scripture was the reality of the event which actually happened thus and not otherwise. Only this misunderstanding of biblical historiography could lead to the scripture passage of Joshua 10,12ff being held against Galileo:

Stand still, O Sun, in Gibeon,
Stand, Moon, in the Vale of Aijalon.

According to the church's interpretation of scripture such a miracle must really have happened. From this the conclusion was drawn that according to biblical teaching the sun must move and the earth stand still. At the time of Galileo exegesis still lacked insight into the special linguistic form of Old Testament historical representation. In Joshua 10,12ff the scriptural authors are more concerned with the poetic glorification of the victory of Joshua than with the exact description of the actual happening — as the context of the passage shows; a little earlier, in Joshua 10,10f this victory is described in the style of the sagas of deliverance: Yahweh confuses the enemy before the sudden appearance of the Israelite army; a storm sent by God makes their flight difficult. In Joshua 10,12ff a song of praise for the victory at Gibeon from the "Book of the Upright" is quoted — and the collectors take no offence at the happening being here described in still more wonderful terms. They do not ask which of the two descriptions is "true" and which not.[55]

We must take into account the strange character of this old historical thinking, though here and there a trait meets us which we also recognize and value in modern historians. Thus the Deuteronomists have an interest in an exact chronology. There are indeed in their work round, symbolic numbers like the forty years of peace after the appearance of a deliverer, but beside these there stand the years in office of the "minor judges", in which no pattern of any kind can be recognized.[56]

Also there was obviously an intention to reproduce with the greatest possible accuracy the dates of the reigns of the kings of Israel and Judah, the synchronizations (comparisons of the times of the reigns in the two states, Israel and Judah) are for that time a sign of astonishing chronological exactitude.

Division of the Course of History into Periods

This work takes in hand yet another task which we also today ascribe to the historians; the past does not appear as a homogeneous unit, but as a sequence of epochs; the time of the conquest of the land is succeeded by the time of the judges, and this by the time of the kings. Joshua's farewell speech (Joshua 23) and that of Samuel (1 Samuel 12) bring the epochs to a solemn close and introduce the new periods of time. In Judges 2,11-23 and 2 Kings 17,7-41 the Deuteronomistic historians themselves give a survey of the epoch of the judges and the time of Israel's kings.

It calls for historical insight to recognize periods of time and to distinguish clearly between them; these authors succeeded in both tasks. The desert wandering began in old times with the crossing of the Red Sea — so the period of the conquest of the land begins with the crossing of the Jordan. The entry into the land is modelled on the exodus from Egypt, in order to emphasise the beginning of a new epoch. The Deuteronomists understand how to give this epoch of the conquest of the land an unmistakable character. It is the time in which Israel strikes fear and terror into all the inhabitants of Canaan. The Deuteronomic historians still do not allow any doubt to arise that the land is to belong to Israel. Yet even in the description of this splendid time the authors do not confine themselves to the miraculous stories of the Jordan crossing, and of the fall of Jericho; they reproduce also the story of the hoodwinking of Israel by the Gibeonites (Joshua 9).

Israel's apostasy from God has a change of the divine plan for history as its consequence. Israel is not able to settle the whole land. So two new facts determine the next epoch, *the time of the judges*; Israel must live with strange peoples and suffer under them (Judges 2,20ff), yet it is protected by judges, whom God repeatedly raises up in the deepest distress.

Even this divine plan miscarries finally because of the people who despise Yahweh and defiantly obtain a king for themselves (1 Samuel 12). *The time of the kings* is marked by two historical facts: God gives to the people the king they long for, and he gives to them Jerusalem as the place of his presence (1 Kings 8,16). Such a percipient division of the course of history was never made in the whole of the ancient orient before the writing of the Deuteronomistic history. At the best the achievement of the Yahwist might be comparable; but he was able to take over the sequence of the time of the fathers, the time of Moses and the time of the occupation of the land from the religious tradition of Israel.[57] The Deuteronomistic historians had themselves to create their structuring of the course of history.

In spite of such singular qualities, which even we are able to appreciate, the Deuteronomistic historical work does not of course depart from the lines of thought characteristic of ancient times. The clear differentiation of historical epochs does not lead to the realization that the people and its institutions have developed and changed. A modern man lives in the consciousness of the historical character of what he sees around him and in himself: there is a history of technology, democracy, science, even ethics are subject to historical transformation. In contrast to this the Hebrews think in totalities. In the seed they see already the tree, in the ancestor they see already the whole people that stems from him. We must reckon with this habit of thought also in the work of the Deuteronomistic historians. The possession of the land is seen together with its conquest. The name of Joshua stands for the whole epoch of the immigration. Even if the ancient sources still allow us to realize that the tribes gradually and singly, or in small bands established themselves in Canaan,[52] the old historians start with the result "Joshua and all Israel" conquer the land (Joshua 10,29.31.34.36 etc.). That Israel is allowed to live in Canaan is a gift that it owes to Yahweh. God does not give his gift gradually:

> All these kings Joshua captured at the same time, and their country with them, for Yahweh the God of Israel fought for Israel (Joshua 10,42).

The difference between lists of tribal boundaries from the time of the judges, and lists of places from the time of the kings, is not worthy of mention for men who see in everything the *one* work of God. When we reflect upon the holistic thinking of the old historians, we can understand also the idea, which seems strange to us, that Joshua did not at once occupy the conquered land, but only divided it after the conclusion of the entire work of conquest (Joshua 13).

The Deuteronomists are thinking along similar lines in their representation of the times of the judges and the kings: they wish to picture the entire time of the judges, the entire time of the kings, as unities, not the multiplicity of different events and figures.

> Whenever Yahweh set up a judge over them, he was with that judge, and kept them safe from their enemies . . . But as soon as the judge was dead, they would relapse into deeper corruption than their forefathers (Judges 2,18f; cf. 1 Samuel 12,9-11).
> They observed the laws and customs of the nations . . . and the example set by the kings of Israel (2 Kings 17,8).

Origin in Exile

These historians took up their stance at a great distance from the events, in order to classify them and interpret them. They did not merely choose freely to distance themselves, external circumstances compelled them to do so. The last event mentioned by the work is the liberation of Jehoiachin (the second-last king of Jerusalem) from prison in Babylon, in the year 562 B.C. — but nothing more is said of the consequences, or rather, of the lack of consequences of this event. From this it may be concluded that the work was concluded shortly after 562. The authors are exiles. They are therefore trying to understand the history of Israel in the light of its catastrophic end.

God's Word and History

This history had begun with a divine promise: God had promised the possession of the land to the fathers of Israel with an oath (Joshua 1,6). Is his word not ineffectual, since Israel is in exile? The Deuteronomistic historical report is attached without visible seam to the older historical writing of Israel, which had treated of the origin of Israel and its immigration into Canaan. The transition is so smooth, that to this day scholars are not agreed among themselves, where the older historical account stops, whether at the end of Deuteronomy, or not until the end of the Book of Joshua. This makes it all the more noticeable how different an interpretation of the history of Israel is presented in this later work. According to the pentateuch God leads Israel to "rest" in the land, but, in contrast, the continuation of this history is full of riddles. Even the older historians could interpret the history of Israel as Yahweh's conversation with Israel; the promise of God determined the course of history. But the Deuteronomistic historians must answer the question, how could this conversation end with the overthrow of Israel: What was left of the power of the divine word of promise?

According to the Deuteronomists the course of history proves not the weakness, but actually the power of God's word. To be sure, God *did* give Israel the land:

None of all the good promises that Yahweh had given to the house of Israel went unfulfilled; they all came true (Joshua 21,45).

God had promised to Israel in its wanderings that it would find rest — this rest the people had found, when it dwelt safe in the land; the rest was bestowed on it again, when God chose in the temple an established place in the midst of Israel.[59]

But the divine word of threat will assert itself in history, with equal power to that of the promises. The Deuteronomic law contains terrible curses on the man who breaks the covenant (Deuteronomy 28).

But the same Yahweh God who has kept his word to you to such good effect can equally bring every kind of evil on you, until he has rooted you out from this good land (Joshua 23,15).

The catastrophe that stands at the end of the history of Israel does not provoke the question: Where now is Israel's God (cf 2 Kings 18,32ff)? On the contrary Yahweh's power reveals itself in this dreadful end of his people. All the curses which were spoken in Deuteronomy against the apostate are fulfilled.

According to the views of the Deuteronomists the time of the kings is specially placed under the divine word of threat. Repeatedly the prophets threaten the apostate kings with death and destruction — and repeatedly the Deuteronomists point out where the word is fulfilled.[60] Sometimes the Deuteronomists require that their readers should have a good memory, if they are to span the arc between the threat and the fulfilment, which can for example stretch from Joshua 6,26 to 1 Kings 16,34.[61] A net of promise or threat and fulfilment is stretched over history, it is most densely woven in the last epoch, the time of the kings. For the Deuteronomists history is activated by the word of God.

This theme of the Deuteronomistic historians gives us an indication concerning the inspiration that underlay their work, which was unique in the environment of its day. The prophets had expected Israel's catastrophe, they had known that they lived in the last times. It was the Israelites themselves, their contemporaries, who were to blame for the end of Israel. Their guilt was the more grievous in the light of the ancient saving acts of God. With this preaching the prophets had drawn attention to the course of history.

The fruit of their activity is the work of the Deuteronomistic historians. Its dependence on the prophets is shown also by the fact that for the Deuteronomists prophetic tradition and Deuteronomic legal tradition are of equal weight. In the reports concerning the fall of Israel and Judah they do not expressly draw attention to the Deuteronomic curses, but to the preceding prophetic words of doom.[61] On the other hand the prophetess Hulda makes urgent reference to the threats of the newly discovered Deuteronomic law (2 Kings 22,15); and the prophets appear as preachers of the law (2 Kings 17,13).

Modern theologians have coined the term "salvation history". We can say that the Deuteronomistic historians with their conception of the action of the word of God in history created a first sketch of "salvation history". We can measure our concept of salvation history against this sketch, and perhaps even correct it. According to the ideas of the ancient historians salvation history is indeed determined by the plan of God, but this itself cannot be read off from the historical events. For example Israel was not given the right to infer from the fact of its conquest of Canaan that "God is with us". The fact is rather that Israel was only enabled to recognize God at work in the occurrence because God had previously told it. The end of Israel might have been estimated as the feebleness of Yahweh, but Yahweh had foretold this end — by this the Deuteronomists were able to recognize in the catastrophe the power of God's punishment.

Today we must frequently admit that historical research has developed another picture of the course of Israel's history than that which the Old Testament offers, Ought we not to limit ourselves to this "correct", critically tested historical picture? This new historical picture by no means makes the historical writing of the Old Testament superfluous. Experiences according to which God promises help beforehand to his people and threatens the apostate with punishment must remain inaccessible to the critical historical discipline. It cannot interpret the events as fulfilment of God's word, it cannot show how God reveals himself in historical events. Anyone who wishes to find salvation history, must seek it in the historial *experiences* of the believing people, not in history itself.

Modern exegetes have asked themselves whether the Deuteronomists were satisfied with explaining the terrible end of Israel, whether they did not inquire about Israel's future. There is only *one* prophetic promise in one work alongside all the threats, and it is all the more striking for that reason: the promise of Nathan (2 Samuel 7). The historians also pay attention to the fulfilment of this promise; Solomon builds the temple, as was foretold, and there are repeatedly successors on David's throne.[62] What does it mean against this background, that the liberation of David's descendant Jehoiachin is the last event which this word records? We are no longer in a position to give a certain answer, since this event is mentioned without commentary in the history itself.

The ancient history of the faith of Israel had this characteristic that it repeatedly succeeded in harmonizing different religious traditions; the promise to the fathers, the possession of the land and the commandments of Sinai. In the Deuteronomistic history two further strands of tradition are linked together, the covenant with David and the choice of Jerusalem. The promise of Nathan, as the Deuteronomists see it, could have meant salvation for the people, if the kings had given an example of loyal obedience to the law, and not one of apostasy.

The Deuteronomistic history was completed by men who had experienced the end of the history of Israel. They stood at a sufficient distance to perceive the unity of the people's history. They unite the manifold variety of the historical traditions of Israel in a conception of astonishing structural integration.

2. THE HISTORICAL BOOK OF THE CHRONICLER

Place in the History of Israel

Up to the exile Israel had retained a trace of political independence, at the last only Judah and Jerusalem. On the other hand the land to which the Jews returned after the edict of Cyrus, formed only an insignificant part of the great Persian empire. Many Jews continued to live in the dispersion; their prosperity depended on the fortunes of the land which happened in each case to have received them. The people of Israel, united by a common history and a common fate, had become the congregation of the Jews, which was chiefly united by its confession of Yahweh. What influence had this transformation on their faith?

In Israel before the exile, faith in Yahweh and the history of the people were closely connected. The settlement, the beginning of the rule of the kings, and the deadly threat posed by the ancient oriental empires, opened ever new perspectives in the relation of Yahweh to his people. Was it not inevitable that this bond of their faith to history would be loosened in the society of the Jews, who were leading their own life apart from the historical happenings of their time?

In this time (at the earliest after 430, more probably about 250), was written the ambitiously designed historical work which spans the course of history from Adam down to the origin and establishment of the post-exilic community. The religious community of the Jews also needed a history-book. It too understood itself only in terms of its memories of the past — not in terms of timeless doctrines. In the historical writings of Israel three groups may be distinguished:

1. The works of "classical" salvation history. The oldest work of this kind is the Yahwist's. In the early times of the kings he traced back the reputation which Israel enjoyed under David and Solomon to the fact that from the times of the tribal ancestors God had led his people according to his plan, and had promised it the land. The purpose of this retrospect upon the past was to make clear the significance and the task of Israel.

2. Historiography under prophetic influence. Under the influence of the pre-exilic prophets Israel learned not only to see God's works in the events of the past, which led to the possession of the land. Even the terrible blows, through which Israel finally lost its reputation and its land, bore witness to God's activity. For this reason the second gap of

295

historians, the Deuteronomists, thought worthy of recording the events which led beyond the classical period of sacred history. Again, the aim is to interpret the present, the catastrophe of the exile in the light of God's plan.

3. Historiography of the post-exilic period. Even for post exilic Judaism Yahweh is not only the God of the past, but the God of the living. The aim of the history of the Chronicler is to demonstrate that in the Jewish community, the work of God, which began in the people of Israel, is still continuing.

Greatly though these three groups of Jewish historiography may differ from one another, when we compare them with the writings of modern historians, their mutual resemblances are equally striking. The purpose of the modern historian is to describe what happened; the only thing of importance for these old historians is to understand their own present.

Position in the Bible

In our Bibles the historical work of the Chronicler cannot at once be recognized as a homogeneous literary form. At first only the last third of the great work was incorporated in the collection of the sacred writings of the Jews, the books of Ezra and Nehemiah; for only these, in the matter of content, went beyond the limits of the Deuteronomic history, which was already contained in this collection. Only later were the two Books of Chronicles added. So the larger first part of the work, the Books of Chronicles, came to stand in the Hebrew Bible after the last part, the Books of Ezra and Nehemiah. Yet it is not hard for the modern reader, judging by similarities of style and interests, and by the conformity of the endings and beginning of books (2 Chronicles 36,22ff, Ezra 1,1ff) to recognize the unity of the work and the original order.

Adaptation of Written Sources

The chief work of the Chronicler consisted in the collection and adaptation of various sources. He represents the course of history from Adam to David in lists of descendants (1 Chronicles 1-9), which he takes from the pentateuch. The story of David takes up a large space (1 Chronicles 11-29, i.e. a third of the Books of Chronicles). Both for the story of Solomon (2 Chronicles 1-9) and the story of the Kings of Judah (2 Chronicles 10-36) the basis is the history of the Deuteronomists. Memoirs of the priest Ezra and the layman Nehemiah, two men of importance for the upbuilding of the post-exilic community, constitute the foundations of the last part.

This characteristic of its origination distinguishes the Chronicler's history clearly from the older historical works. These took their material from written and oral sources of different kinds; their chief achievement was that they formed from various types of material a homogeneous picture of the general course of history. In contrast with this the Books of Chronicles are based on a complete historical work, which they can

296

presume to be known to their readers.[63] Large parts of these are faithfully taken over. What might be the purpose of such a repetition of familiar material? In many passages the work of the Chronicler serves the task of a commentator. Antiquated names are replaced by the modern ones (cf 2 Samuel 8,8 with 1 Chronicles 18,8), obscure passages are made clear. Thus, in their loyalty to the existent tradition, the Deuteronomists had left standing, along side of the narrative of David's victory over Goliath, the information that Elhanan from Bethlehem — and not David — had struck down Goliath (2 Samuel 21,19). The Chronicler believes that this inconsistency could only have arisen from the carelessness of a scribe. He "emends" the words *bēt hallaḥmî 'ēt* (. . . from Bethlehem the . . .) to *'et-laḥmî 'aḥî*: Elhanan slew Lahmi the brother of Goliath). Another example: the Chronicler finds it unfitting that Solomon, the highly honoured king, should have given up towns to the king of Tyre (1 Kings 9,10-14). The older account tells us that the towns did not please Hiram. The Chronicler gives his own interpretation to this sentence: Hiram gave back the towns to Solomon (2 Chronicles 8,1f). By our way of thinking, at least, the text is not interpreted, but something is inserted into it to suit the preconceived opinion of the Chronicler.

Even in more important matters the Chronicler, according to our ideas, goes light-heartedly beyond the given text. In fact, in the last resort, his concern is not merely to comment on the older Deuteronomistic history. He is interested in a question that the older sources which he used could not yet raise. "What right has the Jewish community to which he belongs to understand itself as the community of Yahweh?" Thus he imports the faith and the thoughts of the Jewish post-exilic community into the sources which he is using.

Time and again critical scholarship has been compelled to state that in the biblical histories, historical happenings have not been truly described. Frequently we lay the blame of this on the long periods of oral tradition. In the process of transmission from mouth to mouth, we imagine that the materials were continually undergoing transformation. However, the example of the Chronicler shows that such things can also have another cause.

Above all, the Chronicler has written sources before him; he is a writer, not a story-teller. And yet he does not attempt to give an exact reproduction. Not even the edicts of the Persian kings which he has incorporated in his work, have been left unaltered by him. In Ezra 1 and Ezra 6, the edict of Cyrus about the rebuilding of the temple is cited. This source is so carelessly transmitted that important parts of its content can no longer be clearly understood. It is also hard to reconstruct how large the temple was meant to be. That may perhaps in part be blamed on later copyists who made mistakes in reporting the figures. But it was the Chronicler who treated carelessly the question of the costs, which was important for the source. In Ezra 1 he has so reported the command of

Cyrus, as if the gifts of the Jews and voluntary gifts of other subjects were meant to finance the building, but according to Ezra 6 the Persian crown is to bear the costs. It must cause us still greater surprise that Cyrus speaks as if he knew Deutero-Isaiah:

> Yahweh, the God of heaven has given to me the kingdoms of the earth (Ezra 1,2a)

Compare with this Isaiah 45,1:

> Thus says Yahweh to Cyrus his annointed, Cyrus whom he has taken by the hand, to subdue nations before him.

According to Ezra 1,2b Cyrus traces back to Yahweh the command to build the temple. Compare with this Isaiah 44,28

> I say to Cyrus, "You shall be my shepherd to carry out my purpose, so that Jerusalem may be rebuilt, and the foundations of the temple may be laid.

Today we require of the historian that he should clearly distinguish between the commentary and the reproduction of the facts. In the Chronicler's work the interpretation does not only penetrate the representation of the facts, it is even inserted into documents cited word for word.

Midrash or Historical Work?

So we cannot be surprised when he applies similar techniques in dealing the Deuteronomist's historical work. These techniques were fully developed in Judaism in times after the Chronicler in the midrash literature. A midrash serves the exegesis of the holy scriptures. *Miḏrāš* is derived from *dāraš*, to seek, to investigate. The true meaning of the scripture does not lie open to the light of day; people must eagerly inquire what can be found in them for the needs of the present. Since the holy scriptures are God's word, they have timeless validity; he who seeks tirelessly finds in them an answer to all human problems. Modern exegesis seeks to find the way into the place in the past which was the home of the texts — for the author of a midrash there is no time-interval needing to be bridged. God speaks directly to anyone who is absorbed in meditation on his word. One does not think of asking how the first hearers, for whom a text was originally intended, understood it.

This kind of textual exegesis is already beginning to develop in the Chronicler's work. Yet we must not understand that work as "midrash" on the Books of the Kings. He does not wish to write a commentary, a book about a book. He claims to be reporting on historical events, which contribute to the clarification of his question concerning the origin of the post-exilic community, and in doing this, he bases himself on the Books of the Kings as a source. But neither does he wish to replace the older work. He continually refers his readers to his primary document. His contemporaries are unlike us, they take no offence when two different pictures of the same object are recommended to them as equally excellent.

Judah as all Israel

We must now examine more closely an example of such deviation from the older Deuteronomic work: According to 2 Samuel 2,4 David is anointed in Hebron by the tribe of Judah as the king of Judah; according to 1 Chronicles 11,1 as king over all Israel. How could the Chronicler expect his readers, who also knew the older work to accept such a discrepancy? He does not intend to say anything different from the Book of Samuel; he only proposes to underline the true meaning of that passage, as he has set it forth for a man of his time.

In order to understand this intention of the Chronicler, we must take a look at the whole of his work. When we do this, it becomes clear that the Chronicler is quite convinced that the post-exilic community may fairly see itself as the true Israel. This community will however have consisted almost exclusively of Jews, who after decades of exile were returning home again. The traces of those dispersed out of the ten tribes have been lost. In spite of thus, the Chronicler represents the return in such a manner as if representatives of all twelve tribes had returned (Ezra 6,17; 8,35); the small remnant of the homecomers may feel itself to be "all Israel".

The grounds for the belief that the Jews represent all Israel are found by the Chronicler in history. The ten tribes of the northern kingdom have excluded themselves from the people of Yahweh, from Israel. They were untrue to the kingly house of David, with whom God had made a covenant. By so doing they also turned away from Yahweh himself, and honoured idols; the true worship of God was only to be found in Judah. This judgement about the renegade ten tribes on the one hand, and Judah, the true people of God, on the other hand is made, according to the Chronicler, by the Davidide Ahijah in a speech delivered before a battle between Israel and Judah (2 Chronicles 13,5-12).

He has measured the whole time of the kings by this standard which is offered by this speech. He consistently omits what the Deuteronomistic historian reports concerning the kings of North Israel. This history is no longer the history of Israel, for they have separated themselves from the true Israel. But anyone from the northern kingdom who declares himself for the right worship of Yahweh, as it is practised in Jerusalem, may count himself one of the people of God.[64] Once again we see how the Chronicler introduces into the representation of ancient history the faith of his own time: is not in his day also confession of Yahweh, the common worship of God, the bond that unites the Jews? In contrast with this the differences between the tribes is without significance.

We must know the history of the Chronicler's times in order to understand his interpretation of history. One happening from this late time is specially important for the understanding of his work. The community of the Samaritans came into existence at that time in the former northern kingdom. The remnant of the population of the old Israel that remained in the land did not unite in the worship in the newly erected temple in Jerusalem, but set up their own cult centre on Mount Gerizim. It is principally in opposition to them that the Chronicler insists that as long ago as in David's time Judah alone had represented the true Israel. This thought also moves him on the occasion of the choice of a king in Hebron to replace the "Judah" of the Deuteronomistic work by "all Israel".

In 1 Chronicles 11,1 — the exegesis of 2 Samuel 2,4 — the Chronicler thus used the technique of the midrash. His present experience has taught him that the remnant of the people of Israel, the Jews who returned from exile, are the legitimate heirs of the whole people. This knowledge discloses to him the true meaning of the old text, and he introduces it there: Judah becomes all Israel. Were the Chronicler merely to proclaim his own thought in this manner, his work would be a midrash. But now his work as a whole has the purpose of showing how in the course of history the rights and duties of the people of God were transferred to the Jews: he is not writing a commentary to make things vivid, but a new historical work with a completely new purpose.

David as Central Figure

It is no accident that it should be precisely in the account of David's election to the throne that the Chronicler replaces "Judah" with "all Israel". David has a central place in his picture of the true Israel. He only begins the real historical report with Saul's death. He hurries through the preceding times with the help of lists of generations; what happened before David's time was only a preparation. With David's reign the Chronicler sees that begin, which alone interests him; the Jewish community in Jerusalem and the worship of the temple; the joyful worship of Yahweh, the centre of his life and the life of his Jewish contemporaries. This is the result of history which the Chronicler has before his eyes and from it he interprets the past.

He passes over in silence everything that might tarnish the picture of David and of his son Solomon, David's adultery and the murder of Uriah, the intrigues and revolts of David's sons in the struggle for the throne, the idolatry of Solomon.[65] Had not all this proved itself without result in the course of history? Only the great work of building the temple and the setting up of its worship had consequences lasting into the time of the Chronicler's experience.

Only *one* error of David was not passed over by him, the census of the people (1 Chronicles 21; 2 Samuel 24). For a centrally administered state it is almost a necessity of life to know exactly the powers that are at his disposal; in the first place what interests him is how many men he governs who are capable of bearing arms, how many taxpayers stand in his service. But the people of Israel never understood itself as a "weapon" in the hand of the kings. God alone possessed the people; the king who wished to possess it and count it as a man counts his property, was committing a grave offence. According to old conceptions of the connection between crime and punishment, David ought to be punished in respect of the thing through which he had sinned: his "property", the number of the people is decimated by the plague. Through the purchase of a place of sacrifice and the offering of sacrifices, David can obtain his request from God, that the plague should stop before reaching Jerusalem. This was the place of sacrifice at which later the altar of burnt offering was to stand. So here, according to the Chronicler's ideas, the crime of David turned out to have important historical results lasting into his own time, in which continually burnt-offerings were made at the same place. That is why he includes this report.

But he does not leave it unchanged. In a decisive passage he says what we would judge to be the exact opposite of the report of the older text. According to 2 Samuel 24, "Yahweh incited David against Israel"; for his "anger is kindled against Israel". According to 1 Chronicles 21 Satan appears against Israel, and incites David to number the people. Yet when we understand this alteration from the point of view of the Chronicler, and not from our own, it again becomes evident that the Chronicler does not demand that his hearers should accept contradictory statements. He only expounds the older text more exactly. We take offence at the suggestion that according to 2 Samuel 24 Yahweh incites David to sin. The Chronicler took no offence at the fact that even the temptation to sin came from God. Even for him Israel's faith was unquestioned, that nothing and no one can be so powerful as to influence the human heart without God's permission.[66]

But he can no longer assume that the great king Yahweh demeans himself to play the part of the deceiver himself and directly. Therefore the Chronicler uses a conception which we come to know more exactly in Job 1 and 2. In the court of Yahweh there is one who of his own will has this task; Satan the deceiver and enemy of mankind, stands in the service of Yahweh. The Chronicler thus does not change the older text, he merely explains in what manner Yahweh incites David to commit the sin of numbering the people.

There is a further striking difference from the older text: the vision of the angel and the sacrifice are wonderfully elaborated. In the same way also the report of the dedication of the temple in 2 Chronicles 5,13f can tell of much clearer signs of God's presence than can 1 Kings 8,10. Not only does the cloud enter, but fire also falls from heaven and consumes the sacrifice; all the Israelites see the fire and the glory of Yahweh.

The worship of God is the theme on whose description the Chronicler bestows all his love, he endows it with special splendour. In his time God's presence is no longer experienced in great historical events. All the more does the Chronicler seek to show that in public worship Israel stands in Yahweh's presence: here happen the miracles which Israel once experienced in history.

The Chronicler's predilection for the cultus stands in close connection with his interest in the election of David. 1 Chronicles 22-29 gives much

301

material that is not to be found in the Deuteronomists' work. David is here presented as the decisive organizer of the building and worship of the temple; he is set on a level with Moses. Israel had to prove itself God's people by obeying the laws of Moses "the man of God".[67] Down to the times of the Chronicler the criterion for belonging to God's people was that a man should honour the cult-prescriptions of David "the man of God", and acknowledge his rule.[68] With this the Chronicler is again attacking the community of the Samaritans, who denied the special privileges of the Davidic kingdom and the cultus in Jerusalem.

We might really be surprised that the Chronicler mentions the time of Moses and the Sinai covenant only in the genealogies at the beginning; after all the law of Moses had its place in the centre of Jewish thought. Ezra, an important authority for the Chronicler solemnly declared it to be the law of the Jewish community. The Chronicler does indeed report the reform of the priest Ezra (Nehemiah 8f), but omits at the beginning of his book to mention the covenant of Moses. This peculiarity, on the other hand becomes understandable when we think of the contemporary problems that afflicted the Chronicler. The pentateuch and the legislation of Sinai were recognized just as fully by the Samaritans as by the Jews. It was only the estimate of the Davidic kingship that had kindled to conflict. It is this point of contention which the Chronicler wishes to expose to the light: the covenant of Sinai is recognized by all, so he can pass over it in silence.

Through God's covenant with David, Judah, which remained true to the house of David, was given preference before all Israel — in this the Chronicler can find the legitimation for his conviction that the fellowship of the Jews, to which he belongs, is the heir of all Israel. For this reason, in his adoption of the older texts, he emphasizes all the passages that speak of the nearness of the house of David to God. If the promise of Nathan in the Book of Samuel had assued the continuance and stability of the house of *David*,[69] in 1 Chronicles 17,14, it promises that David's kingship will have perpetual stability in *God's* house and kingdom. Yahweh's kingship, according to the statements of the Chronicler, is to be found in the hand of the Davidide; David and his successors sit on Yahweh's throne.[70]

Yet history taught that God's kingdom could not be realised by David's kingly house:

> But they never ceased to deride his messengers, scorn his words and scoff at his prophets, until the anger of Yahweh burst out against his people and could not be appeased (2 Chronicles 36,16).

Here the Chronicler speaks of the exile as a final termination of the history of Israel; there was nothing in Israel left to save. David's kingdom fell; the survivors were deported. Could God have forsaken his promise to realize his rule among men?

God's Rule in the Jewish Community

In splendid colours Deutero-Isaiah pictured the return from the exile and the beginning of a rule of God in Israel that was never again to be shaken. But the return and the reconstruction were not resplendent events. The new community, its temple and its worship must have seemed modest, even miserable in contrast with what had been — much more in comparison with the expectations that the prophetic promises had awakened.

> Is there anyone still among you who saw this house in its former glory? How does it appear to you now? Does it not seem to you as if it were not there (Haggai 2,3)?

It was precisely this contradiction that kindled all the more the hope of the Jews. Out of the reference to the modest temple or the post-exilic time there grows in the prophet Haggai the great promise:

> Only a small while still, a short time: I will shake heaven and earth, sea and land, I will shake all nations; the treasure of all nations shall come hither, and I will fill this house with glory (Haggai 2,6f).

The eschatological expectation awakened by the prophets lived on even after the exile. Precisely the fact that Israel lived under such needy conditions, was taken for an important sign; now it must be decided, whether the rule of God would reveal itself in full splendour.

The Chronicler sees the new beginning after the exile in quite a different light. To be sure he also knows the hope that God will lead the whole people to the temple (Nehemiah 1,9). But he takes less thought for the splendour of the reign of God than for the way in which the reign of God can be realized in the present modest circumstances. He has emphasized the significance of the royal house of David — but he does not let himself be determined by the hope for the king from David's house. Even in subjection to the Persian rule, even without a king of its own, the community of the Jews can be the place of the rule of God, when they submit to God's commands, and celebrate together the worship of God. With great zeal, the chronicler has always averred that this community is the true Israel. But even in this point he remains a sober realist. He knows that the Jewish community is only an imperfect realization of the people of God — ever and again it must turn to God, renew the covenant and try once more to become in reality what it is:

> We have been disloyal . . . But in spite of this, there is still hope for us. Now, therefore let us make a covenant with our God (Ezra 10,2).

With this sober view of the post-exilic community the Chronicler follows his authorities Ezra and Nehemiah. Commissioned by the Persian government and in full loyalty to it, they both had led the rebuilding; messianic hopes of a return of the kingdom of David had no place in their picture of the Jewish community of the day.

The "memoirs" of these two men served the Chronicler as a source for the time of the rebuilding. Besides these he had but few sources, principally lists from the archives of the temple: a list of the temple vessels (Ezra 1,9ff), for example, and lists of those who returned (Ezra 2; Nehemiah 7). Probably he also found the records in the temple, dealing with the activities of Ezra and Nehemiah. Nehemiah's memoir is composed as a votive gift to the temple. In this report God is addressed:

Remember me for my good, O God! (Nehemiah 13,31).

With the Chronicler's history the category of written histories reaches down to the late age of the Old Testament. Repeatedly new projects came into being in the history of the Old Testament, whose aim was to set in order and interpret the events of history. The faith of Israel experienced God's power at work in the real world of history. For this reason Israel was repeatedly driven to make the attempt to understand the course of history.

FOOTNOTES

1 In Genesis 12,4b-9, we are given a series of such facts; the preceding section which is to be considered here, is clearly distinguished from them.

2 For what follows, cf. Wolff, *Yahwist*, 351ff.

3 The bond with kindred and family gave to the individual and the ancient world a degree of protection which we can hardly imagine today. The stranger must be specially protected by law; in this he is like widows and orphans.

4 On this point cf p.90ff.

5 Genesis 18,1-16 contains such a narrative, which has in view the question of a descendant and the continued existence of the family; cf on this point p.85ff.

6 Five times the word of God at the beginning of Israel's history speaks of "blessing", it is certainly no accident that in the preceding sagas dealing with mankind, which the Yahwist collected together, we encounter the word "curse" five times: Genesis 3,14.17; 4,11; 9,25; 5,29.

7 On this point cf p.268ff.

8 Genesis 22,17; 24,34ff; 26,24; 26,3f; 48,15.

9 Genesis 39,5. The whole of Egypt owes to Joseph its deliverance from the disaster of famine (Genesis 41,46ff); here admittedly the word "blessing" does not occur. It is possible that the Yahwistic version of this report was omitted when his work was being conflated with the Elohist's.

10 Cf 2 Samuel 8.

11 The hearers of the narrators of the sagas may, on the other hand, have laughed over Abraham's deceit; cf Genesis 12,18; Numbers 25,1-4.

12 Genesis 4,26; cf also Genesis 18,25: Yahweh is addressed as "Judge of the whole world".

13 Exodus 12,38 "and a mixed multitude went up with them".

14 Numbers 10,29ff; cf on these questions also p.265-269.

15 On this point see p.265-269.

16 In Genesis 18,1ff the promise of descendants is the goal of the narrative and the heart of the family saga. It is inserted by the Yahwist into narratives to which it did not originally belong; cf Genesis 22,14-18; 28,13f.

17 On the Throne-succession story see p.112ff.

18 Genesis 7,4; Exodus 14,21.

19 Cf on this point p.89ff.

20 Genesis 6,5f; Genesis 7,16; Genesis 18,17f.

21 In Genesis 48 for example E tells of Jacob's special blessing for Ephraim and Manasseh.

22 Hosea 8,5ff; 10,5.

23 Exodus 24; Genesis 18.

24 Genesis 15,28.

25 On these different forms of the legal tradition see p.113ff.

26 Deuteronomy grew out of the seed of the tradition of the law. It is deeply rooted in the law that Moses gave to the people. Through the centuries Moses' law continued to be the plumb-line of the life of faith: it was proclaimed and expounded in public worship, it was continually modified to suit the changing conditions of the times. Thus the Deuteronomic giving of the law grew from the seed planted by Moses. Other law-books also grew from this seed, the Book of the Covenant (Exodus 20,22-23,33) an early precursor of D, and the Holiness Law (Leviticus 17-26). On the handing down of the law cf also p.113ff and p.169.

27 Deuteronomy 13,6.11; 16,12; 18,16; 23,5ff; 24,9.

28 Deuteronomy 16,19 — cf also from the introductions to the law-book, Deuteronomy 8,5; 4,6.

29 Deuteronomy 14,29; 15,1-18; 16,11.14; 20,5ff; 21,14; 22,1ff; 23,16f; 23,25f; 24,6f etc.

30 Hosea 11,1; Deteronomy 14,1. Cf from the introductions to the law-book Deuteronomy 1,31; 8,5.

31 Deuteronomy 7,25,12,30; Hosea 2,7[5]; 4,11ff etc.

32 Cf Deuteronomy 7,10; 8,19; 11,17; the curse in Deuteronomy 28,32 speaks distinctly of exile. These passages may also be additions of later editors, who have already experienced the exile.

33 Cf also, on this pattern of proclamation of the law, p.190ff.

34 On this point cf p.169ff.

35 On the Deuteronomistic historical book see p.286

36 The criteria by means of which the distinction is made between unclean and clean are hard for us to bring under a common denominator: According to Leviticus 5,1-6, for example, a person can become unclean for the following four reasons: because he had heard a curse, has touched a carcase, has touched uncleaness of any sort, has sworn carelessly. Crimes against a neighbour make unclean, but also inadvertent transgressions, even bodily processes and illnesses.

37 Genesis 5,1; 6,9; 10,1; 11,10; 11,27; 25,12; 25,19; 36,1; 36,9; 37,2; Numbers 3,1.

38 Originally it is likely that only seven works were mentioned. In one of the revisions, for theologlical reasons the creation of light had been inserted, separated from the creation of the sun, which was counted among the heathens as the divine bestower of light. A further revision distributed these eight works among the six working-days of the week.

39 This happens in the collection of manna on the sixth day, Israel is, so to speak, compelled by God, to collect an additional supply for the day of rest (Exodus 16,22f).

40 Exodus 19,24.

41 Exodus 6,2ff. According to E also Israel first learned through Moses the name of Yahweh, cf Exodus 3,13ff. On the other hand according to J the faithful among the early fathers already honoured Yahweh (Genesis 4,26). On calling on the name of Yahweh cf p.13ff.

42 1 Samuel 31 tells the story of Saul's death — 2 Samuel 1 of David's mourning for the dead Saul. The story of David's succession to the throne reaches from 2 Samuel 7 to 1 Kings 2. 1 Kings 22,52 introduces king Ahaziah — 2 Kings 1

reproduces a narrative about the prophets, which has to do with Ahaziah.
43 Joshua 24,29 and Judges 2,9 report the death and burial of Joshua. According
to Deuteronomy 31 Joshua is appointed by Moses as the leader of Israel; in
Joshua 1 God himself repeats this commission.
44 E.g. Joshua 23,1-16, the farewell speech of Joshua; 1 Samuel 12, the farewell
speech of Samuel; 1 Kings 8,14-61, Solomon's prayer at the dedication of the
temple.
45 E.g. Joshua 21,43-22,6, retrospect on the conquest of Canaan; Judges 2,11-
23; a forward look to the times of the Judges; 2 Kings 17,7-41 a retrospective
explanation of the fall of Israel.
46 E.g. 1 Samuel 2,27-36; 1 Kings 13,1-3; 1 Kings 21,24-26.
47 E.g. "Love Yahweh, your God" Joshua 22,5; Deuteronomy 6,5 or: "Keeping
God's commandments, walking in his ways", 1 Kings 8,58; Deuteronomy 6,1;
11,32; 12,1.
48 "He did what displeased Yahweh, and walked in the way of his father" 1 Kings
15,26; cf 1 Kings 15,3; 15,11; 15,34; 16,13; 16,19; 16,25; 16,30 etc.
49 On Omri and Ahab cf 1 Kings 16,29ff.
50 Judges 3,11; 3,30; 4,1; 5,31; 6,1; 8,28; 8,33; 10,6; 13,1.
51 Judges 10,1-5; 12,7-14.
52 In mediaeval monasteries there were, for example, books containing the
names of dead persons on behalf of whom a mass was celebrated on the
anniversary of their birthdays. It is only a few years since the importance of these
lists as sources for social history was discovered.
53 Joshua 10,13; 2 Samuel 1,18; 1 Kings 14,19.29; 15,27.23; 31 etc.
54 The rejection of Saul: 1 Samuel 13,8ff-1 Samuel 15.
First meeting of Saul and David: 16,14ff-17,1ff.
David's flight: 19-20.
David's generosity to Saul: 24-26.
David with the Philistines 21,11ff-27.
55 Another example: according to the *song* incorporated in Judges 5 the stars
fight for Israel (verses 20f); according to the corresponding *prose* narrative a
cloudburst assists the victory.
56 Judges 10,1-5; 12,7-14; 22 + 22 + 6 + 7 + 10 + 8 years.
57 On this point see p.190ff and p.275ff.
57 This is revealed to the modern exegete even by the book of Joshua; the district
which Joshua travels through in Joshua 2-10 only includes the territory of the tribe
of Benjamin. What here claims to be the history of the conquest of Canaan by the
whole of Israel, was the tradition of one single tribe.
58 Cf Deuteronomy 12,9ff with Joshua 21,44 and 1 Kings 8,56.
59 Cf 1 Kings 11,29ff with 1 Kings 12,15b, 1 Kings 14,6ff with 1 Kings 14,17f and
with 1 Kings 15, 29, 1 Kings 16,1ff with 1 Kings 16,12, 2 Kings 1,6 with 2 Kings
1,17.
60 Joshua's curse on the man who rebuilds Jericho is not fulfilled until this late
date. A long interval also intervenes between the curse of the man of God on the
altar of Bethel (1 Kings 13,2) and the fulfilment of this curse in 2 Kings 23,16ff.
Elijah's prophecy against Ahab (1 Kings 21,19) is partly fulfilled in 1 Kings 22,28,
but is according to 1 Kings 21,27ff in part still postponed and fully fulfilled in 2
Kings 10.10. Twice a prophetic word is not exactly fulfilled; in its loyalty to the
tradition in spite of this the Deuteronomists reproduce it, although when the
event spoken of occurs, they do not refer back to this: cf 1 Kings 22,17 with 1
Kings 22,35, 2 Kings 22,15ff with 2 Kings 23,29.
61 Cf 2 Kings 21,10ff with 2 Kings 24,2; 2 Kings 17,13.
62 Cf 1 Kings 8,20.24; 1 Kings 11,13; 11,32ff; 15,4; 2 Kings 8,19.

63 In 1 Chronicles 29,29 and 2 Chronicles 9,29 the Books of Samuel and Kings are expressly named as sources. 2 Chronicles 10-36, the history of the Kings of Judah might be taken from a new enlarged edition of these books; this would explain how the Chronicler knows some facts that go beyond the information of the Deuteronomistic history which are often enough confirmed by historical research. In this part of the Chronicler's work we find in the naming of sources eleven slightly divergent titles; yet probably all of them refer to the same book (cf. 2 Chronicles 16,11 etc.; 2 Chronicles 27,7 etc.; 2 Chronicles 20,34; 33,18; 24,27). The parts of the same work, which contain reports concerning the prophets are cited as works of these prophets themselves (2 Chronicles 12,15; 13,22; 20,34; 26,22; 32,32; 33,19).

64 2 Chronciles 11,16; 30,11.18.25; 31,1.

65 In Nehemiah 13,26 on the other hand, he leaves untouched a memory of Solomon's idolatry.

66 Cf Genesis 3,1: The snake is one of the beasts which God has made. Exodus 10,27: God himself "hardens" the heart of Pharaoh, so that he opposes God; Isaiah 6,10; God is so angry with sinful Israel that he proposes to hinder a salvation that might become possible through repentance: instead of the prophet's helping to bring about the repentance of the people, he will contribute to their hardening.

67 Moses the "man of God": 1 Chronicles 23,14; Ezra 3,2. Moses the "servant of God": 1 Chronicles 6,34; 2 Chronicles 24,6.9; Nehemiah 1,8; 9,14; 10,30.

68 David the "man of God": Nehemiah 12,24.36. David the "servant of God": 1 Chronicles 17,4.7.

69 "Your family shall be established and your kingdom shall stand for all time in my sight" (2 Samuel 7,16).

70 Cf 2 Chronicles 13,8; 1 Chronicles 28,5; 29,23; 1 Chronicles 17,14 "But I will give him a sure place in my house and kingdom for all time, and his throne shall be established for ever".

CHAPTER V

THE QUESTION OF THE
UNITY
OF THE OLD TESTAMENT

1. TEXTUAL EXAMPLE: CHRIST, THE IMMANUEL PROMISED BY ISAIAH

(Isaiah 7,14; Matthew 1,22)
1) While Ahaz son of Jotham and grandson of Uzziah was king of Judah, Rezin king of Aram with Pekah son of Remaliah, king of Israel, marched on Jerusalem, but could not force a battle.
2) When the house of Israel heard that the Aramaeans had come to terms with the Ephraimites, king and people were shaken like forest trees in the wind.
3) Then Yahweh said to Isaiah, Go out with your son Shear-jashub (a remnant shall return) to meet Ahaz at the end of the conduit of the Upper Pool by the causeway leading to the Fuller's Field,
4) and say to him, Be on your guard, keep calm; do not be frightened or unmanned by these two smouldering stumps of firewood, because Rezin and his Aramaeans with Remaliah's son are burning with rage.
5) The Aramaeans with Ephraim and Remaliah's son have laid their plans against you, saying,
6) Let us invade Judah and break her spirit; let us make her join with us, and set the son of Tabeel on the throne.
7) Therefore the Lord Yahweh has said:
This shall not happen now, and never shall,
8) for all that the chief city of Aram is Damascus,
and Rezin is the chief of Damascus;
within sixty-five years
Ephraim shall cease to be a nation,
9) for all that Samaria is the chief city of Ephraim,
and Remaliah's son the chief of Samaria.
Have firm faith, or you will not stand firm.
10) Once again Isaiah spoke to Ahaz and said,

311

11) Ask Yahweh your God for a sign, from lowest Sheol or from highest heaven.

12) But Ahaz said, No, I will not put Yahweh to the test by asking for a sign.

13) Then the answer came: Listen, house of David. Are you not content to wear out mens' patience? Must you also wear out the patience of my God?

14) Therefore the Lord himself shall give you a sign: A young woman is with child, and she will bear a son, and will call him Immanuel (God with us).

15) By the time that he has learnt to reject evil and choose good, he will be eating curds and honey;

16) before that child has learnt to reject evil and choose good, desolation will come upon the land before whose two kings you cower now.

17) Yahweh will bring on you, your people, and your house, a time the like of which has not been seen since Ephraim broke away from Judah (the king of Assyria).[1]

Matthew 1,18 tells the origin of Jesus. His mother conceived him by the Holy Spirit; the bridegroom Joseph was informed of this by a messenger of God in a dream. In this wonderful event, according to the words of the gospel, was fulfilled a saying of the prophet Isaiah:

The virgin will conceive and bear a son (Matthew 1,22; Isaiah 7,14).

More than seven hundred years before the conception and birth of Jesus, Isaiah had spoken that word. Of what nature is the bridge, which spans centuries, from the promise to this fulfilment?

Place and Time

When we read the seventh chapter of the Book of Isaiah, it strikes us with what precision the time and place of this word of the prophet are determined: Aram and Israel are invading Judah; at that moment Isaiah, as God's messenger seeks out the king when he is inspecting a position in his town that stands in especial danger. Do not these circumstances in themselves indicate to us that we must not interpret the word about the "son of a virgin" not in the context of a distant future, but in the context of the place and time where it was first spoken?

The birth of the child was to be God's sign for Ahaz. How could Ahaz understand this sign? With this question we must first try to unlock the prophecy. What significance could this promise have in the situation in which it was heard for the first time?

The encounter between Isaiah and Ahaz on the road leading to the Fuller's Field took place in the year 735 B.C. In this year Jotham, the king of Jerusalem and Judah, had died. Ahaz, his twenty-year-old son,[2] was in a desperate situation. The whole of the ancient orient trembled at that time before the "terrifying glare of the god Asshur". Tiglath-pileser, a usurper on the Assyrian throne, a mighty war-lord, had set out to bring all the surrounding lands under the rule of his god. Already all the

312

smaller states in the west, including Israel and Judah, had paid him rich tribute. But this was a heavy burden on the peoples. For this reason king Rezin of Damascus had set up an anti-Assyrian coalition with the Philistines and Edomites, and even the Arabian queen Zabibe. Pekah ben Remaliah, king in Samaria in the northern kingdom of Israel had also joined it. The only weak point was Judah. Jotham and also his son Ahaz regarded this alliance as too risky an adventure. At the beginning of a new reign in Jerusalem the allies thought the moment was favourable to close the gap in the anti-Assyrian alliance. They wished to make a man of their choice king in Jerusalem (Isaiah 7,6). They waged war against Ahaz, and had already driven him back to Jerusalem (Isaiah 7,1). There the king was visiting at that moment a position of essential importance in the siege: "the end of the conduit of the upper pool by the causeway leading to the Fuller's Field" (Isaiah 7,3). At that moment the prophet approached him bearing God's message.

Could Isaiah in this moment of immediate danger have spoken of an event that was not to happen for centuries? Would he not then have spoken to deaf ears? We might even believe that the time and the place would have been as unfavourable as one could think for any word from God. The king was near to losing his throne; how could one expect him to have time to attend to reflections on matters of principle, such as Isaiah brings before him!

Have firm faith, or you will not stand firm (Isaiah 7,9).

Yet certainly Ahaz saw his attitude to Assyria, his measures for defence of the throne and the city, as religious decisions. On the one hand Tiglath-pileser with his conquests was increasing the territory over which the god Asshur ruled.[3] On the other hand the kings of Israel and Damascus wanted to remove the dynasty of David, to which Yahweh had promised enduring stability.[4] To oppose this attack meant, for Ahaz to take Yahweh's word to his ancestor David seriously. In the end, however, he will disregard this purpose, and send a request for help to the king of Assyria.

I am your servant and your son. Come and save me from the king of Aram and from the king of Israel who are attacking me (2 Kings 16,7).

No successor of David should have spoken thus, for Yahweh had promised to the son of David:

I will be his father, and he shall be my son (2 Samuel 7,14).

Reminder of the Tradition

On the road to the Fuller's Field this decision for or against God has not yet been taken. In order to help the king in this decision, Isaiah holds before his eyes the old traditions of the faith. "Establishment" for ever has been promised by God to the house of David (2 Samuel, 7,16) — Isaiah points out to the king that "to be established" and "to believe in God's word" are closely connected.[5] To the reference to the Davidic

313

tradition Isaiah adds a reference to the tradition of the holy war. Once, at the Red Sea God had saved his people, but the people had "looked on in silence" (Exodus 14,14). Isaiah reminds the king also of this:

Be on your guard, keep calm; do not be frightened . . . (Isaiah 7,4).

Exactly thus God had spoken to Joshua before Joshua began the battles for the land. With these reminders Isaiah seeks to give weight to the word that as God's messenger he has to proclaim to Ahaz:

Therefore the Lord Yahweh has said:

"This shall not happen now, and never shall".

Thus he has a clear message of salvation to transmit; the enemy will have no success — there is only one thing Ahaz must guard against, losing his rest, his confidence in Yahweh's word. Ahaz, on the other hand sees himself in a doubly difficult situation. Only in Tiglath-pileser — and the latter's god Asshur — does he believe he will be able to find help against his enemies, who wish to overthrow his house — and with it the ancient word of Yahweh. He believes he must help Yahweh to keep his word of promise — and he seeks help from a strange god.

But Isaiah requires of him to trust that Yahweh is helping him. He offers him all conceivable securites for his message of salvation. Over and above the traditions of the holy war and of the establishment of the house of David, he links up with an old custom; Israel had earlier in times of danger the right to inquire of Yahweh.[7] But Ahaz rejects Isaiah's offer:

I will not ask (Isaiah 7,12).

The Sign for Ahaz

With that, the prophet's patience is at an end; he rebukes the king. But God's patience is not exhausted. Through Isaiah he sends a new message to Ahaz:

Therefore the Lord himself shall give you a sign: A young woman is with child, and she will bear a son, and will call him Immanuel (Isaiah 7,14).

How had Ahaz to understand this sign? Certainly not as a promise that would only be fulfilled in Christ seven hundred years later. He must have been looking out, seeking what help he could find in the present crisis. The prophet too, is certainly not looking forward centuries. He is looking into a near future, which the king will yet experience. The boy, whose birth he indicates, will still be a child when the enemies of Jerusalem will be annihilated (Isaiah 7,16). The prophecy of the end of Aram and Israel was soon fulfilled. Tiglath-pileser came gladly on Ahaz' request for help, smote Aram and Israel and pillaged the land. He made the kingdom of Rezin an Assyrian province, and also a great part of Israel.

Yet for the king who refused to trust God the destruction of his enemies meant not deliverance, but disaster. Isaiah foresees this disaster: terrible times are coming, not only for Israel, but also for Judah (Isaiah 7,17). This prediction of Isaiah also was fulfilled in Ahaz' times.

The voluntary submission to Assyria did indeed secure the continuance of Judah, but made it dependent on Assyria and obliged it to pay heavy tribute.

Strangely, this first interpretation of the word about Immanuel leaves untouched the heart of the saying concerning the birth. At first Isaiah seems to understand the birth of the child only as a point of orientation in time. From this point it can be reckoned when Damascus, Ephraim, and even Judah are to fall into the power of Assyria. Ahaz' decision, to turn for help to Assyria, is completely wrong — that is what the picture of the future shows. But what has the birth of the child to do with that?

The birth of a child is solemnly promised by God — such a joyful message was once received by Sarah and the parents of Samson (Genesis 16,11ff; Judges 13,13 ff). Is not the annunciation of the birth in this case also made to the father? If that were the case, then Isaiah had now another message of salvation to deliver to the king. It ought to have been all the more a cause of joy for Ahaz, when the name of the son was to be "Immanuel — God with us". This child was to be a sign that God was with his people.[8]

Actually Ahaz himself ought to have been a sign of the nearness of God. He was himself descended from the house of David, prolonged the promise given to David. So long as a king of his family ruled on David's throne, God's former promise held good. Yet Ahaz failed. What is more natural than the conjecture that now Isaiah was now promising the young king and his bride a successor, a son, in whom at last would be fulfilled the hopes that were associated with David's house? The birth of this son must for Ahaz be on the one hand a sign, that God remained true to his promise to the house of David, but on the other hand a warning that he himself was no "Immanuel", no king after God's will.[9] Isaiah — angered by Ahaz' refusal to accept God's promise of salvation — underlined this threatening aspect of the birth-proclamation in his further commentary.

How much the meaning of this word has changed, when we see it again in its New Testament context! Matthew 1,22 sees in Christ the Immanuel. This sign from God is not meant only for Ahaz, but for all the faithful of all ages.

Thus we have two interpretations of the same word; the "Christian" one, according to which Isaiah prophesies the coming Messiah, and the "historical" one, which seeks to understand the word of Isaiah in the light of the immediate context of the time. Are these two interpretations mutualy irreconcileable?

The Openness of Isaiah 7,14

Isaiah 7,14 is one of the Old Testament texts which cannot be satisfactorily explained when we look at it from one plane. We have seen what a remarkable discrepancy existed between the prophecy of the birth itself, and the threatening words of Isaiah that accompanied it. Even the prophet himself was in no doubt that the birth of "Immanuel" meant more than a mere threat to Ahaz.

Interpretation in the Context of the Memoir

Soon after the conversation on the road to the Fuller's Field, Isaiah was forced to acknowledge that his attempt to influence Ahaz had failed. The king called on Tiglath-pileser's help, and submitted to him. Had the word of God that Isaiah had delivered to the king, been in vain? Isaiah was not of this opinion. The report of the meeting with Ahaz was incorporated in Isaiah's memoir, in which the record of his early career had been collected, beginning with his call (Isaiah 6-9). Thus Isaiah believed that the promise of Immanuel did not only have a meaning when Ahaz heard it. This word of God must not be forgotten when its first recipient had closed his ears to it.

But how did he wish this word to be further understood? We shall best find an answer to this question if we consider the general context in which Isaiah placed it in the "Memoir". Among these texts we find in 8,5-8 a new threat to those who through fear of Israel and Aram throw themselves into the arms of Tiglath-pileser. This time the word is meant, not for the king, but for the people. Isaiah sees already, how Israel is being overwhelmed by the Assyrian flood. The oracle ends with the shout "O Immanuel". What did Isaiah mean to say by this shout? Did he perhaps wish to ask if the land of Immanuel was going to be lost before the promised king had come?

When he saw the people, that in blind terror of its enemies was not able to trust in God, the prophet might indeed well ask himself this question. But it never came into his mind when he thought of Assyria's superiority. Had not God once in the holy wars sent terror on Israel's enemies and destroyed them? No more do the faithful now need to tremble before the "terrifying splendour of the god Asshur".

> Take note, you nations, and be dismayed
> Listen, all you distant parts of the earth:
> you may arm yourselves but will be dismayed;
> you may arm yourselves but will be dismayed.
> Make your plans, but they will be foiled,
> propose what you please, but it shall not stand;
> for God is with us. (Isaiah 8,9ff).

Isaiah had in vain announced to Ahaz that the plans of Rezin and the son of Remaliah would come to nothing. The king of Israel had not behaved accordingly, but God does not suffer himself to be prevented from fulfilling his word. Now Isaiah turns threateningly upon the nations. "God is with us": the name of the child here becomes a battle-cry; in the faith that "God is with us" the Israelites in the holy war had marched into battle.[10]

As recently as the second world war German soldiers bore on their belt-buckles round the swastika the inscription "God with us". To use this word as a battle-cry seems blasphemy to us. And yet for centuries wars were waged in which both sides drew courage from the faith that God was fighting on their side. Isaiah would have most sternly repudiated this use of his word. To be sure, God leads his people, but no man has the right to say he is fighting God's battle. (That was the mistake of Ahaz, that he believed that he must come to God's help with the political move of an alliance with Assyria.) The memory of the holy war gives no security for all time to come.[11] Isaiah can also use figures from the holy war in the contrary sense: what God once did to Israel's enemies, he is now doing to the apostate people itself.

"God with us" is too narrowly understood if we wish to see in it only the memory of the help in the holy war. It is a brief formula for the faith of Israel.[12] God does not dwell in heaven, and not in the depths of the sea, nor on mountains nor in trees nor in springs, he has no fixed abode save with his people. He went journeying with the people in the desert; he went out to battle with Israel's army in the holy wars. When Yahweh was "not with Israel" (Numbers 14,43; Judges 6,13), it was stricken and brought low. Isaiah 8,10 is to be understood against this background. With the birth of "the maiden's son" the ancient hope of Israel in the presence of God to help was given a new life. The oracle of Isaiah 7,14 is not meant for Ahaz alone. The whole of Israel must gather around the hope here expressed.

Several years later Isaiah had already learnt that for one part of Israel this hope must be given up, apparently finally. Tiglath-pileser, on Ahaz' invitation conquers Damascus and Samaria; his intention is to destroy these countries completely. Aram becomes an Assyrian province; Israel saves only a continuing foothold in the mountainous country of Samaria expelling promptly by a revolt Pekah the enemy of Assyria and replacing the murdered man by Hoshea, a king friendly to Assyria. A great part of the land is however placed under an Assyrian provincial governor (731/30 BC). Isaiah speaks of this in chapter 8, verse 23 [9,1]:

At first Yahweh brought shame to the land of Zebulun and the land of Naphtali . . .

But it is precisely for the inhabitants of these regions which in political reality are excluded from the fellowship of Israel that the ancient hope of Israel in the nearness of God holds good:

. . . But then Jahweh brings to honour the territory of the road to the sea . . . the province of the Gentiles. The people that walk in darkness sees a great light . . . For a boy has been born to us, a son given to us . . . (Isaiah 8,23-9,6 [9,1-7]).

Once again the birth is not an event in the far future. It is to give new hope immediately to the separated part of the people in the Assyrian province. God has given to them a sign that he is with them. In the child of a king once more a bearer of the promise of David is here. On him too is concentrated the hope which Israel from ancient days placed in God's help. Through him God will give the people peace.

Thrice the memoir refers back to the Immanuel promise: (Isaiah 8,5ff; 8,9f; 8,23ff [9,1ff]). This shows that even Isaiah himself did not understand the Immanuel promise as relating to *one* historical moment (the encounter with Ahaz on the road to the Fuller's Field). On the one hand, it arises out of the hope that Israel had already long cherished. It was this ancient hope indeed that had first moved Isaiah to direct this word to king Ahaz. On the other hand, the promise develops further. Just because Isaiah wished with this word to bind Ahaz to the old hope of Israel, the prophet saw himself bound also to transmit this word to all Israel. In the promise of the birth of the child the hope of Israel was to be kept alive, even in the sombre days in which king and people were found wanting, in which the Gentiles had wholly absorbed a part of Israel, and made the other part subject to them. In reality, further, the historical events could not destroy this hope, because it transcended what man can expect in history, it was directed to a "peace without end".

Interpretation by means of Isaiah 11,1ff

Isaiah was yet to learn that even Hezekiah, Ahaz' son and successor, was not "Immanuel". Towards the end of his prophetic life Isaiah was even compelled to see that Assyria by no means shrank back in terror at the battle-cry "God with us". In the year 701 Sennacherib besieged Jerusalem, after ravaging all Judah. But the hope of God's nearness and help did not perish. Isaiah foresees how the Egyptian task-force advances and spreads universal destruction. But even if they were to strike down the tree of the house of David, they would not be able to destroy the hope:

Then a shoot shall grow from the stem of Jesse . . .[13] (Isaiah 10,28-11,5).

Pupils of Isaiah added this poem to the "memoir". By so doing they wished to show how their master understood the word about Immanuel. To be sure, with every new king from David's house the hope is rekindled which God himself lit in Israel, every king who continues to bear the promise made to David, is a sign of God's nearness, but the maintenance of this kingship and its rule is not the essential thing. The only thing of importance is the hope which relies upon God. Even if this ancient great house of rulers perishes, God can carry out his plan; a frail offshoot can have the same significance as formerly the entire tree. The preservation of the royal house of David is not the thing that matters, but the fact that God's spirit is beginning to work (Isaiah 11,2).

Thus it becomes clearer and clearer that the "Immanuel" promise cannot be restricted to a single interpretation. So much hope was placed in the son of Ahaz, that he alone could never be the vehicle of all this hope. With every new king of the house of David it must blaze up again. It even embraced more than any king could fulfil. So in the end the important thing is no longer the preservation of the house of David, but only the mighty activity of God's spirit in a frail "offshoot".

There is an unbridgeable discrepancy between a "historical" and a "Christian" meaning of the word of Isaiah only for those who overlook this singular openness of the Old Testament literary form. Isaiah himself did not understand his promise as a once-for-all cut and dried utterance, but he kept this word of God alive, by ever and again discovering new depths in it.

Interpretation in Matthew

But is not Matthew 1,22 a misunderstanding of the word of Isaiah? The Gospel stresses the virginity of the mother of Immanuel, the miraculous conception without the cooperation of a man — Isaiah speaks of a young maiden who will soon marry and have a child. Isaiah enlarges the meaning of the word about Immanuel, the promise of the birth of a royal child becomes ever more clearly the proclamation of *God's* rule through his chosen one. It becomes clearer and clearer that the hope of which Isaiah speaks cannot be all at once fulfilled and is then disposed of. Does not Matthew 1,22 constrict this word, does it not look on it as the prediction of this one event, the miraculous conception of Jesus?

We have become accustomed to call citations of the Old Testament in the New Testament "proofs from scripture". Nothing was further from the intention of the New Testament writers than the wish to "prove" anything with the help of the Old Testament. Isaiah 7,14 was completely unfitted to prove the virgin birth of Jesus. No Jew had hitherto spoken of the virgin birth of the Messiah — this thought contradicted the expectation of a son of David. Only those who already believed in the miraculous conception of Jesus could discover in Isaiah 7,14 a mysterious reference to it. The already familiar theological teaching about the origin of Jesus thus helped to interpret the Old Testament text — the Old Testament text could not prove the unusual origin of Jesus.

Further, the story of the virgin birth is not told for its own sake; the son so wonderfully begotten is to be called Jesus, which means "God saves". According to the angel's message he is "Saviour of the people". Israel's ancient hope in God's nearness and help appears consequently as the foundation of this narrative. Not in vain does Matthew 1,22 take up also the name of Immanuel in the quotation, though this son is not called "Immanuel". This Jesus, begotten of the spirit, is "God with us", he is born as a sign of the immediate nearness of God. So the purpose of the quotation is not merely to refer to an ancient prediction of the conception of Jesus. On the contrary it serves to arouse reflection on the history of the hope of Israel. This hope has not come to an end with this fulfilment; on the contrary it is filled with new and powerful life.

This man will save his people from its sins (Matthew 1,21).

Schematic Representation

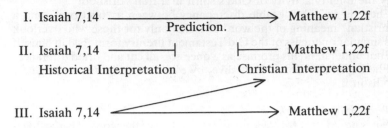

I. Isaiah 7,14 ─────────────→ Matthew 1,22f
Prediction.

II. Isaiah 7,14 ────────┤   ├──── Matthew 1,22f
Historical Interpretation   Christian Interpretation

III. Isaiah 7,14 ◄─────────────→ Matthew 1,22f

So we can neither say that the events of Matthew 1 were predicted in Isaiah 7 (I), nor can we set the "historical" interpretation of the text of Isaiah sheerly against the "Christian" interpretation in Matthew 1,22f (II). The truth is rather that Matthew 1,22f stands within the field that is opened up in Isaiah 7,14, and which had begun to expand more and more even for Isaiah (III).

Summary

In our exegesis of Isaiah 7,14 we started from an angle of inquiry which had not been considered in the previous chapters of this book. In chapters I-IV we attempted to describe and understand Old Testament literary forms as structures with clearly defined outlines. They were examined in the context of the environment in which they originated. Our approach to Isaiah 7,14 was different. Our first interest was the history of the text's influences. In the Gospel of Matthew this passage is quoted with reference to Jesus Christ. When we examined the Old Testament text from this angle we discovered in it a characteristic of a literary form that had not hitherto been observed. We have here an open literary form, what it says is not clearly determined, but unfolds itself. The reason for this lies in the fact that Isaiah 7,14 is a prophetic word of God. According to the biblical way of thinking a word of God is always a living word. The promise of the birth of a child to a young woman had not only something to say to Ahaz who confronted Isaiah on the road to the Fuller's Field, but continued to awaken ever new hopes. When a son was born to Ahaz, Isaiah might have regarded the promise as fulfilled and settled, but the hope that the word of God had awakened was too great to have been fulfilled at one point in time.

The openness of the saying in Isaiah 7,14 is already visible in different ways in the Old Testament:
1. The prophet himself gives further interpretation of the word about Immanuel (cf Isaiah 7,14 in relation to Isaiah 8,8.10; 9,1ff).
2. The promise was set down in writing; it was incorporated in the "memoir". This fact reveals that it was meant to hold good for ever — but that means also alive for ever, and capable of new interpretation.

3. An example of such reinterpretation is given by the work of the redactors who put together the book of the prophet. They added Isaiah 11,1ff to the memoir, a piece from the later years of Isaiah, to the collection of early texts. By so doing they showed that Isaiah 7,14 was to be understood in the sense of that later Messianic promise.

In order rightly to understand this peculiar openness of the literary forms for new interpretations, we have still to note one point. In Isaiah 7,14 already, earlier traditions of Israel are taken up and interpreted to suit a new situation. Only when the promise concerning Immanuel is seen in connection with these older traditions (the promise to David, God's help in the holy war, God's nearness to his people) can we understand that it awakens hopes that reach far beyond the historical moment in which it is spoken.

What is to be observed in this one text, holds good for large parts of the Old Testament; repeatedly we are referred back to older traditions, frequently a text points forward to others which further develop its meaning. This net of relationships, this openness of the texts for new interpretations, makes the Old Testament *one* book, in which in looking at one text we are compelled repeatedly to pay attention to its harmony with others.

2. THE INTERPRETATION OF THE OLD TESTAMENT BY THE OLD TESTAMENT

The Old Testament — one Writing, fulfilled in Christ?

When Christians take the Old Testament into their hands, they naturally read it in the light which the New Testament casts upon it for them. "That the scripture might be fulfilled": this New Testament sentence will at least unconsciously guide them, when they seek to understand the Old Testament. There is here a double pre-understanding. I. The Old Testament appears as "the Scriptures" i.e. as a unity. II. The Old Testament is "fulfilled" by the work of Jesus, it points forward to Christ. Modern exegesis has largely destroyed this understanding of the Old Testament. It has taught us, instead of the *one* voice of the Old Testament revelation, to hear a choir of voices, priests, prophets, wise men, historians and singers, popular narrators and learned men speak to us here. It represents the Old Testament to us, not as one book, but as a whole library of the ancient world. In the preceding chapters we tried to describe the variety of different forms the great number of literary units of the Old Testament.

Modern exegesis does not only call in question the unity of the Old Testament, but also its openness in pointing to Christ. It shows that the Old Testament texts were intended for the men of their times, that they instructed and exhorted them, consoled them and guided them, the authors were not thinking of a distant future.

And yet the two inter-related questions remain: has the Old Testament, that took shape through many centuries, after all come to be *one* book? Does it point beyond itself to one future, one "fulfilment"?

The answer to this double question cannot be briefly given; it can only be investigated and paraphrased from different sides. The "Christian" and the "historical" understanding of the Old Testament cannot be simply harmonized. In this book, up to this point an attempt has been made to understand the Old Testament literature in the light of its history. Even this chapter will not depart from that task. We shall only ask if there are to be found possible points of contact in the Old Testament itself for the Christian interpretation of the Old Testament. The historian can never prove that an event had to come in this way and in no other — here also proof cannot be adduced that the coming of Christ was the necessary fulfilment of Old Testament expectation. We can only ask if it lies within the context of the Old Testament hopes.

From this "historical" angle the coming of Christ appears only as one of many possible answers to the Old Testament. Is that not too light an evaluation to put on the New Testament? Has not God fulfilled and transcended all expectation in Christ? A provisional answer to such doubts can be the counter-question. We believe that perhaps we give the highest evaluation to the Old Testament, when we seek its meaning and its unity in the fact that it is a promise fulfilled in Christ. But does not the promise become useless, when the fulfilment is there? Is not too light a value placed upon the Old Testament, when it is seen from the "Christian" viewpoint?

Points of Contact for the Question about Unity

Thus such fundamental reflections do not here lead to a conclusion. We will rather put the question to the Old Testament. What in the context of the Old Testament do "promise and fulfilment" mean? What characteristics of Old Testament texts indicate that this book forms a unity marked by the hope of a greater future?

There are several points of contact which promise to answer these questions. One of these points is given by the prophetic message of salvation. Does it point to Christ?

A further is provided by the story of the origins of the Old Testament books: we had repeatedly to observe that the authors of the Old Testament and their predecessors, from whom they received the traditions, possessed a great power of assimilation. Individual sagas grew together to form *one* purpose-directed history;[14] — the various traditions of the fathers, of the exodus, of Sinai, and of the capture of the land came together to form *one* creed,[15] the traditions of David and Jerusalem were united with the old substance of the faith.[16] Can we discover the source of this power of synoptic vision? Is there in the Old Testament one point from which it appears as a unity?

Further points of contact, which have not yet come within our field of vision, may be added to these two.

The Bible is a book of written tradition. Why was Israel's holy tradition committed to writing? The oral tradition played an essential part in the long and complicated history of the growth of the Old Testament; but only that part of the tradition which finally became literature is now within our grasp. It would be of special interest to examine prophetic texts with this question. The prophets were orators not writers. They wished to make an immediate impression on their hearers. What was the purpose in writing down their words?

A further point worthy of consideration in this context is given to us in the fact that the Bible which we possess is an ordered unity. Writings of similar kind stand together: the five books of Moses, the historical books, the poetical works from the Psalms to the wisdom writings, the prophets. Who placed these books together and ordered them thus? What were the intentions of these men who put together the Old Testament in its present form? In this manner we approach the question of the unity of the Old Testament "historically" and not on the basis of systematic reflections.

Prospective Summary of Sections 3-7

The following sections concern themselves with the questions raised here.

Section 3 (Promise and fulfilment in the historical traditions of the Old Testament) considers material that was developed already in different chapters from a new viewpoint. What power created the one history of Israel out of the different historical traditions? It was the faith in the word of promise of the one God that directs history. It finds fulfilment, and yet continues to be effectual over and above the fulfilment.

Section 4 (The prophet's message of salvation) asks how we are to understand the prophetic expectation of the future. In two respects it is dependent on the preceding history of Israel. The prophetic message of salvation keeps alive the ancient faith in God's word of promise, it portrays the new salvation in pictures that are provided by the past history.

Section 5 (The continued life of the words of the prophets) shows that we must not see between prophetic word and fulfilment in Christ an empty interval of mere waiting in which people merely conserved the prophetic message, and did not really use it. The prophetic word lived on as a divine word of continuing power.

Section 6 (The beginnings of the study of the scriptures) describes different phenomena of the biblical *literature*. In many points the outlook of those men becomes comprehensible, who first saw the scriptures as a "unity", who contributed to the formation of the Old Testament.

Section 7 (The completion of the Old Testament) concerns itself lastly with the earliest times in which the Old Testament was regarded as a completed entity, to which no more new writings were to be attached. It inquires about the canon of the scriptures. Has the latter a significance for the interpretation of Old Testament texts?

It is an ancient rule of interpretation that an individual text is first to be understood in its context. The following sections are all designed to show that the nearest context of an Old Testament text is the Old Testament, and, indeed, the *whole* Old Testament. No one doubts that the Old Testament contains units of considerable size — the historical works, the individual books of the prophets, etc. Here our concern is to show that the whole Old Testament is a unity, within whose context these larger works and also individual sections alone find their full meaning.

3. PROMISE AND FULFILMENT IN THE HISTORICAL TRADITIONS OF THE OLD TESTAMENT

Promise-Fulfilment: the Heart of Israel's Faith

We are accustomed to see the relation of the Old Testament to the New in terms of the category promise-fulfilment. What was promised in the Old Testament is fulfilled in the New Testament. Yet promise and fulfilment play an essential part even in the Old Testament itself. Indeed, the question "what does promise-fulfilment signify for the Old Testament?" leads us to the very heart of the faith of Israel.

One might think that the question: "What significance do promise and fulfilment have in the Old Testament?" must in the first place be put to the prophetic texts. Did Israel before the prophets not confine itself to looking back on the past? For there salvation had happened, Yahweh had created his people for himself, when he led it out of Egypt. Were not the prophets the first to teach men to expect salvation in the future? The answer is "No": the prophets were not the first to awaken the expectation of salvation. The truth is that Israel created the prophets because expectation of salvation was the heart of its faith.

The prophets did not preach a new faith; they wished to keep the old faith alive in times of crisis. They supported themselves on the older historical and legal tradition.

What is the heart and centre of this tradition? Israel's religious traditions did not stand side by side, as if of equal value. They grouped themselves round the affirmation of faith: Yahweh had delivered Israel from Egypt.[17] The traditions of the fathers were regarded as a prelude to this act: this people of Israel took its rise from Abraham, Isaac and Jacob, therefore God adopted it. The traditions of the desert-wandering, and the conquest of the land were attached; Yahweh had led Israel forth, in order to bring it into the promised land. The traditions of Sinai and the law were included: thus Israel was to respond to God's act of salvation.

How did it come that the tradition of the deliverance from Egypt had the power to draw other traditions to itself and to bind them together in a complete course of history? In many passages of the Old Testament, within the most varied literary categories, the central affirmation of faith concerning the deliverance of Israel from Egypt is repeated. It cannot surprise us, that even Israel's basic commandment, the decalogue, begins with the affirmation of faith.

I am Yahweh, your God, who brought you out of Egypt.

In our catechisms this sentence is abbreviated: "I am the Lord, your God. You shall . . ." The authors of the catechisms wished in this manner to loosen the close connection of the decalogue with Israel, and underline its universality. But in doing so, they altered its meaning. According to the phrasing of the catechism God introduces himself at the beginning of the commandments as the absolute Lord, who tolerates no contradiction; while in the Old Testament he introduces himself as Israel's deliverer. This sentence contains in the utmost brevity Israel's joyful message, the gospel of the Old Testament.

How can we describe this statement about the deliverance as a "message"? It was, after all, known to Israel assembled at Sinai that God had delivered it from Egypt. Can a reference to a known event be a message? Does a message not speak of the unknown, of something yet to come? The first sentence of the basic commandment does not intend merely to remind the hearers of something past. With the deliverance from Egypt, Israel began to be God's people, and Yahweh thereby showed himself as Israel's God. This relation between God and the people remained constant since that time. "God has delivered us from Egypt". This primitive confession of Israel contains not only a statement about the past, but also a hope. The faithful God has been since that beginning Israel's deliverer. Every time when in the course of its history the people got into difficulty, they could take fresh hope and courage from the fact that God had acknowledged his act of deliverance.

I am Yahweh, your God, who brought you out of Egypt.

God's Word and History

Thus the expectation of divine help bases itself on God's word; this was already decisive for the origin of that primitive confession. Israel has not on its own initiative decided to see God's hand in the events of the deliverance from Egypt. The fact was rather that God had promised this deliverance in advance, and therefore, when it happened, Israel could believe that God was the cause. The divine promise is the source of the faith of Israel.

This makes a fundamental distinction between Israel's faith and the mythical religions of the surrounding world. Everything that Israel was and possessed, its freedom and its land, later its kingdom, its town Jerusalem and its temple, it owed to the word of God. The surrounding heathen sought assurance in another manner: the myths told that in primitive times Babylon had been built as the city of the god Marduk,

325

that since primitive times the gods of rain and famine fought with each other. The people, that knows from the myths the movements of the gods, can always move them, to act in the same way. But Israel is unable to support itself on mythical knowledge of the divine world; it receives its certainty only from God's word. God is faithful to this word, Israel can rely on that. Thus "promise" is not one among many other literary forms of the Old Testament — which might be found principally in the prophets. The truth is rather that the heart of Israel's faith is represented in the promise.

Promise-Fulfilment in the Old Testament Compilations

This structure of the faith of Israel is also reflected in the individual literary forms — for example in the Yahwist's history. According to J the beginning of the history of Israel was God's promise to Abraham.[18] The Yahwist found the promise of descendants already in the sagas of the fathers. It was this promise that gave the narratives of the endangering of the tribal mother and her son[19] their tension. A promise of the land fits well into the world of half-nomads in which the scene of the sagas of the fathers is laid. Living on the fringe of the cultivated land, these men had no more urgent wish than to be permitted themselves to live in such a fruitful land. The biblical authors of the pentateuch, who took up these old traditions, were able, with the help of the promise of the land, to span the great arc that extended from the wandering fathers, through the people wandering in the desert, to the conquest of Israel.

Thus it is wrong to see only promise in the Old Testament, and to reserve the fulfilment for the New Testament. Even the stories of the fathers and much more the great written sources of the pentateuch, are built on the principle of promise and fulfilment. Is not the unexpected gift of a son, is not every deliverance of the child and the mother, a partial fulfilment of the promise of descendants? The increase of the people in Egypt, its deliverance from Pharaoh's plan of annihilation, confirms God's faithfulness to his word.

And yet it is singular that these fulfilments do not make the preceding divine word of promise superfluous. There always remains an expectation which must rely upon this word. The Yahwist praises the gift of the land:

> I . . . have come down to rescue them from the power of Egypt, and to bring them up out of that country into a fine, broad land; it is a land flowing with milk and honey (Exodus 3,8.17; 13,5).

Is there a land that can wholly satisfy such an expectation? Must not Israel continue to hope for this promise, when it is already in the land? Even in the time, in which Israel is already living in the good land, it needs the delivering God. The Yahwist himself points this out to us. In the so-called Yahwistic decalogue God adds to the command to make pilgrimage thrice yearly, a promise:

> For I will drive out the nations before you and extend your frontiers,

and no one will covet your land, when you go up three times to enter the presence of the Lord your God (Exodus 34,24).

In order that Israel may serve God undisturbed, it still needs God the deliverer; its hope in the word of God must be continually kept alive. In the fulfilment the promise receives its actualization. The Yahwist lived in the age of David, he was permitted to see the fulfilment of the promise made to Abraham in Genesis 12,1ff. Israel, a great people, possessed the land, it ruled over other peoples, and could tell them of God's blessing. Yet he knew also that the old word of God must have further consequences. In his pre-history he had shown how the whole of mankind had come under the curse — with Abraham the history of blessing for all mankind was to begin; Israel's time of flowering can only be a stage in this history.

The literary form of Deuteronomy also lives in the tension between fulfilment and continuing valid promise. In this book, the people that has already possessed the land for a long time is addressed as if it still stood on the threshold of the promised land. Even the Israel that is already living in the land has not yet reached the goal to which God intends to lead it. For the promise of the land contains more than could be fully satisfied by the mere possession of the land. Deuteronomy speaks of Yahweh there "giving rest"[20] to Israel. But Israel could not find rest, so long as it was forced to share the land with other peoples.

It was no easy question for the faithful in Israel, why the land was still possessed by other peoples. The Old Testament gives here different, contradictory answers. Three of them may be cited: (1) God had promised to extirpate these peoples (Exodus 23,23); but that could only happen gradually otherwise the land would become desolate, so long as Israel had not become strong enough to possess it entirely, and cultivate it alone (Exodus 23,30). (2) Israel had not been true to God's covenant, therefore the peoples should remain in the land as "tormentors" of Israel, and their gods as a "trap" (Judges 2,3). (3) Yet people in Israel also tried still to see something good in the presence of the peoples. God let them remain, in order that in the conflicts with them Israel's later generations should still continue to learn the arts of war (Judges 3,2).

Do not such contrary statements contradict the concept of the unity of the Old Testament? They only do this, if we were to seek for a definite point at which the promise of the land was fulfilled. The Old Testament gives another picture of the fulfilment. An entire history of fulfilment begins with the divine promise. In spite of all false starts and the resistance of men, God's word has its way.

This thought determines the Deuteronomist's history. History is represented as the realization of God's word. The older historical works had shown that the history of Israel as a whole was to be understood in the light of God's word. The Deuteronomist's history follows them in this, but at the same time, it goes beyond them. The representations of the "classical" salvation history up to the conquest of the land, started from the presupposition that God had intended the good land, power, and blessing for his people, and that only the errors of men delayed or even prevented the fulfilment. The Deuteronomists learned from the prophets that all evil for Israel, even the fall of the two kingdoms, is effected by God's word.

We might ask if this did not mean that God had become unfaithful to his promise — after all, the basic promise was the undertaking to be Israel's deliverer (not her destroyer!) But would Yahweh still be Israel's deliverer, if he had confirmed the apostate people in its disobedience through external good fortune? If Israel decides not to be God's people any more, God can only remain faithful to it, if he lets it experience the consequences of its apostasy.

However, the Deuteronomists were not satisfied by asserting that the general course of the history of Israel had been directed by God's word. They also interpreted many individual events as fulfilment of God's words. Everything that happened in Israel's history, counted for them as fulfilment of God's word.

Summary

Israel's faith was essentially trust in God's word of promise. This faith stamped the historical traditions of Israel. The Old Testament works, in which also these traditions have been preserved for us, use repeatedly the extended arc of promise and fulfilment as a structural element. This makes them literary forms of singular openness, which are fundamentally different from modern historical representations. We see past events as unalterable; an historical report depicts facts that cannot any more be altered. The historical reports of the Old Testament have another intention. They bear witness to the fact that all happenings are brought about by God's word of promise, and by so doing, strengthen the faith of Israel, its trust in the word of promise: God's word has already been fulfilled; this shows that it has power also to determine the further course of history.

Thus — precisely through their report about past events — they point the faithful to the future that lies before them. For the fulfilment does not make God's word superfluous. It is only when a word is fulfilled that it becomes evident what further dimensions it still contains. Then for the first time it is revealed that it must also influence the future course of history.

The heart of the historical tradition was the statement: God delivered us from Egypt. This statement records something that is past, but it contains also a prospect for the future: God is for ever our deliverer. From this viewpoint every report about the past becomes a promise, a source of further faith and hope.

4. THE PROPHET'S MESSAGE OF SALVATION

Modern exegesis has taught us to distinguish between the many different voices that find expression in the Old Testament. That is especially important for the understanding of prophetic texts. Often it is important to distinguish the *one* speaker of such a text; for the prophets appeal to their unique and individual mission as the legitimation of their message. Yet there remains the task of paying attention to the way in which one voice harmonizes with the rest. It can even be said that this agreement of the Old Testament authors was more important than the unique individual message that each of them had to deliver in his turn. They did not wish to be original, but to make the faith of the past a living power in the present; each individual stated a message that concerned them all.

The Relationship between Future and Past

This is true also of the prophets' message of salvation. Never previously had anyone in Israel turned so decisively to the future, as did the prophets. They knew indeed how much God had bestowed on the people in the past. But from this point they directed Israel's gaze into the future; there, and not in the past, salvation was to be found.

> Thus says Yahweh, who opened a way in the sea and a path through mighty waters, who drew on chariot and horse to their destruction, a whole army, men of valour; there they lay, never to rise again; they were crushed, snuffed out like a wick. "Cease to dwell on days gone by and to brood over past history. Here and now I will do a new thing; . . . I will make a way even through the wilderness and paths in the barren desert" (Isaiah 43,16-19).

Does not here the prophet appear as a revolutionary innovator, who overturns former religious conceptions? Yahweh is the God who builds roads in the desert, who creates new things where hitherto there was nothing. God himself exhorts men to forget the past. But Deutero-Isaiah does not himself obey this exhortation. He portrays Yahweh as Israel's deliverer from Egypt. On the one hand God challenges Israel to see his unprecedented new work — but on the other hand he portrays this new works as a repetition of the old work of salvation. As once Israel travelled through the desert to the promised land, so again there will be a road through the desert. Is there not here a contradiction?

This radical turning to the future does not cancel out the historical tradition. What it does is to throw light upon the real character of the old religious experience. Then God made a path for Israel in the pathless sea — how should he not now find it possible to realize the impossible, to lead Israel home from exile? The past is to be forgotten — but only in so far as it is past. What remains of importance in the past events is the expectation of salvation that they contained. The past as such is conserved only in memory, and is dead — but Israel must keep alive the old expectation of salvation.

Thus even in the prophets' expectation of the future, loyalty to tradition is a powerful source of faith. The coming salvation has long been on the way; Israel can be sure that it is coming; for Yahweh has always intended to give his people salvation. From this angle we are to understand the peculiar linguistic forms of the prophetic message of salvation; they announce a new work of Yahweh, but picture it with the help of the material that lay to hand in the historical tradition.

The Relation between God's Freedom and his Faithfulness

When the prophets teach men to expect salvation from the future "coming of God", they renew a picture of God by which Israel had for long distinguished itself from the heathen peoples. The heathens knew where the gods were to be found: in heaven, in the depths of the sea, on the mountain of the gods, in trees, springs and groves. But in Israel there was an old tradition of the coming God. Yahweh approached wherever Israel needed his help.[21] This figure made it clear that Yahweh is bound by nothing but his faithfulness, by his own word. He could be found nowhere by his people, but in his word of promise.

Other figures in Israel had come to accompany the figure of the coming God: God sat on his kingly throne in the midst of his court, he dwelt in the temple — but those who used these figures drew attention to the inadequacy of such figures. The temple does not contain Yahweh, his throne towers far above it.[22] Lastly, Ezekiel ventures a bold mixture of the metaphors; the enthroned God is the coming Yahweh; the throne becomes the throne-chariot (Ezekiel 1).

The prophets look for the coming God. They do not confine Yahweh to the salvation that he once bestowed upon Israel, but teach men to expect his future action. In turning radically to the future they keep alive the tradition the freedom of the God, from whom one cannot beforehand expect a quite definite type of behaviour. Traditions can be a burden that blocks the way into the future; it can be necessary to break open their shell in order to make new growth possible. Israel provided an example of this. In Jeremiah 35 the sect of the Rechabites is mentioned. Their adherents believed that they must retain the nomadic life. For example they despised wine as a gift of cultivation, they believed that only so could they rightly serve the God who had encountered the people in the desert. They were not willing to accommodate themselves to Israel's changed situation, which had long since changed from a nomadic life to a life in farms and cities. In spite of all their piety they were thus condemned to insignificance. They had nothing to offer to the solution of *those* problems that at that time were troubling Israel.

To be sure, Jeremiah praised the exemplary loyalty of the Rechabites. But he himself demands another attitude to the past:

These are the words of the Lord: Stop at the cross-roads; look for the ancient paths; ask, "Where is the way that leads to what is good?" Then take that way, and you will find rest for yourselves (Jeremiah 6,16).

It is not because it is past that the past is valuable, but because it shows a viable road, which can be pursued in the present.

The continuing dialogue with its own (and foreign) traditions was the foundation of Israel's spiritual life. It left its stamp upon the literary forms of the Old Testament, and made the many voices of the Old Testament into a single choir.

Even the prophetic promises draw their life from the treasury of tradition. It is just this side of the texts which the Christian reader all too easily overlooks, since above everything he pays attention to the fulfilment of these words in Christ. But by so doing he obscures his vision of their basic structure. Therefore we shall show, by taking some themes dealing with words of promise, how strongly the prophetic vision of the future was guided by tradition. As this is done it will be shown how individual motifs are set free from their original background, and throw light on new aspects of faith, when placed in new and changing contexts.

The Theme of Journeying

The Yahwist makes Israel's history begin by God sending Abram on a journey (Genesis 12,1ff). The goal of the journey is to be the land, that God will show to him; the journey brings Abram nearer to God; it is the first step to the creation of the people of Israel.

The second beginning of the history of Israel is depicted in a similar way. Israel must set forth from Egypt in order to meet God in the desert (Exodus 3,8; 3,17f). This departure will make Israel an independent people.[23] The journey towards God is, however, not concluded by Israel's final settlement in the promised land. Even there, three times a year all Israelites must journey forth, in order to appear before God.[24] Israel must seek nearness to God by means of repeated journeys; in this way it must ever and again become the new people of God.

Deutero-Isaiah consoles the exiled Israelites by referring to these traditions. Israel is a descendant of Abraham, the friend of God. God brought Abraham out of Mesopotamia; he will bring the exiled people from the ends of the earth (Isaiah 41,9).

The prophet also refers to the exodus from Egypt, and further to the third development of the motif of journeying, to the pilgrimages of the people to the holy place. As once the journey to the promised land created the people of Israel, as the pilgrimage to Zion continually reunited the people, so in the near future the journey to Zion will cause a resurrection of the people. Miracles will happen as in the first journey through the desert, and thus a new presence of God will become possible for the rejected.[25]

No Old Testament book represents the return from the exile. But it differed from the expectations of Deutero-Isaiah, it was an insignificant, almost pitiful event, which made no impression. And yet the prophet's word of promise was carefully treasured up. Even the restored Israel knew that the real journey to God and the embodiment of the true people of God lay still in the future.

Finally it understood the journey to God as an event of the last times. This journey was not to make *Israel* alone the people of God. According to the words of the Yahwist Abram was called to go north for the sake of the *peoples*:

In you shall all nations be blessed.

Several related prophetic promises picture how the peoples take part in the journey to God, and how thereby the whole of mankind, united with the people of God, receives peace.[26] Even according to statements of the New Testament we have not yet arrived.

Therefore a Sabbath rest still awaits the people of God (Hebrews 4,9).

The fulfilment of the Old Testament is not the end of the wandering, but only a clearer definition of the goal.

The Theme of the Covenant with God

We do not know when people in Israel began to speak of a covenant of God with the people. But it is certain that historical events gave the impetus. The people surrounding Israel saw men at the mercy of the caprice of the gods, when they did not succeed in influencing the divinized powers of nature by means of magic rites. Israel was different, it could rely on its God; for it had learnt from experience that God was on its side. A word to express this experience is "Covenant".

According to a hypothesis accepted by many exegetes, the first form of the religion of Israel was the faith in the "God of the fathers", a trustful veneration of the God who had revealed himself to the father of the great family as a protecting God, and travelled with him from place to place. We could already describe this personal relation between God and man as a "covenant". "Covenant" was the term used at that time to describe, among other things, the solemnly sealed friendship, the blood-brother-hood, by means of which men came so close to each other, as otherwise only members of a family can (1 Samuel 20,9). The covenant of friendship, like marriage and sonship by adoption, is a kind of "deliber-ately chosen" relationship. According to the prophet Hosea God has voluntarily bound himself to Israel as a bridegroom,[27] as an adopting father, and does not give up this bond, in spite of Israel's failure. In the figures of the marriage with God and the fatherhood of God, Hosea depicts the hope of future salvation (Hosea 2;11). By means of these figures, he illustrates what the "covenant" of God means. Here it becomes clear, that in the covenant God does not cause *something* to be given to the people, but that he gives *himself* to it. "Your God — my people"; the possessive pronouns of the covenant formula are an ex-pression of this nearness of God.[28] In Israel people were astonished that

God could be so close to man. Thus Genesis 15 tells that Abraham only in fear, darkness and "deep sleep" experienced the vision in which God made the covenant with him. In Exodus 24 it is specially mentioned that when the covenant was made, the elders of Israel did not die, but even ate and drank in God's presence.

According to these narratives, rites used in the making of covenants between men also characterized God's covenant with the people; the blood-rite, the feast, even God's solemn curse on himself if he were to break the covenant.[29] This may seem objectionable to us — but Israel thus learnt by experience that God had unreservedly placed himself upon its side. This description discloses further that the covenant with God was not merely a pictorial way of speaking, but was continually experienced anew as an actual reality in public worship.

And yet God's covenant with Israel cannot merely be compared with human covenants of friendship and love. Modern scholarship sees it above all as analogous with old oriental state treaties. Here it is not a matter of a personal bond, what happens is that the stronger party guarantees protection to the weaker and lays obligations on him. This form of covenant appears to be the principal basis of the Sinai covenant, in which God enjoins the law upon Israel. But even here the contract is related to the fact that God has *himself* turned in mercy to the people. He took the initiative in entering into the obligation by taking Israel as his people when he delivered them from Egypt. So life according to the commandments is not a means of achieving salvation — God has promised this in advance — but an expression of the covenant relation. The curses which threaten the apostate (Deuteronomy 28,15ff) are not intended to exact loyalty to the law; the truth is that the apostate shuts himself out from the covenant, and consequently from salvation.

The fundamental pattern of the covenant is thus the covenant of promise: Abraham is promised the land, descendants and the near presence of God (Genesis 15;17). All Israel is privileged to know that it is bound to the saviour God by the Sinai covenant; finally in the covenant with David the continuance of his race and the abiding grace of God are promised (2 Samuel 7).

The prophets live in this history of the divine covenant. When they proclaim disaster for Israel, they base themselves on the curse attached to the covenant. The man who does not accept God's nearness in blessing, will experience God's nearness as disaster:

For you alone have I cared among all the nations of the world;
therefore will I punish you for all your iniquities (Amos 3,2).

If God's covenant had been regarded only as a contract, it could have been broken off through Israel's infringement of the contract. In the threatening words of Hosea this end seems to be announced: the prophet negates the old covenant formula, and the name of God that promised God's nearness.

For you are not my people, and for you I am an "I-am-not-there".[30]

333

Yet the covenant was from the beginning more than a contract; it was a love-covenant of the faithful God. Yahweh cannot forget that he turned to this people, so there comes into being the bold picture of the God who suffers because of the disloyalty and the destruction of his people, who regrets the evil that he himself brought upon Israel.[31] The prophets emphasize that promise, assurance of salvation is the heart of the covenant; in spite of bitter experience they hold fast to the hope of the nearness of the covenant-God. They speak of a new covenant, which will finally unite men with God, so that no more separation is possible. This new covenant is distinguished from the old not because the form of the covenant had altered; on the contrary, God will change man, and make him able to live in agreement with the covenant.[32]

The words of the Last Supper describe Jesus' work as fulfilment of the Old Testament expectation.[33] Yet this fulfilment is not the end of the history of the covenant; on the contrary Christ's covenant meal refers beyond itself to the consummation, in which God creates the new man, who without breach of faith is capable of fellowship with God.

The Theme of God's Kingly Rule

Among their gods the people of the ancient orient knew one king of the gods; as father of all the gods, or as the victor over chaos he towered over the others.

In the older texts of the Old Testament, there are only indications of the conception of the heavenly king. In certain passages Yahweh seems to be addressing his heavenly court; he appears to Jacob as the Lord of a host of messengers.[34] Yet in these passages Yahweh does not receive the title of king. The Old Testament authors obviously were unwilling to give the same name to the Lord of the heavenly court as was given to the heathen divine kings. Yahweh is called king, not as Lord of the heavenly hosts, but as the ruler over Israel.[35] The heathen kings of the gods wrested their mastery over the gods in the primal age, and maintain it when, in the eternal cycle of nature the events of the primal age are repeated. In contrast with this, the God of Israel is king in the historical world, ruler over Israel.

In this tradition stands Isaiah. He represents himself as a messenger, who is sent forth in the place of the heavenly messengers; he is to fulfil the word and the will of the king Yahweh in Israel.[36]

The heathen kings of the gods, the conquerors of chaos, were worshipped as the upholders of a changeless order of the world. By celebrating their kingship the heathen wished to secure the continuance of the creation. In Isaiah 6 Yahweh shows himself as a king of a wholly different kind. He is not the guarantor of stable order, but wishes through his messenger the prophet, to pass judgement on the existing order. Yahweh has not given up his kingship when his people is subjected to foreign domination:

I will reign over you with a strong hand, with arm outstretched and wrath outpoured (Ezekiel 20,33).

An unexpected side of the old tradition is here disclosed: "with strong hand and outstretched arm" Yahweh had once protected Israel from its enemies.[37] But in Ezekiel's time, on the other hand, Yahweh had delivered his people into the hand of the Gentiles. Ezekiel must oppose Jews, who believe that with the fall of Jerusalem Yahweh had ended the covenant with Israel. He emphasizes that Yahweh does not even now give up his claim to rule over Israel. To outward appearance foreigners rule over Israel, but in truth Yahweh remains Israel's king, and rules his people by punishing it.

Even where the prophets expected salvation for the people from Yahweh's kingly rule, Yahweh is not to be compared with Osiris, Marduk, Baal. He is not a God who protects the given order, but a leader to unexpectedly new frontiers. With the cry "Your God is king" Isaiah announces the return of the exiles and the return of God to Zion.

And the whole world from end to end shall see the deliverance of our God (Isaiah 52,10).

The hopes that attach themselves to God's kingly rule far transcend what was at all possible in the time of Deutero-Isaiah. At the same time here opinions which were in part current in Israel are rejected, as if Yahweh's kingship were limited to his people.[38] Deutero-Isaiah, a prophet in exile, had to contend with the claims to sovereignty of strange gods. The kings, who brought Israel into subjection believed that they were extending the territory over which their gods ruled. To this Deutero-Isaiah retorts, Yahweh, "Israel's king and redeemer" has a controversy with the idols and proves their nothingness (Isaiah 43,6).

The thought of God's universal lordship was, however already contained even in the old conception of Yahweh's kingship. The first Isaiah indeed sees Yahweh the king in the temple of Jerusalem, but "his glory fills the whole earth" (Isaiah 6,7).

This thought is developed under the pressure of foreign domination. Yahweh the king is superior to the gods of the peoples, he is ruler and judge of the peoples. This power of God is revealed when all peoples come on pilgrimage to God the king in Jerusalem (Zechariah 14,16f). When God from there gives just judgement and extends his kingdom of peace (Isaiah 2,2ff), when finally he has brought into subjection all the powers in the universe and in history that oppose him (Isaiah 24,21-23). The kingly rule of God was from the beginning a present reality for Israel, it acknowledged Yahweh as its ruler. The prophets show that God's kingly rule remains a reality even when Israel is subjected to the rule of foreign peoples — Yahweh shows himself in his wrath as king over Israel. At the same time he proves his kingly power over the whole world, he guides the foreign peoples and rulers and is far superior to the gods. With this a new dimension was opened up; this kingly rule of God was not only experienced as a present reality, but as a promise for the future, as an indication of the coming kingdom of God.

Jesus stands in this Old Testament tradition. His preaching and his works proclaim that God's kingdom is close at hand.[39]

It repeatedly becomes evident that the Old Testament message of salvation is not made superfluous by Christ, but given new life and fullness. But how is it with the theme of the prophetic promises, which we are accustomed to understand as a direct reference to Christ, the Messianic promises? Have they also still validity now that Christ has come?

The Theme of the Messianic King

The kings of the ancient orient were honoured as bringers of salvation for the people, as administrators or even possessors of divine powers. Israel, on the other hand had to expect its salvation from Yahweh; Yahweh was its king. So kingship was only able to assert itself at a late date in Israel, and only in the teeth of considerable opposition.[40] And yet Israel's expectation of salvation joined hands with the Davidic kingship. How did this come about?

We must not see in this merely a clever political move, that David brought the ark to Jerusalem and planned to build the temple. Certainly by so doing he bound a great part of Israel's populace to his capital and decisively added to the stability of his kingdom. But his action was principally the result of his enthusiastic faith.

> David spun around in the dance with all his powers before Yahweh (2 Samuel 6,14).

He wished to give new life to the old religious traditions of Israel. This wish is acknowledged by the famous promise of the prophet Nathan; Yahweh will not forsake David's house (2 Samuel 7). The prophet Isaiah is evidence that since then the hope of the king persisted. With every king there awakened a new expectation that he at last might be the true king, who would bestow on Israel salvation and the presence of God. Confidence in the coming divine help had always been the heart of this faith; this is the central point of the expectation that links itself with the house of David.

Already Isaiah discloses to our vision the depths of this hope; in the end it reaches beyond history into the last times, for which even we can but look with expectation.[41]

Summary

This list of four themes expressing the prophetic expectation of salvation could be amplified. It is impossible in a small space to deal adequately with the themes of the remnant, the servant of God, of peace, of the city of God, etc. Here we shall confine ourselves to deriving from the material expounded above several characteristics of the prophetic preaching of salvation.

1. The prophetic promises are not be to interpreted merely in the light of

a fulfilment in the New Testament — which would make these promises superfluous — but in the context of a whole history of promises and fulfilments, which will not come to an end before the consummation of the world.

2. The promises of the prophets arise out of the tradition of Israel's past. A salvation is there established that was continually to reassert itself in Israel's history, and has still to show its full splendour.

3. Many pictures of the future stand side by side, some of them mutually incompatible. In Micah 3,12 the destruction of Zion is announced — according to Micah 4,14 and Isaiah 2,2ff the exaltation of Zion is awaited. Isaiah, who proclaims the kingdom of God, at the same time develops the promise of a Davidic king (Isaiah 6-7, 9.11). The theme of a king of salvation, which for the Christian is central to the Old Testament's expectation of salvation, is only one theme among others. When in the time of the exile, the expectation was no longer able to base itself on a royal house, the figure of the servant of God takes its place beside that of the king of salvation;[42] in the post-exilic age, when the infinite distance of God from man becomes a central feature of religious experience, the "Son of man" replaces it.[43] No attempt is made in the Old Testament to harmonize these conceptions.

The prophets paid no attention to such discrepancies, because their purpose was not to give a more or less accurate picture of the future; they wished to show the significance of Israel's ancient hope for the future.

4. But the different themes of the prophetic promises do not stand side by side unrelated. Thus for example Chronicles unites the conceptions of God's kingship and the kingship of David; the descendants of David rule in God's kingdom.[44] The themes of journeying, of God's rule, and of the city of God are linked together in several mutually related promises.[45] The theme of the remnant is an undertone in the messianic promise of Isaiah 11,1ff; according to Zechariah 9,9 the messianic king is humble like the servant of God. Such connections of the themes show how little the expectation of salvation crystallized in one clear-cut form; it is still fluid in the Old Testament; individual currents can unite, take new forms, and separate again — they all belong together in one living context.

5. Promise and fulfilment are not separated from one another by an intervening period of time. The fulfilment begins with the utterance of the promise. For the faithful, God's word is so powerful that something which he has said has to all intents already happened. The promise may be compared with the seed which already contains all the parts of the plant; with it, God has once and for all bestowed salvation. But since the plenitude of this salvation is unfathomable, an end of the history of its fulfilment cannot be foreseen, unless it be in the consummation of the last times. The prophets can thus promise their immediate hearers God's salvation in the present, and at the same time announce the eschatological salvation.

337

6. The tension between the salvation already given in the word of God and its unfolding, which surpasses all expectation, explains to us a singular characteristic of the style of prophetic promises, the prophetic perfect. The Hebrew language has no tenses in the western sense of the word; it only distinguishes verb forms describing finished and unfinished actions. The prophets speak of God's future action in the perfect, in the verb-form of the concluded action. Thus, for example we cannot decide by looking at the verb-form, whether the Immanuel of whom Isaiah 7,14 speaks, is already here, or whether he has yet to come. Deutero-Isaiah used this characteristic of style with remarkable effect; he imitates hymns; the call to praise is connected with the report about the divine action; but the report — in the Perfect — speaks of God's eschatological activity. The future act of God has now already become reality in the word of the prophet. Therefore also, now already, Israel must respond to it with praise.[46]

7. All the peculiar characteristics of the prophetic promises can be traced back to the fact that the promise is God's word. In all the promises the one will of God, and it alone, finds expression. That is the reason why the prophets cannot "predict" the future beforehand. God's will cannot be determined before the event. But on the other hand, for the same reason the prophets can be certain that their word will be accomplished, for they proclaim the work of Yahweh, whom no one can prevent from doing what he has decided to do.

5. THE CONTINUED LIFE OF THE WORDS OF THE PROPHETS

The Literature's Capacity for Change

A work that has come from the hand of an author, is reckoned by us as inviolable. Only the author himself has the right — even a legal right — to change anything in it. In Israel, people had quite a different attitude to literature. The works, which finally were incorporated in the Old Testament, were for long periods counted as still unfinished. We can understand that oral traditions are transformed in the course of time. But in Israel even texts set down in writing remain for a long time fluid; further thought was given to them, and they suffered continual change.

Several factors helped to keep the texts for a long time fluid and alive. One factor was the Hebrew feeling for language. Speakers of Hebrew set but little store by clear conceptual distinctions. On the other hand this language lends itself to indirect hints and suggestions.[47] Such a relation to language must have consequences for the interpretation of texts. The meaning of a text can be easily loosened and remoulded with playful seriousness.

Further, the content which many Old Testament texts were intended to express, leads to their continued vitality and capacity for change. To use a technical term of New Testament exegesis, we could speak of their "kerygmatic structure", of their slant towards proclamation. They conjoin an event with the obligation for the hearers which arises from it. "The time has come, the Kingdom of God is upon you" — event — "repent and believe the Gospel" — obligation (Mark 1,15). Compare with this:

> I . . . have brought you out of the land of Egypt. You shall have no other gods to set against me (Exodus 20,2f).

The purpose of the report about past events is to challenge the hearers to immediate engagement. The Jewish ritual of the passover meal which is still in current use contains the preface which stems from the oldest Jewish traditions:

> In every generation every man must think of himself as if he personally had been brought out of Egypt.

Texts, which not only convey some information, but which, in addition challenge us to behave conformably to it, must remain capable of alteration. They must adapt themselves to other modes of understanding belonging to other men and other times.

In conformity with our ideas of the inviolability of literary works, we are inclined to set a low value of the work of redactors. We can observe, for example, in commentaries of the pentateuch, that the scholars content themselves with separating the written sources from one another, and thus interpreting them. The work of the redactors, who fitted together the basic manuscripts to produce the pentateuch in the form we know, is often held in low esteem. We are not "authorized" — much less obliged, to regard this work of subordinate and second-rate minds as of decisive and ultimate importance. Who indeed would praise a redactional mixture of Schiller's "Maid of Orleans", Shaw's "St. Joan" and Brecht's "St. Johanna of the Slaughter-yards" as an ideal?[48]

Anyone who reads the pentateuch from historical or literary interest does not know how to deal with this fusion of the four written sources into a single work. And yet the judgement noted above of a modern exegete concerning the redactor of the pentateuch is not wholly relevant. Franz Rosenzweig, who together with Buber translated the Old Testament into German, interpreted the sign R, by which the scholars describe the redactor, as "Rabbenu", (our master).

The redactors are neither critical historians nor sensitive literary men, but they are our teachers in the faith. They were able to fuse together four writings which stemmed from different times, because all of them bore witness to the same Lord. From the point of view of the narrative, and certainly historically, the general structure of the pentateuch is questionable. Yet for the faithful it is in all its parts concerned solely with the one God who remains true to himself. This faith precedes and underlies all its literary components; that gave the redactor to form them into one work.

Work of Redaction in Prophetic Books

Other sections deal with the redaction of the pentateuch in greater detail;[49] we shall for that reason not take it here as an example. We shall choose rather to consider the work of redactors in relation to prophetic books.

Here too the exegetes have frequently undervalued the work of the redactors. Often their only concern was to see through the confusion that the redactors have caused, according to our way of thinking. It is not unimportant for interpretation, to know that in Isaiah 1 there stand texts from the latest period of the preaching of Isaiah, that originally the oldest collection of this prophet began with the report of the prophet's call in Isaiah 6, that the five visions of Amos,[50] which are now torn apart, originally formed a coherent report in the first person. Exegetes seek for the original place of the words, but seldom ask why it was changed. Where the redactors come forward with their own ideas, such "contaminations" of the original text are removed, a "textual error", a gloss, a later insertion, is noted, only in order that it may be removed.

In Isaiah 22,1-15 the prophet sees the future fall of Jerusalem, the carefree city, which in all the signs of destruction refuses to see the judgement of God. The climax of the saying is probably verse 8, with the following verses:

(8) Then Yahweh drew the bandage from the *eyes* of Judah, but on that day it *looked* to the armour in the Forest House.

(9a) You *saw* that the cracks in the city of David were many . . .

(11b) But you did not *look* to him who caused this, you did not *look* to him who for long had been ordaining this.

Four times we find "seeing" — twice denied, twice affirmed. This well-planned figure of speech is however disturbed by 9b-11a. A later man, who has experienced the fall of Jerusalem, has amplified the text of Isaiah with a more precise description of the events.

(9b) You gathered the waters of the lower pool. (10) You counted the houses of Jerusalem and pulled them down, in order to strengthen the walls. (11a) You created a reservoir for the waters of the old pool between the two walls.

How could one thus tear apart the old word of the prophet in this way? Is this man a know-all, a philistine who destroys an artistic construction?

As a messenger of God Isaiah had spoken God's word. But God's word is not spoken in vain; it effects what it proclaims. The fall of Jerusalem is so to speak the natural consequence of the old prediction of disaster. Therefore the emendator can speak as if he were himself the prophet. He is not falsifying, but brings the word to its realization in the disastrous event which he experienced. The words of the prophet are transmitted, not as valuable pieces of historical information, but as the living and effectual word of God. What Hosea once had to say in accusation of the northern kingdom is for example applied to Judah by redactors after the destruction of Israel.[51]

When a modern interpreter seeks to understand a text, he tries by various means to convey himself into the time of origin of the text. In contrast with this, the redactors understand the texts in the light of their present circumstances. The prophetic word announces the coming reality — it is only this realization which discloses what the ancient word was trying to say. To us this may seem a "cosmetic emendation" after the event; the redactors saw it in a different light. God himself interprets his word by bringing it to pass.

An example: Isaiah announces the appointment of a new governor in the royal house, who will act according to God's will. This "servant of God", Eliakim, will stand fast like a well-secured tent-peg, and the whole honour (= importance) of his family can depend on him (Isaiah 22,15-23). But soon after this Eliakim was deposed. Isaiah could have put aside the old word of prophecy, because his prediction had turned out to be false. But he did something different. He understood "peg" as a nail that is driven into a wall, and "honour" as weight. The nail fell out because the whole weight of his father's house was hanging on it (22,24ff). The event had shown that the real meaning of the words was different from what was originally thought.

As the prophet here deals with his word, so also do the redactors. It is their chief concern to keep alive the prophetic message entrusted to them, they do not wish merely to conserve it. Nor do they set any store by keeping the words of their master unadulterated. They add pieces from their own time which cause the older words to appear in a new light.[52]

Let us illustrate this procedure by an example, taking Isaiah 12, a hymn of praise of the congregation. Isaiah 12 once concluded a collection of words of Isaiah, which began with the report of Isaiah of his call. For the redactors, as for us, the most significant texts in this collection were the messianic promises in Isaiah 7; 9; and 11, which were ultimately based on the promise to the house of David. For the collectors of these prophetic words, however, who were Jews in exile, the house of David had now but little significance. Yet the thought of the salvation which God had intended for his own people, remains of the utmost importance for them, only they visualize it differently, in the return of the people, in its superiority over Gentile peoples. But this does not mean that the old figure of the Messianic king is pushed aside. It is supplemented by the promise of the return:

The peoples . . . seek after the root of Jesse (Isaiah 11,10).

Instead of replacing the old texts by new ones, the redactors placed the two alongside each other. They knew that the prophetic texts did not wish to make precise predictions; they were willing to leave in God's hands the exact manner in which he would fulfil his promise.

They go even further. Deutero-Isaiah had taught that thanks must be given now in the present for his future saving acts. For, so soon as salvation had been proclaimed, its realization had already begun. This faith, too, the redactors brought into relation to the messianic promises of Isaiah. For this reason, they concluded their collection with a hymn of praise of the congregation.

It is probable that at first Isaiah entrusted his messianic promises only to a small circle of disciples; in Isaiah 12 we have evidence how the hope of the whole community relied upon these texts. Thus the additions of the redactors are by no means merely adulterations of the "genuine" text. They are evidence for the vitality of these texts, for the beginnings of their historical influence, which continues in the New Testament, and finally among ourselves.

Interpretation of Older Prophets

The redactors continue a movement which had begun with the prophets. Jeremiah, for example, had already taken up a word of his predecessor Micah, and reinterpreted it. An attempt was made to bring Jeremiah to trial, because he had announced the destruction of the temple. Then he appealed to Micah:

"In the time of Hezekiah king of Judah, Micah of Moresheth was prophesying and said to all the people of Judah: 'These are the words of Yahweh of Hosts:

Zion shall become a ploughed field,

Jerusalem a heap of ruins,

and the temple-hill rough heath.'[52a]

Did King Hezekiah and all Judah put him to death? Did not the king show reverence for Yahweh and seek to placate him? Then Yahweh relented and revoked the disaster. Are we to bring great disaster on ourselves?" (Jeremiah 26,18).

Jeremiah here does not confine himself to quotation, he interprets the prophetic word. Micah had formulated it as a prediction of evil, Jeremiah understands it as a warning; the evil in the time of Hezekiah was yet again averted. Yet the threat against the temple was not finally lifted. A century later Jeremiah renewed it.

In other cases also, the older prophetic message is familiar to the prophets. Hosea had taken over and transformed the figure of the divine marriage from heathen and mythological conceptions. There it described the natural connection between the rain god and the mother-goddess the earth; in Hosea it becomes a picture of the free personal covenant of God with Israel. Jeremiah takes up again the figures of Israel's adultery and the faithfulness of God in his introductory sermon (Jeremiah 2f). Finally Ezekiel expands the marriage-figure borrowed from Hosea and Jeremiah to a great allegory of the entire history of Israel. Down to the details, we can follow how Ezekiel makes the words of his predecessors his starting-point. In Hosea, God reproached Israel:

For she does not know that it is I who gave her corn, new wine, and oil, I who lavished on her silver and gold which they spent on the Baal (Hosea 2,10[8]).

Ezekiel transforms the reproach into an accusation:

You took the splendid ornaments of gold and silver which I had given you, and made for yourselves male images with whom you committed fornication. . . . You took the food I had given you, the flour, the oil, and the honey, with which I had fed you, and set it before them as an offering of soothing odour (Ezekiel 16,17ff).

Jeremiah had compared Israel, that ran after idols, with the camel in heat:

Snuffing the wind in her lust; who can restrain her in her heat? (Jeremiah 2,24).

Ezekiel tells how Israel ran after Egypt, Assyria, Chaldaea, because it was never "sated",

How fever-hot was your heart, that you did all this! (Ezekiel 16,30).

The Study of Earlier Prophets as Inspiration of Prophetic Speech

The prophets themselves are thus witnesses that the words of the prophets remained unforgotten and powerful. Their figures were elaborated, their words made the theme of ever new meditation.

The longer the history of the Old Testament progressed, the closer becomes the tie with established texts from earlier times. In the time of reconstruction, after the return from the exile, lived a pupil of the second Isaiah; we call him Trito-Isaiah.[53] He used almost exclusively the literary forms of his master, the promises of salvation, the modifications of laments, the eschatological hymns of praise; he employed motifs, conceptions and thoughts of his predecessor — and with the help of all this inherited material he was able to say new things to a changed time. The heart of his message is the message of salvation to Jerusalem:

Arise, Jerusalem, rise clothed in light; your light has come and the glory of Yahweh shines over you. For, though darkness covers the earth and dark night the nations, Yahweh shall shine upon you and over you shall his glory appear; and the nations shall march towards your light and kings towards your sunrise. Lift up your eyes and look all around: they flock together, all of them, and come to you; your sons also shall come from afar, your daughters walking beside them leading the way (Isaiah 60,1-4).

The coming salvation is portrayed in the figure of journeying; God himself, the peoples, and Israel journey to Zion. Deutero-Isaiah too had pictured salvation as the coming of God.

Here is the Lord Yahweh coming in might (Isaiah 40,10).

He had also been the great proclaimer of the return of Israel, he had called to Jerusalem:

Raise your eyes and look around you: see how they assemble, how they are flocking back to you (Isaiah 49,18).

His pupil Trito-Isaiah takes over this sentence, almost word for word (Isaiah 60,4a).

Trito-Isaiah has also the same form of speech as his master; Jerusalem is addressed. It is striking that a promise should be clothed in the literary

343

form of a challenge. The pre-exilic Isaiah had clothed his promises in the form of affirmative statements — this form of statement is more suited to the announcement of future events. But Deutero-Isaiah and his pupils do not merely proclaim, they challenge Zion to look. They speak as if it all depended on Jerusalem's readiness to receive the gift, as if it only needed to look carefully, and could already see the present salvation. These different literary forms of the words of promise correspond to the particular situations of the people to which the prophets are speaking. Before the exile the people still vainly believed itself to be safe in its land, with its temple. They ought to find for themselves the right way to salvation. In their situation the prophet only needs to hold before them the picture of salvation in indicative statements. But Deutero-Isaiah seeks out lovingly the cowed and humiliated people in exile and seeks to win them for a new hope. And the bearing of his pupil confronting the feeble band of the returned exiles is exactly similar; the poor people is challenged to rejoice over its salvation, for through the annunciation of the prophet the time of joy, even in the midst of misery, has already begun.

It is no small thing, that Trito-Isaiah in the post-exilic age, after the return of a small group and a pitiful new beginning, continued to proclaim the great words of salvation of his master. His master had expected that the return home of Israel would be a great miracle:

> Awake, awake, put on your strength, O arm of Yahweh awake as you did long ago, in days gone by . . . The freedmen of Yahweh return home (Isaiah 51,9ff).

The actual events, which fell so far short of these words, had not been able to refute for Trito-Isaiah the words of the master. Trito-Isaiah knew that the miracle still had not happened. What Israel in his day experienced could have been a great disappointment. But Trito-Isaiah saw in it the modest beginning of fulfilment; the great transformation for the better proclaimed its advent. Only a few Jews had returned — but Trito-Isaiah holds fast to the word of the second Isaiah, that all peoples will come to Zion and of their own free choice will bring with them the exiles of Israel (cf Isaiah 49,22). It might be said that his faith in his master had made him blind to everything that his time could have taught him. Yet anyone who reads attentively his sermons about the words of his teacher learns from them that he understood his times. For Deutero-Isaiah the return of the Jews could still be an event that might take place within a foreseeable time. This return was to signal the beginning of the time of God's nearness accompanied by great signs. But Trito-Isaiah's expectation of the coming of God and the beginning of the great time of salvation was no longer connected with a special event. More than the return of Israel he emphasized the pilgrimage of all the peoples to Zion. Deutero-Isaiah had pictured the coming of God with the help of the miracles of the ancient journey through the desert. The pupil wished to show that we are not being true to Deutero-Isaiah's intention when we are on the watch for places where miracles of this kind may happen. For this purpose he introduces another picture for the coming of God, the bright shining of light. That is no longer an event for which we can be on the watch. His hearers are to see that the prophets can only speak of God's coming in pictures. There is no determinate event to which they can refer beforehand, by which we can later exactly identify the coming of God.

From ancient times Israel had tried to depict God's coming as brilliant light. The pre-exilic Isaiah had announced God's salvation as light in the darkness.[55] Trito-Isaiah reaches back behind his master to these older traditions, in order to make intelligible to his contemporaries what Deutero-Isaiah had promised.

Not only Trito-Isaiah, but also the other late prophets lived more and more on the older prophetic traditions. Joel frequently takes up the words of older prophets. A natural catastrophe gave the impulse to his preaching; a plague of locusts had destroyed the entire harvest; Joel teaches that God's work is to be seen in this, the day of Yahweh, on which God reveals his power.

The theme of the day of Yahweh was very old. Amos the oldest of the "written" prophets, had to take action as early as the eighth century against a false conception of the day of Yahweh. It seems to have stemmed from the realm of concepts associated with the holy war: on this day God himself will show his power over all the enemies of Israel, who are also his enemies. It was natural that in times of need the Israelites should set their hope on this day. Amos showed them how dangerous the hope in the day of Yahweh is. He compared those who relied on this day, with people who flee before a lion and run into a bear, with men who take refuge in their house, lean there in relief against the wall, and are bitten by a snake. For when Yahweh reveals his full power, disloyal Israel cannot expect salvation.

Fools who long for the day of Yahweh, what will the day of Yahweh mean to you? It will be darkness, not light (Amos 5,18).

About three hundred years later Joel returned to this message of disaster. On the day of Yahweh nothing but misfortune will come to Israel. The plague of locusts shows that this disaster is not far distant; the day may come at any time.

For the day of Yahweh has come, surely a day of darkness and gloom is upon us, a day of cloud and dense fog (Joel 2,1bf).

Here Joel is not speaking in his own words. He is repeating what he has found in the prophet Zephaniah:

The great day of Yahweh is near, it comes with speed . . . a day of murk and gloom, a day of cloud and dense fog (Zephaniah 1,14f).

The catastrophic plague of locusts had taught Joel that the old words of the prophets had retained their power. The present misfortune is to be understood in this light. He had found in the oracles to the peoples contained in the traditions of Isaiah and Ezekiel words which confront

the power of Babylon and Egypt with the day of Yahweh:
> Woe, woe for the day! for a day is near . . . a day of Yahweh is near (Ezekiel 30,2b f).

> Howl, for the day of Yahweh is at hand; it comes, a mighty blow from Almighty God (Isaiah 13,6).

These words, which were directed against the peoples, become effectual also against the disloyal people of God. Joel quotes them:
> Alas! the day is near, the day of Yahweh: it comes, a mighty destruction from the Almighty (Joel 1,15).

Thus in such quotations it is not always important to the prophet to retain their original meaning. Another example of this is the treatment of a word of Amos by Joel. Amos had come out of Judah into the northern kingdom, to announce destruction to those who disregarded God's law. In the northern kingdom at that time, people were trying by sacrificial gifts of a half-heathenish kind at many shrines to win God to their side, so that he might give fruitfulness to fields and flocks. Amos opposes them with the message of Yahweh, who had chosen Zion (in the southern kingdom):
> Yahweh roars from Zion and thunders from Jerusalem; the shepherds' pastures are scorched and the top of Carmel is dried up (Amos 1,2f).

Through the power of his loud-roaring voice Yahweh will bring not fruitfulness, but famine. According to the message of Amos, this will work disaster in the states of Israel and Judah, and in all the states around them. Before this cry no injustice can prevail among the nations, least of all among the people of God.[56] The experience of hearing this terrible cry of God was probably the crucial experience of Amos; he becomes a prophet in order to bring into action the destructive power of that cry.
> The lion has roared; who is not terrified? The Lord Yahweh has spoken; who will not prophesy? (Amos 3,8).

So far as it is in our power to judge, Amos became a prophet as the result of an immediate shattering experience, the experience of the roaring Yahweh. Joel, in contrast, becomes a prophet through the study of old prophetic texts. He knows that God's cry of evil omen was not only fulfilled in its day through the preaching of Amos in the case of Judah, Israel and the neighbouring peoples. It has the power to bring destruction on the whole world:
> Sun and moon are darkened and the stars forbear to shine. Yahweh roars from Zion and thunders from Jerusalem; heaven and earth shudder . . . (Joel 4[3],15 f).

Still more astonishing than such an expansion of an old prophetic word is its conscious reversal in a quotation. Joel undertakes at the same time two such reversals in chapter 4[3],10. The prophetic promise handed down in Isaiah 2,2ff and Micah 4,1ff pictures God's coming kingdom of peace:

They shall beat their swords into mattocks and their spears into pruning-knives (Isaiah 2,4; Micah 4,3).

Zephaniah pictures the day of Jahweh:

Hark, the day of Yahweh is bitter, there the warrior cries aloud (Zephaniah 1,14).

But Joel cries to the peoples:

Beat your mattocks into swords and your pruning-hooks into spears. Let the weakling say "I am strong" (Joel 4[3],10).

The prophets liked to use the drastic device of reversing familiar conceptions. Amos had proclaimed that the day of Yahweh would be "darkness, not light". His intention had been by such a reversal to protect the true sense of the day of Yahweh from misinterpretation. Now Joel uses the same method in relation to old words of the prophets. The promise of the coming kingdom of peace, could tempt men to see already the fulfilment in such a peace as is possible under a good earthly rule. The threatening words about the day of Yahweh could tempt men all too easily to underestimate the power of the enemies of God. The prophet will not permit the hope of the faithful to be so prematurely satisfied. The power of the peoples is great, their peace quickly turns to war. This state of affairs is revealed, when the day of Yahweh has come, when "the harvest is ripe, the wine-press is full" (Joel 4[3],13). The prophet's intention is by his word to contribute to the speedy revelation of the full power of God. That underlies his challenge to the peoples to reforge their ploughshares into swords. He challenges the powers hostile to God to reveal their true nature.

When Joel can so frequently make reference to words of his predecessors, the presupposition is that these words were already available in written form, and were widely known. When Jeremiah and Ezekiel take up Hosea's marriage-figure, it is possible that they might be drawing on the oral tradition of the followers and pupils of the prophet. But Joel must have had a written version of the prophetic tradition before him.

The Written Version of Prophetic Words

It is really surprising that the words of the prophets were written down at all. The prophets on each occasion received a commission which was confined to one situation. For example, they had to announce God's judgement to the ruler because of one definite transgression, they had to communicate in a unique historical situation God's decision to the people. This is what distinguishes God's word, which these messengers transmit, from God's word in the law, which had to serve for all time as the foundation of Israel's life. The gist of the law was probably set down in writing from the beginning. (The Ten Commandments, as the fundamental document of the covenant between God and the people, are an indication of this).

But the word of the prophets needed to be protected from oblivion only until the judgement had been fulfilled, and the decision of God had realized itself in history. In a transformed situation a new commission of God to a prophet was expected. What reason then had the prophets for writing down their words? It was enough for them when they succeeded in proclaiming them with such urgency, that the hearers received God's word into their hearts.

But frequently the prophets had the painful experience of preaching to deaf ears. The message of doom was not taken seriously. Isaiah even found that his word of deliverance was not accepted by king Ahaz (Isaiah 7). And God's word could not be forgotten until it had been fulfilled! Isaiah infers from this experience that he is no longer to proclaim God's word publicly; it must survive in his family, among his disciples. He withdraws for a while from public activity.

> See, I and the sons whom Yahweh has given me are to be signs and portents in Israel, sent by Yahweh of hosts who dwells on Mount Zion (Isaiah 8,18).

In the prophet himself the word of God lived on, even when no one else in Israel was willing to hear it. There, where the word of the prophet is received, the living power of this word is powerful. For this reason people banished Amos from the land, and believed that so they could avoid the evil that he had prophesied (Amos 7,10ff). The prophet Uriah, who had prophesied against Jerusalem, was put to death, and Jeremiah had almost suffered the same fate.[57] It was believed that when no one was still there, who had received the word of God, that its effect could be stopped.

For this reason the prophets saw themselves compelled to ensure the transmission of the word of God. Isaiah gave to his children names that contained the message: "A-remnant-shall-return" and "Speed-spoil-hasten-plunder" (Isaiah 7,3; 8,3). He collects disciples around him, who will preserve the "witness" (Isaiah 8,16). Finally he even writes a single prophetic word on a large tablet, and in addition to all this collects witnesses and drives home the message so unforgettably that it can no longer be ignored (Isaiah 8,1f; 30,8).

If people feared the spoken message, they feared still more the written word. Jeremiah was forbidden to preach in the temple. Therefore he dictated to his friend Baruch all the messages that he had hitherto delivered, and ordered him to read the scroll publicly in the temple, in order that the people might hear and repent, and the evil be averted (Jeremiah 36). Here we learn for the first time of a prophet becoming a writer — but the writing is only a substitute for preaching, it is intended to have an immediate effect on the writer's contemporaries. The scroll suffers the same fate that threatens the prophet as bearer of the word of God; the king hears it, and burns it bit by bit. The prophetic word is not to be handed on, the divine message of disaster is not to take effect.

The writing down of the words of the prophet is at first only an expedient, necessary among a people that will not hear God's word; this

348

word ought not to be preserved by means of writing, but in the hearts of men.

The prophet Habakkuk sees his task to consist in keeping the words of God alive in his heart, in looking expectantly for their fulfilment, and, indeed holding the ancient messages before God in reproach. Then he receives the command to write down the word of God. This committal of the words of God to writing gives him new confidence. From words that are set down in black and white as in a treaty, God will surely not depart.[58] Thus also for Isaiah the evidence of the word of God once spoken, which he preserved, remained a support in the times when "God concealed himself" (Isaiah 8,16).

The committal to writing of the word of the prophet in Jeremiah 30,2 results from another critical situation; the Jerusalem prophet has to give a message to the exiles.

Thus the word of the prophets was not in the first place intended to receive an unassailable objective verifiable form. As "witness against the disobedient" the committal to writing was intended to keep alive the vital power of the word of God even when no one was willing to hear it, as a kind of contractual assurance its purpose was to give men fresh trust. The committal to writing of the prophetic traditions therefore does not mean petrifaction, but preservation of the living power of the word.

This is pictorially represented in the vision of Ezekiel, the prophet of the exile, on the occasion of his call. At God's command Ezekiel must swallow a scroll, which is full of words of woe (Ezekiel 2,10). The exiles were cut off from the holy places, the feasts and festivals, from all the places in which the traditions of the people were nourished and kept alive. The written word of the tradition was necessary in order to keep their faith alive. That is the significance of this story. When Ezekiel receives his commission in the form of a scroll, he receives with it, as it were, the tradition of the great prophets, to whose number he will henceforth belong. Yet he is not merely to pass on what has been handed down. He must first of all absorb it, it must completely penetrate him. Even here, where the prophetic word is represented as a book, its real *Sitz im Leben* remains the heart of man.

6. THE BEGINNINGS OF THE STUDY OF THE SCRIPTURES

Writings from Exilic and Post-Exilic Times

The destruction of the people of Israel as a consequence of the exile was decisive for the origin of the holy scripture of the Old Testament. The land, which God had bestowed, was lost, and also the temple and the city which he had chosen, and so also the public worship and the festivals in which the presence of God with his people had continually been re-established; the throne of David, which God had confirmed for ever had fallen. Only one fatherland remained to Israel, its tradition. Only in the ancient tradition of his word was Yahweh with his people.

The faithful continued to reflect lovingly upon everything that had remained to them from the old traditions. In this situation there grew up the beginnings of a "scripture" constructed out of the many different sources and traditions. Nearly all the Old Testament books originated in the time of the exile or in the post-exilic time, in which, because of the extremely modest situation of those who had returned home, the exilic situation still remained basically unchanged. It was in the light of their loss of the land that the *Deuteronomic historians* judged the time from Israel's entry into the land down to the exile. It was against the background of the new Jewish community of the temple that the *Chronicler's history* looked back on the time of the kings. The older written sources J and E, together with Deuteronomy, were fitted into the pattern which the priestly document had outlined for the time preceding the entry into the land — the *pentateuch* came into being. Older collections of sayings were put together to form the Book of Proverbs. It was a time of retrospection, whose aim was to take up again all the past, and understand it anew in the context of the present.

Further, the words of the *prophets*, all already existing collections, and all reports which were discovered relating to them, were put together. What had hitherto only been transmitted in a small circle of disciples was now to awaken hope in God's help among the whole people, and gratitude for his promise of salvation.

Reinterpretation of Individual Psalms as Prayers of the Congregation

Even a number of psalms were given a new interpretation by worshippers of the exilic and post-exilic time. There men were so shattered by the fate of their people, that they could no longer use for prayer in the original sense the laments and hymns of praise which the individual worshippers had earlier used in the temple. Of what importance was the misery of one individual person in comparison with the misfortune of the city of God? Psalm 102 contains at the beginning and end (2-12[1-11]; 24-25a[23-24a]) parts from old individual laments, but in the middle stand verses that speak of hope for the deliverance of Jerusalem.

(10[9]) I have eaten ashes for bread and mingled tears with my drink.

(14[13]) Thou wilt arise and have mercy on Zion.

(15[14]) Her very stones are dear to thy servants.

All the laments that one worshipper had ever spoken were now united in the lament about God's departure from his people; all the hope that had ever encouraged one sufferer in Israel, is gathered together in the hope of the new glory of the people and the city of God. The old hymns were read with new eyes. (French exegetes speak of a "re-reading" of the older psalms.) Some examples of this may be adduced in the following pages:

In Psalm 69 an individual bewails his distress to God, praises him for deliverance, and exhorts to congregation to join him. The last verses, 35-7[34-36], must have been added on, when there was a wish to bring before God the distress of the exiled people in the words which earlier had been used by an individual, and when there was a desire to praise him with this old psalm because of the new glory which he had planned to give to Jerusalem.

In Psalm 54 most translations delete an indication of the new reading. In this psalm of individual lament we read "strangers rise up against me". The enemies of an individual have surely scarcely been thus described, therefore modern translators "correct" this passage, by inserting a word of similar sound, which in other contexts describes the enemies of the individual: "Insolent men rise up against me". However, this "textual error" is certainly not a slip of the pen, but a sign that for the later worshippers every distress caused by enemies found its climax in the oppression of Israel by foreign peoples.

Such a reinterpretation of older texts certainly contradicts all the rules of an exact historical and philological interpretation, but it is nearer to the spirit of the old hymns of Israel than our manner of interpretation. The old laments saw as the deepest ground of all distress the withdrawal of God. Illness, persecution and guilt were only indications that God had turned away his face. The distance of God was also experienced by the exiles in their fate, and by those who had returned home in their wretched life. In prayer they continued the search for the distant God, which had begun in the old hymns.

On the other hand, from ancient times all hope which moved the *individual* to spread forth his lament before Yahweh, was based on *Israel's* God and Saviour. And the goal of the *individual* hymn was the song of praise in which the whole *congregation* was meant to join. In lament and praise the individual saw himself given a place in the history of the whole people with its God. This undertone of the old prayers continues to sound, when they are interpreted in the context of the exilic and post-exilic time.[59]

On the basis of such observations there has been an attempt to understand the Psalter as "the hymnbook of the post-exilic community". However this description is not quite correct. To be sure, many psalms, which originally had been the prayers of individuals, were now related to the society. But this reinterpretation is overlain by another one.

Interpretation of the Psalms by the Teachers of Wisdom
A first indication of this other new interpretation is to be obtained from Psalm 1 and Psalm 119. These psalms were once the beginning and end of a collection of psalms. Like the short first psalm the longest psalm of the psalter has also only one theme; joy in the word of God.[60] We see before us religious people from the exilic and post-exilic time, who do not see the source of their faith in the public worship of God by the community, much less in political undertakings for the glory of the

people of God, but in private meditation about the tradition of the people.

The exile meant the annihilation of all the religious institutions of Israel. The faithful were cast back on their own faith. Till then, it had been taken for granted that in salvation and in disaster the individual depended on the society to which he belonged. Now the exilic prophet Ezekiel taught, that everyone had to answer for himself individually to Yahweh (Ezekiel 18).

Up till then, prophets and wise men had been the teachers of Israel. In exile it was possible for the Jews to doubt whether God would reveal himself at all to a prophet in the unclean land of the Gentiles.[61] The priests especially had hardly any possibility of exercising influence, for there was no longer any public worship. But the wise men could give counsel everywhere. The priests had proclaimed God's instructions to the people, the prophets had confronted the whole society of Israel with the choice between salvation and disaster. But the wise men had been concerned less to influence society than to awaken the insight of the individual. All the more must their advice be sought for in this time, in which the individual was left to his own resources. So we find in many passages of the Old Testament traces of the passage of Israel's traditional inheritance through the hands of teachers of wisdom. What had been intended as a message for the whole people of Israel, is recommended by them for the loving acceptance of each of the faithful.

Interpretation of the Scriptures as God's Word

The increasing importance of the wise men did not mean that either the word of the prophets or the law taught by the priests lost their significance. For the word of the prophet was regarded by the faithful as God's word, just as was the word of the priests, the law.[62]

Nor did the historical traditions in this period lose their significance. For they told of God's mighty acts; and the faithful believed that the faithful God was true to what he had once done. Lastly, men saw also in these texts "God's Word". The Hebrew language can translate with the one word "*dābār*", what we call "object", "act", "word", and "event". God's word is already act; what he says, happens. Conversely God's acts are words, through which he gives information about himself, speaks about himself. So it is no matter for surprise, that reports of God's mighty acts were judged to be "God's word".

But it is astonishing that the collectors also understood the psalms as God's word. In the two boundary psalms, Psalm 1 and Psalm 119, they give advice as to how the prayers collected in their book are to be dealt with by Israel. They are to be continually contemplated as the word of God, and taken to heart.

G. von Rad has called the psalms the "answer of Israel" to the work of God. This interpretation of the psalms may indeed seem illuminating to us, the psalms are prayers in which man speaks to God. But how could the Psalms be considered the word of God?

Only a few psalms contain an oracle, an utterance of God,[63] so that this could hardly have been the reason for regarding the whole psalter as "God's word". In order to understand this interpretation of the linguistic form of the psalter, we must once more reflect about the range of significance of "God's word". All reality has its origin in God's word. God even provides for himself the praise that Israel bestows upon him in the psalms:

Thou dost inspire my praise (Psalm 22,26[25]). Thou hast turned my laments into dancing (Psalm 30,12[11]).

In the psalms the worshippers bear witness how God influenced them; this witness was, however, made possible for them by God, when he saved them.

We see, that as early as the time of the origin of the Old Testament, the meaning of older texts was enlarged and understood in a new way. From the literary form: "Prayer; speaking to God" it was possible for the literary form "God's word; God's speaking to man" to be created. Such an enlargement did not arise at random, it was the fruit of meditation about the tradition. In the time of the exile, and after it, the faithful were conscious that the "scriptures" created by them did not consist of dead letters which were rigidly confined to one meaning, but were a living word that should be pondered and accepted in mens' hearts.

Many literary forms in the Old Testament appear to us strange and hard to appropriate. Do not the Jews, who created the Old Testament, show a way in which these old forms may be filled with life for us? Could we not follow their example, and, for example use in prayer the laments of the individual as laments of the whole people of God, or even of mankind, in its god-forsakenness? This could also help us even to make our own the accusations against enemies which otherwise often seem to us downright repellent. Above all, however the faithful worshippers of the time of the exile could see here in an exemplary fashion, that not only careful study, but penetrating meditation and living with the scriptures discloses the meaning of the ancient words.

Composition of Psalms as a Result of Study of the Scriptures

The composer of Psalm 1 praises such association with the "law of Yahweh". His composition is itself an example of a meditation of this kind. Thoughts and figures from quite different parts of scripture are fitted together to make a new psalm. He has taken the theme from Joshua 1,7ff. There, God had bidden Joshua to contemplate the law day and night, in order that he might continually act on obedience to it. The psalmist also envisages life with the law. He does not praise the man whose learning is in his books, who believes that he is doing enough when he reads and studies God's word. He compares the man who diligently contemplates God's law with the tree by the water, which "yields its fruit in season". Here he is using a form of speech of his fraternity, the teachers of wisdom, who love to represent the law-abiding regularities of human life with illustrations from nature. But his immediate model is a word of the prophet Jeremiah, whom he follows even in his choice of words: Jeremiah represents with the picture the vital power of the man who trusts in God: he is like a tree beside the stream, which flourishes even in the heat and in years of drought, keeps its leaves green, and continually bears fruit (Jeremiah 17,7f). But the Psalmist differs from Jeremiah in that he puts the study of God's word in the place of trust in God. For him, continual meditation on the transmitted word of God is an expression of the highest trust in God, the nourishment of living faith. At a first glance, he seems to narrow down the meaning of the words of the prophet. Jeremiah speaks of a tree that is bursting with life, which never ceases to bear fruit. The psalmist is more modest; he speaks of fruits "in due season". The prophet speaks of the vitality of the man, whose life is rooted in God. But at the same time, the poet expands the picture into the realm of the improbable:

Its leaf never withers.

This is a reference to the trees which, according to Ezekiel 47, stand by the river of life. According to this vision, one day a mighty stream will flow out of the city of God, and transform the earth into a Paradise (Ezekiel 47,12). This reference in the context of the psalm must occasion surprise. The loving study of scripture and the eschatological consummation of the world in supreme fertility are linked together. This poet had a very high opinion of his work; meditation on the holy word of God opens the way to the imperishable consummation of salvation.

Psalm 1 praises the man who rejoices in God's word. The psalmist himself is such a man, he proves it by the nature of his composition. He speaks about God's word, by letting this word, scripture speak as far as possible for itself. He avoids his own formulations and speaks in the words of scripture, and in references to older sacred texts.

Consequently among the faithful who meditate upon the word of God handed down to them there is created a new category of psalm. They still use individual motifs of the old categories, but these hymns are no longer prayers of lament and thanksgiving spoken in the temple; it is not possible to understand them as popular laments or hymns. They are not composed for use in the cultus, but for the prayer which the individual says in silence by himself, or for a small group of like-minded worshippers. For by no means everyone can penetrate the meaning of these poems, so carefully are the many references to words of scripture assembled, so laden are the individual verses, or even words, with traditional thoughts, conceptions and figures. Anyone who values originality in a poet, will see in these compositions only "patchwork", put together from quotations from the most diverse passages of scripture. And yet these anthological compositions are given life by a piety which accepts with reverence and meditation everything in which it recognizes the word and work of God.[64]

Such faithful souls there were in Israel until New Testament times. The hymns which Luke includes in his story of Jesus' childhood, the Magnificat and the Benedictus, are composed in the same spirit.

The anthological method of composition corresponds to the inner mood of these psalm writers. The composer of Psalm 119 can repeatedly say of himself that he reflects and meditates upon God's word, that he loves it, and lives according to it. Knowledge of scripture for him is not dry scholarship. All instructive references to words of scripture, all adopted traditions, turn into prayer.

The Scribes

Such compositions prove the spiritual fruitfulness even of the times, in which the Jews lived predominantly looking back upon their tradition. We must not allow the picture given of "scribes and pharisees" in the New Testament distort the picture of Jewish loyalty to scripture. The "scribes and pharisees" arrogantly cut themselves off from the people, they believed that they possessed the true knowledge of scripture, that they were the only true "teachers of Israel"; in so doing they forgot that even the most learned scripture expert, like the simple believer, must remain a student of the word of God.

Beginnings of this professional obscurantism of the scribes are to be found as early as Jesus ben Sirach. This wise man exalts the legal expert far above the artisan. Without those who work with their hands "to be sure no city can be inhabited . . . But in the assembly of the people, they are not consulted". They are neither judges nor rulers. They understand only worldly affairs.

"How different it is with the man who devotes himself to studying the law of the Most High" (Ecclesiasticus 38,24 — 39,1).

This contempt for manual labour is not in the vein of the Hebrew tradition. There, for example the skilful goldsmith, the skilful sailor are counted as "wise".[65] Nor does the arrogance of the scholar find expression in the anthological poems of the scribes. These men did not believe that they already possessed true knowledge; they saw their task rather as continuing deeper reflection about God's word.

The origin of the status of the scriptural scholars is probably to be seen in the school of the writers, the secretaries of the royal court. It was among these men that the wisdom teaching found its first home in Israel. In exile the wise men remained almost the only support of the faithful. Since this time they also turned their attention to the religious tradition of Israel. If hitherto the tradition of the law had had its place in the temple, in the instruction of the people by the priests, we now encounter the figure of the man learned in the law. For the Jewish community of the post-exilic time Ezra had great significance:

He was a scribe learned in the law of Moses . . . Ezra had devoted himself to the study and observance of the law of Yahweh and to teaching statute and ordinance in Israel (Ezra 7,6.10).

He reintroduced in the year 458 B.C. the law of Moses into Jerusalem, in order to build up the community on this basis.

One became a scribe through attending a school; one had later the right to accept pupils oneself. Jesus ben Sirach at the end of his book issues an invitation to attend his school (Ecclesiasticus 51,23). As in ancient Egypt and in Babylon, as still today in the modern Qur'an school and in Jewish bible schools, the instruction in these schools also consisted in learning by heart and repetition in an undertone of texts.[66] Such a school stamps the language of its scholars, every stock-phrase will remind them of words of scripture, they speak in the style of the scripture which they know so well; they can express their own words in the words of scripture. Hence it is understandable if in these circles poems are created which bear the stamp of the spirit and the language of the scripture of Israel.

Poems of the "Scribes" in the Old Testament

In addition to the anthological psalms there are many other texts of the Old Testament which belong to this category.

The introduction to the Book of Proverbs (Proverbs 1-9) was composed by such a scribe.

Koheleth belongs to these authors, a man of striking individuality, who not only has at his disposal an exact knowledge of scripture, but also can speak in the topical style of Gentile literature.

The book of Job was written by a man equally versed in scripture and literature; there is no parallel to his work in the Old Testament. There are even prophetic texts belonging to this group; it is by reflection about older words of the prophets that Joel himself becomes a prophet. We can ascribe to this class also sermons of pupils of the prophets on the texts of their masters, the speeches of Trito-Isaiah and Deutero-Zechariah (Zechariah 9ff).[67]

Finally even the Song of Songs bears the marks of this kind of composition. Its vocabulary is largely taken from older biblical passages; the figures of the king, the shepherd, the flock, the vineyard and garden, of Lebanon, of the night, are to be found in classical prophetic texts. The principal theme of the poem, married love, can be understood against the background of prophetic use of the image of marriage. Could such observations not help to decide the contentious question as to the genre to which this little book belongs? In these songs about the bride and marriage human love becomes an indication of the love that binds together Yahweh and Israel.

Apocalyptic also must take its place here. The visions of the Book of Daniel were a result of the study of the scriptures. A new understanding of the words of Jeremiah concerning the seventy years of misery gave this book its impulse.

356

Midrash

Many literary categories are imbued with the spirit of the scriptures. One of these exclusively serves the understanding of the sacred writings, the midrash, the Bible commentary of ancient times, which has its roots in the compositions of the Old Testament scribes, but is of later date than the Hebrew Old Testament. To be sure, Jesus ben Sirach calls his school a "house of midrash" i.e., a house where scripture is investigated/questioned (*dāraš*)(Ecclesiasticus 51,23). Yet he himself does not yet conceive of the task of the scribe who is to be the product of a school, in such a way as to consist merely of the interpretation of the ancient scriptures. Certainly his first task is,

> To investigate all the wisdom of the past, and to spend his time studying the prophecies,

but he also enters into the service of princes, travels into foreign lands, and lastly himself seeks God in prayer and is filled by him with wisdom.

> He will pour forth wise sayings of his own . . . and dwell on the mysteries he has studied (Ecclesiasticus 39,1ff).

From the study of the sacred scriptures both of men and countries there emerges more than an interpretation of the ancient scriptures; something which is in fact a new work.

The presupposition of the creation of the midrashim is the progressive fixation of the biblical text. At last people no longer ventured, as the redactors had done, so to remodel the sacred texts that they might speak immediately to the present. It was believed that God had revealed himself only in the ancient scriptures, and that no more new scriptures would be bestowed by God. So men endeavoured with eager attention to the details of the ancient texts to disclose the meaning of the divine revelation for the present. One of the last books to be accepted into the Greek canon of the Old Testament is actually an example of this category. Wisdom 10-19 is a commentary on religious history from Adam up to the desert journeying. We are of course very far removed here from what we are accustomed to find in modern scripture commentaries. Instead of immersing itself in the past to which the text belongs, the midrash brings them up to date. It embroiders them with reflections, prolongs them, and seeks edification for its own faith.

In the post-biblical schools of the scribes the study of the law had a central place, for the Jew had continually to do with this word of scripture in his daily life. The exposition of the law was called halakha (*hālak*, to walk). These midrashim showed in what ways people must walk if they desired to follow God's word. There were also the midrashim of the Haggadah, which sought to explain and to make vivid the old texts in a freer and more poetic manner. They knew, for example, how to relate in some detail the biographies of biblical persons where the scanty biblical reports disappoint curiosity. We find a beginning of this already in the Old Testament. In the case of many psalms, the collectors thought up situations which would create a living background to these hymns, and described them in superscriptions. Here repeatedly situations in the life of David attracted the imagination of these interpreters of the psalms. These superscriptions show how vivid the picture of David continued to be in later times. In the Chronicler's history David is surrounded by a shining messianic aura; he is the true ruler on God's throne. But these people who use the psalms in prayer are moved by another trait of the figure of David. David is the worshipper of the psalms of lament, he is the great king, who is persecuted by his own people. He becomes the ideal of the humiliated people of God, which survives the exile under such lamentable conditions. The "meek, the quiet in the land", those who accept their humble lot in piety from God's hand, model themselves on this figure. He is a poor king, as Zechariah 9,9f proclaims him:

humble, and mounted on an ass.

But pious narratives which are composed to explain scripture are not the only components of haggadah. Poetic imagination is given even freer play in narratives that have only a loose connection with biblical facts. Of such pious didactic pictures the Old Testament gives several examples.

Jonah

In the book of "the Twelve Minor Prophets" the Book of Jonah is completely untrue to type. It does not contain prophetic utterances, but a consecutive story about a prophet. Certainly, even at the time of the creation of the Old Testament, this difference in genre was noticed. It is probably a pure accident that the book of Jonah got into the Book of the Twelve Prophets — perhaps because in an earlier copy there was still just room for this little book on the scroll.

The story of the prophet Jonah is clearly a free poetic composition. Miracles are taken for granted as in fairy-tales. Not only the punishment of and deliverance of the prophet, who had to spend three days in the belly of the fish, not only the growth and withering of the gourd within two days, even the central happening, the repentance of the whole city of Nineveh, is an unprecedented event. As in a fairy-tale even the beasts repent like human beings. Three days' journey — sixty miles — according to this story, is the diameter of Nineveh. The writer is clearly indicating to every reader that he has freely invented these details.

Yet, with all this free play of imagination, the narrator feels himself bound to holy scripture. There was, according to 2 Kings 14,25 a prophet Jonah at the time of Jeroboam, only nothing is there told of his life. The narrator makes use of this gap to represent what, according to his conception, a prophet is: an unworthy tool, a messenger of God who himself preaches with effect, even when he does it against his will. It is clear that the narrator had no living experience of prophetism. Jonah under the withered gourd seems like a caricature of Elijah who sat under the broom bush and longed for death (1 Kings 19,4; Jonah 4,8).

This distorted picture of the prophet makes the narrator's intention stand out with all the greater clarity. He quotes in 3,10 the prophet Jeremiah:

> If the nation which I have threatened turns back from its wicked ways, then I shall think better of the evil I had in mind to bring upon it (Jeremiah 18,8-9).

In 4,2 he quotes the word with which Yahweh introduced himself to Moses:

> I will be gracious to whom I will be gracious, and I will have compassion on whom I will have compassion (Exodus 33,19).

His narrative interprets these ancient utterances of God. The only unattractive figure is the Jewish prophet; but the Gentiles listen to God's word.

The narrator had to assert the free choice of God's mercy against strong contrary tendencies in Judaism. This other side can be illustrated by a further didactic fiction of the Old Testament, the Book of Esther. It is evidence of the Jewish rigorism that looked down on the whole world and sought to cut itself off from all others. But it is confronted not only by the book of Jonah, but also by the Book of Ruth in which is told the story of David's descent from the Moabite woman. In earlier days the Yahwist had been inspired by the faith that Israel was only chosen for the sake of the peoples; this faith lived on into late Old Testament times. The Books of Ruth and Jonah probably stem from the same epoch in which the following supplement was added to the Book of Isaiah:

> Assyrians shall come to Egypt and Egyptians to Assyria; both together will worship Yahweh. Then Israel will be the third in the covenant with Egypt and Assyria, a blessing in the centre of the world . . . (Isaiah 19,23-25).

7. THE COMPLETION OF THE OLD TESTAMENT

Anyone who wishes to understand the Old Testament, must survey a period of more than a thousand years.

1) He must immerse himself in the pre-literary beginnings of the Old Testament, both in the everyday life of the people, in its intercourse, its songs, and also in its ordering of society, its worship, its confession of faith, and its prayer. The experiences which created the society of Israel, were here given a fixed form in which they could be handed on. Poems which were created on the occasion of great political events, belong to these forms, as do also the narratives and sayings taken over from parents and grand-parents, which were used in the education of the children in the family. Principles of law with whose help quarrels were settled and social injustice removed, are to be found among these forms as are also prayers of the oppressed or the liberated.

2) A second step leads from these many minor forms, to the picture of the course of the history of the people, in which the forms are brought

together. This too, in its essentials had already been created in the pre-literary age; it had taken shape to the extent that families, clans and tribes were fused together in the one Israel. Public worship was probably the principal place where the many groups experienced themselves as "Israel", and where from their contributions the picture of a history of Israel was formed.

3) However great the influence of the society may be, large parts of the Old Testament can only be understood when the reader attempts to estimate the work of great individuals, beginning with the work of Moses, in whom intersect the lines pointing backwards from the pentateuch, and including the words of the prophets and the books of the Old Testament writers, the composers of the historical works and the wisdom poets of the later period.

4) With that, a first step is taken into the time of the learned epigonoi who collected older texts, handed them down, and kept them alive by their interpretations, and whose own writings were nourished by the spirit of the old traditions.

Such questions however do not yet touch the problem of the unity of the Old Testament. They certainly bring to light cross-connections between the writings of the Old Testament, but can give no answer to the question "How was it that precisely forty-five books were included in the Old Testament?[68] The books of the Old Testament represent only a section of the literary production of Israel in the millenium before the birth of Christ. Why, for example, was the "Book of the Upright" (Joshua 10,13) lost, but the Elohistic work preserved?

Today we can no longer answer such questions, but we are certainly justified in looking for an answer concerning analogous happenings in the better known late period of the Old Testament. For even the latest writings of the Old Testament comprise only a section of a richer literature. The Old Testament was not brought to a close because of a failure in the literary power of Judaism. Many extra-canonical writings, including some still preserved today, continued traditions of the Old Testament, and created new forms. Why were they not included in the canon of holy scripture?

Neither the date of origin of scriptures nor their content provide certain criteria for their inclusion in the Old Testament.[69] There was for a long time disagreement in Judaism about the limits of holy scripture. It included, among the Greek-speaking Jews, five books and some additions[70] more than among the Hebrew-speaking Jews. Many modern exegetes have entirely given up the search for any fundamental unity of structure in the Old Testament; it is "not a single coherent book, but in reality a small library" (Fohrer).

A library can tolerate the admission or removal of books. This is not the case with the Bible: about 100 B.C. Josephus declares that every Jew is prepared to give his life for the proposition that there were not tens of thousands of sacred books, but only twenty-two,[71] whose content is fixed and unalterable. At first glance the selection of the sacred writings seems to us thoroughly capricious. How are we to explain the rigour with which the Jews defended it? Perhaps the story of the creation of the canon of the sacred writings can give us an answer.

The most important impulses to the formation of the Canon lie in the times of the Persians. Strangely enough we hardly know anything about the life of the Jewish community in the time between the rebuilding of the temple and the Macabbean revolt (between 530 and 150 BC). Separated from the Gentiles and left in quiet, without great national pretensions, the Jewish community lived in obscurity. It had leisure to reflect in this withdrawn situation upon its past. The most of the books of the Old Testament were given their final form at that time. Are we then to concede to the Jewish community at the time of the Persian domination the right to fix the norm, for which, from then onwards, every Jew was willing to venture his life?

Nothing was further from the thoughts of the Jewish community, which was establishing itself in the post exilic period, than to set up new norms. If the canon of the sacred writings, which came into existence in their midst, was held to be an authoritative standard for all the faithful, the post-exilic Jews were not the first people to endow it with this authority. Every authority, to which these Jews listened, must rather be able to appeal to the tradition from the time before Israel's overthrow in the Exile. Only so were they sure that in them the old Israel, the chosen covenant-partner of God, lived on. The faith that the old covenant, mediated through Moses, had not been broken in the exile, was central. In the life of the Jewish community therefore, the covenant command-ment, the *Tōrāh*, had a central place. The claims that God had made at Sinai, continued to possess undiminished validity. Nehemiah 8ff de-scribes how the public assembly officially accepted the *Tōrāh*, and renewed the covenant.

Thus the *Tōrāh'* is the heart of the canon, the norm of faith, the pentateuch, the law, which contains God's absolute claim upon his people. The word *Tōrāh* seems even at times to have described the whole collection of the sacred writings; this can be inferred from the fact that John and Paul describe quotations from the prophets and from the psalms as quotations from the "law".

Another description of the Old Testament, which we know from the New Testament is "the law and the prophets". This makes us conjecture that the prophetic books were given an authority of their own, like that of the tradition of the pentateuch. The law had been issued by God for his whole people in all its generations, even in the future. It was from the first taken for granted that it should be passed on. Probably from the beginning Israel also passed it down in written form; a covenant-document was a part of a covenant, with its covenant-duties set down in writing. It is at first glance less obvious that the prophetic word also should be handed down to future generations and set down in writing.

The task of the prophets was to convey God's message to particular historical situations; if conditions changed, a new decision of God was to be awaited. And yet we may probably see in the peculiar character of the words of the prophets itself the reason why they soon became literature, and indeed a sanctified and unassailable literature. The prophets announced the future action of God; they are the harbingers of future events. So it is only natural that a watch is kept for the events that correspond to the prophetic word, that there will be a wish to compare the event with the word that announces it. So long as the event has not happened, the word must be carefully preserved. This alone is a reason why the prophets formulate their message as impressively as possible. Their hearers must remember, when the event announced occurs, that God has foretold it, i.e. has brought it about.

> Who from the beginning made the future known? . . . Have not I long since communicated and proclaimed it? You are my witnesses! (Isaiah 44,7f).

From the word of the prophets the faithful can learn that Yahweh directs world-history according to his will. He has caused the events to be announced beforehand by his prophets, so that everyone may later see that it is he who has brought them to pass. Thus the prophetic word becomes a witness to God's power, which transcends all the powers of history. But the expectations of salvation awakened by the prophets will just as surely be fulfilled as were their threats in the past. For this reason in the end the prophetic word is not assembled and preserved only in the small circles of their supporters, but it becomes God's word for all "Israel". It must be preserved in writing just like the law. This word in fact guides the events in the course of world history until the day of final salvation, in which the meaning of the words of the prophets will be fully disclosed.[72]

The Jews came more and more to the conclusion that both the law and the prophets must be handed down as exactly as possible, without changing "a jot or a tittle". Only thus they believed could they remain united through the law with the beginning, the covenant made at Sinai, and through the prophets continue to travel on the right way to final salvation. There grew up an attitude of rigorous loyalty to the letter of scripture. "No one may keep an uncorrected copy of the Bible, which has not been collated with the normative texts, more than thirty days in his house" demands the Jewish Talmud.

The books of the Old Testament take their stand around "the law" and "the prophets" as their heart. The Deuteronomistic history was reckoned by the Jews as a work composed by prophets, and formed with the actual corpus of the prophetic writings after the five books of Moses the second part of the canon. The third and last part was no longer a coherent structure, it bore only the colourless name "writings"; and contained beside the Psalms the wisdom writings, Daniel, the Books of the Chronicler and the five "megilloth", i.e. the scrolls for five great Jewish festivals. This selection and ordering of the sacred scriptures was already widely recognized when about 100 A.D. the synod of Jamnia (to which place the priests and scribes had fled after the fall of Jerusalem) gave it official recognition.

This meant that another ordering and selection of the scriptures which also had found wide recognition, and was represented by the Septuagint was rejected. Here too law and prophets were central. But here the Deuteronomistic history remained united to the pentateuch. The Deuteronomistic history, indeed, had originally contained the last book of the pentateuch, Deuteronomy, as its first book, and continued with its reports of the occupation of the land, the historical report of the pentateuch. The pentatuech, and the Deuteronomistic history were reckoned to be reports of Israel's past; the psalms and wisdom books followed them as counsels for life in the present; the prophetic books formed the conclusion as a vision of the future. This ordering of the Old Testament canon was adopted by the primitive church.

Thus the history of the Old Testament canon can neither give us assurance concerning the selection of the books that belong to it, nor about their ordering and the meaning of this ordering. But it gives us unmistakable information about what united this collection, and gave it the authority of an immutable norm for the faithful; the word, which God delivered to his people in the law and the prophets — this word must be the norm for the faithful so long as God holds by it.

FOOTNOTES

1 In three places a later editor of this text has inserted explanations; he had already experienced the further course of history, and thinks it necessary to point out at what points this report of the prophet had been confirmed by the events.

2 According to 2 Kings 16,1 Ahaz would have come to the throne a long time before this year. But the numbers given in this verse do not fit in with the otherwise exactly dovetailed chronology of the Books of Kings. The corrections in chronology presupposed here are taken from C. Schedl: "Textkritische Bemerkungen zu den Synchronismen der Könige von Israel und Juda", in VT 12 (1962) 88ff.

3 Tiglath-pileser reports, e.g. on the capture of Gaza ". . . I dragged away his gods, and I erected a statue of my god Ashur in his palace, and a statue of my kingly person. I counted as one of the gods of the land." (Cf "Die Texte Tiglatpilesers III," Editor, E. Vogt, in *Biblica* 1964).

4 2 Samuel 7, the promise of Nathan.

5 Isaiah uses here a pun that cannot be reproduced in translation; he expresses "to believe" and to "remain" with the same Hebrew word-root. We find the same root also in Nathan's promise in a decisive passage. Such puns are for the Hebrews more than mere playfulness; what is linguistically akin is for them essentially related — cf on this point p.24ff.

6 Joshua 8,1; 10,8. A further tradition of which Isaiah reminds the king is probably the election of Jerusalem, which was connected with the election of the house of David. Cf on this point Isaiah 7,8f; this verse requires a continuation: in

Aram Rezin is king, in Samaria Pekah is king; and in Jerusalem? Here Yahweh is king.

7 1 Samuel 10,22; 14,37; 22,10; 23,2 etc.

8 The name Immanuel is not uncommon. In the Papyri from Elephantine we find a similar name: Immanuya, Yahweh-with-us. Isaiah gave his children much more unusual names, in order to proclaim his message with the help of these names. He took his son Shear-jashub ("A remnant shall return") with him when he went to meet Ahaz. By his very name the boy was intended to remind Ahaz of Isaiah's earlier message: for the small remnant of Israel, that turn again to Yahweh, there will be deliverance. Another son of Isaiah bears the name of "Speed-spoil-hasten-plunder" (Isaiah 8,3). We must understand this kind of naming must be understood as a prophetic symbolic action; cf on this point above, p.13ff. Such symbolic actions were natural, because Hebrew names often reflected experiences of the parents. On this point cf p.15ff.

9 The hypothesis that Hezekiah, the son of Ahaz, was the Immanuel proclaimed by Isaiah originated in the old Jewish exegesis. This interpretation would be untenable if the chronology of 2 Kings 16,1 were correct, for according to this passage, Hezekiah must have been born long before the time of the war of Aram and Damascus against Jerusalem (the so-called Syro-Ephraimite war) in the year 735 B.C. On this different chronology, however compare note 2 of this section. Still another hypothesis of the exegetes is that Immanuel was a later son of Isaiah himself. But the prophet's wife was already a mother; she could no longer be called a young maiden, a bride.

10 Judges 6,12; Deuteronomy 20,4; Numbers 14,43; Joshua 1,9; 7,12; 2 Samuel 5,10.

11 Cf on this point above, p.221ff.

12 Cf Psalm 46,8.12; Amos 5,14.

13 Jesse is David's father; this prophetic word refers to the hope given with the promise of Nathan, that there would always be a descendant of David i.e. of Jesse. But when it speaks of Jesse the father, instead of David, we can see therein a suggestion that God can raise up a king even from a non-royal family, as once he did from the family of Jesse.

14 On this point cf above p.275ff.

15 Cf above, p.190ff.

16 Cf above p.286ff.

17 On this point cf p.190ff.

18 Genesis 12,1ff, on this point cf above p.265ff.

19 On this point, cf p.93ff.

20 Deuteronomy 12,9; 25,19.

21 From the tradition that Israel entered into Canaan from the south, originated probably the motif that God, who travelled with the people, repeatedly comes thence; cf Judges 5,5; Deuteronomy 33,2f; Habakkuk 3,1ff. Akin to the motif of the coming God is the motif of the descending God; cf Genesis 11,5.7; Exodus 3,8; Isaiah 31,4; Exodus 19,11.18.20; 34,5; Nehemiah 9,13: information concerning the place from which God descends, is consciously withheld.

22 Cf Isaiah 6: The prophet sees in the temple Yahweh, the king upon his throne — but he towers far above the temple, for even the skirts of his garment fill the whole temple.

23 It is conceivable that the tradition of Abram's departure from Mesopotamia was modelled on the departure from Egypt. Thus probably also the tradition of Abraham's covenant with God was assimilated with the Sinai covenant; cf the appearance of fire in Genesis 15 with the appearance on Sinai; cf further with Genesis 15,7 the preface of the decalogue. Thus the motifs are easily detached

from the original context and fit themselves in a living way to new situations. This "Transposition of motifs" (Gross) is for us a sign of the unity of Old Testament tradition.

24 Exodus 34,23.

25 Isaiah 43,16ff; 48,20f; 49,9f; 52,7-12.

26 Isaiah 2,2ff; Micah 4,1ff; Isaiah 60,3ff.

27 As the adopting father God is clearly represented as the master of the "kinship" covenant, but the same is also true of the figure of marriage, for in the ancient world the husband was the master, who ruled over his wife.

28 Cf Exodus 6,7; Jeremiah 31,33; Exodus 36,28.

29 Exodus 24; Genesis 15. Cf Genesis 31,54; Jeremiah 34,18.

30 Hosea 1,9; on the name of God cf Exodus 3,14; 6,3. God's name Yahweh, interpreted as "I am indeed here (for you)", expresses what is meant by the "covenant" of God. Cf on the name of Yahweh, p.13ff.

31 Hosea 11,8f; Jeremiah 31,20.

32 Jeremiah 31,31ff; Ezekiel 36,26ff.

33 Mark 14,24 and parallels.

34 Genesis 3,22; 11,7 (J); Genesis 1,26 (P); Genesis 28.

35 According to Judges 8,23; 1 Samuel 8,7 Yahweh is king over Israel, therefore it no longer needs a human king.

36 Isaiah 6. The prophet uses a form which we also encounter in 1 Kings, 22; According to that narrative a heavenly being offers himself for the service of king Yahweh in the world. Ezekiel 1ff imitates Isaiah, as does Daniel 7,9ff.

37 Cf Deuteronomy 4,34; 5,15; 26,2; Jeremiah 21,5; 32,17 etc.

38 Deuteronomy 4,19: Yahweh has given the sun and the moon to other peoples, but reserved Israel for himself. Cf also Deuteronomy 29,25: The gods, to whom Israel fell away, were "not intended for it". Cf further the Greek reading of Deuteronomy 32,8f: God divided the peoples among the "sons of the gods", but he laid claim to Israel as his own inheritance.

39 Cf the summary of the preaching of Jesus in Mark 1,15: "The time has come, the Kingdom of God is upon you".

40 Cf Judges 8,23; 1 Samuel 8,7.

41 On this point, cf above p.285ff. The messianic hope unfolded in yet other directions: it will however suffice here if we cite the messianic prophecies of Isaiah. These already show, that the messianic hope included the hope of the final peace of God — and thus points us beyond Christ to the consummation that God himself will bestow.

42 Isaiah 49,1-6; 50,4-9; 52,13-53,12.

43 Daniel 7,13f. This expression contains for Hebrew ears a paradox; For "man" is humble and contemptible in comparison with God's power and greatness.

44 On this point, cf above p.298ff.

45 Isaiah 2,2ff; Isaiah 60,1ff.

46 The eschatological hymns of praise are an original creation of Deutero-Isaiah. Cf also Isaiah 52,9f; 40,9-11 etc.

47 On this point cf p.27ff. and p.52ff.

48 G. Fohrer, *Überlieferung und Geschichte des Exodus*, BZAW 91,5f.

49 Cf above, p.265-278ff. and p.282ff.

50 Amos 7,1-9; 8,1-3; 9,1-4.

51 Cf Hosea 1,7; 4,15; 6,11.

52 Thus it happens that. e.g., in the book of the first Isaiah only the following passages come from the great prophet of Jerusalem himself: Isaiah 1-11 (without 2,2-5; 4,2-6; 11,10-16); 14,24-27; 17,1-14; 18; 19,1-15; 20; 22; 28-32 (without 29,17-24; 30,18-26; 32,1-8); 37,22-29.

52a Cf Micah 3,12.
53 We have his work in Isaiah 56-66: the heart of the work is in 60-62.
54 Cf Exodus 24,9-11; Deuteronomy 33,2; Ezekiel 1,27.
55 Isaiah 9,1[2] "The people that walked in darkness, see a great light".
56 Cf Amos 1,3-2,3. Threats against the peoples; Amos 2,4ff; a threat against Israel and Judah — announced in the same style as the threats against the peoples.
57 Jeremiah 26,20-24; 26,1-19.
58 Habakkuk 2,1-3:
"I will stand at my post,
I will take up my position on the watch-tower,
I will watch to learn what he will say through me,
and what I shall reply when I am challenged.
Then Yahweh made answer;
Write down the vision, inscribe it on tablets,
so that it can easily be read;
for there is still a vision for the appointed time.
At the destined hour it will come in breathless haste,
it will not fail.
If it delays, wait for it;
for when it comes will be no time to linger",
The writing down of the prophetic word in Jeremiah 30,2 meets a different need; the prophet in Jerusalem had to give a message to the exiles.
59 On the individual laments, cf p.155ff.
60 It is true that Psalm 1 speaks of "the law", but "law" is for Israel nothing but God's word, commandment that God has imparted to his own people. Psalm 119 uses many synonyms for "law"; "law" includes the instruction that God gives to his people, the revelation in which he shows himself, the word of help on which man depends.
61 Ezekiel, the prophet of the exile, has to justify his calling as a prophet in the face of such doubts; cf on this point above p.262ff.
62 By their use of the messenger formula "Thus saith Yahweh" the prophets had repeatedly drawn attention to the fact that their word was God's word. From the beginning the law had been understood as God's word, mediated through Moses. On this point, cf Exodus 21,1; 34,28; 24,12; 31,18; 32,15f; Deuteronomy 31,26; 4,2; 13,1 etc.
63 Cf Psalm 2,6; imitation of the prophetic word of God; Psalm 50,5.7ff; imitation of the divine instruction of the law.
64 Anthological compositions among the psalms: Psalms 25; 33; 34; 103; 111; 112; 119; 145.
65 On this point cf p.166ff.
66 Of course in such schools there is a continual noise caused by the repetition of the texts aloud, which often enough results in confusion — hence the expression "A Jews' school".
67 There are poems in the spirit of scripture in the most varied linguistic categories. Further reflections on these compositions are scattered among different chapters in this book. Yet it is not unimportant to see also the unity of these different texts, their common origin in the learning of the scribes.
68 Catholics and Protestants are not agreed about the contents of the Old Testament. Catholic Bibles contain, according to different methods of counting, either forty-six or forty-seven books, Protestant Bibles seven fewer, since Protestants adopt the Hebrew canon, and not the Greek canon. "Canon" is a Greek word, which has been borrowed from the Hebrew (*qāneh* — reed). In Greek it

THE UNITY OF THE OLD TESTAMENT

meant "straight staff" and also the "norm, plumb-line", and in the ancient church the "norm of Christian life". Adopted in Latin as borrowed term, "Canon" came finally to be the church's description for the collection of books that constituted the norm of Christian life.

69 Parts of the apocryphal Book of Enoch are, for example, older than the Book of Daniel, which like Enoch, is an apocalyptic work.

70 Tobit, Judith, 1 and 2 Maccabees, Wisdom, Ecclesiasticus, additions to Daniel and Esther, and Baruch.

71 Josephus came to the number 22, because he put together many books, which we number singly, e.g. the five Books of Moses, or the Book of the Twelve Prophets, 1 and 2 Kings, and 1 and 2 Chronicles. But twenty-two is also the number of letters in the alphabet.

72 Ecclesiasticus 48,22-49,12 is evidence that in the beginning of the second century B.C. the prophetic books were recognized as sacred writings.

General Index

Solomon, 52, 113, 15, 167, 168, 300
Song of Deborah, 163-4
Song of the Harper, 248
Song of Miriam, 163
Song of Songs, 356
songs and prayers, 142-51
songs of praise
    communal, 163-4
    hymns, 164-5
    individual, 162-3
sound, images of, 56-7
speech forms, 4
speeches
    in Deutero-Isaiah, 220-1
    divine, 146-7, 215-16
    warning, 213, 216
spirit world, sagas about, 84
state, and law, 135-6
stratification of texts
    from committal to writing, 104-5
    from oral traditions, 102-4
style
    analysis, 41-52
    doublets, 47-9
    forms of repetition, 50-1
    individual style forms, 42-3
    long sentence structure, 43-7
    preference for the traditional, 41-2
    short-word units, 43
    tension, 44
    triadic forms, 49-50
    subordinate clauses, 43
suffering, 243-4
supplication, prayers of, 151-2

teaching
    193
    teachers of wisdom, 231-54, 351-2
    see also instruction
tehom, 284
Ten Commandments
    124-36, 347
    keeping, 131-2
tension, style and, 44
Terah, 123
thunder, 55
thunderstorms, in Ezekiel's vision, 200-3
Tiamat, 39, 284
Tiglath-pileser, 312, 313, 316, 317
Tobit, 167
Torah, 133-4, 170, 193, 361
Tower of Babel, 73-7, 89, 268

tradition
    78-9
    investigation of the history of, 3-4
    of law, 124-35
traditional style, preference for, 41-2
translations, 6
treaties, Hittite, 130
tree of knowledge, 102-3
tree of life, 102-3
triadic forms, 49-50
Trito-Isaiah, 343-5, 356
truth, 32-3
Twelve Minor Prophets, 358

unity, in the Old Testament, 311-63
Uriah, 38, 113, 115, 116, 300
Utnapishtim, 92

visions, encounters with God, 97, 106, 197-204, 224
vividness, preference for, 52-64
vocation narratives, 118-19, 121

wars, holy, 110-11, 117, 120, 163, 316-17
Wellhausen, Julius, 2, 209
Wen Amon, 208
wheels, in Ezekiel's vision, 205
wisdom
    Book of Job and, 243-4
    didactic poems concerning, 237-40
    divine origin, 235-40
    hiddenness of, 239-40
    and legal tradition, 236-7, 239
    personification, 236-7, 239
    post-exilic age, 237
    and prophetic tradition, 238
    revelation of the mystery of, 231-7
    teachers of, 231-54, 351-2
wisdom literature, 82, 132
wisdom Psalms, 160-1
wisdom sayings
    166-72
    counsel of wise men, 170-2
    Israel's wisdom, 167-8
    of the learned, 168-9
    of the people, 168-9
    proverbs, 169-71
word (dabar), 36-7
word of God, 37-9, 134-5, 325-6, 352-3
word play, 34-6
world, origins of, 80
world picture, 55-6

377

writing, committal, 113-14
written forms, committal to, 104

yadà, 53
Yahweh
anthropomorphism, 61
divine speech, 215-16
encounters with, 224
etymology, 16-17, 23
and Ezekiel's vision, 197-207
freedom and faithfulness, 330-1
gift of land, 194
as God of promise, 57
historicity of the revelation of the
name, 21-3
influence on natural events, 38
the judge, 30, 218-19
kingship, 165-6, 334-6
omnipresence, 107
and the present, 212, 229-30
prophetic similes for, 209

in proverbs, 171
and punishment, 30
salvation, 329-30
significance of name of, 19-20
as statement of God's sovereignty,
20-1
and wisdom, 167-8, 235-40
Yahwist
22, 44, 80, 104, 122, 268-75, 295
anthropomorphism, 275
individual traits, 272
representations of events in the
world, 274-5
sources, 271
texts formulated by, 273-4
work of, 271-5

Zabibe, Queen, 313
Zephaniah, 345
Zion, 165-6, 331, 343-4

Index of Biblical Quotations

ZEPHANIAH
1, 12	209
1, 14f	345
1, 14	347

HAGGAI
2, 3	303
2, 6f	303

ZECHARIAH
9ff	356
9, 9f	358
9, 9	337
14, 16f	335

NEW TESTAMENT

MATTHEW
1	320
1, 18	312
1, 21	319
1, 22f	320
1, 22	311, 312, 315, 319
6, 25ff	151
9, 38	151
27, 46f	28

MARK
1, 12	77
1, 15	339
10, 17-24	159

LUKE
1, 74	148
18, 9-14	159

ACTS
5, 32	36

HEBREWS
4, 9	332

TOBIT
1, 21	168

WISDOM OF SOLOMON
6, 16	239
7, 2	239
9, 4	239
10-19	357

ECCLESIASTICUS
24	238
38, 24-39, 1	355
39, 1ff	357
42, 15-43, 33	112
51, 23	356, 357

1 MACCABEES
3, 3-9	143

NON-BIBLICAL TEXTS

ENUMA ELISH
Tablet 6	90

GILGAMESH
XI, 11	75

KOHELETH
2, 1-11	248
2, 9	249
2, 19	247
3, 10-14	248
3, 11	248
3, 19	248
12, 7b	248